Promoting Successful Integration

EDITORIAL STAFF

Edward A. Lindeke, Colonel (Retired), MSC, US Army
Director, Borden Institute

Vivian Mason
Senior Volume Editor, Borden Institute

Christine Gamboa-Onrubia, MBA
Creative Director and Production Manager, Fineline Graphics, LLC

Published by the
Office of The Surgeon General | Falls Church, Virginia
Borden Institute
US Army Medical Department Center and School
Health Readiness Center of Excellence | Fort Sam Houston, Texas

2018

Library of Congress Cataloging-in-Publication Data

Names: Cooper, Rory A., editor. | Pasquina, Paul F., editor. | Etter, Douglas A., editor. | Borden Institute (U.S.), issuing body.
Title: Promoting successful integration / edited by Rory A. Cooper, Paul F. Pasquina, Douglas A. Etter.
Description: Fort Sam Houston, Texas : Borden Institute, US Army Medical Department Center and School, Health Readiness Center of Excellence ; Falls Church, Virginia : Office of The Surgeon General, United States Army, 2018. | Includes bibliographical references and index. |
Identifiers: LCCN 2018010383 (print) | LCCN 2018011369 (ebook) | ISBN 9780160939839 | ISBN 9780160939846 | ISBN 9780160939853 | ISBN 9780160944758
Subjects: | MESH: Veterans Health | Community Integration | Disabled Persons
Classification: LCC UB369 (ebook) | LCC UB369 (print) | NLM WA 360 | DDC 362.1086/97--dc23
LC record available at Caution-https://lccn.loc.gov/2018010383

For sale by the Superintendent of the Documents, U.S. Government Publishing Office
Internet: bookstore.gpo.gov Phone: toll free (866) 512-1800; DC area (202) 512-1800
Fax: (202) 512-2104 Mail: Stop IDCC, Washington, DC 20402-0001
ISBN No. 978-0-16-094475-8

Promoting Successful Integration

EDITED BY

★ ★ ★

RORY A. COOPER, PhD

PAUL F. PASQUINA, MD, COLONEL (Retired), MC, US ARMY

DOUGLAS A. ETTER, COLONEL (Chaplain), US ARMY

OFFICE OF THE SURGEON GENERAL
Falls Church, Virginia

BORDEN INSTITUTE
Fort Sam Houston, Texas

US ARMY MEDICAL DEPARTMENT CENTER AND SCHOOL
HEALTH READINESS CENTER OF EXCELLENCE
Fort Sam Houston, Texas

THIS BOOK IS DEDICATED TO THE MEN AND WOMEN
OF THE ARMED SERVICES, TO THEIR FAMILIES,
VETERANS, AND THE CIVILIANS WHO SERVE THE
UNITED STATES OF AMERICA TO PROVIDE
FOR FREEDOM AND DEMOCRACY.

★ ★ ★

Authors' Note: In honor of those who have served and sacrificed in defense of our Nation, this book uses
the convention of capitalizing terms for those who served.

Contents

Soldier Profiles

AT THE END OF EACH CHAPTER, a profile is given about Soldiers who have successfully adapted to their impairments and are leading remarkable lives as Soldiers or Army Veterans. These dedicated individuals have overcome numerous physical obstacles, focused on their abilities, committed themselves to optimal recovery, and made important contributions as role models. In order of appearance, they are as follows:

Contributors

Anne E. Barry, MS, CRC

Brian Bilski, BS, Colonel (Retired), US Marine Corps

Shelly Brown, MEd

Steve Bucha, AET

Rebecca P. Cameron, PHD

Cheng-Shiu (Joshua) Chung, PHD

John Coltellaro, ATP

Al Condeluci, MS, PHD

Rory A. Cooper, PHD

Rosemarie Cooper, MPT, ATP

Ron Drach, Sergeant (Retired), US Army

Stanley H. Ducharme, PHD

S. Elaine Eitler, MEd, IAST

Douglas A. Etter, MDiv, MSS, Colonel (Chaplain), US Army

Goeran Fiedler, PHD

Daniel J. Fisher, MHA, Colonel (Retired), US Army

Mary R. Goldberg, PHD

Melva Gooden-Ledbetter, MS

Deepan C. Kamaraj, MD, MS

Twylla Kirchen, PHD, OTR/L

Christina Lacroix, DO

William M. Lake, BS, Colonel (Retired), US Marine Corps

Amy Lane, OTR/L, CDRS

Randy Levander, SFC

Allen Lewis, PHD, CRC

Alissa Ling, MS

Carol Peredo Lopez, AIA

D. Joshua Marino, MS

Amanda McAlpine, NCIDQ, LEED AP

Seth Messinger, PHD

Maria Milleville, MEd

Linda R. Mona, PHD

Amy Mountain, MS

Michael Mushett, MS

Lavinia Fici Pasquina, MS

Paul F. Pasquina, MD, Colonel (Retired), MC, US Army

Patrick Rakszawaski, RA

Amanda Reinsfelder, MS, ATP

Benjamin Salatin, MS

Audrey Schoomaker, RN, BSN, E-RYT

Christina Berchock Shook, PsyD, ABPP

Michelle L. Sporner, PHD, CRC

Adam J. Susmarski, DO, Lieutenant Commander, MC, US Navy

Jeanne Wenos, Ped

Thomas Williams, PHD

Joseph A. Wineman, MHA, DMD, ABGD, Colonel (Retired), US Army

Foreword

BUILDING AND MAINTAINING RESILIENCE among our military and Veteran communities is an essential factor in maintaining the fighting force and in promoting successful reintegration into garrison communities or the civilian sector. Strong families, supportive friendships, and understanding communities are necessary to ensure that our Service Members and Veterans are safe, effective, and successful. Resilience is multifactorial and requires effort on the part of multiple parties; foremost among them is the Service Member and the command structure.

Soldiers, Sailors, Airmen, Marines, and Coast Guardsmen are the military's greatest asset. Their talent, commitment, and tenacity are unmatched by any force in the world. We ask our Service Members and their families to frequently make sacrifices that are difficult for those who have not served in the Armed Forces to understand. They endure repeated deployments, hazardous environments, and long hours away from friends and families. However, they are professionals and serve with honor and deserved pride.

It is the responsibility of the leadership of the Armed Forces and the civilian communities to provide Service Members with the tools and resources they need to succeed on the battlefield. This responsibility remains when they return home to lend their talents to building happy and healthy Families, and when their time of service is completed so that they have every opportunity to contribute to their chosen civilian communities. Whether a person serves for 2 years or 40 years, we must value his or her contributions and patriotism. Less than 1% of Americans are serving in the Armed Forces today, and less than 6% of living Americans have ever served in the military.

The face of the all-volunteer force is different than that of previous generations. The military works as a total force to include active, guard, and reserve components. In addition, the US Public Health Service, the Department of Homeland Security (US Coast Guard), the Department of Veteran Affairs, and first responders have worked with our military at unprecedented levels. Moreover, the US Army, Air Force, and Navy Health Services departments are more integrated and communicate at unprecedented levels. This has facilitated impressive levels of success in the care and reintegration of wounded, injured, and ill Service Members. Survival rates on the battlefield are higher than in any previous conflict, and the accomplishments post-deployment and upon departing military service are impressive. This generation of Veterans has yielded several leaders in politics, government, business, and academia.

Promoting Successful Integration serves as a valuable resource for our Service Members, Military and Veteran leadership, Veterans, Family members, and civilian communities. This book contains extremely helpful information about resilience and reintegration. It also provides concise and practical information for being successful in developing important life skills. The authors have generously shared their knowledge and experience, many of whom have relevant military experience. The chapters include references for readers seeking more information, as well as an end-of-book suggested reading list. This is a book that should be widely read and kept as a reference.

Dr Cooper, Colonel (Retired) Pasquina, and Colonel Etter—all Soldiers —are to be commended for leading this important effort and for assembling this excellent resource. Each of them has been engaged in the care and successful reintegration of Service Members, Veterans, and Families for more than two decades. They are committed professionals who have helped countless individuals, Families, leaders, and communities. *Promoting Successful Integration* is only one of their many contributions. The positive impact that they have had is extraordinary and is reflected in the thousands of people who have benefited from their expertise. They embody the concepts of "Soldier for Life" and "Selfless Service."

LIEUTENANT GENERAL NADJA Y. WEST, MD
THE SURGEON GENERAL
COMMANDING GENERAL, U.S. ARMY MEDICAL COMMAND

Preface

THE STRENGTH AND SUSTAINABILITY OF OUR MILITARY is dependent on the resilience of our Service Members, their families, and our civilian employees. Additionally, the successful reintegration of Service Members back into their families, military garrisons, and civilian communities after each deployment is essential to the continued health of our military and our nation. To those Service Members who become wounded, injured, or ill in service to our nation, we have a nonnegotiable obligation to provide them with an array of tools to assist them in continuing to lead fulfilling lives, and to contribute to their communities and society as a whole. Inarguably, this is a grand undertaking that requires a concerted effort and diligence throughout the Department of Defense (DoD), across the federal government, and within our civilian communities.

The DoD has made considerable strides in understanding and addressing the importance of focusing on resilience and successful reintegration. Each service has created programs that attempt to reach Service Members and their families wherever they may be in their deployment cycle, and in whatever circumstances they may find themselves. Effective programs and resources now exist to help Service Members and their families strengthen relationships, pursue careers, obtain educational opportunities, and manage finances—all aimed at building resilience and facilitating reintegration. Undoubtedly, we have learned much and advanced far in supporting our all-volunteer force and its families. Nevertheless, we must continue to press forward in enhancing and improving these programs—programs that must be adequately resourced and fully integrated throughout all stages of one's service lifecycle in an effort to provide the absolute best resources to our nation's heroes.

This handbook intends to serve as one of those resources. Offering very practical guidance, the book adeptly pulls together a wide variety of tools available to Service Members and their families. Incorporating real-world case studies throughout, the authors have clearly demonstrated that supporting these Service Members and their families truly takes a team effort. Building resilience and a successful reintegration process, as this work proves, depends on the interconnectivity of Service Member, family, and community. The book itself exemplifies this collaborative effort within the DoD, the Department of Veterans Affairs, and numerous other agencies focused on this same mission.

The important work of creating this book would not have been possible without the initiative and dedication of Rory A. Cooper, PhD, Colonel (Chaplain) Douglas A. Etter, and Colonel (Ret) Paul F. Pasquina, MD—all soldiers. I wish to extend my thanks to these gentlemen, all of the authors, the talented staff of the Borden Institute, and, most importantly, to the many Service Members who selflessly shared their personal stories of struggles and successes, as portrayed in the case studies throughout the book. All of these contributors assumed a noble mission, performed valiantly in offering their time and expertise, and have now provided a resource that has the potential to help countless Service Members throughout the coming years.

> Honorable Jessica L. Wright
> Major General (Retired)
> Former Under Secretary of Defense for
>   Personnel and Readiness, Department of Defense
> Former Adjutant General, Pennsylvania,
>   Department of Military and Veterans Affairs

Prologue

AT THE CORE OF MILITARY SERVICE IS ITS PEOPLE. Despite the emphasis on technology and the impact that it can have on shaping military operations, it is people who must ultimately fight our Nation's battles. The people who volunteer to serve in our military are our most valuable asset, and we must take great care to ensure that they are given all the tools and skills necessary to complete their mission. However, when their time in the military comes to an end, they need the resources and guidance to help them succeed as Veterans.

Families and friends are central to the success of our Service Members because they provide the needed stability and security in their lives that enable our Service Members to become more resilient and resourceful in their military duties. Thus, families and friends of our Service Members need to be educated about the challenges and burdens that they will be asked to face, as well as the importance of their service to this country.

This book strives to provide information and to serve as a resource to Service Members across all of the services and at all ranks. It is also an important guide for families and professionals outside of the military who interact with Service Members and Veterans. America has the strongest and best military force in the world, with Service Members who are intelligent, resourceful, talented, and respected. The military is one of the most revered institutions in America, but maintaining this reputation and success requires focused effort and steadfast commitment.

In America, where less than 1% of the citizenry is serving in the military and where less than 6% of living Americans ever served in the military, it is essential to support our Service Members and their families in meaningful and tangible ways. Moreover, it is important to keep our Veterans connected to the military and for them to understand that their service and sacrifice, whether for 2 years or 40 years, are valued and appreciated.

The American public is largely disconnected from the military. Most people do not understand it and are not personally invested in its operation.

The dwindling number of Veterans exacerbates this problem and lessens our most supportive population.

Only 29% of today's youth meet our high standards and are eligible for service. Educational, medical or physical limitations, mental health challenges, or criminal history often rule out the opportunity to serve in the military. Obesity accounts for approximately 31% of disqualifications. Of the 29% of youth who are eligible to serve in the military, less than one in four has a strong desire to serve. Most Americans, while supportive of the military, are not willing to engage even if there is a need for more troops.

The military is a challenging profession, but it is also a proud and distinguished profession that conveys many lifelong benefits to the people who have served, as well as their communities. When compared to their non-Veteran counterparts, Veterans are more likely to volunteer, give to charity, vote, help their neighbors, and participate in service or community organizations. Long after their military service ends, many Veterans choose to continue to help strengthen the Nation by serving as civic leaders in communities across the country. Because of their experience, training, and skills, Veterans are well-suited to provide solutions to some of our Nation's toughest challenges.

Promoting Successful Integration provides an important resource to our military and adds to our knowledge of successful reintegration and resilience. I wish to convey my thanks to Rory A. Cooper, PhD, Colonel (Retired) Paul F. Pasquina, MD, and Colonel (Chaplain) Douglas A. Etter for volunteering their time and expertise to write this important work. They are models of long-term, dedicated, selfless service to a cause greater than themselves. All of the authors and contributors are to be commended for making this book possible because our military's success is built on our Service Members, their families, our civilian employees, and countless volunteers.

RONALD L. GREEN
18TH SERGEANT MAJOR OF THE MARINE CORPS
US MARINE CORPS

Introduction

Our Service Members and their families are incredibly strong,
resilient, and dedicated.

★ ★ ★

LTG ERIC B. SCHOOMAKER, MD, PhD
THE SURGEON GENERAL/THE COMMANDING GENERAL
US ARMY MEDICAL COMMAND

THE GOALS OF THIS BOOK ARE TO EDUCATE, EMPOWER, and elevate
the resilience of Service Members and their families and to help those people
who are transitioning to successfully reintegrate into their chosen civilian
community. It is intended to be useful to Service Members and their families
of all levels and experiences. A theme of the book is that resilience and
successful reintegration are intertwined. Successful reintegration for Service
Members and their families requires resilience. This is due in part to Service
Members, Veterans, and families having experiences that are unfamiliar
to the general public. Over time, the percentage of Americans serving in
uniform has dropped to below 1%, and the percentage of Veterans of who
have served in the military is less than 6% of the American population.
Thus, although most Americans support members of the Armed Forces, few
are familiar with the experiences of Service Members, Veterans, and their
families, which present challenges for reintegration.

There are many facets of building resilience and the promotion of
successful reintegration. Resilience is a family affair, and it can be viewed like
a muscle. It takes regular, targeted work to build and maintain resilience.
Resilience has several components, including physical, mental, social, and
moral components. If any one component is vulnerable, then the Service
Member, Veteran, or family may be at risk. Readiness for transition is
similar to military readiness; it requires knowledge, training, and resources.

When resilient and well prepared, the likelihood of successful reintegration is maximized.

The information in this book is presented in the context of both current programs and the best knowledge available. We hope that this book serves as a valuable tool for learning about the resources and processes that may facilitate each Service Member and his or her family's success. It is also intended to serve as a resource for leaders at all levels.

This book provides information about various transition programs, key federal agencies, Veteran and Military Service Organizations, and the programs and tools that are available to help Service Members and their families. Chapters are written to be broadly accessible, but they are also referenced for people who would like to obtain more in-depth information. Several vignettes are provided about Service Members and Veterans who have faced challenges and addressed them through their resilience. They help to put a human face on the concepts presented in this book.

As a handbook, our intent is to cover a variety of relevant topics, with sufficient depth to provide the reader with working knowledge; but, it is not intended to make people experts in building resilience and successful reintegration. It is expected that this handbook will augment programs and services. Service Members, Veterans, and their families should acquire additional tools or at least refresh their knowledge by reading this book.

Members of the American Armed Forces and their families are remarkably strong and resourceful. They have repeatedly proven that they can rise to every challenge presented to them. Anyone who has served or spent significant time with our members of the Armed Forces and their families understands their commitment to selfless service to something greater than themselves.

We are grateful for this opportunity to continue to serve and to contribute to improving the quality of life for members of the Armed Forces, Veterans, and their families. Each of us has been affected in a very personal way by service in the military, and remains committed to the welfare and success of Military and Veteran families. We are grateful for the support from our families, friends, and colleagues, and for members of the Armed Forces and Veterans with whom we have had the privilege to serve. We will consider ourselves successful if this book proves helpful to military leaders, members of the Armed Forces, Veterans, and their families. It has been an honor to volunteer to serve in the capacity as authors and editors.

Respectfully,
RORY A. COOPER, PhD
COLONEL (RETIRED) PAUL F. PASQUINA, MD
COLONEL (CHAPLAIN) DOUGLAS A. ETTER

Promoting Successful Integration

The Performance Triad.
It summarizes a simple truth about human performance
and well-being: that all of us—no matter who we are,
how old we are, or what we do—need a balance of
three things to build and sustain health.
The three are sleep, activity, and nutrition.

★ ★ ★

LIEUTENANT GENERAL (RETIRED) PATRICIA D. HOROHO
US ARMY SURGEON GENERAL
COMMANDING GENERAL OF THE US ARMY MEDICAL COMMAND
SEPTEMBER 27, 2012

CHAPTER ONE

Framework for Reintegration and Resilience for Service Members and Veterans

RORY A. COOPER, PhD*; PAUL F. PASQUINA, MD†; and
DOUGLAS A. ETTER, MDIV, MSS‡

---

*Director and Senior Career Scientist, Human Engineering Research Laboratories,
Rehabilitation Research and Development Service, US Department of Veterans
Affairs, 6425 Penn Avenue, Pittsburgh, Pennsylvania 15206, and Distinguished
Professor and FISA Foundation–Paralyzed Veterans of America Chair, Department of
Rehabilitation Science and Technology, University of Pittsburgh, 6425 Penn Avenue,
Suite 400, Pittsburgh, Pennsylvania 15206

†Colonel (Retired), Medical Corps, US Army; Chief, Department of Orthopaedics and
Rehabilitation, Walter Reed National Military Medical Center, 4494 North Palmer
Road, Bethesda, Maryland 20889

‡Colonel, US Army; Joint Headquarters Chaplain, Pennsylvania National Guard and
Chief Communications Officer, Lebanon VA Medical Center, 1700 South Lincoln
Avenue, Lebanon, Pennsylvania 17042

INTRODUCTION

Complete freedom from stress is death.

HANS SELYE
FATHER OF STRESS RESEARCH

M ilitary and Veteran communities represent a unique culture within the United States, while at the same time often living among and supporting the broader civilian communities. The exact number of Service Members and Veterans who have had their lives altered by serving during the last decade and beyond is yet unknown, and it will likely take years for the personal costs to be determined because conditions such as traumatic brain injury, posttraumatic stress, orthopedic injuries, and hearing loss are more precisely identified among Military and Veteran populations.[1] More than 2 million US Service Members have been deployed to Iraq or Afghanistan, approximately 27% of whom have been deployed more than once.[2] People serving within the US military represent <1% of the American population.[3] Furthermore, living Military Veterans (individuals who have ever served in uniform as part of the Armed Forces) are only about 6% of the current population of the United States.[4] Therefore, only a small portion of the population has first-hand experience of the challenges faced and sacrifices made by members of the Armed Forces. This prolonged period of war and the operational tempo for Service Members have placed strain on Military families and the Military community. The United States has asked a lot of its Military community. Among the persistent challenges are building and maintaining resilient Service Members, families, Veterans, and communities. The long-term health of Military and Veteran communities is also in part dependent on the successful reintegration of Service Members into the force, with their families, and into their communities.[5] Thus, it is our hypothesis that *resilience and successful reintegration are highly interrelated, and that one cannot be achieved without the other.*

PURPOSE

This handbook is intended to be a source of information for the broad Military community. In this case, the broad Military community includes uniformed Military personnel, family members, civilian personnel of federal agencies, Veterans, and all people who contribute to the success of wounded, injured, and ill Service Members. When Service Members return from a deployment with visible or hidden impairments or challenges, it is important for the entire community to provide support to ameliorate the long-term impact of wounds, injuries, and illnesses that can manifest into permanent disabilities. The information contained herein should help the reader to understand and implement the steps necessary for helping wounded, injured, or ill Service Members and their families to successfully continue their military careers or to become successful as Veterans within civilian communities. A multifaceted approach will be presented, and there is no one single solution that will work for all Service Members. However, the information contained within this handbook should provide insight into the options available and the many pathways that lead to success.

Our definition of disability throughout this handbook is consistent with that of the World Health Organization (WHO) and its International Classification of Functioning, Disability, and Health (ICF). The WHO-ICF model defines an *impairment* as a loss of or a significant reduction of function as a result of biological development or change.[6] For Service Members, impairment and changes in function are frequently the result of wounds, injuries, or illnesses. For example, damage to a limb from an improvised explosive device can require limb salvage or amputation, which leads to a reduction of function over the previous intact limb. Therefore, the person has an *impairment*. A *disability* is the result of the interaction of a person with an impairment with the environment, and the *environment* includes the following:

- *physical environment* (eg, how buildings and communities are designed and built),
- *social environment* (eg, how people respond and is inclusive of people with impairments), and
- *policy environment* (eg, how laws and regulations affect people with impairments and their ability to participate in society).

If the environment is accessible and inclusive, a person's disabilities can be minimized and possibly to a great extent eliminated within that context. For example, if a Service Member has a spinal cord injury and uses a wheelchair, an environment in which everything is accessible from a wheelchair—where colleagues respect him or her and where he or she is treated fairly by the employer—contributes to minimizing the disability.

Wounded, injured, and ill Service Members and their families are part of the tapestry of Military and Veteran communities. Even with impairments, limitations, and differences, they are deserving of respect, inclusion, and integration into our communities. A fundamental theme that readers should consider is that everyone has something to contribute to society and to their communities, including both the Military community of Service Members, their families, and civilian employees of the Armed Forces, as well as the civilian community where Service Members and Veterans live with their families. The concept of "social capital" is another theme within this handbook that will be described in greater detail in a later chapter. This concept emphasizes that communities are composed of groups of people with common beliefs, goals, or physical locations, and that everyone can make a contribution to the culture of the community and ultimately to its success.

GOALS

The overarching goal of this book is to provide the reader with the tools and knowledge to help wounded, injured, and ill Service Members live healthy, happy, and prosperous lives. Another goal is for the reader to gain an understanding of the key factors and current resources that may contribute to successful and fulfilling lives of wounded, injured, and ill Service Members and their families. Furthermore, the current state of knowledge, pathways, programs, and concepts that may help Service Members and their families to pursue and achieve their goals are presented.

One focus of this handbook is to provide practical guidance to Military personnel, families, and civilians on how to build resilience, especially among wounded, injured, and ill Service Members. Resilience and reintegration go hand-in-hand, although few have treated them as such.[7] Ultimately, the goal of resilience is the successful reintegration of soldiers into the Armed Forces, with their families, and into their communities. Another focus of this book is that Service Members, Veterans, and families who are resilient will be more successful in reintegration. Therefore, this handbook is intended to serve as a practical guide based on science, clinical experience, and knowledge of programs for promoting successful reintegration.

STRUCTURE

Reintegration of Service Members with their families, communities, and the Military/Veteran communities is a substantial challenge facing the Department of Defense (DoD), the Department of Veterans Affairs, and the entire United States. This book ties together scientific evidence, clinical knowledge, and practical experience into a handbook accessible to professionals within military medicine and the military population at large, while serving as a resource for Veterans, Service Members, and their families. When Service Members and their families face severe challenges, they may often become overwhelmed. Clinicians, other service providers, and Service Members and their families should all benefit from this reference work.

Each chapter in this handbook is intended to stand alone, while also maintaining consistency with the other chapters. There are scientific and clinical references for each chapter for readers who wish to delve deeper into original source material. However, the information contained within each chapter should be applicable as written.

DEFINITION OF RESILIENCE

Resilience is a topic that has been studied by scientists and clinicians for several decades. Much of the scientific literature has been focused on children and other survivors of abuse.[8] Some of this work is of relevance to the Military population, and recently there has been more work directly related to the Military population.[9] There are also several theories of resilience, as well as definitions of resilience. Thus, we present a definition and description of resilience in the context of this book to provide readers with a framework. The DoD has yet to adopt a unified definition of resilience. When a definition or description is adopted, it may not completely align with our approach. However, the fundamental concepts and components are likely to be similar. The Army's Comprehensive Soldier & Family Fitness Program uses the following definition of resilience: "the ability to grow and thrive in the face of challenges and bounce back from adversity."

In this handbook, we consider resilience to be "the ability to recover from, ameliorate, or avoid the negative effects of risk or adversity." Adversity may be due to

- prolonged separation from friends and family,
- major disasters,
- violence (whether in the home or elsewhere),
- extreme poverty,
- persistent fear of harm for oneself or another,
- trauma (severe injury, illness, or cumulative negative life events), or
- war.

Service Members deployed on hazardous or combat missions often face extreme risk and adversity that place stressors on them, the members of their units, their commanders, their civilian leaders, and their friends and families. Frameworks to build resilience among all potentially affected parties are important, and can help to reduce the negative effects of stress, risk, and adversity. Individuals, families, communities, and organizations that are resilient display positive adaptation despite experiences of significant adversity, risk, or trauma. There are clear examples of Service Members and families who experienced extreme risk and/or adversity to include loss of limb from combat operations, yet who remain strong and even go on to help others. Some such examples are illustrated in this handbook.

FRAMEWORK FOR BUILDING RESILIENCE

Service Members and their families have frequently been endangered by extreme and often complex adversities. This fact requires all of those concerned—including commanders, civilian leaders, healthcare providers, volunteers, Military and Veterans service organizations, and other professionals, as well as families and communities—to confront many challenging issues. Although there is a substantial body of research on resilience, the immediate threats to life or bodily harm, family security, community integrity, and the readiness of the Armed Forces cannot wait for research to provide complete answers before action is taken. Hence, there are multifaceted programs to help build resilience among Service Members, families, and Military communities. The overall framework for building resilience requires a multidimensional approach to building capacity for, processes to, and outcomes of successful adaptation and growth in the face of significant threats to the integrity of the person, family, organization, or community. Programs for resilience need to focus on promoting strength, stability, growth, healthy recovery, function, and adaptation (to include compensatory strategies). The definition of resilience used in the US Army's Ready and Resilient program is as follows: "Resilience is the mental, physical, emotional, and behavioral ability to face and cope with adversity, adapt to change, recover, learn, and grow from setbacks."

The components of resilience can be remembered using the acronym MEPS: Mental, Emotional, Physical, and Spiritual.[10] *Mental* refers to the ability to build a coherent plan with goals and objectives. *Emotional* is the ability to trust in self and the ability to give to others. *Physical* is the ability to accomplish the plan or goal. *Spiritual* is the moral compass (doing the right things for the right reasons). Our framework for building resilience includes the interrelation of several essential components that include adversity, positive adaptation, factors promoting positive responses, and protective factors. There are some individuals who are naturally resilient, and others who require assistance to become more resilient. Moreover, the life course of individuals and families can influence resilience. Intervention strategies for resilience should include the following components:

• minimizing or reducing risk exposure,
• strengthening compensatory strategies,

- increasing factors promoting positive responses,
- having a moderate impact of adversity, and
- boosting protective mechanisms.

People respond differently to the same or similar experiences. There are also some other factors of adversity that should be considered: general dose-effect (closer proximity, relation, or severity of adversity), cognitive awareness of the adversity, the behavior of other people, previous traumatic or adverse experiences, cultural and/or community beliefs/customs, and the context of the adversity (eg, education and sociodemographic factors).[11]

Programs to encourage building resilience should include the following components:

- a program to help individuals, families, and communities frame positive goals;
- emphasis on positive influences and outcomes;
- collection of data on positive indicators of change;
- inclusion of multifactorial approaches (to include tailoring the program to the individual, family, or community); and
- encouragement of collaboration among all stakeholders.

Some people, and even some communities, are able to embrace adversity and turn it into positive energy for change and to continuously improve. Using adversity as a tool for positive growth is often achieved through teamwork and goal setting. The military is very familiar with this concept and uses it quite effectively in training. This is accomplished through a variety of means, such as training in cold or hot weather, training in the rain, or performing a night parachute jump. The US Army Ranger School (Fort Benning, GA) or the US Army Reconnaissance and Surveillance Leaders Course (Fort Benning, GA) exemplifies using adversity to promote positive growth by placing people in extremely challenging circumstances for prolonged periods of time and then recognizing the accomplishments of those Service Members who complete the program. All branches of the military utilize similar models to use adversity as a tool. Entire communities may use similar techniques (eg, by rebuilding a school after a flood or organizing and participating in a run to raise funds for a member of the community in need). Many not-for-profit organizations use a similar model to encourage people to run a marathon or complete a triathlon as a means to support a cause. Even if a person cannot run anymore, that person can train for the Marine Corps Marathon using a handcycle. These approaches encourage people to embrace adversity and to help turn it into a positive force in their lives.

One uplifting example is Terry Fox, who as a young man had to have his leg amputated because of cancer. He chose to face his change in physical ability and how he was perceived by others by running across Canada.[12] Other people have taken on more personal challenges to force themselves to adjust to their "new normal." Then there is Scott Rigsby, who struggled for years with a traumatic brain injury while having one leg amputated and the other with a difficult limb salvage.[13] He had a hard time earning a college degree, maintaining relationships, and managing his finances. Eventually, he came to the conclusion that he should have the salvaged leg amputated and that he needed to change his life. To achieve this and to challenge himself, he set a goal of completing the Hawaiian Ironman Triathlon. Without any prior training or even the appropriate equipment, and after many trials and tribulations, he successfully completed his goal. Scott then wrote a book about his experiences and now works to motivate other people to make positive changes in their lives.

Another uplifting example is Max Cleland. Max is a Vietnam Veteran who had both legs and most of an arm amputated because of wounds received in combat.[14] Despite returning to an America that he found was not accessible physically or socially to someone with his type of injuries, he persevered and set for himself a goal to enter politics and become a US Senator. He ran grassroots campaigns and traveled across the state of Georgia to win a successful bid to the US Senate. He also served as Chief of the Veterans Administration during his career. He set high and seemingly unattainable goals for himself, and achieved them. Despite his successes, he faced many challenges, including requiring treatment for posttraumatic stress decades following his original wounds and after enduring a difficult and unsuccessful reelection campaign. Max used the joy of serving others and making a positive difference in the lives of America's Military Veterans as a tool to make a positive change in his life, as well as in the lives of millions of other people. These individuals set goals to challenge themselves and then pursued them with passion.

Building resilience does not always require making large changes in one's life; sometimes focusing on small things frequently, even daily, can help to increase resilience. A tool used in positive psychology is to use a diary to record three positive notes each day and then to review them once per week.[15] The "good things" that happen in our lives every day often go unnoticed; but, when we write them down, they remind us of our accomplishments and positive experiences. Small things can make a big difference in our outlook toward life and other people. Another simple tool for building resilience is to do something for someone else. Writing a brief, handwritten thank you or congratulatory note to a friend, family member, or even someone you do not know well can make a difference in both the outlook of the sender and the receiver.

FRAMEWORK FOR REINTEGRATION

Reintegration, for the purposes of this book, occurs when Service Members who have become wounded, injured, or ill are successful in becoming loving and valued members of their families and social networks, in continuing with active duty or active guard/reserve, or in assimilating successfully into civilian society as Veterans. For wounded, injured, and ill Service Members to reintegrate into a military unit, their family structure, and the community at large, they need opportunities, accessible goals and resources, and enlightened (and hopefully) welcoming attitudes from the people around them. According to a report produced by the RAND Corporation (Arlington, VA):

> Since 2001, the National Guard and Reserve have been utilized at unprecedented levels to fill key roles in overseas operations, with more than 800,000 reserve component members called to active duty since 9/11. As a result of these increased demands, guard personnel and reservists have experienced more overseas deployments—often in combat situations that extend for long periods or occur in rapid succession. In many cases, this shift in operational tempo places a strain on families, especially as citizen warriors reintegrate back into their civilian lives and return to their civilian jobs after deployment. A smooth reintegration is critical not only for family well-being but also for Military readiness.[16(p1)]

Our approach to successful reintegration is based on the concept of social capital. Although there is no uniform definition of social capital, in this handbook, we will use the following: *Social capital is the strength of the human networks that people have, and how those networks contribute to the sharing or exchange of resources (support, information, influence, finances, etc).*

Each journey begins with the first step, and it takes planning on the part of individuals and communities to attain successful reintegration. One such tool is to set *specific, measurable, attainable, realistic, and time-bound* (SMART) goals.[17] SMART goals help to break down larger aspirations into manageable and achievable tasks that prevent the goalsetter from becoming overwhelmed. SMART goals are concrete and can be precisely defined and therefore more easily targeted. "To become a better person," for example, is not a SMART goal, because it is ill-defined. However, it can be rewritten to "spending more quality time with my family." This goal can be measured in the time together with family and how that time was spent (eg, movies, sports, games, etc). A SMART goal must be something that is achievable from the current vantage point. A series of SMART goals can be chained together to create more ambitious goals. For example, if one of the goals is to take the family on vacation, then planning is required and resources must be committed. The type and location of the vacation will depend on the availability of resources (eg, funds, time, accommodations for any disabilities, and possibly passports). A SMART goal must be realistic; traveling overseas takes more planning and resources than taking a short camping trip to a local state park. Lastly, SMART goals need to be time-bound. The world is full of dreamers who someday are going to do something. SMART goals require setting a date and making a commitment to achieve it. Adjustments can be made for unforeseen events, but then a new date needs to be established. Nearly all great things are accomplished by completing each little step along the way.

The US Marine Corps uses a tool (that originated with the US Army and was originally called the "Leavenworth Order") to help leaders achieve their goals, which can equally be applied to other areas of life for both individuals and organizations. The tool is called a SMEAC, an acronym for Situation, Mission, Execution, Administration, and Communication.[18] These are the items needed to achieve a goal or mission. *Situation* is used to describe current circumstances and obstacles in the way of achieving the *Mission*; support mechanisms to overcome the obstacles are also noted. *Execution* describes the steps that will be taken to accomplish the Mission or to achieve the desired goal; these are essentially subgoals or steps toward the goal that must be acquired. *Administration* is the category in which all of the resources required to accomplish the Mission are listed, including people, gear/equipment, funding, transportation, time, etc. *Communication* consists of people and the methods of conveying information regularly to achieve the desired goal.

At the Semper Fi Odyssey program (Ligonier, PA) participants are taught the tool MA²R*INES³ to help prepare their plan for reintegration into their units or into their home communities.[10] MA²R*INES³ provides a framework for moving forward with reintegration, and helps people and communities to prepare a roadmap to achieve their goals and become more accepting of others and themselves:

M   Mission—What you are going to do and why.
A² Accountability and Attitude—You must be in control of your attitude and hold yourself accountable.
R* Responsibility—You must be responsible for your actions. Are you going to be a giver or a taker?

I Integrity—Completeness. Are you whole in your MEPS (Mental, Emotional, Physical, and Spiritual)?

N Nourish—Is your MEPS balanced enough that you will be able to give to yourself and others? Do you have people that you Value, Accept, Understand, Love, and Trust—VAULT)?

E Energy—It is either positive or negative. Negative energy travels faster than positive energy. Can you provide positive energy in your life?

S³ Synergy, Strive, and SMEAC. Strive to find ways to surround yourself with people and activities that make you and them better.

SOCIAL CAPITAL AS A MODEL FOR SUCCESSFUL REINTEGRATION

The energy I give is equal to the inspiration I provide, which results in the impact I make, which leads to the legacy I leave.

MAJOR GENERAL (RETIRED) T. S. JONES
US MARINE CORPS

The idea of social capital tells us that all people are interconnected and that, through our interactions with one another and the exchange or sharing of resources, communities can become stronger. For wounded, injured, and ill Service Members and their families, a basic premise is that everyone has something to contribute and can add value. This premise must permeate the Military, their families, circle of friends, and communities. An individual's value to his or her community can present in many forms. It can be in terms of knowledge, influence, finances, strength, or relationships. These factors have value and in some cases can even be financially quantified. For example, if a friend purchases a new couch, that person can either pay to have the couch delivered to his or her home or call on friends and family members to help by drawing on his or her social capital. Similarly, when wounded, injured, or ill Service Members move to a new community, they typically wish to make new friends. Most friends are people with shared experiences and/or interests, but this is not enough. Being introduced into a community can be made easier when a trusted member of the community makes the introductions, and this person is using his or her social capital to endorse the new person to other members of the group.

The ultimate goal is for wounded, injured, and ill Service Members to become valued, contributing, happy, healthy, and fulfilled members of their families, circle of friends, and communities. According to the RAND survey, families and Service Members who were most successful with reintegration had the following traits:

> These families felt ready for deployment, had good communication with the Service Member and with the member's unit during his or her time away from home, and tended to be comfortable financially. When the Service Member deployed with his or her own unit and returned home without a combat-related wound, other physical injury, or a psychological issue, readjustment tended to go more smoothly.[16(p1)]

The RAND report also noted that some of the families had problems with reintegration following deployment, and some of their challenges were "emotional or mental health, health care, civilian employment, the spouse/partner relationship, financial or legal matters, child well-being, and education."[16(p1)] For successful reintegration to occur, it is essential to prepare Service Members, families, and friends for reintegration postdeployment, and to involve a wide array of resources from the federal government, not-for-profit organizations, and communities. Frequent communication between all stakeholders has been shown to improve reintegration.[19]

It is important to note that everyone in a community has something to contribute, and this adds to the tapestry that makes up communities. They are essential to successful reintegration. Communities must be transformed so that everyone has a sense of belonging, with Service Members and Veterans being *of* their communities and not simply *part of* them. Communities must strive to create measurable and obvious human gain. Therefore, this requires communities to ask themselves questions such as:

- Can they effectively apply capital?
- Do they have a big enough vision?
- Do they have the capacity to achieve their goals?

Communities need to understand and engage their human capital, intellectual capital, social or network capital, and financial capital to effectively apply social capital to be inclusive of Service Members, Veterans, and their families.

COMMENTS

For wounded, injured, and ill Service Members and their families, resilience, social capital, and reintegration are all inextricably intertwined. It is essential that Service Members and their families be provided the counseling, education, and resources needed to help build their social capital so that they can become and remain resilient, and can successfully reintegrate into their families and circles of friends, into the Military community as desired and appropriate, or into civilian communities either as Veterans or continuing their Military service.

In today's world, it seems that there are more demands placed on everyone's time and that people are available to their families, friends, coworkers, and bosses nearly 24 hours per day. This places demands on our minds and bodies that we are not built to withstand for long periods of time. Good health is built on three pillars: (1) nutrition, (2) activity, and (3) sleep.[20] Too many people eat improperly and do not watch the nutritional content of what they eat; they ingest entirely too much sugar and caffeine. People today, even some Service Members, are at risk for sitting too long daily and not getting enough activity. More is needed than a simple 30-minute workout each morning or afternoon; even simply adding parking further away from the building or taking the stairs can make a big difference in the long run. Sleep is also critical to health and to being effective as a spouse, parent, colleague, and member of the community. At least seven hours of uninterrupted sleep each night is essential to long-term health.[21] This means removing the electronics from the bedroom, taking away the blinking lights, and reducing any noise. Getting a solid night's sleep helps us to stay healthy, remain alert, and make good decisions. Being healthy, fit, and able to make good decisions helps to reinforce key attributes of Military leadership: *character, commitment, and competence.*[22]

Bringing self-awareness, self-care, and mutual support to the center of all activities is key for both resilience and reintegration. For example, science shows that two of the most effective approaches to treating depression are (1) talking to a sympathetic, compassionate, and experienced listener, and (2) doing physical exercise.[23-25] Self-awareness, self-care, and mutual support are tools that can help everyone and should be fully integrated into the community. Community activities in which people with similar experiences and interests can get together and talk can help to remove barriers of isolation and feelings of loneliness.

References

1. U.S. vet's disability filings reach historic rate. USA Today Web site. http://usatoday30.usatoday.com/news/health/story/2012-05-28/Veteran-disability/55250092/1. Accessed July 13, 2014.
2. U.S. veterans: by the numbers. ABC News Web site. http://abcnews.go.com/Politics/us-Veterans-numbers/story?id=14928136. Accessed July 13, 2014.
3. Americans and their military, drifting apart. *New York Times* Web site. http://www.nytimes.com/2013/05/27/opinion/americans-and-their-Military-drifting-apart.html?pagewanted=all&_r=0. Accessed July 13, 2014.
4. Gallup.com. In U.S., 24% of men, 2% of women are veterans. http://www.gallup.com/poll/158729/men-women-Veterans.aspx. Gallup Web site. Accessed July 13, 2014.
5. Doyle ME, Peterson KA. Re-entry and reintegration: returning home after combat. *Psychiatr Q*. 2005;76:361–370.
6. World Health Organization. *How to Use ICF: A Practical Manual for Using the International Classification of Functioning, Disability and Health (ICF)*. Geneva, Switzerland: WHO; 2013.
7. Bowles SV, Bates MJ. Military organizations and programs contributing to resilience building. *Mil Med*. 2010;175:382–385.
8. Richardson GE. The metatheory of resilience and resiliency. *J Clin Psychol*. 2002;58:307–321.
9. Finkel D. *Thank You for Your Service*. Toronto, Ontario, Canada: Bond Street Books; 2013.
10. The Semper Fi Odyssey. *Semper Fi Odyssey Handbook*. Outdoor Odyssey Leadership Academy Web site. http://www.outdoorodyssey.org/leadership-programming/Veteran-programming/semper-fi-odyssey/2013. Accessed July 13, 2014.
11. Aiken AB, Bélanger SAH. *Beyond the Line*. Montreal, Quebec, Canada: McGill-Queen's University Press; 2013.
12. Scrivener L. *Terry Fox: His Story*. Toronto, Ontario, Canada: McClelland & Stewart Ltd; 2000.
13. Rigsby S, Glatzer J. *Unthinkable: The True Story About the First Double Amputee to Complete the World-Famous Hawaiian Ironman Triathlon*. Carol Stream, IL: Tyndale House Foundation; 2009.
14. Cleland M, Raines B. *Heart of a Patriot: How I Found the Courage to Survive Vietnam, Walter Reed and Karl Rove*. New York, NY: Simon and Schuster; 2009.
15. Cohn MA, Fredrickson BL, Brown Sl, Mikels JA, Conway AM. Happiness unpacked: positive emotions increase life satisfaction by building resilience. *Emotion*. 2009;9:361.

16. RAND Corporation. Reintegration after deployment. RAND Corporation Web site. http://www.rand.org/pubs/research_briefs/RB9730/index1.html. Accessed July 13, 2014.

17. Bovend'Eerdt TJ, Thamar JH, Rachel E. Botell, Derick T. Wade. Writing SMART rehabilitation goals and achieving goal attainment scaling: a practical guide. *Clin Rehabil.* 2009;23:352–361.

18. Wiechmann JR. *Marine Corps Leadership Lessons for the Workplace A Case Study* [dissertation]. Lawrence, KS: The University of Kansas; 2011.

19. Downs DA, Murtazashvili I. *Arms and the University: Military Presence and the Civic Education of Non-Military Students.* New York, NY: Cambridge University Press; 2012.

20. Resnick HE, Carter EA, Albia M, Phillips B. Cross-sectional relationship of reported fatigue to obesity, diet, and physical activity: results from the Third National Health and Nutrition Examination Survey. *J Clin Sleep Med.* 2006;2:163–169.

21. Gehrman P, Seelig AD, Jacobson IF, et al. Predeployment sleep duration and insomnia symptoms as risk factors for new-onset mental health disorders following military deployment. *Sleep.* 2013;36:1009–1018.

22. Venturella P. *Character, Competence, and Commitment . . . The Measure of a Leader—Leadership Philosophies, Principles and Observations of a Career Air Force Combat Controller.* Bloomington, IN: AuthorHouse; 2007.

23. Association of the United States Army. Vice chief calls on NCOs to promote Ready and Resilient Campaign. Association of the United States Army Web site. http://www.ausa.org/meetings/2013/AnnualMeeting/Pages/story13.aspx. Accessed July 13, 2014.

24. Segal ZV, Williams MG, Teasdale JD. *Mindfulness-based Cognitive Therapy for Depression.* New York, NY: Guilford Press; 2012.

25. O'Neal HA, Dunn AL, Martinsen EW. Depression and exercise. *Int J Sport Psychol.* 2000;31:110–135.

Lieutenant Colonel (LTC) Steven E. Gventer is currently serving as Commander of the 2nd Squadron, 2nd Cavalry Regiment's Cougar Squadron, in Vilseck, Germany. He assumed command of Cougar 6 on September 1, 2015. Prior to this command, he served at NATO (North Atlantic Treaty Organization) Joint Forces Command in Naples, Italy, and is honored to have been chosen to command a Stryker Cavalry Squadron in Germany in 2016. Gventer was wounded twice leading his Troopers through the volatile streets of Sadr City in Baghdad, Iraq, in 2004–2005 as a Company Commander with Cobra Company, 2-8 Cavalry. In 2004, Gventer (then a Captain) was first shot through the leg while on patrol. A few weeks later, he was wounded by a rocket-propelled grenade while dismounted with his Soldiers. After overcoming these wounds and the surgeries required to repair his right arm and to remove fragments from his shoulder, back, and leg, he again deployed less than a year later as the Aide-de-Camp to the Corps Commander in Iraq.

Gventer was then handpicked to report to Walter Reed Army Medical Center (Washington, DC) in early 2007, and was the first soldier assigned to the new brigade overseeing the care of the Army's Wounded Warriors and their families. He stood up the Army's first Warrior Transition Unit on April 27, 2007, establishing a new set of standards adopted by the Army under the principle of the Warrior Ethos: *I will never leave a fallen comrade.* Upon completion of this command, he assumed responsibilities as the Executive Officer and Advisor to the Commanding General of the Warrior Transition Command that oversaw 36 Warrior Transition Units and 9 Community-Based Warrior Transition Units all over the world, and supported more than 10,000 wounded, ill, or injured soldiers, and 2,500 cadre.

While serving in the USAMEDCOM (US Army Medical Command), LTC Gventer overcame severe complications and a major illness exacerbated by infections from his old wounds. He became a patient in the very system that he helped to improve. After 13 months and several surgeries, LTC Gventer healed and was selected to attend the Australian Command and General Staff College in Canberra, Australia. He was ordered to depart General Staff College 1 month early to deploy with the 3rd Brigade, 1st Cavalry Division, for his third Iraq tour. He served as the S3 for the 3-8 Cavalry at Camp Garry Owen, Iraq. There, the lone battalion conducted operations along the Iranian border in the Maysan Province, closed Camp Garry Owen, and redeployed as part of the last brigade out of Iraq in late 2011.

Upon redeployment to Fort Hood, Texas, Steve was selected to become the 3rd Brigade Operations Officer for the "Greywolf" Armored Brigade Combat Team. During his 15 months as Greywolf 3, LTC Gventer executed the reintegration of the Brigade Combat Team, and planned, resourced, and successfully executed the Armored Brigade  Combat Team's full train-up for a Decisive Action Rotation to the National Training Center for Rotation 13-03.

Gventer joined the Army ("the family business") after working for a few years as a high school teacher and coach. His father retired as a Lieutenant Colonel, and both his sister and brother served as Army officers. In 1998, Gventer enlisted and attended basic training at Fort Jackson, South Carolina, and then Officer Candidate School at Fort Benning, Georgia.

LTC Gventer's awards include the Bronze Star with V-"Valor" Device, the Bronze Star with 2 Oak Leaf Clusters, the Purple Heart with 1 Oak Leaf Cluster, the Defense Meritorious Service Medal, the Meritorious Service Medal with 3 Oak Leaf Clusters, the Army Commendation Medal with 2 Oak Leaf Clusters, the Army Achievement Medal, the National Defense Service Medal, the Iraqi Campaign Medal with 4 stars, the Global War on Terrorism Expeditionary Medal, the Global War on Terrorism Service Medal, the Korea Defense Service Medal, the Army Service Ribbon and the Overseas Service Ribbon with Numeral 5, the Valorous Unit Award, the Meritorious Unit Citation, and the Army Staff Identifier Badge. He has also been awarded the Combat Action Badge. Steve Gventer is also an Eagle Scout.

One of the things that, maybe, the American people are
not as familiar with as we are, . . . is . . . [that]
our work on prosthetics, traumatic brain injury,
medical evacuation has actually had a beneficial
effect, not just for our Servicemen and women, and
their families, but also for the American people at large.

★ ★ ★

GENERAL MARTIN E. DEMPSEY
WARRIOR GAMES
US AIR FORCE ACADEMY
COLORADO SPRINGS, COLORADO
OCTOBER 5, 2014

CHAPTER TWO

Physical Medicine and Rehabilitation

[*]*Lieutenant Commander, Medical Corps, US Navy; Department of Physical Medicine and Rehabilitation, University of Pittsburgh Medical Center, 1400 Locust Street, Pittsburgh, Pennsylvania 15219*

INTRODUCTION

Author Margaret Carty stated, ". . . the nice thing about teamwork is that you always have others on your side."[1(piii)] Throughout its history, the US Military has been, continues to be, and always will be one of the greatest fraternities of men and women (literally and figuratively) fighting side by side with one another to achieve some of the greatest accomplishments our country has ever seen.

Just as the US Military sets the standard for teamwork and camaraderie, the field of Physical Medicine and Rehabilitation has been leading the way in the successful team approach to patient care through the interdisciplinary work of a number of individuals. Each member of this multidisciplinary team works together with the individual Service Member (as well as with one another) to not only formulate the best medical care plan for that member, but also to act as a teammate in the fight for successful rehabilitation and reintegration into the community.

This chapter will explore the expertise of each team member, provide an overview of how the team formulates and carries out a care plan, discuss the benefits of rehabilitation, and note the role of education for Service Members and their families.

THE MULTIDISCIPLINARY REHABILITATION TEAM

The Multidisciplinary Rehabilitation Team consists of the following specialists:

- physiatrists,
- physical therapists,
- occupational therapists,
- speech and language pathologists/therapists,
- recreational therapists,
- rehabilitation nurses,
- social workers,
- mental health workers,
- orthotists and prosthetists,
- exercise physiologists,
- athletic trainers, and
- rehabilitation engineers.

PHYSIATRISTS

Although the physiatrist is often viewed as the director of the Multidisciplinary Rehabilitation Team, the true director of that team is the Service Member. Recovering and reintegrating Service Members are the focal points of every rehabilitation team. By establishing their goals and subsequent feedback, the rehabilitation teams adapt and personalize rehabilitation plans (Figure 2-1).

Physiatrists are medical doctors practicing in the field of Physical Medicine and Rehabilitation. The field dates back to the founding of the American Board of Physical Medicine and Rehabilitation in 1947 and the establishment of Physical Medicine and Rehabilitation as an official field of medicine within the American Medical Association.[2]

However, prior to the official founding of the American Board of Physical Medicine and Rehabilitation, the field can be traced back to World War I. In response to a growing number of wounded soldiers returning home from World War I and an already successful rehabilitation program flourishing in European countries, The Surgeon General in 1917 established the Division of Special Hospitals and Physical Reconstruction based on a similar program conducted at British Army hospitals.[3] Physical reconstruction, which at this time was defined as maximum mental and physical restoration of the individual, flourished. By 1919, there were 45 hospitals throughout the country, and nearly 50,000 returning Veterans had been treated at these facilities.[4]

FIGURE 2-1. *Rehabilitation Interdisciplinary Team.*

OT: *occupational therapist;* PT: *physical therapist;* RT: *recreational therapist;*
SLP: *speech and language therapist.*

Before World War I, there were very few physicians actively practicing physical therapy in the United States. However, after the wars, the civilian sector saw an influx of well-trained personnel in the field.[5]

Two subsequent sentinel events occurred in the 1930–1940s with the advent of World War II, as well as the poliomyelitis epidemic and the associated need for rehabilitation services in these growing populations. Dr Howard Rusk,[6] a lieutenant colonel in the Army Air Corps, is often credited with bringing rehabilitation medicine to the forefront during and after World War II through the reintroduction of active rehabilitation and the resulting success with treating wounded soldiers through early ambulation and exercise following surgery and the treatment of men, not diseases.

Physiatrists specialize in a wide variety of disciplines that are of great importance and applicability to 21st century Service Members and Veterans, including

- traumatic brain injury,
- spinal cord injury,
- musculoskeletal sports medicine,
- polytrauma,
- burns,
- amputation,
- arthritis,
- neurological disorders,
- pain management, and
- stroke.

Figure 2-2. *Taping a patient's knee.*
PHOTOGRAPH: COURTESY OF DALE WILLIAMS.

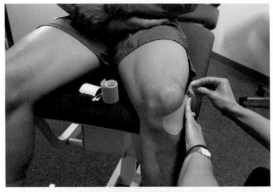

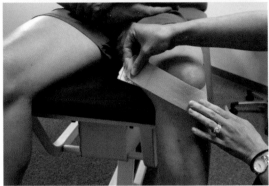

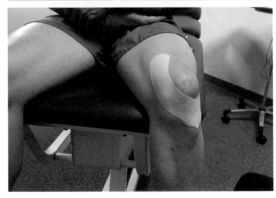

In conjunction with treatment of the aforementioned diagnoses, physiatrists also have unique training in the assessment and prescription of assistive technology from prosthesis to braces to wheelchairs and everything in between that helps maximize an individual's functional independence.

The physiatrist can also take on the role of primary care manager during the inpatient hospital stay of the Service Member/Veteran, as well as assume roles in a variety of situations during outpatient (eg, clinic or deployment setting) care.

PHYSICAL THERAPISTS
Physical therapists (PTs) are specialists in evaluating and treating disorders of the human body primarily by physical means. Whether the condition results from injury, disease, or other causes (eg, trauma), they focus primarily on those individuals who have disturbed function or impairment related to the musculoskeletal, neurological, cardiopulmonary, and integumentary (skin) systems. PTs evaluate the functioning of these systems and apply the appropriate treatment to alleviate pain and improve physical function.[7]

PTs utilize their specialized training to improve an individual's physical function through optimizing one's ability for mobility; transferring to and from a variety of surfaces; and increasing gross motor strength, range of motion, and endurance (Figure 2-2).

OCCUPATIONAL THERAPISTS

Occupational therapists help Service Members participate in the things they want and need to do through the therapeutic use of everyday activities (eg, eating, getting dressed, cooking, etc). Therapy services may include comprehensive evaluations of the client's home and other environments (eg, workplace, school), recommendations for adaptive equipment and associated training in its use, and guidance and education for family members and caregivers.[8]

In Figure 2-3, PerMMA, a robotic wheelchair and arm with mobile wrist and fingers, is designed to aid those with physical impairments complete the activities of daily living.

FIGURE 2-3. *PerMMA is a robotic wheelchair and arm with mobile wrist and fingers. It is designed to aid those with physical impairments complete the activities of daily living.* PHOTOGRAPH: COURTESY OF MICHAEL LAIN.

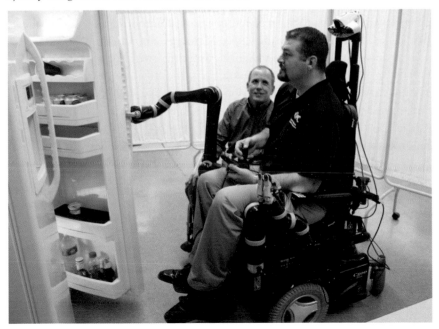

Figure 2-4. *Hand cyclists and a visually impaired runner at the start of the Pittsburgh Marathon.* PHOTOGRAPH: COURTESY OF RONALD ROTH.

Speech and Language Pathologists/Therapists

Speech and language pathologists assess, diagnose, treat, and help to prevent disorders related to speech, language, cognitive communication, and swallowing. These therapists work with Service Members who cannot produce speech sounds or who cannot produce them clearly, those with speech rhythm and fluency problems and swallowing difficulties, those with problems understanding and producing language, and those with cognitive communication impairments (eg, attention, memory, and problem-solving disorders).[9]

Recreational Therapists

Recreational therapists promote play, recreation, and leisure as a means to psychological and physical recovery. These therapists design interventions that include a wide range of modalities and facilitation techniques, including aquatics therapy, wheelchair sports, exercise programs, animal-assisted therapy, and yoga (Figure 2-4).[10]

Rehabilitation Nurses

The goal of rehabilitation nursing is to assist individuals with a disability and/or chronic illness to attain and maintain maximum function. Rehabilitation nurses, in addition to their traditional job requirements, play a unique role in assisting patients in adapting to an altered lifestyle (eg, teaching a patient with a spinal cord injury to properly self-catheterize his/her bladder, teaching a newly diagnosed diabetic patient to administer his/her own insulin prior to returning home, etc).

SOCIAL WORKERS

US Military social workers are officers who enhance unit readiness and the emotional well-being of military personnel, their family members, and other eligible beneficiaries. They provide a wide array of support through clinical counseling, crisis intervention, disaster relief, critical event debriefing, as well as teaching and training in various military settings.[11]

MENTAL HEALTH WORKERS

The Mental Health Rehabilitation Team can be made up of any single, individual, or combination of multiple different aspects of mental health care. Some of the most common members of the rehabilitation team are psychiatrists, psychologists, neuropsychologists, and rehabilitation counselors. These practitioners specialize in a wide variety of diagnostic and treatment methods in numerous diagnoses, including traumatic brain injury, posttraumatic stress disorder, anxiety, depression, anger, as well as relationship and marriage counseling. Further information regarding their integral role in successful integration is addressed in Chapter 4, Psychosocial Factors in Reintegration.

FIGURE 2-5. *Mike Anderson, a Gulf War Veteran and knee disarticulation amputee, is an active participant in a variety of athletic endeavors, including running, CrossFit, obstacle races, and golf.*

ORTHOTISTS AND PROSTHETISTS

Orthotists and prosthetists use state-of-the-art advanced orthotic and prosthetic limb technology for the design and production of orthotic and prosthetic devices. Prosthetic and orthotic devices can be custom manufactured and adjusted by a prosthetist or orthotist who works closely with the rehabilitation team to ensure the best possible fit and utilization (Figure 2-5).[12]

Figure 2-6.
Evaluating aerobic capacity through VO₂ₘₐₓ testing at the Neuromuscular Research Laboratory (Pittsburgh, PA).

PHOTOGRAPH: COURTESY OF CHRIS CONNABOY.

Exercise Physiologists

Exercise physiologists are often divided into two categories: (1) clinical and (2) applied. Applied exercise physiologists manage programs to assess, design, and implement individual and group exercise and fitness programs. Clinical exercise physiologists work under the direction of a physician in the application of physical activity and behavioral interventions in clinical situations where they have been scientifically proven to provide therapeutic or functional benefit (Figure 2-6).[13]

Athletic Trainers

Athletic trainers are healthcare professionals who collaborate with physicians to provide preventative services, emergency care, clinical diagnosis, therapeutic intervention, and rehabilitation of injuries and medical conditions.[14] Athletic trainers are not just beneficial for professional and amateur athletic teams. US Service Members can reap the same benefits from input and collaboration with athletic trainers; the physical and mental rigors placed on the Service Member are not all that dissimilar to their civilian counterparts. A Service Member or military athlete relies on the health and fitness of his/her mind and body to make a living and complete the mission (Figure 2-7).

Rehabilitation Engineers

Rehabilitation engineering involves the use of engineering science and principles to develop technological solutions and devices to assist individuals with disabilities. It also aids in the recovery of physical and cognitive functions lost because of disease or injury. Rehabilitation engineers design and build devices

FIGURE 2-7. *US Army soldier getting his ankle taped by an athletic trainer prior to a training exercise.* PHOTOGRAPH: COURTESY OF DALE WILLIAMS.

FIGURE 2-8. *Human Engineering Research Laboratories at the University of Pittsburgh and US Department of Veterans Affairs (Pittsburgh, PA). The motto is to "continuously improve the mobility and function of people with disabilities through advanced engineering in clinical research and medical rehabilitation." Pictured is HERL's (Human Engineering Research Laboratories') CAREN (Computer Assisted Rehabilitation Environment) system, used to create a virtual reality environment (see Chapter 9). In the foreground is a collection of wheelchairs, including a selection of hand cycling chairs, a rugby chair, and other older and modern manual wheelchairs.* PHOTOGRAPH: COURTESY OF MICHAEL LAIN.

and systems to meet a wide range of needs that can assist individuals with mobility, communication, hearing, vision, and cognition. These tools help people with day-to-day activities and tasks related to employment, independent living, and education (Figure 2-8).[15]

VOCATIONAL REHABILITATION

Vocational rehabilitation provides services to help persons with disabilities prepare for, obtain, or maintain employment.[16] Return to work can be a key component in the rehabilitation process because it can be integral to helping an individual integrate into the community, as well as achieve financial independence. Through vocational rehabilitation, a counselor will meet with the individual and develop an individualized plan to identify the service and needs of the individual to aid in the attainment of returning to the work force. Services can include help in accessing medical care and therapies, job-specific counseling and training, job placement programs, access to additional education, home and job modifications, and even transportation.

THE IMPORTANCE OF SERVICE MEMBER AND FAMILY EDUCATION

The ultimate leader of the Medical Rehabilitation Team is the Service Member (see Figure 2-1). For the team to function at an optimal level and achieve the best outcomes, the leader of the team, in association with his or her family, must take an active role in the planning and continuous adjustment of the rehabilitation care plan. Just like any other aspect of one's personal or professional life, the more educated a person becomes about a particular area or topic, the more effective that person can become at doing his/her job or completing a task. The key here again lies in the team approach of medical rehabilitation. The Service Member and family are not left alone to navigate, investigate, and interpret the wide breadth of rehabilitation medicine. Each member of the rehabilitation team is available to help direct the Service Member in the right direction to find the best and most accurate information available.

REHABILITATION CARE PLAN

The rehabilitation care plan can take place in a variety of settings and roles to aid in the recuperation of the Service Member from the inpatient hospital setting to the outpatient community office setting.

When initially integrated into the Medical Rehabilitation Team in the inpatient hospital setting, each of the previously described members of the team will meet with the Service Member for an initial evaluation. At that time, the rehabilitation team members will meet with the Service Member *and* family members to evaluate previous function and current function, as well as to discuss functional goals for the future. Once each member of the team has had an opportunity to complete an initial evaluation with the Service Member, they will meet all together as a Medical Rehabilitation Team and again at regular intervals. These meetings allow team members to share their individual knowledge and expertise to formulate recommendations for the best way forward to achieve the Service Member's goals.

Throughout this process, team members will also routinely meet on numerous occasions—in between more formal group meetings—to discuss thoughts and insight on how to progress forward toward success. All the while, the individual Service Member is adding the key ingredient to the team: insight into what *is* or perhaps what *is not* working and how to progress forward to achieve the goals that have been set. Keep in mind that the rehabilitation care plan is one of great fluidity and flexibility (perhaps better known in the Marines and Navy as "Semper Gumby") and can be molded and manipulated to fit the individual as he/she progresses. Thus, it is not a rigid and unchangeable format that cannot be adjusted after its initial establishment.

The rehabilitation care plan can also be applied in the outpatient community setting either as continuity of care after discharge from the hospital or independently through consultation. After discharge from the hospital, the physiatrist will continue to work with the rehabilitation team through a variety of formats to ensure continued success. A physiatrist also plays a role in the Service Member's reintegration by working in conjunction with other medical providers to contribute a unique perspective through a variety of formats, including a comprehensive neuromusculoskeletal physical evaluation, assessment and prescriptions of assistive technologies, and electrodiagnostic studies.

Electrodiagnostic studies include a two-part examination with a series of small electrical shocks to test the function of nerves and a needle portion in which a small, thin needle is placed into muscles to evaluate for proper functioning. The physiatrist can then interpret and evaluate this information to identify potential nerve and muscle diagnoses like carpal tunnel syndrome, as well as monitor health and recovery after injury during the rehabilitation process.

SUMMARY

"From the hottest forge comes the hardest steel."

Unknown

The 21st century American Service Member has faced great adversity and has not just survived, but has thrived in this setting. Oftentimes, when a Service Member first reports to rehabilitation, he/she is at, near, or beginning the recovery from a low point, a valley, and potentially one of the darkest and most trying moments. It is through these most difficult and challenging of times that one is forged and molded into the most resilient and strongest of individuals. Those who go through this transition will become a pillar of the strongest US steel and should know that there will be an entire team—the rehabilitation team—right beside them, working and cheering for each and every individual Soldier, Sailor, Airman, and Marine to succeed!

References

1. Parcon P. *Develop Your Team Building Skills*. New Delhi, India: Lotus Press; 2007.

2. Opitz JL, Folz TJ, Gelfman R, Peters DJ. The history of physical medicine and rehabilitation as recorded in the diary of Dr. Frank Krusen: part 1. Gathering momentum (the years before 1942). *Arch Phys Med Rehabil*. 1997;78:442–445.

3. Heaton L. *Army Medical Specialist Corps*. Washington, DC: U.S. Army Surgeon General's Office; 1968.

4. Lynch C, Weed FW, McAfee L. *The Medical Department of the United States Army in the World War*. Washington, DC: U.S. Army Surgeon General's Office; 1923–1929.

5. Kovács R. *Electrotherapy and Light Therapy With the Essentials of Hydrotherapy and Mechanotherapy*. 4th ed. Philadelphia, PA: Lea & Febiger; 1942.

6. Rusk HA. The growth and development of rehabilitation medicine. *Arch Phys Med Rehabil*. 1969;50:463–466.

7. University of Kansas Medical School Physical Therapy and Rehabilitation Science Web site. http://www.kumc.edu/school-of-health-professions/physical-therapy-and-rehabilitation-science.html. Accessed August 31, 2014.

8. American Occupational Therapy Association, Inc. AOTA Web site. www.aota.org. Accessed September 1, 2014.

9. University of Redlands Web site. http://www.redlands.edu/. Accessed September 1, 2014.

10. Temple University College of Health Professions and Social Work. Department of Rehabilitation Sciences Web site. http://chpsw.temple.edu/rs/home. Accessed September 1, 2014.

11. US Army. US Army Careers and Jobs: Social Worker (73A). Go Army Web site. http://www.goarmy.com/careers-and-jobs/amedd-categories/medical-service-corps-jobs/social-worker.html. Accessed September 10, 2014.

12. Walter Reed National Military Medical Center. WRNMMC: Prosthetic Orthotic Service Web site. http://www.wrnmmc.capmed.mil/. Accessed September 14, 2014.

13. Commission on Accreditation of Allied Health Education Programs. CAAHEP Web site. http://www.caahep.org/. Accessed September 11, 2014.

14. National Athletic Training Association. NATA Web site. http://www.nata.org/athletic-Training. Accessed September 8, 2014.

15. National Institute of Biomedical Imaging and Bioengineering. NIBIB Web site. http://www.nibib.nih.gov/. Accessed September 9, 2014.

16. Commonwealth of Pennsylvania. Pennsylvania Department of Labor & Industry Web site. http://www.dli.state.pa.us/portal/server.pt/community/vocational_rehabilitation/. Accessed December 15, 2014.

RETIRED STAFF SERGEANT MICHAEL KACER grew up in the small town of Waymart, Pennsylvania. Just as he was about to graduate from high school, he decided to join the Pennsylvania Army National Guard for discipline and direction. Shortly after graduating from Fort Benning Infantry Basic and Advanced Individual Training, he returned home to start his citizen soldier life in the National Guard. After three long years trying to figure out if the military was the right life choice for him, September 11, 2001 occurred and decided it for him. He was a lost soul who now found direction. However, after his first deployment, Kacer succumbed to depression. Bouncing from job to job, fighting alcoholism, and never starting college, Kacer felt helpless until another opportunity to deploy occurred. Lost and aware that he needed a restart in his life, he took the deployment.

What was supposed to be a 12- to 18-month deployment became nearly a 23-month deployment. Shortly after bouncing around from camp to camp, his unit (the 2/103 Armor of the 55th Brigade, 28th Infantry Division (M)) fought and worked alongside the 2nd Battalion, 5th Marines Regiment, 1st Marine Division in Fallujah, Iraq, providing support on route patrols, outer cordon security, explosive ordnance disposal, and check points for people and vehicles entering and leaving the city. His unit also became the first unit in Operation Iraqi Freedom/Operation Enduring Freedom to receive a cross-service combat patch.

In 2007, after finally starting to settle down, Kacer volunteered for his last deployment. Little did he know that his life was about to change. At the beginning of his deployment, he was promoted to Staff Sergeant. In a Staff Sergeant-heavy platoon, he was a team leader working alongside the

Navy Providential Reconstruction Team. On June 18, 2008, Kacer and his fellow soldiers were playing spades in a building on a combat outpost when insurgents began firing 110-mm Chinese rockets into the combat operations post. Kacer was unable to react when one of the rockets came in through a window and hit the wall next to him, resulting in a 6-inch fracture across the back of his head, three broken ribs, two collapsed lungs, severed intestines, and his left arm amputated above the elbow. Following his injury, Kacer again fell into a "lost state of mind." The hardest thing for him to deal with were not only his injuries or upcoming divorce, but also the loss of his medic and mechanic, and the subsequent survivor's guilt that resulted from these losses.

Recuperating at Walter Reed National Military Medical Center (Bethesda, MD), help arrived for Kacer in the form of sports therapy. "The folks at Walter Reed pushed me to compete, due to my competitive nature," said Kacer. "For me, competition and training are not just about recovery or physical fitness, it's more about being in control of myself."

Staff Sergeant Kacer is part of a small group of wounded soldiers who have not only spent long hours of rehabilitation to regain a sense of normalcy, but

EVERYONE WOULD UNDERSTAND IF I QUIT..

EXCEPT ME!

SSG MIKE KACER
55TH ABCT, 28TH ID
WOUNDED IN AFGHANISTAN
ROCKET ATTACK 2008

have also taken their recovery to new levels. Since his injury, Michael has been an active member of the Achilles Freedom Team, Hope for Warriors, and Disabled Sports USA. He has made Paralympic Track and Field Nationals every year since 2011 (just barely missing Worlds in 2013). He completed two New York City Marathons, 3 Army Ten Milers, the Boston Marathon, 3 Bataan Death Marches, 3 Warrior Games (medaling in 10 of 15 individual events), 5 Hope & Possibilities Five Milers, the Chicago Marathon, the Detroit Half Marathon, the Disney Half Marathon, and 9 Tough Mudders, just to name a few of his outstanding athletic accomplishments. Currently, however, he has put all other races on hold as he trains at West Point for the 2016 Paralympics in Rio de Janeiro, Brazil.

Kacer says that, "Each injury has left its scars both physical, emotional, and/or mental. However, when I get in the pool, or on the track, the only thing that can be seen is my competitiveness and the desire to win. I hope I will be able to show my ability and also that just because people are injured doesn't mean they are limited."

There are those who speak about you who say,

'he lost an arm, he lost a leg, she lost her sight . . . ,'

I object. You gave your arm. You gave your leg.

You gave your sight.

As gifts to your Nation. That we might live in freedom.

Thank you. And to your families.

Families of the fallen and families of the wounded.

You sacrificed in ways that those of us who

have not walked in your shoes can only imagine.

★ ★ ★

GENERAL PETER PACE
CENTER FOR THE INTREPID
SAN ANTONIO, TEXAS

CHAPTER THREE

The Promise of the Future: Assistive Technology, Transportation, and Emerging Technologies

ROSEMARIE COOPER, MPT, ATP[*]; CHENG-SHIU
(JOSHUA) CHUNG, PhD[†]; JOHN COLTELLARO, ATP[‡]; CHRISTINA
LACROIX, DO[§]; AMY LANE, OTR/L, CDRS[¥]; ALISSA LING, MS[¶];
AMANDA REINSFELDER, MS, ATP[#]; BENJAMIN SALATIN, MS[**]; AND
GOERAN FIEDLER, PhD[††]

---

[*]Assistant Professor, Department of Rehabilitation Science and Technology, University of Pittsburgh, and Director, Center for Assistive Technology, Forbes Tower, Suite 3010, 5600 Forbes Avenue, Pittsburgh, Pennsylvania 15213

[†]Postdoctoral Researcher, Department of Rehabilitation Science and Technology, University of Pittsburgh, Human Engineering Research Laboratories, VA Pittsburgh Healthcare System, 6425 Penn Avenue, Suite 400, Pittsburgh, Pennsylvania 15206

[‡]Rehabilitation Engineer, Center for Assistive Technology, Forbes Tower, Suite 3010, Pittsburgh, Pennsylvania 15213

[§]Acting Assistant Service Chief, Director of Outpatient Services, Director of Mobility Clinic, and Staff, Physical Medicine and Rehabilitation, Walter Reed National Military Medical Center, 8901 Rockville Pike, Bethesda, Maryland 20889

[¥]Instructor, Department of Rehabilitation Science and Technology, University of Pittsburgh, Suite 3010 Forbes Tower, 3600 Forbes Avenue at Atwood, Pittsburgh, Pennsylvania 15213

¶*Student, Department of Physical Medicine and Rehabilitation, Uniformed Services University of the Health Sciences, 4301 Jones Bridge Road, Bethesda, Maryland 20814*

#*Assistive Technology Specialist, Walter Reed National Military Medical Center, Building 19, 1st Floor, Room 1313, 4954 North Palmer Road, Bethesda, Maryland 20889*

***Rehabilitation Engineer, Department of Physical Medicine and Rehabilitation, Virginia Commonwealth University, 1223 East Marshall Street, Richmond, Virginia 23298 and Hunter Holmes McGuire VA Medical Center, 1201 Broad Rock Boulevard, Richmond, Virginia 23224*

††*Assistant Professor, Department of Rehabilitation Science and Technology, University of Pittsburgh, 6425 Penn Avenue, Suite 403, Pittsburgh, Pennsylvania 15206*

INTRODUCTION

D isability sustained during military service presents a major challenge facing Service Members and Veterans, as well as their families. Physical and/or cognitive injuries are life-changing and may have emotionally devastating effects on both the person who has sustained injury and the family of the injured person. To successfully reintegrate into the community, injured Service Members or Veterans must discover their "new normal," however they choose to define it.

Assistive technology (AT) can be a critical part of finding this new normal. Physical or cognitive impairments that at first may be perceived as highly limiting at best and insurmountable at worst can actually be compensated for. With the appropriate AT and guidance of qualified AT professionals, Service Members and Veterans are able to successfully rejoin the community, participate fully in family life, and partake in activities they have always enjoyed. Some Service Members are even able to return to active duty.

This chapter will provide a practical insight into the range of AT applications for individuals who have experienced physical, sensory, and cognitive impairments as a result of traumatic and nontraumatic injuries and disease. An important step to ensure appropriate selection of AT is to start with an AT team that consists of qualified AT professionals who have a keen interest in including and encouraging active participation of the end user in the AT evaluation and selection process. Sections covered in this chapter include clinical case examples of

- AT interventions in wheelchair seating and mobility,
- adaptive driving,
- computer access,
- cognitive technologies,
- orthotics and prosthetics, and
- emerging technologies (as they apply to independent community living and enhancement of performance for recreational, educational, and professional activities).

Actual clients were the basis for the case examples. In certain instances, additional details were added to help clarify the effect of the technology.

SEATING AND MOBILITY

Service Members and Veterans with severe mobility impairments, such as lower extremity amputation or spinal cord injury, can achieve independence in daily life with the help of AT devices (eg, wheelchairs, assistive driving controls, and specialized computer applications). The process begins with a thorough assessment by a team of AT professionals, by trial and error, and with a series of more precise adjustments. The prescribed mobility solutions will lead to the fullest possible autonomy for the AT user.

As the following examples illustrate (eg, ultralight manual wheelchairs, power wheelchairs, super lightweight manual wheelchairs, adaptive driving, and computer access), better mobility solutions result in more complete reintegration into the community.

ULTRALIGHT MANUAL WHEELCHAIRS

Case Example: Katie

An active 23-year-old undergraduate student with tetraplegia following a C5–C7 spinal cord injury first arrived at the Center for Assistive Technology (Pittsburgh, PA) for modifications to her 16-inch width x 16-inch depth (16″w x 16″d) ultralight manual wheelchair that was equipped with push rim-activated power assist wheels for mobility. Since arriving at the university, she experienced difficulties in maneuvering this chair around her apartment and through the narrow doors and hallways on campus. Because her chair was only 2 years old, she assumed that she would not qualify for a new chair. However, because she had multiple inches of extra space between the frame and her hips, she wanted to see if her current chair could at least be modified to allow her to get around and maneuver better at home and in school. The physical therapist, together with the rehabilitation technology supplier, discussed options with Katie and decided that a smaller-sized (14″w x 16″d) wheelchair frame would meet her needs.

When Katie transferred to a 14″w x 16″d ultralight manual wheelchair, she immediately reported increased comfort because of the better fit and significant ease with self-propulsion due to the axle position. The smaller space between the wheels then aligned with her shoulders. A letter of medical necessity was submitted to Katie's insurance company. One month later, she was seen for a final fitting and delivery of her new retrofitted 14″w x 16″d ultralight manual wheelchair equipped with power assist wheels. The power assist was necessary for her to be able to traverse the hilly university terrain. It allowed her to push for long distances up and down slopes, and over semi-uneven terrain with less effort. The overall lighter wheelchair frame allowed her to continue with active self-propulsion of a manual wheelchair and to incorporate the benefits of an ultralight manual wheelchair into her active and independent lifestyle.

Case Example: John

A 35-year-old, full-time employed civil engineer, husband, and father—with amputations of both legs above the knees—came to the Center for Assistive Technology to inquire about assistive devices to supplement his prosthetic legs, which he felt were limiting his functional mobility. John needed to be able to maneuver a chair over uneven recreational outdoor terrain (eg, playgrounds, sports fields, family theme parks) and rougher terrain at construction sites. He was not interested in a power wheelchair because he preferred active self-propulsion of a manual wheelchair, and a power wheelchair would also limit the flexible transportation and vehicle options he needed for work. John tested one of the demo ultralight manual wheelchairs equipped with durable lightweight carbon-fiber wheels and quick-release options. Because he would have to transfer in and out of his car multiple times, the lighter the components John would have to manipulate, the less strain on his upper extremities. The wheels were equipped with ergonomically designed hand rims to reduce the risk of repetitive strain injury to wrist joints, and to protect the hand from injuries and lacerations.

Once positioned in the demo chair, he reported increased comfort and experienced significant ease with self-propulsion. John was provided with the opportunity to use this demo chair for a 1-week, in-home trial to allow him to incorporate and evaluate its features during his daily mobility-related activities at home and at work. He spent significant time learning the center of gravity adjustment and its effect on the responsiveness and "tippiness" of the chair. This was important because his center of gravity would be different when using the chair *with* and *without* his prosthetic legs. Based on John's positive feedback of the in-home trial, a letter of medical necessity was submitted to his insurance company.

One month later, he was seen for a final fitting and training with his new ultralight manual wheelchair. John was instructed in appropriate semicircular propulsion, and he received "wheelie" training. He was able to hold and control the wheelie after 10 minutes of supported practice. He now has the ideal supplemental mobility device option to let him accomplish the high-energy–consuming activities for raising his young son and for doing field work at construction sites.

POWER WHEELCHAIRS

Case Example (continued): Katie

Katie also owned a 3-year-old power wheelchair equipped with power seat functions, including power tilt/recline/elevating leg rests and seat elevator, that she received on discharge from rehabilitation. This chair was appropriate at a time when her C5–C7 spinal cord injury was still very recent, and she was still adjusting to her new physical limitations. Being able to spend more time in her chair was important for Katie because she liked controlling her own schedule and joining activities with her friends and family. Thus, the power seat functions were important to her.

She frequently used the power tilt after her therapist had explained to her the benefits of gravity-assisted positioning that increases stability and decreases fatigue. Also, the seat elevator allowed Katie to independently change her seat height levels at tables, restaurant counters, desks, and work surfaces. Reaching counters and cabinets were essential for her to participate in food preparation and to access storage cabinets and freezer contents. With the adjustable seating, she could reach into a washer and dryer, reach across a stove safely, push elevator buttons, and use ATMs. It also helped to manage the pain in her neck/back so that she could raise herself for eye-to-eye contact during social interactions without having to look up all the time.

SUPER LIGHTWEIGHT MANUAL WHEELCHAIRS

Case Example (continued): Katie

Katie returned to the Center for Assistive Technology in December 2013 to find out if there was a super lightweight manual wheelchair on the market that she could possibly lift into a sedan-type vehicle. Although Katie was independent in driving her minivan, she was considering obtaining a smaller vehicle to use on campus and during local outings with her friends. With her goal in mind, we introduced her to a super lightweight carbon-fiber manual wheelchair (8 lbs total weight with wheels). By significantly reducing the weight of the wheelchair, Katie had enough strength to

- self-propel the chair,
- transfer into a smaller vehicle, and
- load and stow the super lightweight chair into a vehicle cabin.

This chair will help her to achieve her goal of simplifying her reliance on autoadaptive equipment and vehicle modifications, and potentially reduce the need for purchasing costly vehicle technology.

ADAPTIVE DRIVING

Case Example (continued): Katie
Katie had expressed an interest in exploring independent transportation options and was referred to the driver rehabilitation evaluation program to determine her transportation needs. During the course of the evaluation, she determined that she preferred using push-right, angle-style hand controls to operate the gas and brake pedals. She also determined that she would need a trip-in steering device because of her hand function.

During Katie's vehicle selection process, various vehicle options were reviewed. A significant consideration was Katie's active lifestyle—her interchanging use of two wheelchairs and multiple recreational devices that would need to be transported. A lowered floor minivan with an entrance ramp allowed her greater options to

- use either of her wheelchairs,
- transport equipment,
- travel comfortably to her long-distance destinations, and
- supply traveling space for family and friends.

With the support of her family and funding sources, she was able to purchase a used, lowered floor ramp minivan. When using her new power assist wheels, she was able to independently propel herself up the ramp of the minivan, secure her wheelchair using a crash-tested securement system, transfer into a driver's power base seat, and then drive using her adaptive driving equipment.

Case Example (continued): John

John also participated in a driver rehabilitation evaluation program to determine his transportation needs and goals. He was shown push-rock hand controls to operate the gas and brake pedals, as well as a spinner knob to steer. He questioned the possibility of using his prosthetic legs in lieu of the adaptive equipment to operate the gas, brake, and clutch in his work truck. John was advised that it was not generally recommended to use his prosthesis to access the vehicle's pedals because of the loss of sensory awareness, limited control of knee and ankle mobility, and potential misstrike on the pedals. He was satisfied with the rationale for using adaptive driving equipment and quickly adjusted to driving with the controls.

At the time of the on-road evaluation, John was not using his prosthetic legs, but he had to transfer from his manual wheelchair to the driver's seat. Both John and his seating team remembered that he needed to independently break down and secure his wheelchair during periods of time when he would not be ambulatory. John realized the options and expenses in modifying his manual transmission vehicle, and admitted that his truck was quite old and that he would prefer to obtain a new vehicle. He was able to identify a four-wheel-drive SUV (sports utility vehicle) that he could easily transfer into if he was walking, yet had ample space to store his new ultra lightweight wheelchair as needed. John was able to progress quickly through the driving training program, become licensed to drive with the devices, and had the vehicle modifications completed in his new SUV. He was quite satisfied with the ability to use the vehicle with or without his wheelchair, for both work and personal use.

COMPUTER ACCESS

Case Example (continued): Katie

Katie was also introduced to various ATs that could benefit her that had computer access and could assist her in completing her college assignments. Although Katie could use a laptop computer keyboard, her typing speed was significantly slower because of her injury. Therefore, Katie was introduced to voice recognition software. Katie demonstrated the voice and breathing skills, as well as the cognitive abilities, required to become a very efficient user of voice recognition technology. Katie was also introduced to the Smartpen (Livescribe, Inc, Oakland, CA) to help compensate for her slower handwriting speed. The Smartpen is a unique device that records the audio from a lecture or meeting and matches the audio file to what was written at that moment. Katie felt this technology would really help with classroom note-taking.

COGNITIVE ASSISTIVE TECHNOLOGIES

AT is comprised of two main parts: (1) the actual tangible tool (including specific software/applications where applicable) and (2) the services provided to teach a person how to use that tool. Generally speaking, AT is considered to be any tool that can increase the independence of an individual to accomplish a desired goal.[1]

Cognitive ATs are tools that help a person who has trouble with managing everyday cognitive activities (eg, maintaining a calendar/schedule or a current task list, finding one's destination when traveling, remembering where the car was parked, etc). Some people may have difficulty physically speaking a particular word or cannot think of the word at all. Still other people may have decreased dexterity, which means that they may not physically be able to complete tasks as they were completed preinjury. A variety of cognitive ATs could be used to accomplish each of these tasks.[2]

Case Example: Jim

For Jim, checking his smartphone is a vital part of his daily routine because the alerts help him get through his day. He is able to remember to enter down when he has to complete tasks and when his appointments occur. However, he is unable to remember to check his schedule; thus, his phone becomes AT when it reminds him to look at his calendar, which he would not be able to do without the alarms that sound at the appropriate times. If Jim works in a secure facility and is unable to take his phone with him into work, *the environment changes the effectiveness* of his strategy to manage his appointments and task list. A solution might be to use the calendar on his computer at work, or he could print out the current copy of his electronic calendar on his phone and carry the paper copy with him. If Jim has to schedule an appointment that affects his home life, he could email himself the details to add to his calendar at home. Therefore, any AT solution must also consider the environment in which the person is planning to accomplish a task.

Rehabilitation after an injury, especially a brain injury, requires a team approach.[3] The team is centered on the individual, who can offer valuable insights from his or her perspective to expedite recovery from the brain injury. As noted in Chapter 2 (Physical Medicine and Rehabilitation), the multidisciplinary team will most likely include a mixture of the following specialists:

- a physiatrist (or a doctor specializing in working with trauma to the body),

- an occupational therapist,
- a physical therapist,
- a speech language pathologist,
- a recreation therapist,
- nurse case managers,
- vocational rehabilitation counselors,
- personal care assistants, and
- a rehabilitation engineer/technologist or certified AT professional.

Additional related discipline specialists may also participate on the team as appropriate. Communication among members of the team is vital for the patient to receive high-quality care. As a part of this multidisciplinary team, patients and their families should be confident in advocating for clear explanations or any unaddressed concerns. Some individuals with traumatic brain injuries may not realize the extent of their new inabilities and challenges until they return to a routine similar to the preinjury routine.[4] With the Warrior Transition Command system implemented by the Army in 2009,[3] and in collaboration with the vocational rehabilitation counselor and the appropriate therapists, patients are able to apply the skills and tools learned from the rehabilitation team in supervised work settings. Any challenges that surface can be addressed by the team to help the individual understand the situation and discuss options for the future.

Case Example (Team Approach): Mark

Mark is an inpatient who has a delay in understanding speech. In addition, it is very difficult for him to move any of his body parts, and he is unable to speak. The physical therapist works with Mark to strengthen the muscles he does have control over. The speech language pathologist helps determine how much Mark is actually able to comprehend and the accuracy of his answers. The speech language pathologist is also able to determine that he can accurately answer yes and no, and can decipher whether he has a method to express yes and no. The AT specialist works with the physical therapist, the speech language pathologist, and the occupational therapist to determine that he is able to independently control his left thumb and his right foot. The AT specialist found a lever switch that he can activate with his foot and an infrared switch that can be activated when he raises his thumb. The switches are connected to a communication device that plays a recorded message of yes and no when he moves his thumb or foot. Adjustments are made as necessary throughout the process (eg, switch placement or switch type). The occupational therapist practices with Mark to work the muscles and answer questions with yes and no. The entire team works together to help Mark strengthen his skills to independently answer questions. Once he has mastered responding yes and no, he will be set up to control his environment, which could include changing channels on the television.

Healing occurs when multiple facets of the brain are engaged, such as requiring the person to complete physical tasks in addition to cognitive tasks.[5] Therapists and members of the rehabilitation team can use electronics with touch interfaces and interactive video technology (computers) to customize an individual's care plan.[5,6] Virtual environments can be customized to target the needs of a particular patient by focusing on the specific goals of that patient and the rehabilitation team. Computer programs used in therapy can provide feedback to users as necessary, measure where users are looking to complete a task, or require patients to complete a task by focusing on a side they might tend to neglect (ie, left or right).[5,6] Computer programs can also be used, in collaboration with the rehabilitation team, to strengthen cognitive skills by adjusting difficulty levels that are appropriate to the individual user.[4]

Because every person is unique, different tools need to be used to provide independence.[7] *Feature matching*, a system that matches the needs of the patient with the specific abilities of available tools, is used to determine which tool will be the appropriate fit for an individual's characteristics.[8] People have different strengths and weaknesses, and devices have different features and specifications. Although the most advanced technology may be appropriate for some, it is important to understand that simple tools can also have a significant impact (eg, a notebook or a voice recorder to help a person remember important facts).[8]

Case Example: Feature Matching
Jim has difficulty remembering his appointments and uses an electronic tablet to manage his medical appointments. However, the best solution for Jane might be to use a paper planner with color-coded pens to help her stay organized.

Automated reminders can be set to alert users for important events or tasks that need to be completed. For people who frequently lose their keys, a retracting keychain that can be tethered to a backpack, belt loop, or purse would help them meet the goal of not misplacing keys. An electronic wireless leash that sounds an alarm when a cell phone has been left behind would help someone remember a cell phone. As an alternate solution to not misplacing an important item (eg, a cell phone), a retracting keychain could be fastened to the cell phone with Velcro. Options exist for each challenge a person faces, and it is important to remember that solutions range from simple to more advanced.

With smartphones more easily available for end users, applications can serve as AT or alternate tools to accomplish a specific task.[9] If an individual is going to the grocery store, he or she could carry a notepad. However, if the person frequently leaves the notepad but not his or her cell phone behind, grocery items could be stored in an application designed for tracking shopping lists. Some people note that applications can be synced to a cloud system, which could be monitored/edited by a family member in real-time from another location. Calendars and task lists can also be managed electronically from a smartphone.

A person who has difficulty with auditory processing might be able to understand a conversation with visual captions.[10] Captions are available for telephone conversations, large meetings, or presentations through captioned telephone services or CART (Communication Access Realtime Translation).[11]

Individuals who have difficulty typing can use mainstream speech recognition technology to speak into a phone or computer, as noted in the previous case example with Katie. If dictation is a problem because of difficulties with vocabulary, specialized predictive software programs are available. Specialized software is programmed to prompt users with a menu of options that change with every word entered. If the user is unsure of the words on the list, words can be "hovered" over in order to hear and see them used in a sample phrase.

Technology constantly changes at a rapid pace, and the way it is applied in a rehabilitation setting is evolving.[12-15] A primary resource for all individuals is an AT professional, a therapist, or a medical provider (see the Rehabilitation Engineering and Assistive Technology Society of North America [RESNA]; www.resna.org). For individuals who are active duty Service Members, medical treatment facilities may have an AT professional ready to answer any questions. Veterans with a service-connected injury could access a Veterans Affairs facility for assistance. All individuals (including the general public) are able to access their local state AT resource center for free information regarding any AT questions. Current information for local resource centers can be found by state at the Association of Assistive Technology Act Programs (www.ataporg.org/states.html).

Learning about AT is a team effort. There is no instant answer, and feedback is important. As noted in the beginning of this section, AT includes the services that support the actual tool. Sharing where an individual is having difficulty will help the AT professional pinpoint the barriers that need to be addressed. Once the barriers are identified, specific solutions can be implemented. If the suggested solutions are not working, the AT professional will continue to explore additional options until a successful solution has been identified.[16] Some software programs, such as speech recognition software that types what is spoken, might be frustrating without proper instruction. An AT specialist will work with patients to help them learn the proper techniques for using the recommended software or tools. To find a certified AT professional registered through RESNA, visit the RESNA Web site.

ORTHOTICS AND PROSTHETICS

Orthotic devices are attached or applied to the external surface of the body. They are used to improve function, restrict or enforce motion, or support a body segment. This is done by supporting, immobilizing, or treating muscles, joints, or skeletal parts that are weak, ineffective, deformed, or injured. A *prosthetic device* is an artificial device used to replace a missing body part. Both of these categories of AT devices are important tools in the reintegration of injured Veterans and Service Members into community life. These tools make it possible to perform activities of daily living (ADLs) essential to the emotional and physical well-being of the injured person, thus leading to greater independence and self-esteem.

ORTHOTICS
Orthotic devices are commonly divided into upper limb orthotic devices, lower limb orthotic devices, and spinal orthoses.

- *Upper limb orthotic devices* include devices for the entire upper extremity and are used for many other conditions, including sports injuries, neurological conditions (eg, stroke and spinal cord injuries), and even burns. They are often known as splints or braces.
- *Lower limb orthotic devices* attach to the lower extremities to assist ambulation, transfers, and mobility. They range from simple arch supports bought from a local pharmacy to more complicated devices.
- *Spinal orthoses* are used to stabilize and support the spine. A simple spinal orthotic is a soft collar given to patients after a whiplash injury. These devices are used for patient comfort, but sturdier examples are made to support a patient's spine after injury or surgery.

The rehabilitation team involved in the patient's care—including the doctor, physical therapist (PT), and occupational therapist (OT)—decides if a patient needs an orthotic device. More complicated devices usually require a prescription from the patient's doctor. Often, a patient's PT or OT can construct and fit these devices, particularly if they are made of softer materials. More complicated devices are usually constructed by orthotists. A certified orthotist has extensive training in the proper fit and fabrication of these devices, has undergone additional residency training, and has taken a national examination for certification supplied by the American Board for Certification in Orthotics, Prosthetics, & Pedorthics (Alexandria, VA; www.abcop.org).

In more recent years, prefabricated orthotic devices have become more common. These devices, made in various sizes, can be fitted to patients often with little or no adjustment. However, these are usually more appropriate for simpler issues and a more standard body size because custom orthotics are considered to have better fit and control.

Use of prefabricated components has also been beneficial to the development of next-generation orthotic devices on the other end of the spectrum. Dynamic exoskeletal orthoses serve the purpose of replacing lost muscle function. Their sophisticated actuator and control mechanisms exceed the capabilities of conventional passive devices, as the provided joint torques can be tailored exactly to the requirements in any given gait cycle phase. One prime example is the Intrepid Dynamic Exoskeleton Orthotic (IDEO), an energy-storing ankle-foot orthosis that was developed at the Center for the Intrepid (CFI; San Antonio, TX), and has since been demonstrated to significantly improve rehabilitation outcomes in patients with high-energy lower extremity trauma.[17] Powered exoskeleton technology continues to make advances as well, driven in large part by military research efforts. The main applications of this technology include the enhancement of physical performance of soldiers in the battlefield and the rehabilitation of patients after severe neuromuscular injuries. As we see breakthroughs in one area, the other area benefits as well.

Although the doctors, therapists, and other members of the rehabilitation team can answer any questions that patients may have about their orthotic devices, more information can be found at the American Board for Certification in Orthotics, Prosthetics, & Pedorthics and at the Orthotic and Prosthetic Activities Foundation (Charlotte, NC; www.opafonline.org).

PROSTHETICS
Because prosthetic devices can replace any missing body part, technically artificial eyes, implanted teeth, and even replacement heart valves can be considered prosthetic devices. However, for the purposes of this chapter, we will restrict our discussion to devices that replace missing limbs. With these exclusions, upper extremity prosthetic devices perform the functions of a

missing finger, hand, or arm. Lower extremity prosthetic devices perform the functions of a missing toe, foot, or leg.

The rehabilitation team involved in the patient's care—including the doctor, PT, and OT—decides if a patient needs a prosthetic device. Prosthetic devices require a prescription from the patient's doctor and are constructed by prosthetists. A prosthetist has extensive training in patient evaluation, prosthesis design, fabrication, fitting, and modification to treat limb loss for purposes of restoring physiological function and/or cosmetics. This professional has usually undergone additional residency training and has taken a national examination for certification given by the American Board for Certification in Orthotics, Prosthetics, & Pedorthics.

There are four major categories of upper extremity prosthetic devices:

1. A *passive* upper limb prosthetic device is primarily cosmetic, but also functions as a brace for the task of the upper limb. It is sometimes used when the patient does not have enough strength to operate a device.
2. A *body-powered* prosthetic device uses the strength and range of motion of the remainder of the patient's limb to control the prosthetic device. Body-powered systems are usually more durable and are usually able to bear more weight.
3. An *externally powered system* uses an outside power source (usually a battery) to move and control the prosthetic device. The patient controls the function through muscle contractions, thus inducing myoelectric signals that are registered by skin contact electrodes implemented in the socket. These devices are usually heavier and require more maintenance.
4. A *hybrid system* is what its name implies; it uses both an outside power source and the patient's own strength to operate the device. This is sometimes chosen to reduce the weight of the device. An example of this would be a body-powered shoulder accompanied with an externally powered elbow.

Common levels of upper extremity amputation include the following:

*   *partial hand* (through the bones of the hand),
*   *wrist disarticulation* (through the wrist joint),
*   *transradial* (through the bones of the forearm),
*   *elbow disarticulation* (through the elbow joint),
*   *transhumeral* (through the bone of the upper arm),
*   *shoulder disarticulation* (through the shoulder joint), and
*   *forequarter amputation* (through the entire shoulder, including shoulder blade and collarbone).

With either extreme of amputation—partial hand amputation and fore-quarter amputation—prosthetic devices are rarely used. In the case of partial hand amputation, this is most often due to the patient's ability to compensate for the missing part, as well as current limitations of the device (eg, lack of sensation). In the case of forequarter amputation, the device required is often too heavy, and there are limited options available for controlling it. In both cases, many patients are fitted with light, primarily cosmetic, prosthetic devices.

Wrist disarticulation prosthetic devices are usually well tolerated by patients. They are fitted over the patient's remaining forearm bones (radius and ulna) and are fairly functional because this level still permits full rotation (pronation and supination) of the wrist. At this amputation level, however, it is difficult to make the prosthetic limb the same length as the remaining limb on the opposite side (which patients often desire because of concerns about appearance). Thus, there is usually not a separate wrist joint provided in the prosthetic device. If there is a wrist joint, it is not externally powered because there is no extra room for a power supply. (Externally powered wrist joints are usually considered in the case of bilateral upper extremity amputees.) These wrist joints are usually manually manipulated by the patient with the opposing limb and are held in the desired place either by friction with a *friction device wrist* or by locking it into place with a *locking device wrist*.

In terms of transradial amputation prosthetic devices, there are several common options for levels of amputation in the radius or forearm bone. In terms of functionality and the prosthetic device chosen, the "long" transradial amputations (distal third of the radius) are similar to wrist disarticulations, and the "short" transradial amputations (proximal third of the radius) are similar to elbow disarticulations. However, in most typical cases, the prosthetic device can be fitted over the radius and ulna and is therefore self-suspending (not needing an outside harness or other device to keep the prosthetic device affixed, although there is usually a harness to control the terminal device). Common types of these self-suspending sockets are the *Muenster socket* and the *split socket*. These devices are usually well-tolerated by patients and are extremely functional.

Elbow disarticulation prosthetic devices usually have excellent weight-bearing capability and stability due to their support from the socket. Although the functionality of this level is excellent, cosmetic appearance is usually a problem because the artificial elbow is usually asymmetric to the other side. An artificial elbow joint, when present, is usually an *externally locking elbow* (which locks from the outside) because there is not enough space for an internally locking elbow.

Humeral amputation, in the same way as a transradial amputation, varies in functionality and in prosthetic choices depending on length. Very *long* humeral amputations have many of the same benefits and disadvantages as elbow disarticulations. With amputation at this level, suspension is more challenging because the end of the humerus has been lost. Very *short* humeral amputations are challenging (although not impossible) to fit and control the device because of loss of strength and leverage. Often, a harness system must be implemented. Either externally locking or internally locking (locking from the inside) elbows can be used at this level.

Shoulder disarticulations have the most prosthetic device components of any commonly fitted amputation levels to replace all the joints below. Often a *complete-enclosure socket,* which encloses the limb to the chest, is used. Unfortunately, it is difficult to fit, and there may be issues with heat dissipation. Another option is a rigid *X-frame shoulder socket* that stays closely applied to the torso. It is usually lighter and cooler for the patient.

Case Example: Leroy

The otherwise healthy patient lost his right hand due to a war injury in Afghanistan at age 28. As an accomplished and decorated soldier, his rehabilitation goal is to rejoin the military. Initial recovery at a US Army hospital in Germany included surgery and hospitalization for additional bullet wounds and fragment injuries suffered during combat. Early prosthesis fitting is further delayed by reamputation surgery to remove part of the wrist to allow the use of a prosthetic hand with wrist joint, a decision jointly made by the patient, his surgeon at Carl R. Darnall Army Medical Center (Fort Hood, TX), and his prosthetist. Leroy's good overall physical constitution and determined mindset of an active soldier supports an ambitious approach to prosthetic rehabilitation. In addition to receiving a conventional body-powered hook prosthesis, the patient is deemed a candidate for an advanced myoelectric hand. Features of such devices now include individually movable fingers that conform to the shape of a grasped object; controllable speed and force of hand motion that allows proper grasping of objects of different weight and fragility; and performance of quick motions (eg, catching a ball in midair) and programmable moving and gripping patterns that mimic the human hand and that can be selected via the smartphone app. Leroy needs to learn and practice the control mechanism for a multitude of functions, which entails purposeful contractions of the remaining muscles in his arm to generate the signals that the hand's microprocessor and electromotors translate into motion. Some of the control algorithms are intended to be intuitively accessible, for instance, by providing proportional response to the magnitude of contractions detected. Others require a retraining of the physiological muscle activation patterns; the signal for wrist rotation, for instance, may be a co-contraction of hand flexors and extensors, something that most resembles the pattern for opening a fist. With diligent training, Leroy soon masters the operation of his new prosthetic hand and concludes his long road to rehabilitation about 10 months after his initial injury. He reenlists and continues his Army career as a liaison officer, assisting injured Service Members and their families.

As is the case in upper limb loss, the difficulty of prosthetic rehabilitation increases steeply with the level of amputation of the lower limb. The further proximal an amputation is performed, the greater the loss of functional joints and muscles, and the smaller the residual limb structure needed for suspension and control of the prosthetic device. Although limb prostheses may be abandoned because patients consider them either unnecessary or impractical, such occurrences are much less common in lower limb prosthetics than upper limb prosthetics. In most cases, the decision not to use a prosthesis requires a person with lower limb loss to resort to bilateral crutches or wheeled mobility for ambulation, both of which are often more debilitating than even a poorly functioning artificial leg.

There are several different types of artificial foot/ankle systems:

- A *solid-ankle, cushion-heel (SACH) foot* is a solid foot without articulations. The cushion in the heel of this artificial foot, when loaded by a patient's weight, imitates the normal plantarflexion (movement of the foot that flexes the foot or toes downward toward the sole) of the human foot, but does not allow any motion in any other direction.
- A *single-axis foot* is an artificial foot with an axis that allows for both plantarflexion and dorsiflexion (movement of the foot that extends the foot upward), but no motion in any other direction.
- A *multiaxis foot* has motion in several planes, like a normal human foot.
- A *dynamic response foot* acts similarly to a spring, as weight-bearing loads it to return energy back to the user.
- A *hydraulic ankle* provides adjustable resistance to dorsi- and plantarflexion, allowing seamless adaptation to sloped walking surfaces.
- A *microprocessor-controlled ankle* offers similar functionality as modern hydraulic ankles in addition to active regulation of the ankle angle that increases ground clearance in the swing phase and helps with activities such as stair climbing.
- A *powered ankle* replaces the lost function of the foot plantar flexors. Unlike any of the aforementioned systems, such a device provides active push-off force at every step and thus helps reduce asymmetry and metabolic cost of prosthesis gait.

- *Sprint feet and other sport-specific designs* are dedicated to facilitating athletic activity. They are generally not very versatile, but can help approximate able-bodied performance in narrowly defined athletic disciplines.

Likewise, there are also several types of prosthetic knees in lower extremity devices:

- An *outside (single-pivot) hinge* is an artificial knee joint with one direction of motion applied to the outside of the prosthetic device.
- A *single-axis* artificial knee joint has only one direction of motion (motion type), and is controlled by alignment and voluntary control.
- A *polycentric* joint has more than one axis of rotation. This has the advantage that the instantaneous center of rotation can be outside the geometry of the device, which helps increase buckling resistance and/or proper knee axis alignment in long residuals.
- A *weight-activated stance* has a friction braking system, preventing further knee-bending when weight is applied. A *manual-locking* joint has a manual switch release for flexion.
- A *hydraulic knee* unit allows the accurate adjustment of flexion and extension resistances over a wide spectrum, thus providing efficient swing phase control for walking at higher speeds, as well as dynamic stance phase control that enables controlled knee flexion under weight to prevent or mitigate accidental falls.
- A *microprocessor knee* has a microprocessor that adjusts friction in the artificial joint in response to the speed of walking. In combination with a hydraulic unit, the processor substantially increases fall safety by employing sophisticated stance phase activation roles.
- A *powered knee* is equipped with a large battery and actuator to replace the quadriceps muscle in providing active knee extension. Because prosthesis knee extension during gait is generally achievable by hip motion and gravity, powered knees are usually indicated for moderate activity patients who cannot generate a hip movement.

There are many common types of lower extremity amputation, each with its own considerations for appropriate prosthetics:

- A *partial foot* can be an amputation removing as little as a toe. Solutions for the missing part of the foot can be as simple as a custom foot orthotic device with toe filler. For higher foot amputation levels, an orthopedic shoe with a wide toe box is required. Sometimes a steel shank is built into such shoes for further support or a *rocker-bottom sole* (a sole with a rounded bottom) is added to unload the residual foot. Additionally, with some amputations, an ankle-foot orthosis is needed to help with functional length.

- A *Symes amputation level* is an ankle disarticulation with the fat pad of the heel attached. Usually, this level of amputation allows for some weight-bearing on a long residual limb without a prosthetic device. Challenges arise from prosthetic fitting, primarily with encompassing the wide bulbous shape of the residual limb and making the prosthetic device equal in length to the opposite foot (usually a SACH foot is chosen for these patients).

- *Transtibial amputation* is through the lower leg below the knee, and very often has a successful fitting and functional outcome. There is no need for knee joint components, and patients have many choices for componentry, unlike Symes or knee disarticulation levels.

- A *knee disarticulation* creates an excellent weight-bearing surface on the end of the femur (upper leg bone). A prosthetic device may cause the two knees to be unequal, which often causes issues when the patient attempts to kneel or sit in close contact. This also causes some limitation in artificial knee choices.

- A *transfemoral amputation* often has excellent results, despite the fact that there are additional components at this higher amputation level. Very long transfemoral amputations are fitted similarly to knee disarticulations, and very short transfemoral amputations are more challenging because they are more similar to hip disarticulations in functionality.

- *Hip disarticulation* removes the entire femur, but leaves the pelvis intact and is often difficult to fit. Many components in the prosthetic device increase the weight of the device. Socket design often requires that the socket wraps entirely around the pelvis so that the belt system is commonly used for suspension. Often, the prosthetic device must be shorter than the remaining limb to assist with clearance, and to prevent knee buckling and falling.

- A *hemipelvectomy* is a resection of the lower half of the pelvis. Results vary, depending on how much bone is removed postamputation, which can range from limited removal to removal of most of the hip bone. If much of the pelvis is intact, the fitting principles are similar to that of hip disarticulation. If very little pelvic bone remains, socket design will depend on the patient's individual anatomical limitations.

- A *hemicorporectomy* is the amputation of both lower limbs and pelvis below the L4 and L5 levels. These patients usually do not use ambulation as a primary form of mobility; however, they may be fitted with a socket to assist in wheelchair sitting and prevent development of skin ulceration. Some individuals may also be able to ambulate short distances with a walker. These patients may be fitted with devices with manual-locking knees for maximum stability.

A key element of any limb prosthesis is the socket that encapsulates the residual limb and provides weight transfer, suspension, and control without reducing patient comfort or joint range of motion. Those sockets are custom fitted in a multistep process involving various check sockets and optimization sessions with a prosthetist. To reconcile such diverging objectives as tight fit and comfort, various suspension systems have been developed, using the basic function principles of hydrostatic pressure, vacuum, and material compliance. Many modern prosthesis sockets have a layered design where the inner layer, or "liner," is made of comparably soft material (eg, silicon or polyurethane gel) that provides comfortable, full-surface contact and the outer layer (often a carbon fiber laminate) is rigid enough for stability and protection. The liner and outer socket are donned in sequence and connected through a locking mechanism or, increasingly in recent years, by means of an elevated vacuum maintained by a battery-powered pump. Specific considerations affect the design of sockets for particular amputation levels, depending on the available pressure-tolerant areas of the residual limb and the required range of motion of the adjacent joint.

Case Example: Mike

Injured at age 38 from a bomb blast while serving in Afghanistan, Mike is left with a below-knee amputation of his right leg and debilitating burst fractures in his left foot that have an increasingly poor healing prognosis. His rehabilitation goal is to become an independent community ambulatory who can play with his young children and engage in outdoor activities, such as hunting and fishing. After 2 years of healing complications in his remaining leg, he is faced with a decision: continue his rehabilitation efforts with the damaged left leg or opt for another amputation and bilateral prostheses. After intensive consultations with his family and rehabilitation team at Brooke Army Medical Center (San Antonio, TX), which includes a thorough study of prosthetics options, he decides for optional amputation surgery. Recovery after this planned procedure progresses quickly, and an early postoperative prosthesis is fitted within days of the amputation. Those prostheses are designed to easily accommodate the changes in volume and the load-bearing capacity of the residual limb that are typical in the aftermath of a surgical procedure. A compliant foot is prescribed initially to help Mike balance on his two prosthetic legs. Later, the feet on both legs will be replaced with stiffer carbon fiber models that provide the necessary resistance and energy storage to walk briskly, but require more active balancing because they have a smaller area of contact with the floor. Definitive prostheses are built once the residual limb has stabilized and matured after about 6 months. Mike is aware that walking on two prostheses demands much more energy than able-bodied walking, but he is reluctant to switch to powered foot ankle systems that could help mitigate this drawback.[18] The feet's added weight, necessity to frequently charge batteries, and comparably high sensitivity to moisture and extreme temperatures appear incompatible with his desired active lifestyle.

For any amputation level, without exception, the patient should undergo preprosthetic training and then extensive training with PT and OT to effectively use the prosthetic device. Optimizing the rehabilitation regimen has been the topic of research efforts for many years. The US Military has assumed a leading role in this realm, establishing dedicated facilities where interdisciplinary teams of rehabilitation specialists utilize the latest technology to enable the best possible outcomes for wounded Service Members and Veterans. The CFI, located at Brooke Army Medical Center (San Antonio, TX), provides state-of-the-art amputee care through an in-house prosthetics laboratory, physical and occupational therapy facilities, and a number of military-specific training devices. Among the equipment is a virtual reality training system known as the Computer Assisted Rehabilitation Environment (CAREN). An elevated platform holding a split-belt treadmill can be tilted and rotated by means of a large hydraulic system to simulate a variety of natural surface conditions. It is surrounded by a dome-like projection screen in which computer-generated environments are displayed to provide the perfect illusion of any real-life scenario the rehabilitation patient may encounter, including combat and other military missions. The site's personnel and equipment resources combine with the willpower and resilience of the patients to regularly achieve rehabilitation outcomes that would have been impossible just years ago.

Although the doctor, therapists, and other members of the rehabilitation team can answer any questions that patients may have about their prosthetic devices, more information can be found at the same Web sites listed in the section on orthotics. For more information on amputation and prosthetics, see www.amputee-online.com and www.amputee-coalition.org.

THREE-DIMENSIONAL PRINTING

One of the newest tools that AT professionals have in their arsenal of equipment is three-dimensional (3D) printing. 3D printers take materials such as plastic or metal—which usually come in resin, wire, or powder form—and melt them into computer-designed physical objects layer by layer. The printed object is very light and very strong, which makes it ideal to use for AT devices of all kinds.

Case Example: Bill

Bill is a Veteran in his late 50s who worked as a programmer for the Department of Defense. One day, on his way to work, he was involved in a car accident that left him with a spinal cord injury. He now functions as a person with a C4-level tetraplegic injury, unable to move anything below his neck. Bill came to the AT Center at the Hunter Holmes McGuire Veterans Administration Medical Center in Richmond, Virginia, to receive a full AT evaluation. He very much wanted to get back to his work as a programmer, if at all possible. The AT treatment team included an OT and a rehabilitation engineer. Bill was seen by the AT team almost every day during his stay at McGuire. One of the cutting-edge tools that the AT team had at their disposal was a 3D printer that created parts designed on a computer out of tough, nontoxic ABS (acrylonitrile butadiene styrene) plastic (the same plastic LEGOs [Billund, Denmark] are made from). The following examples show several instances during the AT service delivery process for Bill wherein the rehabilitation engineer decided to use 3D printing to create custom parts that would have been cost- or time-prohibitive in any other way.

Bill's new shower wheelchair did not allow for armrest height adjustment. Because Bill was having problems with very tight shoulder and neck muscles, which were causing him a lot of pain, the OT wanted Bill's arms raised 2 inches to alleviate excessive downward pull on his shoulders. Requesting custom-height armrests from the vendor would have been the best option, but there was not enough time for a custom order, so the team decided to fabricate a spacer that would raise his armrests. Because the spacer had to be waterproof, the materials of choice were aluminum or plastic. The quickest and best-looking solution was to design a custom spacer that was 3D-printed in plastic. The rehabilitation engineer designed a 3D computer model of the spacer based on measurements from the shower wheelchair and printed the spacer on the 3D printer. Once the spacer was installed on one side of the shower wheelchair to confirm that it fit, the other side was 3D-printed and installed. Bill was then able to practice bathing with his modified shower wheelchair before leaving the hospital.

Bill came to the computer access evaluation with an iPhone and an iPad. The iPhone could use Siri for voice control, but the iPad was not new enough. At a previous hospital, Bill had started using a mouthstick to control the iPad, so this was where the AT team started. The iPhone and iPad were mounted to his Permobil M400 Corpus 3G Power Wheelchair (Lebanon, TN) with pieces from the reconfigurable REHAdapt Mounting System (REHAdapt North America, St Augustine, FL; http://www.rehadapt.com/). The devices were positioned so that Bill could reach them with his mouthstick; however, his mouthstick had no holder. The OT fashioned a holder out of a foam tube and attempted to tape it to the iPad mount, but this did not hold the mouthstick reliably. So, before the next day's appointment, the rehabilitation engineer took the OT's foam holder design and 3D-printed a copy of it, but added an extra part so the holder would be able to interface with the REHAdapt Mounting System to keep it firmly in place. As before, 3D printing was chosen for this situation because it was the quickest option to provide a custom part for evaluation. Bill tried the mouthstick with the holder for a couple of days and eventually decided to explore other options because the required neck movements proved too painful to reliably access his devices.

At the conclusion of the computer access evaluation, Bill decided that his preferred option was to use Bluetooth switches to control his iPad and computer. These Bluetooth switches were controlled via his wheelchair's output modules that were controlled by Bill's Sip and Puff commands. The plan was to use two switches for scanning in iOS 7 on his iPad and two switches for left/right clicking on his desktop PC. Mouse cursor control was provided by a head tracking device mounted on his large screen monitor. To install the two Bluetooth modules and add a power supply, the rehabilitation engineer decided that an easily accessible enclosure was needed. The Bluetooth modules needed to be accessible because Bill's caregiver would need to pair the Bluetooth module to his desktop PC at home. 3D printing was chosen as the way to make a custom enclosure because no other option could provide the high level of finished quality with customization and speed. The rehabilitation engineer designed and 3D-printed a custom enclosure with a magnetic latching lid to hold the Bluetooth modules and their associated wiring. The power supply for the modules was mounted under the wheelchair seat, and all the wiring was neatly secured to limit any possibilities of wires being pulled.

After leaving McGuire, Bill has continued becoming more proficient at using the Sip and Puff control on his wheelchair to control his iPad and desktop computer at home. He is currently going through the process of acquiring an adapted van so that he can drive himself to work. Once Bill has reliable transportation in place, he hopes that, in the near future, he will be able to continue working in a similar capacity at his former job.

EMERGING TECHNOLOGIES

As technologies continue to evolve, researchers seek assistive solutions not only for moving from point A to point B, but also for assisting in the performance of ADLs. This includes using intelligent coaching to aid with daily routines or wheelchair usage, mobility enhancement that can overcome difficult environments, and robotic manipulation for moving objects and housework. These new technologies are in position to be commercialized now or within the next few years, and each could have major transformative effects on the lives of injured Service Members and Veterans.

FIGURE 3-1. *Virtual Seating Coach, tablet version and smartphone version.*

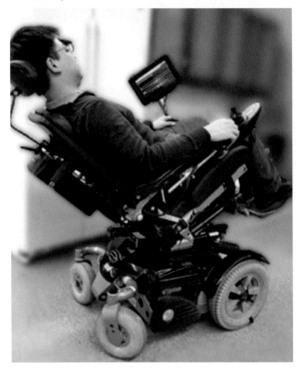

INTELLIGENT COACHING

Intelligent coaching helps users in two ways: (1) by providing appropriate suggestions or instructions based on contextual awareness and (2) by educating users within their daily activities. Two examples are (1) the Virtual Seating Coach (VSC) and (2) the Cueing Kitchen. The VSC (Permobil, Inc, Lebanon, TN) gives power wheelchair users guidance in using their seating functions effectively during the day, even when they are driving. The Cueing Kitchen coaches individuals with traumatic brain injury in completing everyday kitchen tasks (Figure 3-1).

Virtual Seating Coach and Phone App

The VSC[19,20] provides an intelligent, tailored reminder that helps to educate power wheelchair users about appropriate power seating function (PSF)

FIGURE 3-2. *Snapshot of the application on the Virtual Seating Coach smartphone version.* PHOTOGRAPH: COURTESY OF THE HUMAN ENGINEERING RESEARCH LABORATORIES, UNIVERSITY OF PITTSBURGH.

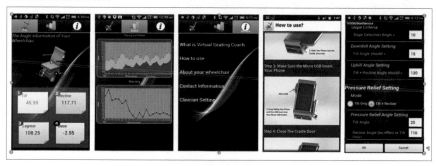

usage to meet their pressure-relieving needs. It contains sensors to monitor the current PSF angles and environmental situations. Unlike a regular reminder, the VSC can modify its messages according to context awareness and give instructions based on PSF usage (Figure 3-2). For example, if the VSC user is resting on a slope, the VSC guides the user to adjust the PSF step by step to a safer sitting posture and reminds the user to wait to perform pressure relief until the chair is resting on a flat surface.

As shown in Figure 3-2, the VSC smartphone version[20,21] is a phone cradle attached to the armrest. It uses a built-in gyro sensor and additional accelerometers to detect the PSF. An Android application (see Figure 3-2) was developed to detect and record PSF usages. This app also includes instructions for PSF and wheelchair usage. Clinicians may modify the reminder and warning configurations remotely to meet each user's needs. This intelligent coaching system expands personal care and training into each individual's daily living situations.

Cueing Kitchen

The Cueing Kitchen[22] (Figures 3-3 to 3-5), developed by the Human Engineering Research Laboratories at the University of Pittsburgh, is an intelligent coaching system built within a kitchen to assist with independent meal preparation for people with difficulties in attention, cognition, memory, and executive functions. The Cueing Kitchen contains an integrated centralized control network with various types of built-in sensors and prompting components. The Cueing Kitchen can

- guide the user through steps to prepare a recipe,
- direct the user to find the ingredients' location,

[TOP] FIGURE 3-3. *The Cueing Kitchen is a basic residential kitchen cabinet layout with major appliances. This layout is modified with low-cost and adaptable portable or wireless sensing and cueing technologies that work with any modern kitchen design.* PHOTOGRAPH: COURTESY OF THE HUMAN ENGINEERING RESEARCH LABORATORIES, UNIVERSITY OF PITTSBURGH.

[MIDDLE] FIGURE 3-4. *The Cueing Kitchen is able to prompt individuals through multistep tasks in a timely and systematic manner.* PHOTOGRAPH: COURTESY OF THE HUMAN ENGINEERING RESEARCH LABORATORIES, UNIVERSITY OF PITTSBURGH.

[BOTTOM] FIGURE 3-5. *Interactive Island set up: Touch Interactor (area where pasta box is positioned), Count Interactor (area where salt and pepper are positioned), and Coverage Interactor (area where apples are positioned).* PHOTOGRAPH: COURTESY OF THE HUMAN ENGINEERING RESEARCH LABORATORIES, UNIVERSITY OF PITTSBURGH.

- protect the user from unsafe appliance use, and eventually
- enable the user to prepare a meal independently.

MOBILITY ENHANCEMENT

Wheelchairs increase mobility functions in users who have ambulatory difficulties. However, there are still architectural barriers in users' homes and environments. These physical environmental barriers—such as curbs, stairs, or doorsteps—may hinder electrical powered wheelchair (EPW) users from visiting friends and family or performing daily activities. Mobility enhancement is focused on reducing these barriers by creating wheelchairs that can overcome difficult terrains. The TopChair-S (TopChair SAS, Montrabé, France) is a commercialized EPW that includes an additional track system, and the Me-Bot (Mobility Enhancement Robotic Wheelchair;

FIGURE 3-6. *The MeBot (Mobility Enhancement Robotic Wheelchair) is a wheelchair that climbs stairs and traverses difficult environments.* PHOTOGRAPH: COURTESY OF THE HUMAN ENGINEERING RESEARCH LABORATORIES, UNIVERSITY OF PITTSBURGH.

Human Engineering Research Laboratories, University of Pittsburgh) is a wheelchair that has six independently moving wheels. Both of these have been developed to assist EPW users with traversing architectural barriers within their living environments.

TopChair-S

The TopChair-S is a power wheelchair available in the European market, designed for indoor and outdoor use. Invented by French scientist Hervé le Masne, the TopChair-S is designed for complete patient autonomy and includes the ability to climb stairs and curbs. The rear wheel–driven chair contains four wheels and a caterpillar track. The two rear wheels are powered and are used to move on flat terrain. The two tracks are for maneuvering around obstacles. There are sensors that detect the first and last step of a set of stairs, which then automatically adjusts the speed and maneuverability of the wheelchair.

The TopChair-S has two driving configurations: (1) regular wheelchair mode and (2) climbing mode. Although it is used in the climbing function, the four wheels are lifted above the caterpillar track. This chair is capable of climbing obstacles up to 8 inches. The required width for the TopChair-S to climb up and down stairs is at least 29.5 inches wide, but preferably 31.5 inches wide. The landing area must be at least 45.3 inches in length. The seat is secured in the horizontal position by an electromechanical actuator while climbing the slope of the terrain.[23]

MeBot

The MeBot mobile base uses a six-wheel design, similar to many current EPWs (Figure 3-6). The MeBot's dimensions were designed to be similar to those of a standard powered wheelchair, taking the ISO (International Organization for Standardization)/RESNA standard into consideration. It is designed to climb steps and drive over challenging surfaces (eg, cross slopes and steep hills); study of the kinematic simulation has shown that the MeBot could successfully climb up an 8-inch curb. In addition, the MeBot can also perform lateral pressure relief and maintain a level seat under uneven surfaces and cross slopes.[24,25]

ROBOTIC MANIPULATION

As reported in the consensus report *Americans with Disabilities: 2010,*[26] about 20 million people (8.2%) in the United States have difficulties with tasks using their upper extremities (eg, lifting or grasping). In addition, among the elderly population 65 years or older, the proportion is much higher: 23.8%. Two commercialized assistive robotic arms—(1) iARM (intelligent Assistive Robotic Manipulator; Exact Dynamics, Didam, The Netherlands) and (2) the JACO Robotic Manipulator (Kinova, Boisbriand, Canada)—can be mounted on a wheelchair to assist wheelchair users in lifting and grasping during ADLs[27]; they can also be mounted on a stationary base. The Kitchen-Bot[28] (Human Engineering Research Laboratories, University of Pittsburgh) is an assistive manipulator that is mounted on an overhead track to help individuals with upper extremity impairments perform kitchen tasks. The Personal Mobility and Manipulation Appliance (PerMMA; Human Engineering Research Laboratories, University of Pittsburgh) integrates bimanual manipulation with a standard EPW to enhance the quality of life for people with severe physical impairments.[26,27–31] Finally, the IMES (implantable myoelectric sensor) robotic arm is operated directly by a user via electromagnetic implants and muscle twitches.

The iARM and the JACO Robotic Manipulator

The iARM (intelligent Assistive Robotic Manipulator) and the JACO Robotic Manipulator, two commercialized assistive robotic manipulators, are available in the United States. Both mimic the range of motion of human arms and have

FIGURE 3-7. *iARM is a commercialized wheelchair-mounted robotic manipulator with a two-fingered grip. It can be controlled by keypad, joystick, or single-button switches.* PHOTOGRAPH: COURTESY OF THE HUMAN ENGINEERING RESEARCH LABORATORIES, UNIVERSITY OF PITTSBURGH.

FIGURE 3-8. *The JACO manipulator is a wheelchair-mounted robotic manipulator. It has a three-fingered hand that can group objects using either two or three fingers.* PHOTOGRAPH: COURTESY OF THE HUMAN ENGINEERING RESEARCH LABORATORIES, UNIVERSITY OF PITTSBURGH.

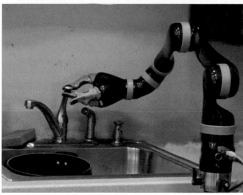

FIGURE 3-9. *The KitchenBot is an overhead, track-mounted manipulator designed to aid individuals with physical impairments complete common kitchen tasks (eg, meal preparation, cleanup, etc).* PHOTOGRAPH: COURTESY OF THE HUMAN ENGINEERING RESEARCH LABORATORIES, UNIVERSITY OF PITTSBURGH.

minimized fold-in positions that retract the manipulator when not in use.[32]
The iARM (Figure 3-7)

- is a six degrees-of-freedom robotic arm with two-fingered hands;
- is an upgraded version of the Manus ARM (Exact Dynamics, Didam, The Netherlands);
- is lighter than the Manus ARM, mainly because of the removal of gravity compensation springs; and
- can be controlled via keypad, joystick, single-button switches, or Android app (iMove) through Bluetooth communication.[33]

The JACO Robotic Manipulator (Figure 3-8)

- is a wheelchair-mounted robotic manipulator,
- is also composed of six interlinked segments with a three-fingered hand,
- is controlled by a three degrees-of-freedom proportional joystick, and
- has additional control interfaces (eg, single-button switches) that can be connected through a universal interface box.[34,35]

KitchenBot
The KitchenBot (Figure 3-9), developed by the Human Engineering Research Laboratories at the University of Pittsburgh, is an overhead, track-mounted manipulator designed to aid individuals with upper extremity impairments with common kitchen tasks (eg, meal preparation and cleanup). It can be integrated into the individual's kitchen for those who require the next level of assistance beyond a caregiver. The initial prototype design is transferable for use in residential homes with standard building materials. Additionally, the low-profile track requires little space above cabinets for installation consistent with typical residential kitchens.[28]

PerMMA
Personal Mobility and Manipulation Appliance (PerMMA) is the first wheelchair to integrate bimanual manipulation for enhancing the quality of life for people with severe physical impairments (Figure 3-10). PerMMA integrates both a smart-powered wheelchair and two dexterous robotic arms to assist its users in completing essential mobility and manipulation tasks during basic and instrumental ADLs.[31]

PerMMA aims to improve functional performance and independence with three integrated user interfaces:

1. *Local control interface*—the local user has full control of PerMMA; the user can move both robotic manipulators along the track using a track control box and operate them with a touch pad.
2. *Remote control interface*—the remote operator can conduct both robotic manipulators using either the haptic joysticks or the keyboard.
3. *Cooperative control interface*—the local user and a remote operator work together to complete mobility and manipulation tasks.

PerMMA was evaluated with end users in completing basic ADL tasks. Fifteen participants with both lower and upper extremity impairments were recruited to operate PerMMA and complete ADL tasks. Thirteen participants successfully completed at least one task with both modes. Results of a questionnaire showed that the majority of the participants thought that PerMMA was easy to learn and easy to use. Participants also thought that PerMMA would make their lives easier and using PerMMA in their daily lives would not be embarrassing or cause any invasion of their privacy.[25,29–31]

FIGURE 3-10. *PerMMA is a fully robotic mobility and manipulation device for people with disabilities. It is designed to accommodate a wide variety of custom and off-the-shelf interfaces.* PHOTOGRAPH: COURTESY OF THE HUMAN ENGINEERING RESEARCH LABORATORIES, UNIVERSITY OF PITTSBURGH.

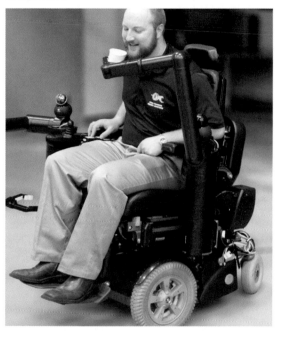

Targeted Muscle Reinnervation

Targeted muscle reinnervation (TMR) is a promising approach to the problem of obtaining the multiple myoelectric signals that are required for operation of advanced upper limb prostheses.[36] The issue is pronounced in people with an amputation at the shoulder level or higher; multiple prosthetic joints need to be controlled with very limited remaining muscles. TMR entails the deliberate surgical implantation of nerve endings that were made obsolete by the amputation into existing muscle tissue, which is commonly the pectoralis. The reimplanted nerves enable distinct contractions of small segments of this muscle, which generates a multitude of separate myoelectric signals that can be recorded with conventional skin electrodes. By using the nerves to control prosthesis motions that resemble the motions caused by their respective originally innervated muscles, the system is very intuitive to use.

Osteointegration

Various complications may arise from prolonged use of prosthetic sockets, including skin damage, restricted blood circulation, joint contractures, muscle atrophy, and bone degeneration. A possible approach to attaching a prosthesis to the limb without a socket was derived from dental medicine. Osteo-integration entails the implantation of a metal anchor in the cut end of the residual bone.[37] Part of this anchor protrudes through the skin and provides an attachment point for the more distal components of a prosthesis. The system has been tested with some success in Europe and has recently been FDA (US Food and Drug Administration)-approved for clinical trials in the United States. It is widely assumed that its indication will be limited by the specific requirements on density and length of the available residual bone and the meticulous hygiene regimen needed to prevent infections at the continuously damaged skin around the metal anchor.

Implantable Myoelectric Sensor Robotic Arm

The implantable myoelectric sensor (IMES) robotic arm is the most advanced technology ready for clinical use. To make learning the new techniques of this prosthesis easier, the patient activates the robotic hand with muscle twitches. This arm uses magnetic field lines to operate, and the coils of wire wrapped in a solenoid loop that are encased inside a carbon-fiber shell conduct the electric muscle signals from the implants to the mechanical hand to induce movement. A magnetic field is generated from electromagnetic implants in the patient's limb. These implants are surgically put in the muscles in specific places, depending on which muscle movements coordinate to which hand movements. The implants pick up the electric pulses from the muscles and carry that to the prosthesis. The prosthesis also has a battery box that attaches to the outside. Because regular muscle movements to move a real hand also move a prosthetic hand, it is also easier to learn how adapt to the prosthesis.

SUMMARY

Assistive technology encompasses a wide variety of tools that can give Veterans and Service Members with disabilities the ability to participate fully in life. Because each individual will have differing degrees and types of disability, it is important for Veterans and Service Members and their families to consult with qualified assistive technology professionals to help them select and use the technologies that will best help them reintegrate into the community.

REFERENCE

1. Cook AM, Hussey SM, Sasser M. *Assistive Technologies: Principles and Practice.* St Louis, MO: Mosby-Year Book, Inc; 1995.

2. Angelo J. Factors affecting the use of a single switch with assistive technology devices. *J Rehabil Res Dev.* 2000;37(5):591–598.

3. Cooper RA, Pasquina P, Drach R, eds. *Warrior Transition Leader: Medical Rehabilitation Handbook.* Fort Detrick, MD: Borden Institute; 2011.

4. Lumosity, Lumos Labs, Inc. The Human Cognition Project. http://hcp.lumosity.com/research/neuroscience. Accessed October 22, 2013.

5. Confalonieri M, Tomasi P, Depaul M, et al. Neuro-physical rehabilitation by means of novel touch technologies. *Stud Health Technol Inform.* 2013;189: 158–163.

6. Martinez-Mareno JM, Solana J, Sánchez R, et al. Cognitive neurorehabilitation based on interactive video technology. *Stud Health Technol Inform.* 2013;190:27–29.

7. Maiti S, Kumar KHBG, Castellani CA, O'Reilly R, Singh SM. Ontogenetic de novo copy number variations (CNVs) as a source of genetic individuality: studies on two families with MZD twins for schizophrenia. *PLoS ONE.* 2011;6(3):e17125.

8. Scherer MJ. Assessing the benefits of using assistive technologies and other supports for thinking, remembering and learning. *Disabil Rehabil.* 2005;27(13): 731–739.

9. Georgia Technical University. App finder. http://www.gatfl.org/favorite-search.php. Accessed September 14, 2015.

10. Northwestern University. Accessible NU. http://www.northwestern.edu/disability/faculty/strategies/hearing-loss.html. Accessed September 14, 2015.

11. National Association for the Deaf. Communication access realtime translation. http://www.nad.org/issues/technology/captioning/cart. Accessed September 14, 2015.

12. Eghdam A, Scholl J, Bartfai A, Koch S. Information and communication technology to support self-management of patients with mild acquired cognitive impairments: systematic review. *J Med Internet Res* 2012;14(6):e159.

13. Jamieson M, Cullen B, McGee-Lennon M, Brewster S, Evans JJ. The efficacy of cognitive prosthetic technology for people with memory impairments: a systematic review and meta-analysis. *Neuropsychol Rehabil.* 2014;24(3–4):419–444.

14. De Joode EA, Van Heugten CM, Verhey FR, Van Boxtel MP. Effectiveness of an electronic cognitive aid in patients with acquired brain injury: a multicentre randomised parallel-group study. *Neuropsychol Rehabil.* 2013;23(1):133–156.

15. Seelye AM, Schmitter-Edgecombe M, Das B, Cook DJ. Application of cognitive rehabilitation theory to the development of smart prompting technologies. *IEEE Rev Biomed Eng.* 2012;5:29–44.

16. Wisconsin Assistive Technology Initiative. The WATI Assessment Package. http://wati.org/content/supports/free/pdf/WATI%20Assessment.pdf. Accessed October 12, 2013.

17. Patzkowski JC, Blanck RV, Owens JG, et al. Comparative effect of orthosis design on functional performance. *J Bone Joint Surg.* 2012;94:507–515.

18. Wright DA, Marks L, Payne RC. A comparative study of the physiological costs of walking in ten bilateral amputees. *Prosthet Orthot Int.* 2008;32:57–67.

19. Liu HY, Cooper R, Cooper RA, et al. Seating virtual coach: a smart reminder for power seat function usage. *Technol. Disabil. (Special Issue on Quality of Life Technology).* 2010;22(1–2):53–60.

20. Wu Y, Liu H, Brown J, Kelleher A, Cooper RA. A smartphone application for improving powered seat functions usage: a preliminary test. In: *Proceedings of the RESNA Annual Conference 2013*; Alexandria, VA: Rehabilitation Engineering and Assistive Technology Society of North America; 2013:2–5.

21. Wu Y. Call up a seat. *PN.* 2013;8:30–32.

22. Mahajan HP, Ding D, Wang J, Ni SX, Telson J. Toward developing a "cueing kitchen" for people with traumatic brain injury. In: *Proceedings of the RESNA Annual Conference 2013*; Alexandria, VA: Rehabilitation Engineering and Assistive Technology Society of North America; 2013.

23. Laffont I, Guillon B, Fermanian C, et al. Evaluation of a stair-climbing power wheelchair in 25 people with tetraplegia. *Arch Phys Med Rehabil.* 2008;89(10):1958–1964.

24. Candiotti J, Wang H, Chung CS, Shino M, Cooper RA. Design and development of a step climbing sequence for a novel electric powered wheelchair. In: *Proceedings of the RESNA Annual Conference 2012*; Alexandria, VA: Rehabilitation Engineering and Assistive Technology Society of North America; 2012.

25. Wang H, Grindle GG, Candiotti J, et al. The Personal Mobility and Manipulation Appliance (PerMMA): a robotic wheelchair with advanced mobility and manipulation. *Conf Proc IEEE Eng Med Biol Soc.* 2012;2012:3324–3327.

26. Brault MW. Americans with disabilities: 2010. Household economic studies. *Curr Pop Rep.* 2012:70–131.

27. Chung CS, Wang H, Cooper RA. Functional assessment and performance evaluation for assistive robotic manipulators: literature review. *J Spinal Cord Med.* 2013;36(4):273–289.

28. Telson J, Ding D, McCartney M, Cooper RA. Preliminary design of an overhead kitchen robot appliance. In: *Proceedings of the RESNA Annual Conference 2013*; Alexandria, VA: Rehabilitation Engineering and Assistive Technology Society of North America; 2013.

29. Wang H, Xu J, Grindle G, et al. Performance evaluation of the Personal Mobility and Manipulation Appliance (PerMMA). *Med Eng Phys.* 2013;35(11):1613–1619.

30. Xu J, Grindle GG, Salatin B, Vazquez JJ, Cooper RA. Enhanced bimanual manipulation assistance with the Personal Mobility and Manipulation Appliance (PerMMA). In: 2010 IEEE/RSJ International Conference on Intelligent Robots and Systems; Taipei, Taiwan: Institute of Electrical and Electronics Engineers/Robotics Society of Japan; 2010:5042–5047.

31. Cooper RA, Grindle GG, Vazquez J, et al. Personal Mobility and Manipulation Appliance—design, development, and initial testing. *Proc IEEE.* 2012;100(8):2505–2511.

32. Chung CS, Cooper RA. Literature review of wheelchair-mounted robotic manipulation: user interface and end-user evaluation. In: *Proceedings of the RESNA Annual Conference 2011*; Alexandria, VA: Rehabilitation Engineering and Assistive Technology Society of North America; 2011.

33. Wakita Y, Yamanobe M, Nagata K, Clerc M. Evaluation of single switch interface with robot arm to help disabled people daily life. In: 18th IEEE International Symposium on Robot and Human Interactive Communication; New York, NY: Institute of Electrical and Electronics Engineers; 2009:429.

34. Maheu V, Archambault PS, Frappier J, Routhier F. Evaluation of the JACO robotic arm: clinico-economic study for powered wheelchair users with upper-extremity disabilities. In: The IEEE International Conference on Rehabilitation Robotics 2011; New York, NY: Institute of Electrical and Electronics Engineers; 2011:1–5.

35. Routhier F, Archambault PS. Usability of a joystick-controlled six degrees-of-freedom robotic manipulator In: *Proceedings of the RESNA Annual Conference 2010*. Alexandria, VA: Rehabilitation Engineering and Assistive Technology Society of North America; 2010:1–7.

36. Kuiken TA, Li G, Lock BA, et al. Targeted muscle reinnervation for real-time myoelectric control of multifunction artificial arms. *JAMA.* 2009;301:619–628.

37. Van de Meent H, Hopman MT, Frölke JP. Walking ability and quality of life in subjects with transfemoral amputation: a comparison of osseointegration with socket prostheses. *Arch Phys Med Rehabil.* 2013;94:2174–2178.

JOHN J. FARLEY, III ("JACK"), JUDGE (RETIRED), US COURT OF APPEALS FOR VETERANS CLAIMS On January 10, 1969, an enemy 82 mm mortar round landed "gimme" distance from Jack Farley at FSB (Forward Support Battalion) Pershing in Vietnam. Two weeks later, he arrived at Walter Reed Army Medical Center in a full-body cast, sporting more than 100 wire sutures and missing his right leg above the knee. He spent the next 14 months relearning how to walk.

Jack was a 1964 graduate from the College of the Holy Cross, where he captained the freshman and varsity lacrosse teams. In 1966, he received his MBA from Columbia University Graduate School of Business. Following his

retirement from the Army as a
Captain in 1970 due to 100%
disability, Jack was the first
student admitted to the charter
class of the Hofstra University
School of Law—where he was
the founding Editor-in-Chief
of the *Hofstra Law Review*—
graduated first in his class, and
received his JD degree cum laude
in 1973.

Jack spent 17 years as a US
Department of Justice litigator,
rising to become a director
of the Torts Branch, a Senior
Executive Service member, and
the Founding President of the Department of Justice Senior Executive Service
Chapter. He was responsible for, *inter alia*, defending national security cases
and the massive asbestos litigation, as well as representing federal employees
sued personally for common law torts and constitutional violations. In
September 1989, Jack was nominated by President George H. W. Bush and
confirmed 1 week later by the Senate to a 15-year term as one of the founding
judges of the US Court of Appeals for Veterans Claims. After serving as a
senior judge for seven additional years, he retired in 2012. Ever resilient,
Jack recently co-founded an information technology company (n2grate
Government Technology Solutions, LLC), which assists federal agencies in
their pursuit of complex data center and cloud integration strategies.

If his postmilitary vocation was the law, Jack's avocation has been serving
Veterans. Since 2003, Jack has been a fixture at Walter Reed helping to
establish the rehabilitation program for our Wounded Warrior amputees.
He has been a daily amputee peer visitor for many of the more than 1,380
Amputee-Warriors during Operation Iraqi Freedom, Operation Enduring
Freedom, and Operation New Dawn. In addition, he has trained and certified
more than 125 amputee peer visitors at Walter Reed and Brooke Army
Medical Center.

Jack has joined Wounded Warriors in completing eight Marine Corps Marathons, as well as the New York City and Palm Beaches Marathon, on a handcycle. He has also taught disabled Veterans of World War II, Korea, Vietnam, Bosnia, Somalia, Iraq, and Afghanistan as a volunteer downhill ski instructor for more than 20 years at the Veterans Administration/Disabled American Veterans Winter Sports Clinic in Colorado. As he tells the amputees the first time they attack a mountain on skis, or a snowboard, or a monoski, "Once you conquer this, there is nothing you cannot accomplish."

Jack's decorations include the Bronze Star Medal with Combat "V," three Oak Leaf Clusters; the Purple Heart Medal with Oak Leaf Cluster; and the Army Commendation Medal. He received the Dean's Award for Distinguished Hofstra Law School Alumni, as well as the Distinguished Alumni Medal. Jack was the first chair of the Veterans Law Section of the Federal Bar Association, is in the Massapequa High School Hall of Fame, and received the In Hoc Signo Award from the College of the Holy Cross. The Paralyzed Veterans of America presented him with the Harry A. Schweikert, Jr. Disability Awareness Award in August 2007.

As they recover from these life-altering wounds,
my vision is that the Department of Defense,
the [Department of Veterans Affairs] and the rest of America
figure out a way to take care of these young people
and their families for the rest of their lives.
In many cases, they are trying to figure out what they
want to be for the rest of their lives, and
their choices have changed.

★ ★ ★

ADMIRAL MIKE MULLEN
UNION LEAGUE
PHILADELPHIA, PENNSYLVANIA
APRIL 29, 2008

CHAPTER FOUR

Psychosocial Factors in Reintegration

MICHELLE L. SPORNER, PhD, CRC,* and
ANNE E. BARRY, MS, CRC†

*Assistant Professor, Rehabilitation Counseling, School of Health and Rehabilitation Sciences, University of Pittsburgh, 5049 Forbes Tower, Pittsburgh, Pennsylvania 15260

†Rehabilitation Counselor, Office of Vocational Rehabilitation, 531 Penn Avenue, Pittsburgh, Pennsylvania 15222

INTRODUCTION

To address the reintegration of Veterans and Service Members, it is helpful to understand more about the psychosocial adjustment of those who have served. The military creates a unique subculture that has established norms, values, and behaviors. From the time Service Members enlist, complete basic training, and finish their Military Occupation Specialties training, they will have adapted to this culture and its own survival of the fittest. For those who serve in the infantry and see combat, an added layer of stress and demands are connected to this unique environment. Adaptive stress reactions are created and then reinforced in the tense and sometimes hostile environments that translate into survival, victory, and mission complete status. Once a soldier is taken out of that context, he or she will find that the behaviors, organization, and priorities that proved successful in the military may not translate successfully to civilian culture. This chapter will provide an overview of factors affecting adjustment, particularly resilience, traumatic brain injury (TBI), and posttraumatic stress disorder (PTSD). Special emphasis will be placed on counseling approaches that may help promote successful reintegration.

PSYCHOSOCIAL ADJUSTMENT

Military Service Member to Veteran and Civilian

Regardless of whether a Service Member has deployed, or if he or she sustained an injury or disability, transitioning from the military into civilian culture can be challenging. Members of the United States military belong to a unique culture and take great pride in their military identity. While individuals are in the service, the military places special emphasis on the values of duty, honor, loyalty, and commitment to comrades, unit, and Nation.[1] Military identity promotes the ideas of self-sacrifice, discipline, obedience to legitimate authority, and belief in a merit-based rewards system.[2] Although these values are vital to the safety and functioning of the military unit, these values are in conflict with more individualistic, liberty-based civic values that embrace materialism and autonomy. Individuals who are in the midst of transitioning out of the military often feel as if they are caught between two worlds, which may result in feeling alienated from friends and family members and experiencing an identity crisis.[1] As a result, for some Service Members, the process and experience of transitioning out of the military and back into the civilian world can be challenging.

The deployment experience itself adds another dimension to adjustment. Service Members face many challenges as a result of deployment, including being away from family and important events, deteriorating relationships, or experiencing personal change for the worse.[3] Service Members may also encounter negative reactions as a result of personally experienced trauma (eg, taking a life, being shot at, seeing/handling corpses, having a colleague killed or seriously wounded, etc).[4] These experiences may linger with a Service Member long after the deployment. Deployments during the conflicts in Iraq and Afghanistan were longer and more frequent than in previous conflicts, adding to the potential for Service Members to experience these personal traumas.[5] In addition to this increased frequency, the time between deployments was also much shorter.

Although most people readily recognize the negative reactions to deployment, it is important to note that there may be several positive reactions. For example, some Service Members reported that during deployment, they experienced self-improvement, had time to think, were able to help others, and had the opportunity to experience another culture.[3] Further discussion on the impact of culture in the military is discussed in Chapter 16 (Culture and Reintegration of Veterans).

Risk Factors for Adjustment Difficulties

Reports indicate that there is a high rate of depression, PTSD, TBI, anxiety disorders, and substance use disorders in Service Members who have been deployed.[6,7] Additionally, it has been reported that Soldiers are more likely to experience higher levels of psychological problems (eg, acute stress) when they experience high or intense levels of combat (eg, being attacked, ambushed, or killing the enemy).[8] Risk factors for adjustment difficulties include combat experience and can be classified into five categories:

1. fighting,
2. killing,
3. threat to oneself,
4. death or injury of others, and
5. other atrocities.[9]

Longer deployments or multiple deployments may indicate additional risk factors. Soldiers who were deployed for at least 7 months reported the following as concerns: lack of time off, lack of privacy or personal space, separation from family, and long deployment lengths.[10] Additionally, for individuals in the military, suicide is the second leading cause of death.[11]

Forty-five percent of Iraq and Afghanistan War Veterans are seeking compensation for their service-connected disability.[12] Returning from combat can act as a risk factor in transition, but the system of care and benefits that awaits a service-connected Veteran can also be a risk factor itself. There is an unfortunate reality that develops when benefits are provided to those who are given the label of "disabled." For some, that label and status of disability will create a dependency on government disability compensation. Although this compensation is undoubtedly deserved, what was intended as a temporary assistance becomes a lifelong disincentive. Those who accept government support as their sole earnings are forgoing the optimization of skills and gifts that could be used in the civilian workforce.[12]

It is noteworthy that Veterans of the Iraq and Afghanistan Wars are more educated than the typical American. The majority of these Veterans have a high school diploma or GED equivalent, and >80% of officers have at least a bachelor's degree. In addition to education, these Veterans are held to higher mental and physical standards than the typical American. Moreover, this en-

Exhibit 4-1. *Distribution of Service-Connected Disability Ratings*

SERVICE-CONNECTED DISABILITY RATINGS (%)	PERCENTAGE OF VETERANS
0–20	28
30–40	26
50–60	21
70–80	17
>80	8
= 100%	4

tirely volunteer-era military includes record numbers of Reserve or National Guard individuals, which assumes that Service Members are older and more educated.[12]

When a Veteran transitions to civilian life with a service-connected disability, it should not be assumed that his or her status disallows that Veteran to engage in a gainful, active, productive lifestyle and career. In Exhibit 4-1, the service-connected disability ratings are given in increments of 10%, and the average-awarded, service-connected percentages for Iraq and Afghanistan Veterans are also shown.[12]

Although the technology and advancements in medicine for the care of war wounds are unprecedented, the injuries that result from combat and war wounds are not to be taken lightly. However, caution needs to be utilized when interpreting the definition of "disability" as the military defines it. Military disability and civilian disability can be very different concepts because they are rooted in two different models. The civilian world has transitioned *from* the medical model (to which the military maintains residual roots) *to* a social-biopsychosocial model of disability. In this model of disability, the person is considered holistically, inclusive of their strengths, their limitations, and contextual factors. This differs from the medical model in that it does not focus on the impairment or diagnosis. Clinicians and counselors are trained and equipped to work with individual Veterans to assess their strengths as well as obstacles and also find suitable employment that provides meaning and rewarding activity to life. In this case, employment can serve as a therapeutic outlet for Veterans to once again find meaning in their lives after returning from war. The bottom line is the fine distinction between capacity and performance. Capacity is defined as *the best an individual is expected to do,* whereas performance is defined as *what the individual actually does and what the individual actually achieves.* The goal should always be to minimize the gap that exists between these two factors. Additionally, the same significance and attention should be given to the performance factor as has been given to the capacity number placed on a disability claim form.[12]

TRAUMATIC BRAIN INJURY

According to the Department of Defense (DoD) and the Department of Veterans Affairs (VA), the definition for determining whether a Service Member has sustained a TBI is "a traumatically induced structural injury and/or physiological disruption of brain function as a result of an external force that is indicated by new onset or worsening of at least one . . . clinical sign immediately following the event."[13(p16)] The Clinical Practice Guidelines identify clinical signs as

- any period of loss of or a decreased level of consciousness (loss of consciousness),
- any loss of memory for events immediately before or after the injury (post-traumatic amnesia),
- any alteration in mental state at the time of the injury (confusion, disorientation, slowed thinking, etc) (alteration of consciousness/mental state),
- neurological deficits (weakness, loss of balance, change in vision, praxis, paresis/plegia, sensory loss, aphasia, etc) that may or may not be transient, and
- intracranial lesion.[13(p16)]

From 2000 to 2013, the DoD reported diagnosing 294,172 Service Members with mild-to-severe TBI not only as a result of deployment, but also in nondeployed settings. Sources of nondeployment-related TBI include motor vehicle accidents, sports, other recreation activities, and military training.[14]

The impact of sustaining a TBI and the resulting associated long-term consequences have been well documented. A TBI may result in physical, cognitive, sensory, language and communication, affective, and behavioral disturbances that may have both short-term and long-term consequences. Due to the complex nature of the brain and the functions the brain is designed to carry out, disruptions that result from TBI are interrelated and are closely connected, thus making it difficult to narrow the nature of the problem to one domain. Additionally, effects from TBI may affect individuals' quality of life, especially in the personal, social, and vocational domains. A general overview of the consequences of a TBI is provided based on the categorization of functional limitations into cognitive, neurobehavioral, sensory, and somatic domains.

Common cognitive dysfunctions following TBI include difficulties with

- memory,
- attention,

- language,
- visuospatial perception,
- sensory motor integration,
- affect recognition,
- communication,
- speed of processing, and
- executive function.[15–17]

Neurobehavioral and emotional disorders have been the least studied and understood, despite clinical agreement that significant problems are present.[16] Research has, however, identified large disturbances in emotion and behavior post-TBI. Furthermore, disorders of behavior and emotion after TBI are the most frequently reported problem by family members, friends, and caregivers.[18]

When an individual sustains a TBI, he or she may experience significant changes in equilibrium and somatosensory perception.[17] Commonly reported sensory disruptions reported in TBI include blurred vision, dizziness, and fatigue.[16] Additionally, persons may experience sensitivity to light and noise, balance problems, and transient neurological abnormalities.[19] In moderate and severe TBI, seizures are a common long-term problem.[20] Research has also shown that survivors of TBI often have a high prevalence rate of chronic headaches.[16,21]

POSTTRAUMATIC STRESS DISORDER

Posttraumatic stress disorder (PTSD) is another common consequence of war zone deployment.[22] According to the American Psychiatric Association (APA; Arlington, VA), PTSD is characterized by the development of specific symptoms following exposure to an extreme traumatic stressor. This exposure may include direct involvement in an actual or threatened death event or serious injury or threat to one's physical integrity. These traumatic stressors can also include witnessing events that involve death or serious injury or learning of an unexpected death of a close friend.[23] For Service Members or Veterans to be diagnosed with PTSD, they must meet the following criteria:

- exposure to one or more traumatic events,
- recurrent intrusive distressing memories,
- avoidance of stimuli associated with the traumatic event,
- negative alterations in cognitions and mood,

- marked alteration in arousal (hypervigilance), and
- reckless or self-destructive behavior.

Recurrent intrusive memories often occur as flashbacks or bad dreams, thus reliving the trauma.[24]

Individuals who have PTSD often spend a lot of time and energy avoiding activities, situations, or people who are associated with the traumatic event and, as a result, avoid any thoughts or feelings that are associated with these events.[23] In everyday life, these avoidance behaviors manifest as feeling emotionally numb or having strong feelings of guilt or worry. Individuals who have PTSD may also lose interest in activities they previously found enjoyable. For example, if driving through a crowded city reminds a person of his or her patrols, that person may have difficulty driving to work or driving to areas of the city to visit others.[24] Individuals may also have symptoms of hyperarousal that served them well while they were deployed. However, when an individual returns home, it can be difficult to turn off this constant alertness that may result in an individual being easily startled, being constantly on edge, or having significant sleep difficulties or outbursts of anger.[24] It is common for previously deployed Service Members with PTSD to express survivor's guilt or guilty feelings about the things they needed to do to survive their combat deployment.[23]

The prevalence rates for PTSD following deployment vary. According to the RAND Corporation (Arlington, VA) study, approximately 14% of all Service Members who served during Operation Enduring Freedom (OEF)/Operation Iraqi Freedom (OIF) have PTSD,[25] whereas rates for Service Members who deployed to Iraq range anywhere from 9.8% to 19.9%[6,7,26] Comparatively, the prevalence of PTSD in the general US population is approximately 4% to 8%.[22,23] It is important to note that female Soldiers were found to be 2.5 times more likely to develop PTSD compared with male Soldiers.[27]

PTSD is an important outcome to consider because it can affect the whole person, causing difficulties and disruptions in psychosocial and occupational functioning and overall well-being.[22,28] Additionally, PTSD has been found to decrease quality of life for Veterans of the OEF/OIF cohort.[22]

Additional Factors Affecting Adjustment

The Office of the Army Surgeon General estimated that 12% of soldiers had anxiety and depression disorders after their first deployment. As soldiers continue to deploy multiple times, these rates increase to approximately 27% after a third deployment.[29] Additional psychological health issues may include anger and aggressive behaviors, as well as guilt or shame.[30]

Ground troops (usually Soldiers and Marines) are more likely to report PTSD and depression than are Sailors and Airmen.[29] Further, female military personnel, enlisted personnel, Hispanics, and those not currently on active duty—including members of the Guard and Reserve and those who have retired—are most likely to report PTSD and depression. Adding an additional layer of challenges, Military Veterans who have sustained a TBI are three times more likely to also have PTSD.[31]

Eighty percent of individuals who have been diagnosed with PTSD also experience additional co-morbid psychiatric disorders, most frequently substance use disorders, depression, and anxiety.[32] Additionally, PTSD is often associated with suicidal ideation and suicide attempts, as well as other chronic medical conditions such as arthritis and headaches. PTSD and TBI are also associated with self-reported disturbances in sleep. OEF/OIF Veterans with PTSD also report psychosocial difficulties, as well as difficulties with family, peers, work, money, and school.[33]

For individuals transitioning out of the military, lack of social or familial support, fears of the future, pain, and substance abuse may also make the transition process for Service Members more challenging.

MANIFESTATIONS OF ADJUSTMENT DIFFICULTIES

Many Veterans and Service Members experience difficulties as they transition into a civilian life. These challenges include marital difficulties, financial difficulties, alcohol or substance abuse problems, medical problems,[34] anxiety and depression,[35] homelessness, and motor vehicle accidents.[36] Even more troubling, the 2013 unemployment rate for Veterans who have served since September 2001 was 8.8% for men and 9.6% for women, compared with 7.5% and 6.8% for their respective non-Veteran cohorts. This indicates that many Veterans experience difficulty finding civilian employment.[37]

In addition to transition difficulties faced by returning Service Members and Veterans, participation can be further impacted as a result of some of the challenges associated with TBI and PTSD.

POSTTRAUMATIC STRESS DISORDER

Service Members with PTSD have an increased likelihood of being unemployed and have a decreased likelihood of being employed after participating in work therapy.[38,39] Additionally, while many Veterans experience homelessness, PTSD is associated with an 85% greater risk of becoming homeless again in the future.[40] Further, PTSD is associated with a variety of problems across social and interpersonal functioning, marital functioning, parental and family functioning, and occupational functioning. PTSD is also related to career and work difficulties, and Veterans with PTSD having an increased likelihood of accomplishing less, being limited in the type of work, and having difficulty performing work.[41] Research has also shown that PTSD is associated with lower life satisfaction and overall well-being.[22] Veterans who screened positive for PTSD or depression were twice as likely to report alcohol misuse compared with Veterans who did not have PTSD or depression.[42]

TRAUMATIC BRAIN INJURY

Service Members and Veterans with TBI face challenges in their day-to-day lives. There are several psychosocial implications of acquiring a brain injury. When persons sustain a TBI, they may experience difficulty adjusting to their new disability and may face challenges with recognizing problems they are now experiencing and continue to see themselves as their old selves. Adjustment to disability after sustaining a TBI depends on the severity and location of the injury, as well as the available social and family support, educational attainment, and premorbid functioning.[43] For individuals who sustain moderate or severe TBIs, emotional problems are common, specifically lower frustration tolerance, agitation, excessive use of profanity, aggression, and potentially destructive behaviors. Additional emotional conditions that individuals experience after TBI may include anger, anxiety, depression, and low self-esteem.[44] These common emotional challenges often negatively impact social relationships and can increase social problems because persons may become overdependent on others; become tangential in their talking; and display immature behavior, such as an inappropriate use of humor or inappropriate sexual behaviors.[44]

Return to work following TBI can also be challenging due to the complex interaction of physical, cognitive, and emotional demands associated with work.[45] As a result, a large set of individuals with TBI are unemployed or underemployed,[46] with approximately only 40% returning to work rates 1 to 2 years after TBI.[47] Work plays an important role in people's lives and when individuals are unable to return to work, they are more likely to have negative psychosocial adjustments and increased health problems. Further, unemployment for individuals with TBI may lead to a decreased level of satisfaction with life, failure to successfully reintegrate into their community, economic dependency, and an increase in secondary disability.[48,49]

SUICIDE

The suicide rate for Service Members across all branches has risen, with the Army and the Marine Corps having the greatest rise since 2001.[11] Traditionally, suicide rates among military personnel were lower than the general population. However, starting in 2009, the suicide rate in the military surpassed the civilian rate. In 2001, the suicide rate for Service Members was 9 per 100,000; yet, in 2009, that number had risen to 24 per 100,000.[50] Further, an estimated 6% of active duty members have attempted suicide.[51]

According to the Defense Centers of Excellence for Psychological Health and Traumatic Brain Injury (Arlington, VA), warning signs for suicide can include the following:

- thinking about or talking about hurting or killing him/herself;
- threatening to hurt or kill him/herself;
- talking or writing about death, dying, or suicide;
- looking for ways to harm him/herself, such as seeking pills or firearms;
- undergoing increased substance use/abuse;
- having feelings of hopelessness or having no sense of purpose;
- being unable to sleep or oversleeping;
- withdrawing from friends, family, or society;
- experiencing excessive rage, anger, or desire for revenge;
- having feelings of anxiety or agitation; and
- experiencing dramatic changes in mood.[52]

It is important to note that Service Members and Veterans who have untreated PTSD, depression, and TBI are more likely to attempt suicide.[53] Risk factors that may increase a Service Member's or Veteran's likelihood of committing suicide include the following:

- male gender;
- Caucasian race;
- E-1 to E-2 rank;
- younger than 25 years of age;
- GED/less than a high school education;
- divorced;
- regular component—including those on active duty in the Army, Navy, Air Force, and Marine Corps;
- drug and alcohol abuse;
- relationship problems; and
- legal, administrative, and financial problems.[52]

KEY FACTORS TO SUPPORT ADJUSTMENT
Previous research has found that, among individuals who have experienced traumatic events, roughly 30% to 70% report positive change.[54] Social sup-

ports and intimate relationships may protect against developing PTSD or act as a moderating factor against PTSD symptomatology.[27] It is hypothesized that when an individual is faced with a stressful event, he or she seeks out support from others to help reduce or regulate this distress.[55] Further, these intimate relationships may help facilitate the development of coping skills that can be utilized during times of separation or prolonged stress (deployments).[56] Additional protective factors that have been found to have a direct relationship to unit well-being and may serve as a buffer between deployment stressors and behavioral health outcomes include supportive leadership, unit cohesion, and perceived readiness.[10,57,58]

Resilience factors have been shown to protect against the negative effects of depression. These aspects of resilience include positive emotions, cognitive flexibility, meaning-making, and active coping.[59] With respect to PTSD, social support has been found to be the strongest protector against PTSD.[60,61] Furthermore, individuals who perceive themselves as having a high level of social support have been linked to having higher levels of resilience.[62]

In a recent survey of OEF and OIF Veterans, individuals who had lower levels of unit support and postdeployment social support were identified as having a higher rate of PTSD and increased depressive symptoms, as well as decreased resilience and psychosocial functioning.[33] However, positive appraisals of one's military service may serve as a buffer against combat-related PTSD symptoms.[8] Service Members who describe a positive appraisal of their military service may view their deployments and combat as a necessary part of their service, as well as an opportunity for growth.[63] The positive view of military service, in addition to having a view that the Service Member is supported by his or her military leaders, may promote a positive identification with the military and may encourage individuals who have experienced trauma to reach out to other Service Members who have also experienced combat trauma.[64] This process may lead to finding a positive meaning in the trauma and encourage a healthy coping style with that trauma.

COUNSELING AND REHABILITATION INTERVENTION

POSTTRAUMATIC STRESS DISORDER

Only approximately one-half of the Service Members who met screening criteria for PTSD or major depression actually reported seeking psychological or counseling services within the previous 12 months.[25] It has been reported, however, that only one-quarter of active duty troops with psychiatric diagnoses actually receive treatment services,[6] and approximately 57% of individuals who suspected they had a TBI never saw a medical professional for that injury.[25]

In general, both the civilian and military cultures in America discourage people from seeking medical help or mental health services for cognitive and psychological disorders, but this is often more pronounced for Service Members and Veterans. Service Members often report fear of negative effects on careers, personal stigmatization, and potential loss of peers' confidence as significant and powerful reasons to avoid professional help.[65] When individuals do not receive the appropriate services for cognitive and psychological trauma, there are grave and negative implications for future health, including substance abuse and suicide, poor work outcomes, and relationship and family success.[5,65] Although Service Members may report more concerns about seeking or following through with treatment, there are many interventions that have been proven effective for Service Members and Veterans during the transition process, including individual counseling, group counseling, and support groups.

For Veterans with PTSD, the current gold standard of treatment is cognitive behavioral therapy (CBT).[32] CBT is effective in treating both acute and chronic PTSD, particularly through prolonged exposure therapy, cognitive processing therapy, and eye movement desensitization and reprocessing.[66] The overall process of change that occurs through CBT is the modifying of cognitive distortions that are associated with PTSD.[67] Another CBT intervention that is effective is stress inoculation training. The VA/DoD Clinical Practice Guidelines for the treatment of PTSD recommend components of exposure and cognitive restructuring therapies.[68] While CBT is effective in treating PTSD, there is a high dropout rate, and the nonresponse rate is approximately 50%.[69] Additionally, individuals with co-morbid TBI may not benefit from CBT because of the high-level cognitive requirements; however, several case studies indicate that CBT may be a promising treatment for individuals with both TBI and PTSD, but more research is still needed.[70]

There are also many advantages to group-based therapy for the treatment of PTSD. Economically speaking, the VA or other service providers benefit from group therapy approaches because of the increasing number of returning Soldiers who will be in need of these services. From a clinical perspective, the reliable evidence of the advantages of group-based treatment for those who have PTSD is growing. One advantage that is seen in group-based, exposure-style treatments is the validation that can be experienced through hearing other combat Veterans' struggles. The validation and empathy experienced in the group can establish a sense of normalcy that can be a strong catalyst for recovery.[71]

Two prominent therapy interventions for this population include
(1) group-based exposure therapy and (2) trauma-focus group therapy.
The most common interventions in both types of treatment include:

- a psychoeducational element,
- a focal trauma narrative presentation,
- repeated exposure,
- interpersonal skills training, and
- relapse prevention.

Another component that is usually included is cognitive restructuring. Most
treatments of PTSD stem from the cognitive therapy school that has been
proven reliable and effective because it is an evidence-based practice. Education and cognitive interventions are integral in the treatment of PTSD and
enable traumatic experiences to be reintegrated into a nondistorted
schemata of understanding.[72]

Traumatic Brain Injury

Cognitive rehabilitation is the gold standard of intervention for individuals
who have TBI. Cognitive rehabilitation is a systematic, functionally oriented
service of therapeutic cognitive activities and an understanding of the person's
behavioral deficits. Functional changes are achieved by directing cognitive
rehabilitation services to reinforce, strengthen, or reestablish previously
learned patterns of behavior, or by establishing new patterns of cognitive
activity or mechanisms to compensate for impaired neurological systems.
A major goal of cognitive rehabilitation is to provide interventions that lessen
the cognitive impairment itself or that lessen the disabling effect of cognitive
impairments.[73,74] Cognitive rehabilitation gained popularity in the United
States after World Wars I and II to treat injured Service Members. It focused
on compensatory and restorative cognitive rehabilitation and has now
become a fundamental component of TBI rehabilitation.[75,76]

Suicide Prevention

One way to help prevent suicides among military personnel and Veterans is
through the DoD's ACE (Ask, Care, Escort) framework (http://realwarriors.
net). By using these three simple steps, individuals who interact with Service
Members and Veterans, particularly family members, may have some basic
steps to help guide how they talk with that person.

1. *Ask* the Service Member or Veteran about his or her suicidal thoughts. Individuals working with Service Members and Veterans should know the suicide warning signs and have the courage to ask the person about their thoughts in a calm manner.
2. *Care* for the person by staying calm and nonjudgmental while actively listening to the details they share. At this time, individuals should also remove any objects that may pose a danger to the Service Member or Veteran.
3. *Escort* the Service Member or Veteran (if it is suspected that he or she is suicidal) to a chaplain or to a behavioral health professional.

In case of an emergency, the National Suicide Prevention Lifeline (1-800-273-TALK [8255] and press 1 for Veterans) will always react immediately. Feel free to call 911 in an emergency.

Each military branch has created a suicide prevention program specific to the needs of its Service Members. Additionally, the DoD has identified the importance of resiliency training as an effort to decrease the number of suicides and suicide attempts. Resiliency is just one component of the broader concept of positive psychology.

POSITIVE PSYCHOLOGY

For Service Members prior to deployment, as well as in the transition period, positive psychology interventions may be useful. Positive psychology is the study of how positive subjective experiences and positive individual traits can improve quality of life and may prevent pathology in the face of negative experiences.[77] At an individual level, positive psychology focuses on the subjective value individuals place on their experiences. It further includes an examination of past well-being, contentment, and satisfaction. Additionally, it focuses on future hope and optimism, as well as present flow and happiness.[77] Characteristics of resilience include gratitude, hope, kindness, leadership, love, spirituality, and teamwork.[78] While traditional counseling and psychology approaches often look at mediating negative consequences associated with psychological problems, positive psychology is a strength-based approach that aims to foster excellence. Positive psychology is not designed to replace traditional counseling, nor does it deny the human pain, weaknesses, and disorders people face. Rather, it offers a complete view of human life in both happiness and suffering.[79]

The Army tested a Comprehensive Soldier and Family Fitness program consisting of three parts: (1) a psychological fitness test, (2) resilience training, and (3) courses on training others to be resilient.[4,80] Individuals initially assess their strengths through the Global Assessment Tool, which measures emotional, family, social, and spiritual fitness. High scores for these criteria indicate a lower potential for anxiety and depression.[80] As of 2011, more than 900,000 Soldiers had taken this assessment.

After completing the assessment, Soldiers then take a course on post-traumatic growth, as well as additional optional courses on emotional, family, social, and spiritual fitness. The mandatory posttraumatic growth module teaches soldiers about five elements that contribute to this growth:

1. understanding the response to trauma and its relationship to the normal responses, and how this differs from symptoms of PTSD and are not character defects;
2. reducing anxiety by controlling intrusive thoughts;
3. engaging in constructive self-disclosure and not keeping their story hidden or bottled up;
4. creating a new story that redefines trauma as an experience that changes a person's views on loss and gain, vulnerability, and strength; and
5. articulating life principles, such as creating a new identity and being altruistic.[80]

The final and most important component is the training to teach others how to embrace resilience. Master resilience trainers and resiliency training assistants are taught how to train others in their units about resiliency. The master resilience training includes three parts that cover (1) building mental toughness, (2) building signature strengths, and (3) building strong relationships.

Another approach the Army is taking to increase resilience is through the Comprehensive Soldier and Family Fitness resilience training. This training is a component of the Army's Ready and Resilient Campaign and aims to improve the physical and psychological health of Soldiers and their families. Training is provided through "Five Dimensions of Strength," which include

1. physical,
2. emotional,
3. social,
4. spiritual, and
5. family strength.[81]

The Army's Ready and Resilient Campaign is an integrated and comprehensive approach to increasing individual and unit readiness and resilience.[82]

According to the Mental Health Advisory Team 9, soldiers who report getting some resilience training prior to their deployments reported lower rates of stress than those who did not receive any resilience training.

BARRIERS TO ACCESSING COUNSELING SERVICES

For Service Members and Veterans with PTSD, several challenges exist that often prevent individuals from participating in treatment. Many Veterans reported challenges in engaging in the counseling process, with a decision to seek treatment, including concerns about treatment (40%), emotional readiness for treatment (35%), stigma (16%), and logistical issues (8%) being cited as reasons for not beginning treatment.[83] Other reasons may include

- negative career repercussions,
- inability to receive a security clearance,
- concerns about confidentiality,
- concerns about side effects of medications,
- preferred reliance on family and friends, and
- perceived lack of effectiveness of the medications as barriers to receiving mental healthcare for formerly deployed Military personnel.[25]

A group of OEF/OIF combat Veterans reported that perceived stereotypes exist around PTSD, including labels such as being dangerous/violent or crazy and a belief that combat Veterans are responsible for having PTSD.[84] They also reported not seeking treatment to avoid being labeled as having a mental illness. Once individuals engaged in treatment, they reported resisting these stereotypes, but still reported challenges with reintegrating into society and acknowledged the fact that other combat Veterans best understood their experiences.[84] As a result, peer-based groups may encourage Veterans to engage in treatment sooner.

SUMMARY

This chapter provides an overview of some of the challenges Service Members and Veterans face as they transition from the military to the civilian world, taking into consideration military cultural changes that may impact this transition. In addition to the challenges Service Members may face, the other complications that deployment experiences bring, particularly PTSD and TBI, are also highlighted. The transition process cannot only be examined through the Service Member or Veteran's perspective. Further emphasis should be placed on the unique challenges this group and their social support network face. Counselors and other healthcare providers should be trained or provided with more information about these specific cultural factors. Although counseling interventions are beneficial in treating psychosocial adjustment issues, positive psychology interventions such as resilience training aim to teach skills that may serve people during stressful times. Veterans and Service Members have dedicated much more than their time. Therefore, an increased effort is needed to utilize approaches that aid this group to transition smoothly into their next chapter.

REFERENCES

1. Demers A. When Veterans return: the role of community in reintegration. *J Loss Trauma*. 2011;16:160–179.

2. Collins J. The complex context of American military culture: a practitioner's view. *Washington Q*. 1998;21:213–226.

3. Newby JH, McCarroll JE, Ursano RJ, Fan Z, Shigemura J, Tucker-Harris Y. Positive and negative consequences of a military deployment. *Mil Med*. 2005;170:815–819.

4. Cornum R, Matthews MD, Seligman MEP. Comprehensive soldier fitness: building resilience in a challenging institutional context. *Am Psychol*. 2011;66:4–9.

5. Tanelian TL, Jaycox L. Summary. In: Tanelian TL, Jaycox L, eds. *Invisible Wounds of War: Psychological and Cognitive Injuries, Their Consequences, and Services to Assist Recovery*. Santa Monica, CA: RAND Corporation; 2008: xix–xxxiii.

6. Hoge CW, Auchterlonie JL, Milliken CS. Mental health problems, use of mental health services, and attrition from military service after returning from deployment to Iraq or Afghanistan. *JAMA*. 2006;295:1023–1032.

7. Hoge CW, Castro CA, Messer SC, McGurk D, Cotting DI, Koffman RL. Combat duty in Iraq and Afghanistan, mental health problems, and barriers to care. *N Engl J Med*. 2004;351:13–22.

8. Dohrenwend BP, Turner JB, Turse NA, Adams BG, Koenen KC, Marshall R. The psychological risks of Vietnam for U.S. veterans: a revisit with new data and methods. *Science*. 2006;313:979–982.

9. Fontana A, Rosenheck R. Psychological benefits and liabilities of traumatic exposure in the war zone. *J Trauma Stress*. 1998;11:485–503. doi: 10.1023/A:1024452612412

10. Mental Health Advisory Team 9. Operation Enduring Freedom (OEF) 2013. Army Medicine Web site. http://armymedicine.mil/Documents/MHAT_9_OEF_Report.pdf. Accessed January 15, 2014.

11. Ramchand R, Acosta J, Burns RM, Jaycox LH, Pernin CG. *The War Within: Preventing Suicide in the U.S. Military.* Santa Monica, CA: RAND Corporation; 2011.

12. Gade D. A better way to help Veterans. *National Affairs, Summer 2013.* National Affairs Web site. http://www.nationalaffairs.com/publications/detail/a-better-way-to-help-veterans. Accessed January 15, 2014.

13. Department of Veterans Affairs and Department of Defense. VA/DOD Clinical Practice Guidelines for Management of Concussion/Mild Traumatic Brain Injury. Veterans Affairs Web site. http://www.healthquality.va.gov/mtbi/concussion_mtbi_full_1_0.pdf. Accessed February 3, 2010.

14. Defense and Veterans Brain Injury Center. DVBIC Web site. http://dvbic.dcoe.mil/dod-worldwide-numbers-tbi. Accessed January 15, 2014.

15. Levine M. Issues in neurobehavioral assessment of mild head injury. *Cogn Rehabil.* 1988;6:14–20.

16. Borgaro SR, Prigatano GP, Kwasnica C, Rexer JL. Cognitive and affective sequelae in complicated and uncomplicated mild traumatic brain injury. *Brain Injury.* 2003;17:189–198. doi:10.1080/0269905021000013183

17. Halbauer JD, Ashford JW, Zietzer JM, Adamson MM, Lew HL, Yesavage JA. Neuropsychiatric diagnosis and management of chronic sequela of war-related mild to moderate traumatic brain injury. *J Rehabil Res Dev.* 2009;46:757–796. doi:10.1682/JRRD.2008.08.0119

18. Marsh NV, Kersel DA, Havill JH, Sleigh JW. Caregiver burden at 1 year following server traumatic brain injury. *Brain Injury.* 1998;12:1045–1059. doi:10.1080/026990598121954

19. Prigatano GP. Personality disturbances associated with traumatic brain injury. *J Clin Consult Clin Psychol.* 1992;60:360–368.

20. Gordon WA, Zafonte R, Cicerone K, et al. Traumatic brain injury rehabilitation: state of the science. *Am J Phys Med Rehabil.* 2006;85:343–382. doi:10.1097/01.phm.0000202106.01654.61

21. Hall RC, Hall RC, Chapman MJ. Definition, diagnosis, and forensic implications of postconcussional syndrome. *Psychosomatics.* 2005;46:195–202.

22. Schnurr PP, Lunney CA, Bovin MJ, Marx BP. Posttraumatic stress disorder and quality of life: extension of findings to veterans of the wars in Iraq and Afghanistan. *Clin Psychol Rev.* 2009;29:727–735.

23. American Psychiatric Association. *Diagnostic and Statistical Manual of Mental Disorders.* Fifth edition. Washington, DC: American Psychiatric Publishing; 2013.

24. National Institute of Mental Health. Post-traumatic stress disorder. NIMH Web site. http://www.nimh.nih.gov/health/topics/post-traumatic-stress-disorder-ptsd/index.shtml. Accessed January 15, 2014.

25. Schell TL, Marshall GN. Survey of individuals previously deployed for OEF/OIF. In: Tanielian TL, Jaycox L, eds. *Invisible Wounds of War: Psychological and Cognitive Injuries, Their Consequences, and Services to Assist Recovery.* Santa Monica, CA: RAND Corporation; 2008: 87–116.

26. Milliken CS, Auchterlonie JL, Hoge CW. Longitudinal assessment of mental health problems among active and reserve component soldiers returning from the Iraq war. *JAMA*. 2007;298:2141–2148.

27. Skopp NA, Reger MA, Reger GM, Mishkind MC. The role of intimate relationships, appraisals of military service, and gender on the deployment of posttraumatic stress symptoms following Iraq deployment. *J Trauma Stress*. 2011;24:277–286.

28. Schnurr PP, Hayes AF, Lunney CA, McFall M, Uddo M. Longitudinal analysis of the relationship between symptoms and quality of life in veterans treated for posttraumatic stress disorder. *J Consult Clin Psychol*. 2006;74:707–713.

29. Kaplan A. Untreated vets: a 'gathering storm' of PTSD/depression. *Psychiatric Times*. 2008;25:12–13.

30. Department of Veterans Affairs. Mental illness research, education and clinical centers post-deployment stress: what families should know, what families can do. Veterans Affairs Web site. http://www.mirecc.va.gov/Coaching/PostDeployment-Stress_Families.pdf. U.S. Department of Accessed January 15, 2014.

31. Carlson KF, Nelson D, Orazem R, Nugent S, Cifu DX, Sayer NA. Psychiatric diagnoses among Iraq and Afghanistan war veterans screened for deployment-related traumatic brain injury. *J Trauma Stress*. 2010;23:17–24.

32. Tanev KS, Pentel KZ, Kredlow MA, Charney ME. PTSD and TBI co-morbidity: scope, clinical presentation and treatment options. *Brain Injury*. 2014;28:261–270.

33. Pietrzak RH, Goldstein MB, Malley JC, Rivers JC, Southwick SM. Structure of posttraumatic stress disorder symptoms and psychosocial functioning in veterans of Operation Enduring Freedom and Iraqi Freedom. *Psychiatr Res*. 2010;178:323–329.

34. Resnik LJ, Allen SM. Using International Classification of Functioning, Disability and Health to understand challenges in community reintegration of injured veterans. *J Rehabil Res Dev*. 2007;44:991–1006.

35. Doyle ME, Peterson KA. Re-entry and reintegration: returning home after combat. *Psychiatr Q*. 2005;76:361–370.

36. Hooper TI, Debakey SF, Bellis KS, et al. Understanding the effect of deployment on the risk of fatal motor vehicle crashes: a nested case-control study of fatalities in Gulf War era veterans, 1991–1995. *Accid Anal Prev*. 2006;38:518–525.

37. Bureau of Labor Statistics. Employment situation of veterans news release. BLS Web site. http://www.bls.gov/news.release/vet.htm. Accessed January 15, 2014.

38. Smith MW, Schnurr PP, Rosenheck RM. Employment outcomes and PTSD symptom severity. *Mental Health Serv Res*. 2005;7:89–101.

39. Resnick SG, Rosenheck RA. Posttraumatic stress disorder and employment in veterans participating in Veterans Health Administration Compensated Work Therapy. *J Rehabil Res Dev*. 2008;45:427–436.

40. O'Connell MJ, Kasprow W, Rosenheck RA. Rates and risk factors for homelessness after successful housing in a sample of formerly homeless veterans. *Psychiatr Serv.* 2008;59:268–275.
41. Rona RJ, Jones M, Iverson A, et al. The impact of posttraumatic stress disorder on impairment in the UK military at the time of the Iraq war. *J Psychiatr Res.* 2009;43:649–655.
42. Jakupcak M, Tull MT, McDermott MJ, Kaysen D, Hunt S, Simpson T. PTSD symptom clusters in relationship to alcohol misuse among Iraq and Afghanistan war veterans seeking post-deployment VA health care. *Addict Behav.* 2010;35:840–843.
43. Falvo DR. *Medical and Psychosocial Aspects of Chronic Illness and Disability.* Burlington, MA: Jones & Bartlett Learning; 2014.
44. Department of Veterans Affairs. *Traumatic Brain Injury: Independent Study Course.* Washington, DC: United States Government Printing Office; 2010.
45. Dawson DR, Schwarts ML, Winocur G, Stuss DT. Return to productivity following brain injury: cognitive, psychological, physical, spiritual and environmental correlates. *Disabil Rehabil.* 2007;29:301–313.
46. Doctor JN, Castro J, Temkin NR, Fraser RT, Machamer JE, Dikmen SS. Worker's risk of unemployment after traumatic brain injury: a normed comparison. *J Int Neuropsychol Soc.* 2005;11:747–752.
47. Van Velzen J, Van Bennekom A, Edelaar M, Slutter J, Frings-Dresen M. How many people return to work after acquired brain injury? A systematic review. *Brain Injury.* 2009;23:473–488.
48. Keyser-Marcus L, Bricout J, Wehman P, et al. Acute predictors of return to employment after traumatic brain injury: a longitudinal follow-up. *Arch Phys Med Rehabil.* 2002;83:635–641.
49. O'Neill J, Hibbard MR, Brown M, et al. The effect of employment on quality of life and community integration after traumatic brain injury. *J Head Trauma Rehabil.* 1998;3:68–79.
50. Tarabay J. Suicide rivals the battlefield in toll on U.S. military. NPR Web site. http://www.npr.org/templates/story/story.php?storyId=127860466. Accessed January 15, 2014.
51. Bray RM, Pemberton MR, Hourani LL, et al. Department of Defense. Survey of health related behaviors among active duty military personnel. Tricare Web site. http://www.tricare.mil/2008HealthBehaviors.pdf. Accessed January 15, 2014.
52. Defense Centers of Excellence for Psychological Health and Traumatic Brain Injury. Risk and protective factors. DCoE Web site. http://www.dcoe.mil/content/navigation/documents/dcoe%20fact%20sheet%20risk%20and%20protective%20factors.pdf. Accessed January 15, 2014.
53. Hosek J. How is deployment to Iraq and Afghanistan affecting U.S. service members and their families? In: Tanielian TL, Jaycox L, eds. *The Invisible Wounds of War: Psychological and Cognitive Injuries Among Veterans of Iraq and Afghanistan.* Santa Monica, CA: RAND Corporation; 2008: 19–26.

54. Linley PA, Joseph S. Positive change following trauma and adversity: a review. *J Trauma Stress*. 2004;17:11–21.
55. Hazan C, Gur-Yaish N, Campa M. What does it mean to be attached? In: Rholes WS, Simpson JA, eds. *Adult Attachment: Theory, Research, and Clinical Implication*. New York, NY: Guilford Press; 2004: 55–85.
56. Orthner DK, Rose R. Work separation demands and spouse psychological well-being. *Fam Relat*. 2009;58:392–403.
57. Bliese PD. Social climates: drivers of soldier well-being and resilience. In: Adler AB, Castro CA, Britt TW, eds. *Military Life: The Psychology of Serving in Peace and Combat: Operational Stress*. Vol 2. Westport, CT: Praeger Security International; 2006.
58. Bliese PD, Castro CA. The soldier adaptation model (SAM): applications to peacekeeping research. In: Britt TW, Adler AB, eds. *The Psychology of the Peacekeeper*. Westport, CT: Praeger; 2003.
59. Southwick SM, Vythilingam M, Charney DS. The psychobiology of depression and resilience to stress: implications for prevention and treatment. *Clin Psychol*. 2005;1:255–291.
60. Brewin CR, Andrews B, Valentine JD. Meta-analysis of risk factors for post-traumatic stress disorder in trauma-exposed adults. *J Consult Clin Psychol*. 2000;68:748–766.
61. Ozer EJ, Best SR, Lipsey TL, Weiss DS. Predictors of posttraumatic stress disorder and symptoms in adults: a meta-analysis. *Psychol Bull*. 2003;129:52–73.
62. Bonnano GA. Loss, trauma, and human resilience: have we underestimated the human capacity to thrive after extremely aversive events? *Am Psychol*. 2004;59:20–28.
63. Jennings PA, Aldwin CM, Levenson MR, Avron S, Mroczek DK. Combat exposure, perceived benefits of military service, and wisdom later in life. Findings from the normative aging study. *Res Aging*. 2006;28:115–134.
64. Folkman S, Moskowitz JT. Positive affect and the other side of coping. *Am Psychol*. 2000;55:647–654.
65. Kelty R, Kleykamp M, Segal DR. The military and the transition to adulthood. *Future Child*. 2010;20:181–207.
66. Kar N. Cognitive behavioral therapy for the treatment of posttraumatic stress disorder: a review. *Neuropsychiatr Dis Treat*. 2011;7:167–181.
67. Hembree EA, Foat EB. Posttraumatic stress disorder: psychological factors and psychosocial interventions. *J Clin Psychiat*. 2000;61:33–39.
68. Department of Veterans Affairs/Department of Defense. *VA/DoD Clinical Practice Guidelines for Management of Post-traumatic Stress Disorder*. Version 2.0. Washington, DC: The Management of Post-Traumatic Stress Working Group; 2010.
69. Schottenbauer MA, Glass CR, Arnkoff DB, Tendick V, Gray SH. Nonresponse and dropout rates in outcome studies on PTSD: review and methodological considerations. *Psychiatry*. 2008;71:134–168.

70. McMillan TM, Williams WH, Bryant R. Post-traumatic stress disorder and traumatic brain injury: a review of causal mechanisms, assessment, and treatment. *Neuropsychol Rehabil.* 2003;13:149–164.

71. Ready DJ, Sylvers P, Worley V, Butt J, Mascaro N, Bradley B. Suicide prevention resources for military families. Real Warriors Web site. http://www.realwarriors. net/family/support/preventsuicide.php#_edn2. Accessed February 1, 2014.

72. Lubin H, Loris M, Burt J, Johnson D. Efficacy of psychoeducational group therapy in reducing symptoms of posttraumatic stress disorder among multiply traumatized women. *Am J Psychiatry.* 1998;155:1172–1177.

73. Committee on Cognitive Rehabilitation Therapy for Traumatic Brain Injury. Defining cognitive rehabilitation therapy. In: Koehler R, Wilhelm EE, Shoulson I, eds. *Cognitive Rehabilitation Therapy for Traumatic Brain Injury.* Washington, DC: National Academic Press; 2011: 75–87.

74. Bergquist TF, Malec JF. Psychology: current practice and training issues in treatment of cognitive dysfunction. *Neurorehabilitation.* 1998;8:49–56. doi: 10.1016/ S1053–8135(96)00208–9

75. Boake C. A history of cognitive rehabilitation of head-injured patients, 1915 to 1980. *J Head Trauma Rehabil.* 1989;4:1–8.

76. Parente R, Herrmann D. *Retraining Cognition: Techniques and Applications.* Austin, TX: PRO-ED; 1996.

77. Seligman MEP, Csikszentmihalyi M. Positive psychology: an introduction. *Am Psychol.* 2000;55:5–14.

78. Peterson C, Seligman MEP. Character strengths before and after September 11. *Psychol Sci.* 2003;14:381–384.

79. Seligman MEP, Steen TA, Park N, Peterson C. Positive psychology progress: empirical validation of interventions. *Am Psychol.* 2005;60:410–421.

80. Seligman MEP. Building resilience: what business can learn from a pioneering army program for fostering post-traumatic growth. *Harv Bus Rev.* 2011;April:100–106.

81. United States Army. Comprehensive Soldier & Family Fitness. CSF2 Web site. http://csf2.army.mil/index.html. Accessed February 1, 2014.

82. United States Army. Ready and Resilient Campaign. US Army Web site. http:// www.army.mil/readyandresilient. Accessed February 1, 2014.

83. Stecker T, Shiner B, Watts BV, Jones M. Treatment-seeking barriers for veterans of the Iraq and Afghanistan conflicts who screen positive for PTSD. *Psychiatr Serv.* 2013;64:280–283.

84. Mittal D, Drummond KL, Blevins D, Curran G, Corrigan P, Sullivan G. Stigma associated with PTSD: perceptions of treatment seeking combat veterans. *Psychiatr Rehabil J.* 2013;36:86–92.

Private First Class (PFC) Steve Domitrovich grew up in Aliquippa, a small town on the outskirts of Pittsburgh, Pennsylvania. He was born the son of two hard-working Croatian immigrants and was part of a family that included 12 brothers and sisters.

In 1943, he was drafted into the US Army and went to California for training. Later, he became a medic. As an 18-year-old, he fondly recalled his first driving lesson, in which his training instructor asked his class, "Who here has a license? (All but one soldier raised his hand.) Who here does not have a license? (Only one person raised his hand.) Great, you're our driver!" Shortly

thereafter, he was behind the wheel of his first vehicle. He went around the track countless times, grinding the gears of the ambulance until he finally got it down pat.

Originally, PFC Domitrovich had come ashore on the beaches of Utah as a member of the 479th Ambulance Company. In December 1944, he later found himself in the midst of what was later known as the Battle of the Bulge. He was a medic in the 575th Ambulance Company with a group of American units.

On December 17, 1944, near the town of Malmedy, Belgium, a German SS (Schutzstaffel) Division ambushed his convoy and took him and more than 100 other prisoners of war (POWs) captive. After being captured, PFC Domitrovich presented his Geneva Convention card that identified him as a medic. The SS processing soldier said, "Nix good" and tossed the card aside. The POWs were then led to a field and placed in lines. The SS backed up a truck and uncovered a crew-served machine gun. The SS troops went up and down the lines of soldiers collecting identification cards and dog tags from all the American Soldiers. It was during this collection process that Domitrovich stepped forward undetected from his line to the line directly in front of him, which had already been searched by the German SS troops, thus allowing him to keep his forms of identification.

What occurred next was one of the greatest known atrocities to American Soldiers. The SS troops finished their collection process and immediately opened fire. Domitrovich recalls to this day very clearly hearing a voice telling him to "fall!" He quickly fell to the ground and played dead. When the firing ended, he was surrounded by blood-soaked bodies and the sounds of dying men moaning for God and their mothers.

He lay there listening to the footsteps of the SS as they walked along the writhing bodies laughing and mocking the maimed American Soldiers. He also heard shots from their pistols. As the footsteps grew closer, a boot was placed next to Domitrovich's head. He remained still and held his breath for what seemed like an eternity. Fleeting thoughts ran through his head about his family and how they would take the news of his death. He prayed to God that if he was able to survive, he would attend Sunday Mass every week for the rest of his life.

A pistol went off, and blood covered his face, but it was not his own. The SS troops moved on and eventually left the area, leaving behind a field of executed American Soldiers. Domitrovich remained still in freezing

temperatures until he felt safe enough to open his eyes and stand up. He will never forget the sight of all those bodies strewn about the field, including in the adjacent fields where men were mowed down trying to flee execution.

Steve and a handful of other fortunate soldiers who miraculously survived gathered together and walked dazed to a nearby hilltop where they came upon an American patrol in the valley below. Ultimately, he finished out his participation in the Battle of the Bulge and supported Allied troops.

Domitrovich returned home to his family in Aliquippa, Pennsylvania. He has used the atrocities that took place that fateful day in Malmedy to catalyze and motivate himself to appreciate every moment of every day. He also met the love of his life, his wife Helen, a Greek immigrant living in Aliquippa. Steve opened his own small business, a dairy mart that he ran with his family for more than 30 years before finally retiring at the age of 70. He became an integral member of their small community, a town in which it would be very difficult to not run across a person who did not fondly know the unforgettable personality that is Steve Domitrovich. He has two children and two grandchildren, as well as numerous nieces and nephews. He has spent his days in retirement with his family and enthusiastically cheering for his favorite Pittsburgh sports teams. Steve's story has been featured in multiple books and on various Web sites, as well as immortalized in paintings.

Still to this day—since December 1944—he has not missed a Sunday Mass!

*I am proud to serve with such dedicated
Soldiers, families, and civilians and I'm inspired by
their resilience, sacrifice, and dedicated service
to our mission at home and abroad.*

★ ★ ★

GENERAL DANIEL B. ALLYN
VICE-CHIEF OF THE STAFF OF THE ARMY

CHAPTER FIVE

Spirituality and Reintegration: Building Strength, Fortitude, Optimism, and Connection

DOUGLAS A. ETTER, MDiv, MSS*; AMY MOUNTAIN, MS†; and
AUDREY SCHOOMAKER, RN, BSN, E-RYT‡

---

*Colonel, US Army; Joint Headquarters Chaplain, Pennsylvania National Guard and
Chief Communications Officer, Lebanon VA Medical Center, 1700 South Lincoln
Avenue, Lebanon, Pennsylvania 17042

†Director of Business Resources, Sysco Central Pennsylvania, LLC, 3905 Corey Road,
Harrisburg, Pennsylvania 17109

‡Integrative Health Specialist, Consortium for Health and Military Performance
(CHAMP), Human Performance Research Center, Uniformed Services University of
the Health Sciences, 4301 Jones Bridge Road, Bethesda, Maryland 20814

INTRODUCTION

*The Soldier's heart, the Soldier's spirit, the Soldier's soul are everything.
Unless the Soldier's soul sustains him he cannot be relied upon
and will fail himself, and his commander, and his country in the end.*

GENERAL GEORGE C. MARSHALL
US ARMY, CHIEF OF STAFF
(1939–1945)

Human beings are remarkably complicated. Although we are composed of various chemicals and compounds, many claim that we are more than just the sum of these parts. Specifically, they suggest that there is an element beyond our physical, emotional, or intellectual composition. Many people call this element the *soul*, *spirit*, or *life force*. There is little scientific evidence that such an element exists within human beings; however, there is an enormous collection of secondary literary, religious, psychological, historical, cultural, and empirical evidence that suggests such an element does exist. Therefore, it is not the purpose of this chapter to prove or disprove the existence of the human soul; rather, its existence is a presupposition of this chapter.

There are also two more presuppositions of this chapter:

1. We are convinced that spiritual growth is possible. Just as people can improve their physical well-being through a variety of exercises and practices (eg, aerobics, strength and flexibility training, good nutrition, and proper sleep habits), people can also improve their spiritual well-being.
2. We are asserting that there is not a single correct pathway or platform to develop one's spirituality.

Despite our many similarities, human beings are very complex; something that helps one person develop his or her spirituality may hinder another person's growth. What appeals to one might repel another. Each person must find the right pathway, platform, or combination to assist in his or her own spiritual growth and development. Thus, the purpose of this chapter is threefold:

1. to provide empirical scientific data that demonstrates the positive benefits of spiritual development;
2. to share a variety of pathways or platforms that one can use to increase or enhance spiritual development; and
3. to suggest other resources in which the reader can learn more about spiritual development, resiliency, and reintegration.

KEY CONCEPTS AND DATA

According to the journal *Military Medicine,*

> . . . the scientific study of spirituality and health is a very new field. There has been a five-fold increase in research on spirituality and religion, which from 1990–2007 reflects the growing increase in this topic within healthcare and psychology and spirituality.[1(p73)]

Before progressing to the scientific data, however, it is important to define certain key terms. The term *spirituality* can be confusing and easily misunderstood. For this reason, we have adopted a working definition of spirituality provided by Wong et al[2] that is drawn from an earlier work by Benson et al.[3] In this chapter, spirituality is defined as "the intrinsic human capacity for self-transcendence, in which, the self is embedded in something greater than the self, including the sacred,"[2(pp205–206)] and that motivates "the search for connectedness, meaning, purpose, and contribution."[2(pp205–206)] Spirituality is contrasted with *religiosity*, which is defined as, "one's relationship with a particular faith tradition or doctrine about a divine other or supernatural power."[2(p267)]

Additional key terms in this chapter include meaning, values, transcendence, and connection.

- *Meaning* refers to defining, making sense, understanding, or accepting situations or events in life. It also may refer to a driving or foundational motive that provides a sense of purpose or reason to think, speak, or behave in a certain manner. It provides an answer to the "why" questions in life.
- *Values* are cherished beliefs and standards that provide a framework through which a person may think, speak, or behave. Values provide a person with a "moral compass," indicating for that person what is right or wrong. These are the principles through which one perceives and defines his or her world.
- *Transcendence* relates to that which is beyond one's self. It includes an awareness and appreciation of the vastness of the universe, as well as an awareness of or belief in a force, spiritual being, higher power, or entity that is beyond, outside, or greater than one's self.
- *Connection* refers to the link or perceived link that one has with other human beings, other living organisms, the earth, the universe, or a force, spiritual being, higher power, or entity that is beyond, outside of, or

greater than one's self. It can also relate to one's understanding of our interdependence with others, as well as with the world at large.

Dr Harold Koenig, MD—Director of the Center for Spirituality, Theology, and Health; and Professor of Psychiatry and Behavioral Sciences and Associate Professor of Medicine at Duke University—reviewed 724 quantitative research studies examining the relation between religion and mental health in five areas: (1) depression, (2) suicide, (3) anxiety, (4) psychotic disorders, and (5) substance abuse.[4] The majority of these studies (476 of them) reported statistically significant positive associations between spirituality or practicing a religion and the ability to cope. Koenig states,

> Religious beliefs provide a sense of meaning and purpose during difficult life circumstances that assist with psychological integration; they usually promote a positive world view that is optimistic and hopeful; they provide role models in sacred writings that facilitate acceptance of suffering; they give people a sense of indirect control over circumstances, reducing the need for personal control; and they offer a community of support, both human and divine, to help reduce isolation and loneliness. Unlike many other coping resources, religion is available to anyone at any time, regardless of financial, social, physical, or mental circumstances.[4(p285)]

Additionally, Smith et al,[5] in their review of spirituality and resilience studies, state that

> . . . healthy spirituality may be related to increases in both resilience and positive emotions and that resilience and positive emotions may have a reciprocal influence on each other.[5(p450)]

The benefits of a positive and deep spirituality cannot be denied or ignored. There is a mountain of scientific evidence that supports the contribution of spiritual practices and well-being to physical, psychological, and social well-being. According to the book *Spiritual Resilience: Renewing the Soldier's Mind,*[6] numerous research studies show that spiritual practices increase health and physical well-being, psychological and emotional well-being, and family and social well-being.[7] Consequently, it is clear that although the existence of a human soul, spirit, or life force cannot be scientifically proven, a healthy positive spirituality can have numerous benefits on one's overall health. It is one more tool in the Service Member's toolbox that can and should be leveraged to assist Warriors as they reintegrate into their circles of family, friends, acquaintances, neighborhoods, coworkers, civic organizations, volunteer service organizations, and other communities to which they belong or hope to belong.

PATHWAYS OR PLATFORMS TO HELP DEVELOP OR DEEPEN ONE'S SPIRITUALITY

As noted previously, spirituality and religious observance are not the same. One may be a spiritual person without being religious or, conversely, one may be religious without having a deep spirituality. In this section, various pathways or platforms are discussed that can help develop or deepen one's spirituality, such as:

- prayer,
- sacred writings,
- meditation,
- storytelling or journaling,
- service,
- alms,
- spiritual direction,
- fasting,
- yoga, and
- artistic expression.

PRAYER

Prayer is not an old woman's idle amusement. Properly understood and applied, it is the most potent instrument of action.

MAHATMA GANDHI

INDIAN POLITICAL ACTIVIST (1869–1948)

It is not an accident that prayer is the first pathway or platform we offer as a means to deepen one's spirituality. Many people believe that prayer is the most basic method of developing spirituality. Some even argue that prayer is instinctual. However, despite certain exceptions, prayer is a discipline that can be practiced by anyone, at any time, and anywhere. Some faith groups believe prayers may be more efficacious, depending on who is offering the prayer and where they are offering the prayer. But, prayer is almost universally seen as a practice that is available to all humanity.

At its most fundamental level, prayer is best described as a form of communication. It is communication between human beings and that which they identify as God, a god, a natural force, a spiritual force, Mother Earth, or something greater or beyond themselves. It can involve adoration, confession, thanksgiving, and supplications. It can be deliberate or spontaneous. Prayer can follow prescribed formats based on different traditions or cultures or it can be wide open and enable the person "to go where Spirit leads." Prayer can be performed corporately as a group (with or without a leader) or by individuals. It can be done at prescribed times or destinations, or it can be done when one is emotionally, intellectually, or spiritually moved to say or offer a prayer.

Prayers may even involve different tangible objects, sacred items, or other materials (eg, books, candles, prayer beads, incense, etc). They can be vocalized in words or songs. Prayers may also be offered silently. Some traditions include repetitions in their individual and corporate prayers; other traditions steer clear of repetition. The common threads that run through the wide diversity of beliefs, traditions, and cultures are threefold:

1. A higher power exists.
2. This higher power commands, demands, or offers prayer as an avenue by which human beings may seek divine wisdom, guidance, or power.
3. The practice of prayer leads people to become better; that is, by practicing the discipline of prayer, they become more compassionate, empathetic, sympathetic, sensitive, kind, merciful, focused, and thoughtful.

Although it is beyond the limitations of this chapter to provide specific methodologies on the wide range of how various traditions or cultures practice prayer, we can offer a few general guidelines. For specific ways to practice prayer according to specific belief systems, consult a religious leader from that tradition or consider observing the following:

- *Find space that is conducive to prayer* (ie, distractions should be minimized in order to maximize focus). This selected space may also provide a sense of calm, inspiration, or both. The space can be one created by human hands or be one that occurs in the natural environment.
- *Prepare for prayer.* In some traditions, this means moving through certain rituals physically, emotionally, or intellectually to reach a preferred state for prayer, whether it means to be cleansed, centered, or connected to the faith community or others. It may involve elements like water, music, or sacred items. Sometimes, the preparation can take just a few moments, and at other times and in other traditions, it can take much longer.

- *Assume a comfortable position*, whether sitting, standing, kneeling, or lying prostrate. Depending on the religious tradition, hands may be folded, raised, or placed across the chest or at the sides. Different religious systems also permit accommodations for those individuals who may be physically challenged or unable to follow their tradition's prescribed methods.
- *Begin prayer*. It may be initiated by singing, saying prescribed statements, performing certain actions, or reading from prayer books or sacred scriptures. Follow the tradition that is most comfortable and that is most meaningful. In group or directed prayer, there may be times when each individual may offer his or her own prayers. These prayers should reflect the genuine desires of the heart.
- *Conclude prayer*. Individuals may once again be encouraged to move through certain rituals to officially end this time. Their prayers may be concluded with certain phrases, words, or actions.

The most important thing to remember is to find a prayer tradition that resonates with you, one that is comfortable, and one that can be practiced routinely. Prayer is most beneficial when it becomes part of a normal routine.

SACRED WRITINGS

When we follow the counsel of our leaders to read and
study the scriptures, benefits and blessings of many kinds come to us.
This is the most profitable of all study in which we could engage.

HOWARD W. HUNTER
ATTORNEY (1907–1995)

Every major religion has written materials that contain its traditions, beliefs, philosophies, instructions, and rituals. Some religions believe these texts are the very word of God. Others acknowledge they are the teaching or instruction of their leaders or founders. Yet some religions believe that these texts should be widely distributed, while others believe the texts should be reserved only for adherents of their faith or certain individuals within their tradition. Oftentimes, these writings will be translated into a variety of languages to give greater access to more individuals. Yet, in other situations, the writings are only considered to be sacred in their original language. The common theme that runs through all of these texts is their authority and instruction in relation to the faith that claims them. There is often, although not always, stern warnings against adding to or subtracting from the texts.

Whatever faith one embraces, it should be acknowledged that all of these religious texts contain wisdom, guidance, and advice, which if followed can lead to a fuller, richer, and happier life. The wisdom, instruction, and inspiration found within these texts are major reasons that we encourage Warriors who are reintegrating into their communities and who are seeking to build their spiritual resiliency to intentionally involve themselves in this type of study because there is so much to be gained.

But how should one go about studying the sacred texts of his or her faith? As in the section on prayer, we encourage Warriors to seek out religious leaders, teachers, or scholars in the tradition that specifically interests them. Different faiths suggest different approaches to the study of sacred texts. If, however, one is seeking general guidance, then we offer the following suggestions.

- Find a place and time to read or study without distraction. Interruptions should be avoided if at all possible. Pause for a few moments to separate yourself from all concerns in order to focus on the text. If your tradition encourages it, pray to receive divine guidance.
- Read slowly and deliberately according to your tradition. Some faiths encourage the texts to be read aloud, even if one is alone, and other faiths permit the texts to be read silently. Still some faiths demand that the reading be done in its original "tongue," whereas other faiths permit reading in the reader's "native tongue."
- Ask yourself these questions:
  — What is this telling me about God or the Divine?
  — What is it teaching me about humanity?
  — What is it telling me about myself?
  — What is the proper response to what I have read?
- Take time to offer prayers or to journal about your experience. Journaling has the added benefit of the person being able to return to it and to see again the inspiration or instruction perceived through personal study.

The simple truth is that Warriors would do well to avail themselves of the wisdom, instruction, and guidance of these sacred texts. They have provided information and inspiration to countless people and can do the same for today's Warrior.

MEDITATION

*Meditation is the life of the soul; action, the soul of meditation;
and honor, the reward of action.*

FRANCIS QUARLES
ENGLISH POET (1592–1644)

The practice of meditation, active for centuries in the Eastern tradition, has had a popular following in Western culture for less than a century. People who practice meditation do so for many reasons:

- to consciously increase nonanalytical attention,
- to emphasize and engender positivity,
- to increase the internal capacity for healing, and
- to reduce symptoms of pain and alleviate discomfort.

Many people meditate simply to create a quiet place of solitary focus and to develop a serene, internal ability to dispel random or mindless thoughts and ruminations. Advocates of meditation say the ability to calm thoughts and focus the mind through meditation is a life-changing experience. This fairly simple and low-cost practice, essentially available to anyone who seeks to learn the techniques, is believed to be a powerful and healing tool—one that can conquer the cacophony of thoughts that often serves as a barrier to pursuing and achieving a life of meaning.

Initially, meditation was conceived within the religious framework of Eastern cultures. Prayer and meditation are still linked today as personal activities designed to quiet inner conflict and open mind and soul to the influence from a different power typically not thought to be emanating from the individual. Although many types of techniques exist, the family of meditation practice falls generally into three specific categories:

1. concentrative meditation,
2. mindfulness meditation, or
3. contemplative meditation.

As the term conveys, *concentrative meditation*, on one hand, focuses on a specific object or concept. Sometimes a word, phrase, or mantra is the tool. The goal is to focus thought in a nonanalytical way, using the sole object as an aid to prevent distracting intellectual or emotional noise from interfering with the session. *Mindfulness meditation*, on the other hand, applies a broader technique in which the individual remains aware of the environment (ie, sounds, scents, etc), but prevents definitions or judgments about it—that is, the person is conscious of the environment, but does not ruminate or engage in targeted thinking about anything that he or she might hear, sense, smell, or feel. *Contemplative meditation* seeks to create a quiet place where the individual can engage with the presence of a higher power, whether interpreted as the presence of God or some other religious/nonreligious entity. This model applies aspects of concentrative and mindfulness meditations, in that the individual is focusing on the potential of engaging with a specific entity or source of power, as well as creating an open mind that allows greater awareness.

When an individual chooses to meditate, he or she may follow a number of common rituals to prepare for each session. Although meditation practices differ, most techniques are easily adapted to any environment. Consider these techniques and suggestions:

- Begin with brief sessions lasting a few minutes and build to longer periods.
- Be aware that some meditation sessions may be more successful or beneficial than others.
- Ask a friend or family member who meditates to lead a session.
- Wear comfortable clothing that does not restrict movement.
- Choose a physical position that is comfortable and supports the back, hips, and neck whether sitting, fully reclining, leaning against a wall, or standing.
- Select a quiet location: A brightly lit patio sheltered from the elements; a dark, comfortable interior room; or a park or garden that offers privacy.
- Choose the same time of day to meditate: Morning meditation can prepare the individual to meet each day with focus; mid-day meditation can help reduce stress and anxiety that has built up during the day; and evening meditation may support the reduction of tension, thus enabling more restful sleep.
- Utilize a meditation audio or video track: Essential sounds like rain, wind, or waves are commonly used as background elements; bells or chimes are often used to signal pacing during the session; a meditation track can be recorded using sounds, voices, or music that is personally meaningful.

STORYTELLING OR JOURNALING

*Storytelling reveals meaning without committing the
error of defining it.*

HANNAH ARENDT
GERMAN HISTORIAN (1906–1975)

How often are favorite stories told over and over, with the storyteller relishing the details and possibly even gaining greater insight into different aspects of the tale unrealized in earlier versions? The history of storytelling is as long and diverse as humankind. In most cultures, the telling of stories—either orally or in written form—serves as documentation of the past and may come to play an important function in that culture's future. Although generally we might consider storytelling a form of entertainment, one of the major properties of self-disclosure may be healing, particularly for those who have suffered trauma.

More than 95% of emotional experiences are typically shared within a few hours.[8] Although talking about traumatic events may be the norm for many people, some experiences are too difficult to share in conversation with others. Under these circumstances, storytelling through writing—often referred to as "journaling" in the psychotherapy field—can serve as a therapeutic tool to help individuals explore trauma without attempting to define or solve it.

The benefits of therapeutic writing can result in emotional, cognitive, and social improvements. An individual who has experienced trauma may have difficulty disclosing the incident, resulting in isolation and depression. Because of overwhelming emotions, many individuals find themselves inhibited from disclosing the experience. A research effort documented that individuals who experienced a significant and specific traumatic incident and did not disclose it were more likely to have significant health issues over an extended period of time, including hospitalization, ulcers, and high blood pressure.[9] Because talking about trauma may not come easily, writing can act as an emotionally safe way in which to disclose the incident, even if no one ever reads the writer's words. The process of releasing the trauma through words may foster an emotional release, and the writer may find some relief in sharing the incident, if only on a piece of paper or a computer screen.

Gestalt psychologists' views of perception reveal that when individuals experience trauma, they disconnect from their core identity. The disconnect from "themselves" continues to deepen as they repress thoughts and feelings about the trauma.[10] The unfortunate outcome is often that individuals who have experienced trauma behave in exactly a manner that prevents them from processing what happened; they cannot confront the experience in their minds or through their emotions. This cognitive challenge may not be resolved easily. Writing or storytelling, however, can provide a structured and prescribed process for documenting experiences that may help the writer realize possible connections that occurred during trauma. Even if there is no indication of a cause and effect related to the trauma, documenting it through storytelling may help the individual gain a sense of control and predictability by evaluating the experience through writing and recording the circumstances in his or her own words, without fear of reprisal or judgment.

From a social perspective, the isolation an individual experiences in the wake of a trauma incident only exacerbates the inherent instinct to retreat and withdraw from contact with the outside world. However, writing circles mirror the conversational and social structure of book clubs, in which participants write on an assigned topic and share their stories with members of the group. Not only have members of writing circles expressed satisfaction with the personal insights gained by writing together, but also they report receiving immediate benefit from the feedback and input provided by other members of the circle in response to sharing stories. An added benefit with technology advances is that many writing circles are virtual and do not require members to travel to be able to write and share stories.

Another benefit of therapeutic writing is not actually the writing process itself, but the preparation to write. The rituals that writers often engage in prior to writing serve as a kind of meditation. Going through the same motions every time an individual tells a story may create an environment of control and order, particularly if the outcome of the trauma incident was a sense of chaos or unpredictability. Some rituals storytellers might use to prepare themselves include the following:

- Create a quiet place in which to write—a home office, a comfortable chair, or a corner in a favorite room.
- Choose to tell your story at the same time every day—dedicate a half-hour that is your time to think about your story, tell it, or write about it.
- Fuel yourself with a favorite cup of coffee or tea.
- Begin your writing or storytelling session with physical rituals, such as stretching exercises or deep breathing techniques.
- Reward yourself for completing a story with a pleasurable activity, such as reading, meeting a friend for coffee, or taking a bike ride.

Service Members who are reintegrating into their communities may think about whether storytelling or writing is an activity they want to pursue and should consider the following:

- Use a digital recorder to talk about your story instead of telling it to another person.
- Tell or write your story with a different beginning or ending, and evaluate your thoughts and feelings about the impact.

Think over these questions:

- If you could tell anyone your story, who would it be?
- Is your story something that you want future generations to hear or read?
- How can someone benefit or learn from hearing or reading your story?
- How might sharing your story prevent something negative or bad from happening to someone?
- Might there be a time in the future when you no longer want or need to write or tell your story?

SERVICE

*In the end, the number of prayers we say
may contribute to our happiness, but the number of prayers we answer
may be of even greater importance.*

DIETER FRIEDRICH UCHTDORF
GERMAN AVIATOR (1940–)

For centuries, human beings have helped one another, demonstrating a long-standing legacy of altruistic behavior. There are countless examples of individuals—both famous and not—throughout history for whom service to people and community represented a life philosophy. Milton S Hershey (1857–1945) was a leading figure in philanthropy and gave economic and educational support to the community of central Pennsylvania. Mother Teresa (1910–1997) was an international symbol for selflessness and the power of collective service to those in great need. Myriad other individuals— ranging from Clara Brown (1800–1885) to Andrew Carnegie (1835–1919) and from Dana Reeve (1961–2006) to J P Morgan, Jr (1867–1943)—have committed time, energy, money, and other valuable personal resources for the honorable purpose of helping humankind and the broader society.

Social and psychological research have identified several underlying motivators for why we help others. The most common altruistic motivator is what researchers call an "other-oriented emotional reaction," typically defined as empathy, compassion, sympathy, or sometimes, pity.[11] For decades, philosophers and psychologists have written about empathy as the primary foundation for why humans continue to help one another without expectation of anything in return. Two other motivators—perhaps not as familiar to the general public—have been suggested: (1) collectivism and (2) principlism. *Collectivism*, on one hand, stems from the need to benefit a group as a whole, which is thought to be connected to our need for group identity. *Principlism*, on the other hand, is defined by the instinct to act simply to uphold a broad and impersonal moral principle, such as justice.

Regardless of the motivation that moves someone to help another person, the benefit from giving and being in service to individuals or a community has been well documented. Because empathy can motivate behavior to give to others, therapeutic programs are now suggesting the use of empathy-based tactics directed toward enhancing positive social interactions. These practices are very different from traditional therapy programs that often focus on controlling or inhibiting negative behavior. Instead, empathy-based tactics encourage developing a broader perspective and improving interpersonal relationships through the pursuit of common goals. Empathy-based tactics are also being used to reduce negative attitudes toward groups of people who are stigmatized by various factors, including gender, race, culture, and military service.

There are thousands of groups and organizations that provide service opportunities, from nonprofits, schools, and foundations to churches and other faith-based institutions. Many resources exist to identify and select a cause that can benefit from your expertise. In considering if you want to engage in service to individuals or the broader community, think about the following questions as you weigh your options:

- What do you enjoy doing in your free time that could benefit others?
- Is there a specific mental or physical health issue in your background that you would like to resolve? If so, is there a nonprofit organization located in your community that could benefit from your experience with a specific issue?
- What unique expertise or experience have you gained that could benefit someone else?
- What type of service work could include your partner and/or family?
- How much time or money do you want to commit in service to individuals or your community?

Alms

Prayer carries us half way to God,
fasting brings us to the door of His palace, and
alms-giving procures us admission.

THE QURAN
(C. 651 AD)

Alms can be defined as money, goods, or certain sentiments given to others. Almost all faith traditions encourage or even require their adherents to participate in sharing their material resources with those in need. The word *alms* comes from an old English word, *ælmes*, which can be translated as mercy. Therefore, when one is giving alms, that individual is also showing mercy and/or respect. Many traditions suggest that because God shows humanity mercy, it is incumbent upon the entire human race to show mercy, kindness, and respect to others. This may be accomplished through the giving of alms.

Alms-giving can be done voluntarily or as an act of obligation. Some faith traditions (eg, Judaism, Christianity, and Islam) establish guidelines as to what percentage of one's income or business resources should be given as alms. Other faith traditions (eg, Buddhism or Hinduism) restrict financial dispersements and instead encourage the distribution and sharing of food and drink. It is important for Warriors to discuss with others who share their faith tradition, the rationale, expectations, and options for alms-giving.

One common thread that weaves the various tapestries of alms-giving together is that alms should be given secretly or privately. They should not be given because of a desire to show off, to impress others, or to gain something for oneself. Instead, alms should be given discreetly without the desire of seeking the praise or approval of others. One should not seek reward or recognition for oneself while sharing what is that person's. Thus, the amount of one's gift is not as important as the purity or sympathy of one's heart. The more pure or more sympathetic the gift, the better. Various traditions suggest that the giver will be rewarded for his or her altruistic behavior. Some traditions believe that the reward will come in this life, others believe it will come in the next life, and still other traditions believe there will be a combination of the two.

There are a wide variety of methods that can be used to donate alms, depending on one's faith tradition and community's culture. There are also an almost seemingly endless number of recipients to whom one may donate, again depending on the traditions and teaching of one's faith community. Some methods encourage giving only to charities within their own religious tradition, other methods encourage a broad array of charitable possibilities, and other methods permit secular nonprofit organizations or charities. The Warrior and his or her loved ones will be best served by seeking the counsel of authorities within their tradition. Nevertheless, we still offer the following words of counsel:

- *Do your due diligence.* In other words, verify that the charity, organization, or person to whom you intend to donate is legitimate and not simply seeking to play on your heartstrings to steal from you. Be sure that the receiver will use the gifts wisely. Some charities have higher overhead and thus fewer dollars reaching their intended audiences.
- *Follow your heart or personal interest (if permissible within your faith tradition) to the charity of your choice.* Perhaps you would rather give to a Wounded Warriors fund than a religious charity or maybe give to some other 501(c)(3). When you donate to a 501(c)(3), your donation can be written off on your tax return. Be sure to consult your tax preparer for specific details.
- *Consider including your favorite charity in your will.* Gifts of this type can have a long and lasting legacy. Consult your financial advisor or attorney for details. Whatever decisions you make, and although it may seem counterintuitive, many people from a variety of faith traditions will testify that the more they give away, the more they have.

Spiritual Direction

> *What we need to do is bring the director into contact with*
> *our real self, as best we can, and not fear to let him see what is false in*
> *our false self. . . . We must let the director know what we really think,*
> *what we really feel, and what we really desire, even when*
> *these things are not altogether honorable. . . . Hence, we should*
> *approach direction in a spirit of humility and compunction,*
> *ready to manifest things of which we are not proud.*

> Thomas Merton
> Trappist Monk (1915–1968)

Long before personal trainers existed for athletes or personal financial advisers sprang onto the scene to assist investors, spiritual guides or directors were teaching neophyte seekers the deeper truths and mysteries of their faith. The spiritual guides or directors did not claim to possess all knowledge or all truth. They possessed knowledge, wisdom, and patience and gladly invested themselves in their students or devotees to make their experience of faith richer or deeper. Together, the director and devotee explore the various ways in which God may be touching the devotee's life; calling the devotee to action; and bringing the devotee to a place of more meaningful peace, joy, service, and satisfaction. Although a guide and seeker may discuss relationships, finances, work, and other aspects of life, the guide is not a counselor, therapist, or financial advisor. Guides are deeply contemplative people who are committed to assisting other people grow closer to their God, find deeper meaning in life, and tell their personal stories in ways that reveal the movement of the Holy. It is this focus on seeing life through the lens of the Divine and always returning each conversation to the Divine that distinguishes spiritual direction from other forms of mentor and mentee relationships.

Spiritual directors can be found in almost every faith tradition, although they may be called by different names or titles. Some traditions are even beginning to steer away from the verbiage "spiritual direction" because they interpret such language as pedantic or condescending. They prefer to describe the relationship as a spiritual friendship or companionship. Whatever the case may be,

> The director is one who knows and sympathizes, who makes allowances, who understands circumstances, who is not in a hurry, who is patiently and humbly waiting for indications of God's action in the soul. He is concerned not just with this or that urgent problem, this or that sin, but with the whole life of the soul. He is not interested merely in our actions. He is much more interested in the basic attitudes of our soul, our inmost aspirations, our way of meeting difficulties, our mode of responding to good and evil. In a word, the director is interested in our very self, in all its uniqueness, its pitiable misery and its breathtaking greatness. A true director can never get over the awe he feels in the presence of a person, an immortal soul. . . .[12(p21)]

For those who are interested in such a relationship or seek a deeper, more meaningful way of seeing and describing the movement and mystery of God in their lives, we offer the following suggestions:

- Before you seek a spiritual guide or director, spend time contemplating what you are seeking or what you hope to achieve from spiritual direction. You should also ask the following questions:
  — Are you ready or prepared to invest yourself as will be required by your spiritual guide?

— Are you prepared for the brutal honesty required?
— Are you prepared to invest the necessary time?
— Are you prepared to immerse yourself totally in this platform of growth and discovery?

- Once you know what you are hoping to achieve, gain, or experience from spiritual direction, and you know that you are willing to pay the price required, you can begin to seek a guide. You might ask the leaders of your community of faith for their recommendations. You can ask friends or other adherents to your faith where they have found spiritual guides. You might also search online according to your particular tradition.

- Once you have found spiritual directors who meet your desired religious affiliations, meet with them. Discuss your hopes and aspirations. Test the waters to see if you intuitively trust and respect them. There may be times during the course of your direction when you are uncomfortable, and you must be sure you can completely trust this person.

Fasting

I fast for greater physical and mental efficiency.

Plato
Greek Philosopher and
Mathematician (428–348 bce)

Making the conscious decision not to eat, for a prescribed period of time (*fasting*), is an increasingly popular method by which to cleanse and rebalance the physiological structure of the body. Therapeutic fasting is a treatment philosophy advocated by the International Association of Hygienic Physicians (IAHP; Youngstown, OH), an association comprised of primary care physicians who specialize in the supervision of therapeutic fasting. Certified members must be a licensed medical doctor, chiropractor, or osteopath who has completed a minimum 6-month residency program in an accredited institution specializing in therapeutic fasting.

There are many forms of fasting or cleansing available to consumers, using juices and supplements, specific food groups, and different combinations of ingredients and additives. Anyone considering entering into a fasting or cleansing program should have a forthright conversation with his or her primary care physician to discuss the positive and negative implications of a fasting program. For the purposes of this chapter, therapeutic fasting, as defined by the IAHP, will be the primary focus. It is defined as *abstinence from all substances, except for pure water, under conditions of complete rest and with the supervision of an IAHP-certified physician.*[13]

Physicians who attend to fasting under the IAHP guidelines identify therapeutic fasting as a tool for isolating issues within the body and stimulating an acute response to address the issues. If the body is focusing solely on processing only pure water and sitting at complete rest, it is more likely to target a directed and intense response to a specific symptom or condition. Often, therapeutic fasting is recommended for patients with an acute illness, and that fasting process is designed to isolate and address particular symptoms.[13] Therapeutic fasting has been successful in treating patients with chronic illnesses. It has also been used as a tool to create a clean, physiological foundation for the patient to engage in treatment.

When a patient is fasting, the body undergoes a purification of its tissue, organs, and metabolic processes. This process allows the body to let stressed and abused areas slough off any abnormal elements and return to a clean state. Scientific and medical literature contain hundreds of references on the use and implications of therapeutic fasting. The practice has been used extensively, and successfully, in the treatment of a variety of conditions—including obesity, diabetes, cancer, and autoimmune diseases—applied to psychiatric disorders (eg, schizophrenia), and utilized as a desensitization tool in the treatment of hypersensitivity and allergies.

Many people associate fasting with the concept of rejuvenating and "cleaning house," both mentally and physically. Often accompanied by meditative practices, fasting can provide a medically sound tool for eliminating accumulated debris in the body's systems and supporting a heightened internal focus on emotional, intellectual, and physical wellness.

When considering a fasting regimen:

- Consult your primary care physician first, before selecting a fasting or cleansing process.
- Follow all directions and guidelines associated with any specific fasting program.
- Monitor a fasting program as determined by your doctor's recommendation.
- Ask a friend or family member to participate in the program with you, for support and as a resource to discuss your progress and outcome.

Yoga

Blessed are the flexible, for they shall not be bent out of shape.

Anonymous

There are estimates that somewhere between 15 and 20 million Americans practice yoga.[13] At its core, the word *yoga* means to "yoke, to unite, to join together" and can provide a bridge from the body to one's own inner wisdom.[14] Beyond the pain relief, boost in mental performance, stress reduction, and overall strength and flexibility it claims to offer,[15,16] yoga is a tool people can draw upon to deepen their connection with their inner spirit. The practice of yoga is one tool for providing a timeless answer for those who quest for a deeper meaning in life and who desire abiding peace. Yoga classes are offered on many military installations. From elite Soldier–athletes who use yoga to build strength and flexibility to those recovering from posttraumatic stress disorder and other war injuries, the 4,000-year-old tradition of yoga offers resilience-building skills for Service Members, Veterans, and their families.

There are many forms and specific practices of yoga. Hot yoga classes offer fast-moving posture flows, and therapeutic yoga helps to rehabilitate people recovering from physical injuries. Other yoga classes emphasize balancing the nervous system before building strength in order to relieve stress, anxiety, depression, or even posttraumatic stress disorder. The many different styles and techniques of yoga offer something for everyone. The inner focus; the combination of practicing breathing exercises; and the practice of moving the body into poses with mindful, compassionate, present-moment awareness is part of the recipe that creates a sense of ease, calm, openness, strength, and flexibility in both body and mind.

For the purpose of reintegration, offering therapeutic, trauma-sensitive yoga classes invites a sense of safety or "groundedness" in one's inner self. It can foster a deep connection internally to one's spiritual side, thus connecting or yoking that person's soul to God—however that individual sees God. It also bolsters a sense of community when offered on military installations where practitioners share the gifts of practice together. Consider the following story of a military wife:

> Our life was somewhat chaotic. While raising three young kids with moves every year or two (once moved four years in a row), it was my job to keep the home together and children educated in good schools as we packed and unpacked one year to the next. I was under so much pressure—way more than I understood. I lost my faith as I felt like God

wasn't listening to me. I had a lot of pain, and not much less sorrow. My husband's work kept him away far too much for the kids and me. I stepped onto a yoga mat with some skepticism to experience almost immediate relief from my endless aching back. I felt a quiet in my body and soul that had left me. That sense of stillness returned my soul to life, and inspired me—with far more peace and wholeness than I had felt in years. (Name withheld by request, oral communication, January 2013.)

For people who are seeking another tool for their toolbox to assist with inner healing, resilience-building, and stress management while reintegrating after deployment, yoga may just be the answer.

ARTISTIC EXPRESSION
The purpose of art is washing the dust of daily life off our souls.

PABLO PICASSO
SPANISH ARTIST (1881–1973)

The link between being creative and expressing emotion has a long and complex history. Creativity has been defined as a neocortical activity, whereas emotions are often considered, psychologically speaking, as a "lower" form of thought process. Many scientists, psychologists, psychiatrists, and other professionals across different areas of expertise have studied the connection between expressing creativity through artistic pursuits and the impact it has on emotions. Regardless of what historical and academic research document, the end result is this: for thousands of years, artists have created works that have changed their lives and the lives of others who experienced or viewed their art.

So, how can creativity and expressing emotions and thoughts through the creative process be helpful? The American Art Therapy Association (Alexandria, VA) defines the practice as a mental health profession in which clients—facilitated by the art therapist—use art media, the creative process, and any resulting artwork to

- explore their feelings,
- reconcile emotional conflicts,
- foster self-awareness,
- manage behavior and addictions,
- develop social skills,
- improve reality orientation,
- reduce anxiety, and
- increase self-esteem.

Exhibit 5-1. *Available Resources on Spirituality*

PRAYER

Online resources:
- http://www.churchofengland.org/prayer-worship/learnpray.aspx
- http://www.arabacademy.com/en/downloads/learn-how-to-pray
- http://www.myjewishlearning.com/practices/Ritual/Prayer.shtml

Books:
- Bennet S. *Wisdom Walk: Nine Practices for Creating Peace and Balance from the World's Spiritual Traditions.* Novato, CA: New World Library; 2007.
- Blythe TA. *50 Ways to Pray: Practices from Many Traditions and Times.* Nashville, TN: Abington Press; 2006.

SACRED WRITINGS

Online resources:
- http://www.faithology.com/
- http://www.sacred-texts.com/index.htm

MEDITATION

Myriad resources exist on meditation, ranging from its history and practice to specific techniques. Searching the Internet will result in a number of sites to explore. Essential health and wellness information are cited on the National Institutes of Health and the Mayo Clinic sites. Two sites— (1) Learning Meditation and (2) Zen Habits—offer, respectively, free downloadable meditation sessions and specific calming and focus tactics for beginners. In-depth information about the therapeutic effects of meditation can be found in numerous scientific and academic journals, including the *American Journal of Psychotherapy*, the *Journal of Counseling Psychology*, the *Journal of Social Behavior and Personality*, etc.

Health and wellness:
- http://nccam.nih.gov/health/meditation/overview.htm
- http://www.mayoclinic.com/health/meditation/HQ01070

Free tools and techniques:
- http://www.learningmeditation.com (offers downloadable meditation sessions)
- http://zenhabits.net/meditation-for-beginners-20-practical-tips-for-quieting-the-mind

STORYTELLING OR JOURNALING

Resources for storytelling and journaling:
- Andrew EJ. *Writing the Sacred Journey: The Art and Practice of Spiritual Memoir.* Boston, MA: Skinner House Books; 2005.
- Jepson J. *Writing as a Sacred Path: A Practical Guide to Writing with Passion and Purpose.* Berkeley, CA: Ten Speed Press; 2008.
- Shapiro R. *Writing—The Sacred Art: Beyond the Page to Spiritual Practice.* Woodstock, VT: Skylight Paths Publishing; 2012.

SERVICE

Online resources:
- www.serve.gov—The Corporation for National and Community Service provides information and opportunities to engage in community service at local and national levels.
- www.charitynavigator.org—Charity Navigator is a comprehensive Web site that provides information about the viability and transparency of nonprofit organizations, helping volunteers to select the right charity for their interest.
- www.unitedway.org—Visit the United Way agency for your specific community. Agencies like the United Way offer specific days of service during the year that are organized by local coordinators and designed to introduce individuals to ongoing community service options.

ALMS-GIVING

Online resources:
- http://www.allahsword.com/free_islamic_books_zakah.html
- http://www.catholiceducation.org/articles/apologetics/ap0413.htm
- http://www.telegraph.co.uk/travel/destinations/asia/laos/9808241/Luang-Prabang-Respecting-the-alms-giving-ritual.html

SPIRITUAL DIRECTION

Online resources:
- http://www.shalem.org/index.php/resources/publications/pamphlets-on spiritual-direction/spiritual-direction
- http://www.rootedinspirit.org/spiritual-direction/definition/
- http://www.sdiworld.org/find-a-spiritual-director/what-is-spiritual-direction

Books:
- Merton T. Thomas Merton: *Spiritual Direction and Meditation*. Collegeville, MN: The Order of St. Benedict, Inc; 1960.
- Nouwen HJM. *Wisdom for the Long Walk of Faith*. New York, NY: Harper Collins Publishers; 2006.
- Vest N, ed. *Tending the Holy: Spiritual Direction Across Traditions*. Harrisburg, PA: Morehouse Publishers; 2003.

FASTING

Online resources:
- http://www.healthpromoting.com/learning-center/articles/fasting
- http://www.ncbl.nlm.nih.gov/pmc/articles/PMC1274154/
- http://www.cancer.org/treatment/treatmentsandsideeffects/complementaryandalternativemedicine/dietandnutrition/fasting

YOGA

Online resource:
- http://www.yogajournal.com/category/beginners/

Books:
- Feuerstein G, Payne L, eds. *Yoga for Dummies*, 2nd ed. Indianapolis, IN: Wiley Publishing House; 2010.
- Perlmutter L. *The Heart and Science of Yoga*. Averill Park, NY: AMI Publishing; 2005.

ART

Suggestions for learning more about art as a spiritual discipline:
- Visit www.arttherapy.org—The American Association for Art Therapy has more information about the history of art therapy, recommendations for local art therapy resources, and details about the education and certification requirements for certified art therapists.
- For the artist who simply wants to explore art as a therapeutic tool, a number of books can be found online, such as *Art as Therapy* by Alain de Botton and John Armstrong (London, UK: Phaidon Press; 2013), which serves as a tool for the reader to use art as a way to explore and interpret daily life challenges.
- Local craft stores and art schools are resources for classes or sessions. Look for class listings that include "interpretive" or "process" in the title.
- Visit www.artastherapy.com—Art as Therapy offers various artistic works to explore when facing questions about life, work, self, and love, along with other topics.

Documented art therapy results have been realized for patients experiencing cognitive decline. In addition, aggressive behavior has decreased through the use of art therapy.

Whether experiencing art by putting a paintbrush to paper, molding a clay figure, layering colored sand in a glass jar, or beating on drums, the creative process allows the artist to focus on an activity that creates a window for evaluating emotions from afar—often enabling the artist to resolve thoughts about those emotions. Some have described the process of creating art as a state of meditation, away from day-to-day stressors. The end result of creating the art, regardless of the finished product, often provides a feeling of accomplishment and satisfaction for the artist.

The American Art Therapy Association offers extensive background and information about art therapy options. It recommends seeking a trained and certified art therapist, particularly if the process involves treating fragile patients working out deep-seated issues. In these situations, art therapy must be performed in a private environment that allows patients to safely forget the outside world and express their innermost feelings.

RESOURCES

The number of resources available to develop one's own spirituality is virtually unlimited. As noted previously, we encourage Warriors and their loved ones to seek the guidance of leaders, teachers, and guides within their own traditions or the traditions that interest them to gain instruction related to these spiritual disciplines. The resources listed in Exhibit 5-1 should not be considered an endorsement of these products, materials, books, or sites. They are simply starting points for the beginner seeker, but many more are available. Consult your faith tradition's authorities for further guidance.

SUMMARY

There is no single best pathway or platform to develop one's spirituality. Because human beings are so complex, despite our many similarities, what helps one person develop his or her spirituality may hinder another person's growth. What appeals to one might repel another. Each person must find the right pathway, platform, or combination to assist with individual spiritual growth and development. This chapter provided empirical scientific data that demonstrate the positive benefits of spiritual development; shared a variety of pathways or platforms that Warriors and their families can use to increase or enhance their spiritual development; and suggested resources in which the reader can learn more about spiritual development, resiliency, and reintegration. Consider using the long-accepted practice of deepening your spirituality to accomplish this goal. Not only may you find your spirit renewed, but you may also find your life changed in ways you never anticipated.

REFERENCES
1. Hufford DJ, Fritts MJ, Rhodes JE. Spiritual fitness. *Mil Med.* 2010;175(8 suppl):73–87.
2. Wong YJ, Rew L, Slaikeu KD. A systematic review of recent research on adolescent religiosity/spirituality and mental health. *Issues Ment Health Nurs.* 2006;27:161–183.
3. Benson PL, Roehlkepartain EC, Rude SP. Spiritual development in childhood and adolescence: toward a field of inquiry. *Appl Dev Sci.* 2003;7:205–213.
4. Koenig H. Research on religion, spirituality, and mental health: a review. *Can J Psychiatry.* 2009;54:283–291.
5. Smith BW, Ortiz JA, Wiggins KT, Bernard JF, Dalen J. Spirituality, resilience, and positive emotions. In: Miller LJ, ed. *Oxford Handbook of Psychology and Spirituality.* Oxford, UK: Oxford University Press; 2012.
6. The Army Chaplaincy. *Spiritual Resilience: Renewing the Soldier's Mind.* Fort Jackson, SC: Center for Spiritual Leadership; 2009. Professional Bulletin of the Unit Ministry Team 16-09-2.
7. Brinsfield JW, Baktis P. The human, spiritual, and ethical dimensions of leadership in preparation for combat. In: Marshall J, Franks FM, eds. *The Future of the Army Profession.* Boston, MA: McGraw-Hill Companies, Inc; 2005: 463–490.

8. Rime B. Mental rumination, social sharing and the recovery from emotional exposure. In: Pennebaker JW, ed. *Emotion Disclosure and Health*. Washington, DC: American Psychological Association; 1995: 271–291.
9. Pennebaker JW. *Opening Up: The Healing Power of Expressing Emotions* (rev ed). New York, NY: Guilford; 1997.
10. Helson H. The psychology of Gestalt. *Am J Psychol.* 1925;36:494–526.
11. Batson CD. The empathy-altruism hypothesis. In: Weiner IB, Craighead WE, eds. *The Corsini Encyclopedia of Psychology*, Vol 1, 4th ed. Hoboken, NJ: John Wiley & Sons; 2010: 71.
12. Merton T. *Thomas Merton: Spiritual Direction and Meditation*. Collegeville, MN: The Order of St. Benedict, Inc; 1960: 21.
13. Goldhamer A. Therapeutic fasting: an introduction to the benefits of a professionally supervised fast. TrueNorth Health Center, Santa Rosa, CA, May 30, 2010. http://www.healthpromoting.com/learning-center/articles/therapeutic-fasting.
14. Payne L, Feuerstein G. *Yoga for Dummies*, 2nd ed. Indianapolis, IN: Wiley; 2010.
15. Pearlmutter L, Pearlmutter JC. *The Heart and Science of Yoga: A Blueprint for Peace, Happiness and Freedom from Fear*. Averill Park, NY: AMI Publishing; 2005.
16. McCall T. *Yoga as Medicine: The Yogic Prescription for Health and Healing*. New York, NY: Random House; 2007.

SERGEANT (SGT) MILES KAMSON has found a way to embody a lively and very optimistic character that serves as a springboard for everyone he meets. SGT Kamson is a current active duty Soldier in the 1st Squadron, 104th Cavalry Regiment in the Pennsylvania National Guard. He was retained in the military after a severe motorcycle accident in which he lost his left leg above the knee. He continues to serve honorably, showing Soldiers that once we are Warriors, we can never be anything less.

SGT Kamson was born in Philadelphia, Pennsylvania, where he encountered poverty, violence, and drugs in his neighborhood. He enlisted in the Pennsylvania Army National Guard directly out of high school in 2006 when our country was at war. In 2007, he was called to active duty and deployed to Sinai, Arab Republic of Egypt. In 2009, once he returned home and back to being a traditional drilling Soldier, he pursued a college degree at Temple University. Quickly derailed because of a motorcycle accident in 2010, he not only fought for his life, but also fought for his mind and career. This began his toughest fight.

SGT Kamson asked himself many times, "How can I be an asset to my commander with just one leg?" He has since served as a Battalion Career Counselor, Resilience Trainer Assistant, and Retention Non-commissioned Officer. In his community, he has volunteered as an Amputee Peer Visitor, Blood Drive Coordinator, and Red Cross Disaster Action Team member. SGT Kamson's road to reintegration was no easy trip, and every day remains a battle. He believes the world has given him so much that he can never stop giving back.

Not defined by his amputation, he uses patience, perseverance, professionalism, and pride to repeatedly conquer obstacles that make him resilient. SGT Kamson will never quit. He is not only an irreplaceable asset to his

Commander, but also his unit, his community, and his country.

SGT Kamson's awards and decorations include two Army Commendation Medals, Army Achievement Medal, National Defense Service Medal, Global War on Terrorism Expeditionary and Service Medals, Armed Forces Reserve Medal with M Device, Army Service Ribbon, Overseas Service Ribbon, Multinational Force and Observers Medal, Army Superior Unit Award, Noncommissioned Officer Professional Development Ribbon, Pennsylvania Recruiting and Retention Medal, and the Army Reserve Components Achievement Medal.

*One of my main priorities is taking care of our
Soldiers, Airmen, and their families. They are the foundation
of our force and I am committed to their safety and well-being.
Overall our families are resilient and cope with the
stresses of deployments. Deployment is an extremely stressful
time for all of our families. Each family is unique,
so the circumstances of deployments affect them differently.
Typically, they turn to various sources of support; with friends,
family members, their spouse, Family Support Groups, and
other family readiness personnel.*

★ ★ ★

GENERAL FRANK J. GRASS
CHIEF OF THE NATIONAL GUARD BUREAU
MARCH 14, 2014

CHAPTER SIX

The Role of Friends and Family in Reintegration: Building Insights and Strategies That Promote Reintegration and Resiliency

CHRISTINA BERCHOCK SHOOK, PsyD, ABPP*

*Clinical Psychologist, Behavioral Health Consultation Liaison and Primary Care Mental Health Integration Program Leader, Lebanon VA Medical Center, 1700 South Lincoln Avenue, Lebanon, Pennsylvania 17042

INTRODUCTION

The wars in Iraq and Afghanistan have created significant stressors for Military Service Members and their families. According to the Department of Defense,[1] more than three million family members have been affected by the deployment of more than two million troops to the Iraq and Afghanistan theaters. The challenges of reintegration on families are significant, given that 50% of Military personnel are married, 40% have children, and 64% of Military families live on military bases in more than 4,000 communities throughout the United States.[1] In addition, the duration of operations during the conflicts in Iraq and Afghanistan resulted in the deployment of unprecedented numbers of National Guard and Reserve forces. On average, National Guard and Reserve personnel are more likely to be older, partnered, and parenting, compared with their active duty counterparts.[2] In addition, multiple and longer deployments have been a hallmark of the conflicts in Iraq and Afghanistan. The duration of operations, the high operational tempo, the unprecedented numbers of military Service Members involved, as well as the extensive use of National Guard and Reserve personnel in these conflicts, have highlighted the need for services to promote resiliency and reintegration efforts for those transitioning back to civilian and family life.

Family and social relationships are impacted tremendously during the process of reintegration. As Service Members work to readjust to civilian life, their families, friends, and communities must also adjust to changes in the Service Member. Thus, the aims of this chapter are to describe the most common concerns related to negotiating family and social relationships throughout the deployment cycle, provide an overview of strategies to improve reintegration efforts in the domains of family and social relationships, and share resources designed to help Service Members and their families promote reintegration more successfully.

NEGOTIATING RELATIONSHIPS THROUGHOUT THE DEPLOYMENT CYCLE

FAMILY

The resiliency of our Service Members and their families cannot be overstated. Military families proactively manage and adapt to unique stressors, including deployments, frequent relocations, and reconfigurations of the family system. Nevertheless, the prolonged duration of the Iraq and Afghanistan conflicts has contributed to multiple and longer deployments for Service Members and their families, which has resulted in increased challenges with reintegration. Deployments strain family relationships as spouses and children attempt to cope with the absence of a parent, fear of death or injury to a loved one, high levels of stress, and significant changes in the psychological and emotional well-being of the returning Service Member.[3-5]

Despite these challenges, the majority of Service Members and their families demonstrate positive adaptation during and after deployment.[6] Although we do not have a complete understanding of what distinguishes families who adapt positively from families who adapt negatively, it appears that the most robust protective factors for positively adapting to stressors are sensitive and responsive parenting and supportive family and social networks.[7] Simply, the healthier the Service Member and family members are emotionally, spiritually, physically, and psychologically, the more resilient they are to stressors during the deployment cycle.

To understand more fully how deployment impacts family relationships, it is important to discuss the basic dynamics of family attachment. Attachment is defined as how human beings respond within relationships when hurt, separated from loved ones, or perceiving a threat.[8] Family attachments are inherently impacted by the deployment cycle because the deployment constitutes a threat to all family members' sense of safety, causes separation from loved ones, and results in powerful emotional responses.

Attachment styles—or the way in which individuals respond in relationships when they are hurt, separated, or threatened—are developed early in life. They provide internal working models of how to cope with stress, regulate emotions, and interact in close relationships.[9] Individuals with *secure or positive attachment styles* (which are characterized by healthy communication, loving and supportive relationships, and strong emotional well-being) generally cope and adapt more easily to stress. These individuals have high self-efficacy and psychological well-being, are more likely to have secure relationships with their spouses, and provide sensitive and responsive parenting, all of which contributes to secure attachment and interpersonal relationships for their children. In contrast, individuals with *insecure attachment styles* demonstrate anxiety and avoidance in their relationships. Individuals with *a history of rejection by early caregivers* develop internal working models characterized by

- distrust,
- avoidance,
- denial, and
- minimization of emotions to cope in relationships.

However, individuals with *a history of inconsistent or intrusive early caregivers* develop relationships characterized by

- fears of abandonment,
- exaggerated emotional reactions, and
- dependency.

Any combination of these unhealthy attachment styles can result in confusion, fear, ineffectiveness, and the inability to develop effective coping strategies for stress and healthy relationships in adulthood.[10]

Strength and the overall health of family attachment relationships are important in promoting resiliency during the deployment cycle. When Service Members and their families are notified of deployment, the way that they respond to the anticipated separation is impacted by their degree of attachment to one another and the overall health of the family relationships. Regardless of attachment styles, it is completely normal for all family members to experience anxiety, tension, and a sense of sadness and impending loss that may contribute to marital and family conflict, interference with parenting and family routines, and subsequent negative behaviors from children (eg, fear responses and acting-out behaviors).[11]

During deployment, family members often experience a sense of abandonment, numbness, mood and sleep problems, as well as anger and resentment.[11] Upon return from deployment, Service Members and their families must resume civilian life and the multiple roles and responsibilities they have as partner, parent, employee, coworker, and friend. At the same time, the entire family may also be coping with a Service Member facing physical injuries and/or mental and behavioral health concerns (eg, depression, substance use, posttraumatic stress disorder [PTSD], or traumatic brain injury [TBI]) that further complicate the process of reintegration. All of these factors inevitably place stress on family relationships; but families characterized by healthy, strong, supportive family attachment relationships often demonstrate more resiliency throughout the deployment cycle. Understanding the unique reactions of each member of the family can be helpful in learning how to promote healthier, stronger, and more resilient family relationships.

Nondeployed Spouse/Parent Reactions

The nondeployed spouse/parent assumes responsibility for raising children, running the household, and maintaining the integrity of the home during a deployment. Spouses of Military members report that deployment results in loss of emotional support, loneliness, role overload, role shifts, and concerns about the safety and well-being of the deployed spouse.[12] The response of the nondeployed spouse/parent is associated with a variety of coping and emotional reactions that contribute to different outcomes for the family.

A positive, healthy, and secure attachment style or mindset serves as a buffer against maladaptive responses to stress, and activates the individual to utilize internal sources of strength and external support systems.[13] This adaptive coping response contributes to the spouse/parent's ability to maintain psychological well-being, provides responsive parenting, and establishes new functional family processes in the absence of the deployed parent.[10] In contrast, nondeployed spouses/parents with unhealthy attachment and interpersonal relationship styles often become distressed and find that their coping strategies break down under the added stress of loss of emotional support, loneliness, financial strain, role shifts, and single parenthood.[10]

Differences in attachment styles and stress responses affect the psychological functioning of the nondeployed spouse/parent, which in turn affects the entire family. A growing body of research shows increased risk for psychological distress in the nondeployed spouse/parent during deployment, which is associated with higher rates of depression, sleep disturbance, anxiety, acute stress reactions, and adjustment disorders.[14] It is likely that the increased rates of abuse perpetrated by spouses who remain at home during deployment[15] are associated with extremely elevated levels of emotional distress and lack of healthy coping skills among nondeployed spouses/parents. Thus, healthy coping strategies and interpersonal relationships promote adaptive stress responses, support positive parenting, and help to maintain psychological well-being among nondeployed spouses/parents during the deployment phase.

After deployment, during the process of reintegration, the family has to reorganize and shift roles to accommodate the return of the deployed parent. It is inevitable that this period of time will cause stress, confusion, and disagreement about role shifts, child-rearing, decision-making, and control. The major tasks of redefining family roles and managing strong emotions represent some of the greatest challenges during the process of reintegration. If the nondeployed spouse/parent functionally or emotionally excluded the deployed spouse/parent from the family system, there will likely be a power struggle to reassert previous family roles that the nondeployed spouse/parent resents because it means giving up hard-earned independence and decision-making authority.[11] Subsequently, the parenting unit and the diligence of both parents/spouses in redefining roles are immensely important in promoting successful reintegration. Families that maintain psychological health, flexibility, good communication, supportive relationships, and healthy boundaries during deployment typically are most successful with the reintegration process.

Children's Reactions

Research suggests that many children exhibit high levels of resilience throughout the deployment cycle; however, more frequent or longer deployments result in some military parents being absent for large portions of their children's lives.[16] Separation from a key attachment figure because of deployment represents a significant loss for a child, and the child's response to this loss will vary depending on their developmental stage, degree of attachment with the deployed parent, and the overall psychological and behavioral functioning of the nondeployed parent.[10] There is a wealth of literature documenting the adverse psychosocial impact of deployment on children. For instance, the children of deployed parents demonstrate increased rates of anxiety, withdrawal, anger, conduct, and depression symptoms.[4,17]

In response to deployment, younger children tend to exhibit more difficulty with deployment and reintegration transitions. They are more likely to exhibit fear and regressive behaviors (eg, clinginess, crying, wetting the bed, etc),[11] whereas older school-age and adolescent children may experience emotional dysregulation, anger, aggression, sense of abandonment, withdrawal, or academic difficulties.[5,18] The negative impact of the deploying parent's departure is minimized when children feel securely attached to a nondeployed parent who copes adaptively and maintains responsive and stable parenting practices. Nondeploying parents who are unable to cope adaptively or modify family structure and routines may find that children respond with discomfort, distress, and emotional and behavioral dysregulation.

The same factors that influence a child's response before and during deployment are also important during the reintegration process. It is typical for children to display a range of emotions and behaviors during this time. Very young children will often respond to the return of the deployed parent with normal fear responses, whereas older children may remain detached and ignore the returned parent for a period of time.[10] Generally, the longer the duration of deployment separation, the greater the length of readjustment.[17] Children who were securely attached and had healthy relationships prior to deployment are more likely to adapt and settle into a positive relationship with a returned parent who demonstrates healthy adjustment.[10] In contrast, children who did not have healthy attachment relationships prior to deployment will be at the most increased risk for difficulties, such as anxiety, depression, anger, and oppositional behavior.[10] Secure attachment relationships with the deployed parent and the nondeployed parent, as well as healthy coping skills, will ultimately serve as the most protective and advantageous in facilitating adaptation to reintegration.

Deployed Spouse/Parent Reactions

Most Service Members demonstrate remarkable resilience when facing a range of challenges at all stages of the deployment cycle. Nevertheless, reintegrating to civilian life following return from a combat deployment can often be the most difficult stage to navigate. Upon return from deployment, Service Members may have to renegotiate multiple roles and responsibilities as

- partner,
- parent,
- employee,
- coworker, and
- friend.

Simultaneously, they may also face physical injuries and/or mental and behavioral health concerns (eg, depression, PTSD, TBI, etc) that further complicate the process of reintegration and can be significantly associated with parenting impairment.[19]

During deployment, Service Members develop and strengthen their vigilance and responsiveness to danger while suppressing strong emotions and fears. These abilities, while undoubtedly adaptive in combat, may result in difficulty adjusting to family life and the civilian world. Moreover, these responses that were once adaptive may now increase volatility; argumentativeness; and negative, coerced interactions within the family unit. Returning Service Members are at greater risk for difficulties with family relationships, parenting, and child adjustment, particularly if they are experiencing psychological problems.

The health and strength of family relationships and the way in which the family responds to stress can mediate how much psychological difficulty the deployed spouse/parent will experience. A healthy and secure attachment relationship with the entire family system is associated with better adaptation upon return from deployment, and contributes to more effective coping throughout the deployment cycle. In contrast, Service Members who have unhealthy family relationships and poor coping skills are more likely to experience difficulty with reintegration, especially when they are experiencing mental health concerns.

Service Members with trauma symptoms and PTSD are more likely to exhibit anger, fear, avoidance of intimacy and emotional expression, hostility, and denial, which negatively impacts the romantic relationship and the ability to bond and remain attached to children.[13,20-22] Research with combat Veterans has shown that PTSD symptoms (eg, numbing and arousal) are especially predictive of family distress, and anger is associated with troubled family relationships and secondary traumatization (ie, vicarious traumatization) among family members.[23]

In addition, the use of substances and sleep disturbance in combination with psychological problems after deployment can contribute to an increased tendency for the Service Member to be physically present in the family unit, but essentially absent from the family emotionally and functionally.[10] This situation represents an ambiguous loss for families and affects their reorganization and adaptation due to the lack of clarity regarding family roles and boundaries. This creates further confusion, disorganization, tension, and chaos within the home environment.[12,24] Ultimately, this also creates a situation in which the family is confused and without a healthy sense of organization, which results in greater tension, exacerbation of the Service Member's psychological symptoms, and further problematic family interactions. The degree to which a deployed spouse/parent can effectively reintegrate will be related to the degree in which psychological symptoms impact his or her parenting skills, as well as the health of the relationship with the nondeployed spouse, the degree of parental attachment with children, and the level of hostility and disorganization within the home.

STRATEGIES FOR IMPROVING
RELATIONSHIPS AND REINTEGRATION

Family Relationships and Resiliency

Given the wealth of literature identifying the strong associations between individual health and family health,[25,26] it is crucial for Service Members and their families to have opportunities to not only understand the impact of deployment on themselves, but also to avail themselves of the initiatives that support them in reintegrating more successfully. Recommendations from the Defense Centers of Excellence for Psychological Health and Traumatic Brain Injury[27] to improve total force fitness, as well as the Department of Defense's[1] pledge to strengthen Military Families, have resulted in a more holistic approach to reintegration programs. Studies suggest that strengthening and supporting parenting in Military Families for the nondeployed parent/spouse and the deployed Service Member can support the entire family unit's adjustment during and following deployment.

Integrative community care for Service Members and their families to strengthen resilience skills and promote more seamless transitional assistance has become the focus of many military organizations.[28] These programs focus on resiliency training because higher levels of resilience are associated with more personal growth, less distrust in others and the world, increased self-esteem and optimism, improved self-control, and less avoidance of negative emotion.[29] In addition, the strength of family relationships plays an important role in the development of Military–Family resiliency.[10] Thus, military organizations and programs designed to build Military–Family resiliency emphasize effectively adapting to stress and maintaining physical and psychological well-being within the individual, the family, and the community.[30]

To enhance and strengthen family relationships and resiliency, an overview of strategies is provided that emphasizes the role of the family attachment network in promoting resilient family processes.[10] When seeking to improve family resiliency and strengthen the family unit, consider the following strategies:

- *Strengthen the family belief system*—Families adapt well to deployment when they are able to find meaning in deployment.
  - Military Families exhibit higher levels of functioning when they display optimism for the future, a sense of mastery, spiritual philosophies, and a positive outlook on military life and its purpose. This includes patriotism and a sense of pride in the deployed spouse/parent.

— Families can talk about how they were changed by the experience of deployment, which promotes empathy and understanding.

— Families can talk about how the family has grown stronger from the deployment experience, and focus on plans and goals for the future.

— Storytelling, drawing family pictures, and reading children's books about deployment are healthy ways that parents can alleviate stress associated with a deployment for their children. This also creates opportunities for children to communicate about their experience during the deployment cycle.

— Families can create scrapbooks about deployment that include letters, pictures, artwork, and writings to and from family members during the deployment. This helps to reconnect the family and create a family story of the time spent apart.

- *Improve organizational patterns and problem-solving*—Family roles and responsibilities inevitably shift during deployment and postdeployment. Reestablishing mutual support and a "secure family base" that provides all family members with a sense of feeling cared for contributes to better overall family functioning. To facilitate adjustment:

— Frame transitions as opportunities for couples/families to create a new normal, and renegotiate roles and tasks of family members. Maintain an open mind about traditional gender roles. Acknowledge that roles change and fluctuate to adjust successfully. Couples with flexible gender roles fare better in adjusting to a deployment.

— Maintain simple routines, such as family meals and bedtime rituals.

— Consider creating new rituals to replace lost ones. Parents should also maintain a strong hierarchical organization with clear structure and boundaries inside the family, as well as between the family and the outside world.

- *Mobilize family resources*—Establish a support network between the family and the outside world.

— This network allows the family to benefit from social and economic resources.

— Extended family and friends, as well as community and military support organizations, can serve an important role in supporting the family both during and after deployment.

— Explore opportunities to connect with the Military community, other Military Families, and with the deployed Service Member via online forums that support and enhance the flow of information and provide support, outreach, and information to family members.

- *Improve the quantity and quality of communication*—Communicating openly about emotions and with honesty enhances family functioning and displays the importance of expression of feelings to children. Children and adults should be encouraged to express their feelings about impending deployment throughout the deployment process and upon return of the deployed parent/spouse.
    — It is important to avoid the tendency to "shut down" emotional expression within the family because it limits the ability of family members to support one another and obtain assistance from outside the family.
    — Adolescents are especially perceptive of heightened negative family emotions and conflict during deployment, and will often choose to withhold their emotions as an attempt to minimize conflict. It is important that they are encouraged to express their own emotions and thoughts throughout the deployment cycle.
    — Encouraging open, honest, and healthy communication also provides opportunities for the returning Service Member to reengage with the family after deployment.
    — Although there are practical limitations on communication during deployment, avoid cutting off contact between family members and the deployed spouse, if possible. Although some families who close off communication are able to establish a fairly organized system during deployment, they tend to have more difficulty during reintegration.
- *Maintain an emotional and psychological presence*—The stress of deployment and the assumption of new roles for nondeployed parents can be overwhelming.
    — Nondeployed parents can practice mindfulness-based exercises aimed at increasing one's present awareness or the capacity to be present and pay attention to their children, family members, and themselves. Paying attention to the responses of children and their emotions is vital to building healthy relationships and moderating emotions.
    — Nondeployed parents can also work to keep a strong bond with the absent parent. The ways in which this can be done are varied. You are limited only by your own creativity.
- *Define new roles and promote healthy parent–child boundaries*—Nondeployed parents are responsible for filling in the roles and responsibilities of the deployed spouse/parent. Defining clear roles and boundaries for the family during deployment helps to reduce confusion, while promoting task completion and adaptive reorganization of the family system.

— Role reversals and enmeshment (ie, unclear boundaries) can be destructive to parent–child relationships and adaptation. Avoid spousification (ie, parent turns to child for companionship, friendship, and intimacy) and parentification (eg, excessive caregiving responsibility for siblings).

— Some degree of assistance from older children contributes to positive adaptation and functioning during deployment, but avoid extensive parent–child role reversals and enmeshment because it can have a negative impact on the psychological well-being of children and all family members.

• *Attend a retreat focused on postdeployment reintegration that provides a holistic approach to enhancing community-building and resilience*—The Coming Home Project has been recognized as a model program,[27] and it provides retreats to Veterans, Service Members, their families, and professional care providers.

— Activities are presented in a variety of formats, including large group meetings and instruction, small peer-based support and discussion groups, and free individual and family time.

— Also offered is psychoeducational training in wellness (eg, relaxation, mindfulness, parenting, and couples communication).

STRENGTHENING PARENTING

To build healthy families that are resilient and promote more successful well-being during deployment and reintegration, it is necessary to strengthen parenting in military families as a means to support children and their parents. Decades of developmental research have demonstrated the importance of parenting for children's healthy development and promoting children's resilience.[31] Effective parenting is critical for mediating deployment-related stressors and child adjustment. Effective parenting practices provide a protective buffer for children and youth during the deployment cycle.

Parent management training interventions have strong evidence for their efficacy and effectiveness,[32] and they focus on enhancing positive parenting practices. Following separation due to deployment, parents often have difficulty reestablishing their roles within the family and working collaboratively to co-parent. It is tremendously important that parents collaborate to set rules, develop routines, and reestablish roles to successfully promote reintegration as a family. Parents must have joint goals for their children, practice effective and balanced discipline strategies, and problem-solve parenting challenges as a cohesive parenting unit.

One unique, empirically supported program that is modified specifically for National Guard and Reserve military families is the After Deployment: Adaptive Parenting Tools (ADAPT) program.[2] This parent training program targets school-age children and focuses on military culture and the influence of combat stress reactions while seeking to enhance five positive parenting practices: (1) skill encouragement, (2) positive involvement, (3) family problem-solving, (4) monitoring, and (5) effective discipline. The ADAPT program is unique in that it also accounts for the challenges associated with parenting after combat, accounting for the unique experience of the deployed parent in a combat zone. Most Service Members understand and recognize the challenges of reintegration in that, while deployed in a combat zone, it is crucial to maintain order, vigilance, and readiness for action at any time. Although these skills contribute to life-saving action when needed and are highly valued in a combat zone, they can contribute to difficulties, such as increased volatility and argumentativeness within the family unit upon return from deployment. When returning to one's family, Service Members must learn to adapt their emotional responsiveness and readiness, as well as recalibrate patience with their children, partners, and the civilian world.

To enhance and strengthen parenting, it is necessary to develop parenting skills, encourage positive parental involvement, enhance problem-solving as a family, monitor child behaviors effectively, and promote effective discipline strategies. It is helpful to consider addressing family stress and parenting throughout the entire deployment cycle: predeployment, deployment, and postdeployment/reintegration. An overview of practical strategies is provided and is consistent with those promoted in the ADAPT program[2] because it is tailored specifically for Service Members and focuses on the influence of combat stress. When seeking to improve parenting practices and strengthen the family unit throughout the deployment cycle, consider the following strategies:

- *Build healthy emotional responding within the family*—Parents can socialize their children in healthy emotional responding to reduce children's deployment-related anxiety and other adjustment difficulties. It is normal to worry during deployment, but parents can learn and understand children's cognitive capacities and how much information children can absorb at particular developmental stages. Parents can also teach their children skills for talking about their feelings related to deployment and utilizing media and other resources directed at children facing the deployment cycle. These resources are most beneficial when the family views or reads them together.

- *Build mindfulness skills*—Parents can learn to control and regulate their own emotional responses through the use of mindfulness exercises. Mindfulness-based exercises are aimed at increasing one's present awareness, or the capacity to be present and pay attention. In terms of parenting and families, it is important for Service Members to be present and pay attention to family members, as well as their children. Paying attention to the responses of children and their emotions is vital to building healthy relationships with them.
- *Build resilience within the family*—Parents can learn to promote coping skills for stress and teach the family how to utilize these skills together. In addition, the family is encouraged to identify their own strengths as a military family and promote the use of these skills as a unit.
- *Teach new behaviors and guide children effectively*—Parents can encourage the cooperation of children through utilization of effective parenting directions, as well as teaching new behaviors for managing life. Parents are role models for children and their first teachers. The importance of effective teaching strategies, as well as the use of positive reinforcement contingent on desired behavioral responses, is very important.
  - Learn to set consistent limits with children and identify effective versus ineffective discipline strategies.
  - Establish family rules and strategies for managing undesirable and negative behaviors.
  - Communicate effectively within the family by encouraging active listening skills, having family meetings, and learning to moderate strong emotions.
  - Manage conflict in a healthy manner through the use of assertive communication skills.
- *Develop family problem-solving skills to anticipate and address stressful events and family conflicts that are inevitable during the deployment cycle*—Parents can teach their children problem-solving skills that increase communication and provide a method for solving everyday conflicts in a cooperative manner. Problem-solving reduces anxiety in children by increasing predictability and self-efficacy. When children feel prepared with skills they can use to manage problems, they feel more secure, confident, and stable during periods of transition.
- *Create positive family activities*—It is important to create positive family activities that develop the family unit and encourage group cohesion and fun.
- *Promote school success*—Parents can work to be positively involved in the academic development of their children. It is important to ensure that

the school administration understands and is sensitive to the process of reintegration, and that parents communicate effectively with the school regarding deployment.

- *Plan for the future*—Parents can plan family events to continue to build cohesion as a family unit. Planning for the future also involves being mindful about preparing children and partners about future deployments so that there is a balance between "work" and family time.

MENTAL AND BEHAVIORAL HEALTH

Family members and friends play an important role in the care and rehabilitation of individuals with behavioral and mental health conditions. Service Members returning home from deployment often have increased rates of depression, anxiety, suicidal ideation, interpersonal conflict, aggressiveness, PTSD, TBI, and substance use disorders.[33] More specifically, Department of Defense data show that, among soldiers returning from combat operations in Iraq, 27.7% of active duty and 35.5% of National Guard and Reserve component Service Members screened positive for clinically significant mental health concerns (PTSD, depression, suicidal ideation, interpersonal conflict, or aggressive ideation) 3 to 6 months after returning from deployment.[34] Despite the awareness of mental health concerns among Service Members, many families and friends struggle with assisting the Service Member who is seeking help—or failing to seek help—during the reintegration process.

Anxiety, Depression, Posttraumatic Stress Disorder, and Substance Use

It is not uncommon to experience symptoms of anxiety and depression in response to significant stressors. Exposure to combat while deployed places the human body and brain under a large amount of stress, which can subsequently result in acute readjustment reactions that consist of symptoms of anxiety, depression, sleep disturbance, irritability, or difficulty concentrating. For most Service Members, over time, these symptoms naturally resolve on their own. In fact, the majority of combat-exposed Service Members will not develop long-term mental health problems at all.[35] Nevertheless, with multiple deployments and repeated combat exposure, the incidence of anxiety, depression, and PTSD begins to increase. Multiple exposures to combat stress and the subsequent impact on the body and mind often result in a shift from more acute stress symptoms to more chronic and persistent symptoms of anxiety, depression, and PTSD.

As previously described, symptoms of anxiety, PTSD, and depression are associated with poor family functioning during postdeployment readjustment.

Common concerns associated with PTSD, depression, and substance use include the following:

- increased role confusion,
- emotional numbing,
- parenting difficulties,
- relationship dissatisfaction,
- poor cohesion within the family unit,
- problems outside the home, and
- physical aggression.[36]

Some Service Members engage in adrenaline-seeking behaviors to re-create the intense emotions experienced in combat by playing violent video games, driving recklessly, or using illicit substances to experience a high similar to combat.[37] In addition, irritability and anger outbursts interfere with the ability to reconnect with family and friends, and result in low frustration tolerance. Clark and Messer[37] suggest that Service Members who feel out of control or overwhelmed by anger may act out and attempt to assert power and control in their relationships that may lead to domestic violence, child maltreatment, or physical altercations.

Research shows that, for Service Members experiencing PTSD, the active avoidance and emotional numbing symptoms are most closely associated with family functioning problems and difficulties with readjustment in the postdeployment stage.[38,39] When Service Members avoid conversations about trauma that would engender feelings of closeness, or activities that friends and family may have once enjoyed together, their loved ones subsequently feel physically and emotionally disconnected. Often, this is a significant change from predeployment functioning, which can further exacerbate relationship problems, alienate friends and family, and prevent successful reintegration.

Service Members, family members, and friends can use a number of strategies to successfully navigate the challenges of postdeployment stress, anxiety, depression, and PTSD. The level of intervention or strategy used will depend on the severity and chronicity of the mental and behavioral health concerns. Service Members, family members, and friends seeking to improve overall mental health and address symptoms of anxiety, depression, substance use, and PTSD may wish to consider the following strategies:

- *Manage strong emotions by learning skills that help to deescalate powerful feelings*—Working with feelings and emotions can often help people to overcome their problems/issues and improve their mental health.

— Relaxation strategies (eg, deep breathing, visual imagery, and progressive muscle relaxation) are effective for managing strong emotions and reducing the nervous system response to anxiety and tension.

— Mindfulness-based stress reduction[40] techniques incorporate focusing and building awareness to manage stress, illness, psychological distress, and promote wellness.

— Cognitive behavioral therapy is a powerful type of psychotherapy that can help with learning how to change your thoughts, emotions, and behavioral responses to stressors.

— Spiritual practices or meditation are also helpful tools to reassure and assist with deescalating power feelings (discussed in depth in the previous chapter).

— Conflict disengagement strategies (eg, time-out) help to avoid the negative consequences of explosive anger outbursts.

- *Address avoidance and emotional numbing in relationships*—It is important for friends and family to engage in activities aimed at strengthening relationships through healthy emotional expression and the creation of closeness.

— Recognize that it is normal to have challenges with emotional reconnection. Go slowly and give everyone permission to adjust at their own pace.

— Try to reconnect at an emotional level with yourself and with others. Letting down the wall can cause feelings of uncertainty, but with time it gets easier.

— Take time for families and friends to recognize that everyone has changed, and getting to know each other again takes time and energy.

— Take time to engage in activities that family and friends shared before deployment.

— Plan family nights, date nights, and activities with friends to support emotional reconnection.

- *Seek conjoint family and couples therapy if you are having trouble reconnecting as a family*—If partners are finding that they feel emotionally and physically disconnected and struggling with improving this on their own, it is important to seek outside counsel on methods to improve the marital and/or family relationship. Couples counselors can assist with helping partners to improve their relationship using strategies to enhance communication, emotional connection, physical exercises, and relationship guidance.

- *Stimulate aspirations for betterment*—Seek out opportunities for psychological, spiritual, and social growth. This may manifest in the form of educational pursuits, occupational achievement, or a rededication to family life.
- *Seek support groups for Service Members, Military Families, and friends who are coping with mental and behavioral health concerns*—Often, Service Members miss the structure and camaraderie of military service, and find it helpful to be around other Service Members who are struggling with managing their own mental and/or behavioral health concerns. Support groups are ideal for family, friends, and Service Members to experience a sense of community and shared experience.
- *Seek mental and/or behavioral health assessment from a professional if you are having difficulty managing symptoms*—There are evidence-based treatments available for depression, anxiety, PTSD, and substance use disorders.
  — Research supports the use of cognitive behavioral therapy[41] and interpersonal therapies for treating depression, anxiety, family/relationship distress, and substance use concerns. Mental health concerns can be treated individually or conjointly with family members present.
  — There is strong research evidence supporting the use of cognitive behavioral therapies, such as prolonged exposure therapy and cognitive processing therapy, for the treatment of PTSD.[42]

Traumatic Brain Injury

In addition to exposure to combat and the trauma of witnessing difficult events, many of the men and women serving in Iraq and Afghanistan have experienced a TBI. TBI is often associated with changes in mood and behavior (eg, depression, anxiety, impulsiveness, and memory impairment). Most Service Members with a TBI recover within the first few months following injury with minimal intervention. Individuals with more moderate-to-severe or penetrating brain injuries will typically improve; however, the recovery process is often more unpredictable and indeterminate. Family and friends play an important role in the recovery and rehabilitation of Service Members with brain injuries given the emotional, cognitive, physical, social, and vocational impact associated with TBI. Family and friends experience the impact of TBI in all of these domains and may have difficulty adapting to the changes they see in their loved ones. Adjustments and accommodations may need to be made for the injured person. For Service Members with more severe injuries, family members may assume the role of lifelong caregiver. The shifting of roles within the family can be a difficult process and require flexibility, resilience, and a strong support system. Service Members, family members, and caregivers seeking to adapt to living with an individual with TBI and/ or who are seeking to enhance and strengthen the family unit may wish to consider the following strategies:

- *Learn more about TBI*—Brain injuries can be difficult to diagnose, but advanced neuroimaging and neuropsychological evaluations can assist in the diagnostic process.
  - Most people recover from TBI quickly and completely, whereas others require more intensive rehabilitation. Learning more about treatment and recovery from TBI is one of the most valuable things a Service Member and his or her loved ones can do for themselves.
  - A neuropsychological evaluation can provide insight into the brain areas impacted by injury and provide valuable recommendations for functional adaptations that help Service Members and their families.
- *Manage symptoms of TBI*—Cognitive, emotional, and behavioral changes in the brain after TBI can disrupt multiple domains of a Service Member's life.
  - Building awareness of the common cognitive, emotional, and behavioral changes that a Service Member will experience can be beneficial to family, friends, and caregivers. With insight as to why a loved one has changed comes the ability to develop an understanding of how to adapt as a family unit to more successfully support the Service Member in recovery.
  - Assessment and treatment are important. Treatment may include cognitive rehabilitation, adaptations within the home, psychotherapy, academic accommodations, or vocational rehabilitation.
- *Promote recovery*—For most people with TBI, life will return to normal, or a new normal, over time. Not all brain injuries are alike, and recovery rates vary depending on the severity of injury. Even individuals with severe brain injuries can have fulfilling and meaningful lives.
  - Family and friends can promote the return to normal functioning by talking about the changes they have witnessed and having open dialogue about the proactive strategies they are using to promote reintegration into the family and civilian life.
  - TBI recovery programs exist throughout the country and offer invaluable resources.
  - Talk to children about TBI and involve them in the recovery process. It is important that children understand that the family is learning to

cope as a unit. Promoting family coping skills for stress and teaching children how to utilize these skills as a family helps to build the cohesion of the family unit and to adapt to the changes they are experiencing within the family.

- *Utilize caregiver support*—Becoming a caregiver for a Service Member with a moderate-to-severe brain injury is typically an unexpected event. Caregivers often feel unprepared for their new role and have difficulty adapting to the sudden change of lifestyle, as well as the impact on the family unit.

  — Caregivers can experience innumerable strong emotions while adjusting to life after a TBI. Feeling discouraged or overwhelmed is normal, and it is important to seek support.

  — It is important to have friends and family members to talk to about your feelings. Talking about your stress and anxiety can help relieve it.

  — It is also important to think about joining a support group for other families affected by TBI.

  — The Department of Veterans Affairs offers caregiver support programs at all Veterans Affairs medical centers.

  — It is essential to engage in self-care activities, such as relaxation, exercise, maintaining a healthy diet, and engaging in enjoyable activities.

  — It is important to accept help from others, and enlist family or friends to allow for you to have a few hours "off duty" as a caregiver.

  — If stress, anxiety, or sadness begin to escalate, seek professional help from a psychologist, counselor, or spiritual leader.

HOW TO FACILITATE HELP

Despite recognition of mental health and readjustment concerns among Service Members, families, and friends, it can be challenging to begin talking about mental health concerns and how to seek help. Service Members report multiple barriers to seeking help: societal stigma about mental health; a military culture that promotes the warrior ethos of loyalty, strength, self-sacrifice, and intolerance of weakness; fear that unit leaders and peers will view them as weak or lose confidence in them; concern over loss of rank, promotion, or career stability; skepticism about the effectiveness of mental health treatment and medication; and perceived difficulties in navigating the military or Veteran healthcare systems.[43]

Service Members, family members, and friends seeking to facilitate mental health treatment may wish to consider the following:

- Recognizing and accepting mental health concerns and the need for help are often the first steps.
- Enhancing treatment-encouraging beliefs, such as "getting help is okay," eases the anxiety of asking for help.
- Identifying resources available for treatment reduces the perception that care is not available or accessible.
- Utilizing your entire social network to encourage the Service Member's participation in mental health treatment can be the impetus for the Service Member to reach out for treatment.

Family and friends often report concerns related to how they should best talk to and encourage Service Members to seek help. Research shows that the most common dilemmas loved ones face when talking to Service Members about seeking help are: getting the Service Member to recognize that he or she is having problems without implying that the Service Member is not "normal"; convincing the Service Member to seek help without implying weakness; being persistent, but also patient; and wanting the Service Member to open up without implying that the family or friend understands what he or she is going through.[43]

The following strategies are a resource for assisting families and friends in talking to their loved ones about seeking help for mental health and readjustment concerns:

When to talk

- Be mindful about when/how much to talk. Make choices about when and how often to discuss the topic to prevent the Service Member from withdrawing or avoiding.
- Be available when the Service Member is ready to talk. Make it clear that you are available and willing to communicate on the Service Member's terms.

How to talk

- Communicate care and commitment: "I am here no matter what."
- Be polite and show respect by modulating your tone of voice.
- Listen without judgment. Focus on listening rather than talking and share that the Service Member will not be judged for sharing how he or she feels and thinks.

How to frame talk

- Frame things positively. Frame help-seeking as a way to become healthy, happy, and productive rather than as a way to attempt to treat a deficiency or illness within the Service Member.
- Frame things cooperatively. Frame help-seeking as an opportunity to work on the problem together as a partnership.

Where to turn

- Enlist the help of third parties. Call on friends, other Service Members, or extended family to speak to the Service Member about symptoms and help-seeking.
- Use prayer. Families and friends of Service Members frequently suggest using prayer as a means to cope and as strength. There are other spiritual practices that can also help. These can be found in Chapter 5.
- Treat yourself positively. Family members and friends must take care of themselves so that they are healthy enough to care for the Service Member. This may involve seeking help for yourself even if the Service Member refuses and recognizing that it is not your fault if the Service Member is not ready to seek help at this time.

There are coaching and support services available to assist family members and friends of Service Members in obtaining help for their loved ones. Patience, early intervention, and support are key in reducing the development of chronic mental health problems and negative outcomes for families during the deployment cycle. The negative impact of deployment on Service Members and their families can be buffered by encouraging the overall health and well-being of the entire family unit, and by encouraging families to seek effective interventions when needed.

REINTEGRATION RESOURCES FOR SERVICE MEMBERS AND THEIR FAMILIES

A range of interventions and services are available to support Service Members and their families throughout the deployment cycle and beyond. Accessing these resources and services is vital in promoting the overall health, well-being, and resiliency of Military Families. The resources provided represent the more robust and evidence-based interventions available to our Nation's Military Service Members and their families.

Broad and Comprehensive Websites

- *After Deployment*—This website is tailored for Service Members and their families to provide wellness resources for the military community. This extensive website offers resources that cover a wealth of topics (including but not limited to) on mind, body, spirit, family, community, finances, and work. Website: http://afterdeployment.dcoe.mil/

- *Department of Defense Military Family Support*—Caring for military families has become a national priority with the launch of the White House's "Strengthening Our Military Families" initiative and the related "Joining Forces" campaign. This website provides regular updates on all Department of Defense and related efforts to help improve the lives of military families. Website: http://www.usa4militaryfamilies.dod.mil/

- *Deployment Health Clinical Center*—This center provides a gateway to information on deployment, health, and healthcare for healthcare providers, Service Members, Veterans, and their families. Website: http://www.pdhealth.mil/

- *Military OneSource*—This site offers a central hub and resource for the military community to browse topics related to military life, deployment, parenting, relocating, retirement, and much more. Website: http://www.militaryonesource.mil/

- *National Resource Directory*—The Department of Veterans Affairs and the Department of Defense provide this directory to connect Wounded Warriors, Service Members, Veterans, their families, and caregivers with resources, support, and education. Website: https://www.ebenefits.va.gov/ebenefits/nrd

- *The Real Warriors Campaign*—This campaign is an initiative launched by the Defense Centers of Excellence for Psychological Health and Traumatic Brain Injury to promote the processes of building resilience, facilitating recovery, and supporting reintegration of returning Service Members, Veterans, and their families. Website: http://www.realwarriors.net/

- *US Army Family Readiness Group*—Family Readiness Groups within the US Army, the US Army Reserve, and the Army National Guard communities are command-sponsored organizations of family members, volunteers, soldiers, and civilian employees associated with a particular unit. They provide activities and support to enhance the flow of information, increase the resiliency of unit soldiers and their families, and provide practical tools for adjusting to deployments. Website: https://www.armyfrg.org

- *Yellow Ribbon Reintegration Program*—This program provides National Guard and Reserve Service Members and their families with deployment cycle information, resources, programs, services, and referrals. Programs include webinars and courses on strengthening resiliency, helping military families, preparing for deployment, and more. Website: http://www. yellowribbon.mil/yrrp
- *Warrior Gateway*—This website caters to the unique needs of Service Members and Military Families by providing a virtual community center equipped with consolidated and validated resources for connecting, learning, and communicating with others before, during, and after deployment. Website: http://www.warriorgateway.org/

CAREGIVER SUPPORT

- *Defense and Veterans Brain Injury Center*—The Center's mission is to serve active duty military, their beneficiaries, and Veterans with TBIs through state-of-the-art clinical care, innovative clinical research initiatives and educational programs, and support for force health protection services. The program offers family and caregiver support throughout the country and at military medical centers. Website: http://dvbic.dcoe.mil/audience/family-friends
- *Department of Veterans Affairs*—This organization has caregiver support programs and services nationwide at their Veterans Affairs Medical Centers. The programs are available both in and out of the home to help support and care for Veterans. Website: http://www.caregiver.va.gov/

EDUCATION AND EMPLOYMENT

- *Education and Employment Initiative*—This initiative is a Department of Defense program. It assists wounded, ill, and injured Service Members early in their recovery process to identify their skills and match them with the education and career opportunities that will help them successfully transition to civilian life. Website: http://warriorcare.dodlive.mil/wounded-warrior-resources/e2i/
- *Operation Warfighter*—This program is a Department of Defense internship program that matches qualified wounded, ill, and injured Service Members with nonfunded federal internships for them to gain valuable work experience during their recovery and rehabilitation. Website: http://warriorcare.dodlive.mil/wounded-warrior-resources/operation-warfighter/

Operation Enduring Freedom/Operation Iraqi Freedom/ Operation New Dawn Resources

- *Department of Veterans Affairs*—This organization offers cost-free medical care for any condition related to service in the Iraq/Afghanistan theater for 5 years after the date of discharge or release. Website: http://www.oefoif.va.gov/

Mental and Behavioral Health

- *Center for the Study of Traumatic Stress*—This is one of the Nation's oldest and most highly regarded academic-based organizations dedicated to advancing trauma-informed knowledge, leadership, and methodologies. Resources, publications, and more are available. Website: http://www.cstsonline.org/
- *Coaching into Care*—This Veterans Affairs program offers free, confidential, telephone-based coaching services for family members who would like to help a Veteran seek mental health care. Coaches work with families to help them discover new ways to talk with a Veteran in their lives about their concerns and about treatment options. Website: http://www.mirecc.va.gov/coaching/
- *Department of Veterans Affairs*—This organization offers an expansive array of mental and behavioral health services to Veterans and their families. Veterans receive coordinated care, mental health treatment coordinators, evidence-based psychotherapies, and personalized treatment plans developed to focus on recovery, reintegration, and wellness. Website: http://www.mentalhealth.va.gov/VAMentalHealthGroup.asp
- *Department of Veterans Affairs Vet Centers*—These centers serve combat Veterans, Service Members, and Military Families by providing no-cost visits for readjustment counseling, military sexual trauma counseling, and bereavement counseling services. Website: http://www.vetcenter.va.gov/
- *InTransition*—This is a free, voluntary program with coaches who provide psychological health care support to Service Members, Veterans, and their healthcare providers during times of transition. Website: http://intransition.dcoe.mil/
- *Military and Veterans Crisis Line*—This hotline is available for military Service Members, Veterans, families, and caregivers in crisis. It puts individuals in touch with the support of trained professionals 24 hours a day through a toll-free number or online chat. Phone: 800–273–8255, press 1
- *Mindfulness-Based Stress Reduction*—This program is a well-defined and systematic patient-centered educational approach that uses relatively

intensive training in mindfulness meditation as the core of a program to teach people how to take better care of themselves and live healthier and more adaptive lives. Website: http://www.umassmed.edu/cfm/stress-reduction/

- *National Center for Posttraumatic Stress Disorder*—This is a special center within the Department of Veterans Affairs created to advance the clinical care and social welfare of America's Veterans through research, education, and training in science, diagnosis, and treatment of PTSD and stress-related disorders. Website: http://www.ptsd.va.gov/
- *PTSD Coach*—This app is a mobile phone application for Veterans, Service Members, and others to learn about PTSD symptoms and treatment, track their symptoms, and develop tools for coping. It is available online as well as on Apple and Android devices. Website: http://www.ptsd.va.gov/public/materials/apps/PTSDCoach.asp

PARENTING AND CHILDREN
- *Department of Veterans Affairs*—This organization offers parenting resources and tools, including online training and education for Service Members, families, and their loved ones. Website: http://www.veterantraining.va.gov/parenting/
- *After Deployment, Adaptive Parenting Tools (ADAPT)*—This program aims to strengthen parenting skills. Website: http://www.cehd.umn.edu/fsos/projects/adapt/default.asp
- *Love and Logic*—There are excellent curricula available for parents related to the topics of discipline and expectations, including the Parenting with Love and Logic series of books. Website: https://www.loveandlogic.com/
- *Military Kids Connect*—This is an online community for military children (6–17 years old) that provides access to age-appropriate resources to support children dealing with the unique psychological challenges of military life. Website: http://militarykidsconnect.dcoe.mil/
- *Talk, Listen, Connect*—Sesame Street's program designed for military families offers strategies and resources to help children through difficult periods of transition and separation that can come with military service. Website: http://www.sesamestreet.org/parents/topicsandactivities/toolkits/tlc

POSTDEPLOYMENT RETREAT
- *Coming Home Project*—This project is a nonprofit organization devoted to providing retreats that emphasize expert, compassionate care, support,

education, and stress management tools for Iraq and Afghanistan Veterans, Service Members, their families, and their care providers. Website: http://www.cominghomeproject.net/

Traumatic Brain Injury

*   *Concussion Coach*—This is a mobile phone application for Veterans, Service Members, and others who have experienced a mild-to-moderate concussion. It provides portable tools to assess symptoms and to facilitate use of coping strategies. It is available for Apple devices. Website: https://itunes.apple.com/us/app/concussion-coach/id713590872
*   *Defense Centers of Excellence Outreach Center*—This center is designed to provide a source of psychological health and TBI information and resources for Service Members, families, friends, and clinicians. The center is available 24 hours per day, 7 days per week via phone, chat, or email. Website: http://www.dcoe.mil/Families/Help.aspx
*   *Defense and Veterans Brain Injury Center*—This center's mission is to serve active duty military, their beneficiaries, and Veterans with TBIs through state-of-the-art clinical care, innovative clinical research initiatives and educational programs, and support for force health protection services. Website: http://dvbic.dcoe.mil/
*   *Department of Veterans Affairs*—The Veterans Affairs Polytrauma/TBI System of Care is an integrated network of specialized rehabilitation programs dedicated to serving Veterans and Service Members with both combat and civilian-related TBI and polytrauma. Services include interdisciplinary evaluation and treatment, case management, patient and family education and training, psychosocial support, and advanced rehabilitation and prosthetic technologies. Website: http://www.polytrauma.va.gov/

SUMMARY

Recognizing and responding to the needs of Service Members, Military Families, and their communities can improve the overall health and well-being of our military force. Family and social relationships are impacted tremendously during predeployment, deployment, and postdeployment reintegration into civilian life. Although the majority of Service Members, families, and friends adapt appropriately during the deployment cycle and demonstrate a great degree of resilience, there are also some who struggle with the process. The goal of this chapter was to provide insight to readers about the various challenges and changing dynamics related to renegotiating relationships throughout the deployment cycle, as well as provide strategies aimed at improving resiliency and reintegration for Service Members, families, and friends. Although the deployment cycle can be a challenge, it also provides an opportunity to learn, to develop coping skills, and to enhance a sense of cohesion and shared purpose in relationships. As Service Members work to readjust to civilian life, their families, friends, and communities must also adjust to changes in the Service Member and themselves. It is hoped that this chapter serves as a resource for helping Service Members, families, and communities promote reintegration of our nation's heroes more successfully.

REFERENCES

1. US Government. Strengthening our military families. http://www.dol.gov/dol/milfamilies/strengthening_our_military_families.pdf. Updated 2011. Accessed September 28, 2015.
2. Gewirtz AH, Pinna KL, Hanson SK, Brockberg D. Promoting parenting to support reintegrating military families: After Deployment, Adaptive Parenting Tools. *Psychol Serv*. 2014;11:31–40.
3. Cozza SJ, Chun RS, Polo JA. Military families and children during Operation Iraqi Freedom. *Psychiatr Q*. 2005;76:371–378.
4. Flake EM, Davis B, Johnson P, Middleton L. The psychosocial effects of deployment on military children. *J Develop Behav Pediatr*. 2009;30:271–278.
5. Huebner AJ, Mancini JA, Wilcox RM, Grass SR, Grass GA. Parental deployment and youth in military families: exploring uncertainty and ambiguous loss. *Fam Relat*. 2007;56:112–122.
6. Peterson C, Park N, Castro CA. Assessment for the U.S. Army Comprehensive Soldier Fitness Program: The Global Assessment Tool. *Am Psychol*. 2011; 66:10–18.
7. Charuvastra A, Cloitre M. Social bonds and posttraumatic stress disorder. *Ann Rev Psychol*. 2008;59:301–328.
8. Waters E, Corcoran D, Anafarta M. Attachment, other relationships, and the theory that all good things go together. *Hum Dev*. 2005;48:80–84.
9. Bowlby J. *Attachment and Loss: Volume 3. Loss, Sadness and Depression*. New York, NY: Basic Books; 1980.
10. Riggs SA, Riggs DS. Risk and resilience in military families experiencing deployment: the role of the family attachment network. *J Fam Psychol*. 2011;25:675–687.
11. Military.com. The emotional cycle of deployment: military family perspective. Miltary.com website. http://www.military.com/spouse/military-deployment/dealing-with-deployment/emotional-cycle-of-deployment-military-family.html. Accessed September 28, 2015.
12. Faber AJ, Willerton E, Clymer SR, MacDermid SM, Weiss HM. Ambiguous absence, ambiguous presence: a qualitative study of military reserve families in

wartime. *J Fam Psychol.* 2008;22:222–230.

13. Mikulincer M, Shaver, PR. *Attachment in Adulthood: Structure, Dynamics, and Change.* New York, NY: Guilford; 2007.

14. Mansfield AJ, Kaufman JS, Marshall SW, Gaynes BN, Morrisey JP, Engel CC. Deployment and the use of mental health services among U.S. Army wives. *N Engl J Med.* 2010;362:101–109.

15. Rentz E, Martin SL, Gibbs DA, Clinton-Sherrod M, Hardison J, Marshall SW. Family violence in the military: a review of the literature. *Trauma Violence Abuse.* 2006;7:93–108.

16. Lester P, Peterson K, Reeves J, et al. The long war and parental combat deployment: effects on military children and at-home spouses. *J Am Acad Child Adolesc Psychiatry.* 2010;49:310–320.

17. Chandra A, Lara-Cinisomo S, Jaycox LT, et al. Children on the homefront: the experience of children from military families. *Pediatrics.* 2010;125:541–561.

18. Lincoln A, Swift E, Shorteno-Fraser M. Psychological adjustment and treatment of children and families with parents deployed in military combat. *J Clin Psychol.* 2008;64:984–992.

19. Gewirtz AH, Polusny MA, DeGarmo D, Kaylis A, Erbes C. Posttraumatic stress symptoms among National Guard soldiers deployed to Iraq: associations with parent behaviors and couple adjustment. *J Consult Clin Psychol.* 2010;78;599–610.

20. Ghafoori B, Wierholzer RW, Howsepian B, Boardman A. The role of adult attachment, parental bonding, and spiritual love in adjustment to military trauma. *J Trauma Dissociation.* 2008;9:85–106.

21. Renaud EF. The attachment characteristics of combat veterans with PTSD. *Traumatology.* 2008;14:1–12.

22. Scaturo D, Hayman P. The impact of combat trauma across the family life cycle: clinical considerations. *J Trauma Stress.* 1992;5:273–288.

23. Galovski T, Lyons JA. Psychological sequelae of combat violence: a review of the impact of PTSD on the veteran's family and possible interventions. *Aggress Violent Behav.* 2004;9:477–501.

24. Dekel R, Goldblatt H, Keidar M, Solomon Z, Polliack M. Being a wife of a veteran with posttraumatic stress disorder. *Family Relat.* 2005;54:24–36.

25. Dekel R, Solomon Z, Bleich A. Emotional distress and marital adjustment of caregivers: contribution of level of impairment and appraised burden. *Anxiety Stress Coping.* 2005;18:71-82.

26. Palmer C. A theory of risk and resilience factors in military families. *Mil Psychol.* 2008;20:205–217.

27. Defense Centers of Excellence. *A Review of Post-deployment Reintegration: Evidence, Challenges, and Strategies for Program Development.* Arlington, VA: US Department of Defense; 2012.

28. Bobrow J, Cook E, Knowles C, Vieten C. Coming all the way home: integrative

community care for those who serve. *Psychol Serv.* 2013;10:137–144.

29. Schok ML, Kleber RJ, Lensvelt-Mulders GJLM. A model of resilience and meaning after military deployment: personal resources in making sense of war and peacekeeping experiences. *Aging Mental Health.* 2010;14:328–338.
30. Bowles SV, Bates MJ. Military organizations and programs contributing to resilience building. *Mil Med.* 2010;175:382–385.
31. Masten AS. Ordinary magic: resilience processes in development. *Am Psychol.* 2001;56:227–238.
32. Kazdin AE. Parent management training: evidence, outcomes, and issues. *J Am Acad Child Adolesc Psychiatry.* 1997;36:1349–1356.
33. Hoge CW, Auchterlonie JL, Milliken CS. Mental health problems, use of mental health services, and attrition from military service after returning from deployment to Iraq or Afghanistan. *JAMA.* 2006;295:1023–1032.
34. Milliken CS, Auchterlonie JL, Hoge CW. Longitudinal assessment of mental health problems among active and reserve component soldiers returning from the Iraq war. *JAMA.* 2007;298:2141–2148.
35. Hoge CW, Castro CA, Messer SC, McGurk D, Cotting DL, Koffman RL. Combat duty in Iraq and Afghanistan, mental health problems, and barriers to care. *N Engl J Med.* 2004;351:13–22.
36. Possemato K, Pratt A, Barrie K, Ouimette P. Family functioning in recent combat veterans with posttraumatic stress disorder and alcohol misuse. *Traumatology.* 2015. Online First Publication.
37. Bowling UB, Sherman MD. Welcoming them home: supporting service members and their families in navigating the tasks of reintegration. *Profess Psychol Res Pract.* 2008;39:451–458.
38. Zerach G, Solomon Z, Horesh D, En-Dor T. Family cohesion and posttraumatic intrusion and avoidance among war veterans: a 20-year longitudinal study. *Social Psychiatry Psychiatr Epidemiol.* 2013;48:205–214.
39. Erbes CR, Meis LA, Polusny MA, Compton JS. Couple adjustment and posttraumatic stress disorder symptoms in National Guard veterans of the Iraq war. *J Fam Psychol.* 2011;25:479–487.
40. Kabat Zinn J. Mindfulness meditation: what it is, what it isn't, and its role in health care and medicine. In: Haruki Y, Ishii Y, Suzuki M, eds. *Comparative and Psychological Study on Meditation.* Delft, The Netherlands: Eburon; 1996: 161–169.
41. Beck A, Rush J, Shaw B, Emery G. *Cognitive Therapy of Depression.* New York, NY: Guilford Press; 1979.
42. National Center for PTSD. Overview of psychotherapy for PTSD. http://www.ptsd.va.gov/professional/treatment/overview/overview-treatment-research.asp. Accessed July 30, 2015.
43. Wilson SR, Gettings PE, Hall ED, Pastor RG. Dilemmas families face in talking with returning U.S. military service members about seeking professional help for mental health issues. *Health Commun.* 2015;30:772–783.

Lieutenant Colonel (LtCol) Tim Maxwell "After a while, my unit, the 24th Marine Expeditionary Unit, who had just returned from Iraq, went back to work. But my abilities had not improved. I tried. Believe me. I tried to get involved in the upcoming operations. I tried to be  more productive. I tried to be useful in some way. But I could not, and that was unpleasant. I was a Warrior! At least, I used to be. And so, to spend my time productively, I started going to the hospital at Camp Lejeune. I met and chatted with Marines who had been sent there directly. I learned that these Marines would not be in this hospital forever. When they got out, their unit would still be deployed. I wondered what they were going to do. One thing led to another and, somehow, I had an idea."

LtCol Tim Maxwell, US Marine Corps (Retired)—well educated, accomplished triathlete, and leader—suffered a severe penetrating traumatic brain injury on October 7, 2004 in Iraq. The lessons he learned from his convalescence and recuperation inspired the formation of both Maxwell Hall (the US Marine Corps Wounded Warrior Barracks) and the Marine Corps Wounded Warrior Regiment.

While serving as the 24th Marine Expeditionary Unit Operations Officer during his sixth and final deployment, LtCol Maxwell's base was mortared, and the left side of his brain was damaged by fragments. During the initial phase of LtCol Maxwell's lifelong recovery—an additional left arm injury and enduring physical (right side), cognitive, and psychological challenges subsequent to the brain injury—he discovered that he did better when surrounded by other Wounded Warriors because they truly understood what he was going through, just as he had understood them.

"In those first months, as soon as he could sit up in a wheelchair, he was visiting other Wounded Warriors. He continued to do this at the Veterans'

Hospital and with General [James] Amos on trips to various military hospitals," noted his wife, Shannon.

The experience of sharing his frustrations and victories with his fellow Marines, as well as recognizing that the time he spent by himself was not helpful to his recovery, led LtCol Maxwell in 2005 to present the idea of the US Marine Corps Wounded Warrior Barracks (now named "Maxwell Hall" in his honor) to then II Marine Expeditionary Force Commander, Lieutenant General James Amos. With fellow wounded Marines, then Gunnery Sergeant Ken Barnes and Chief Warrant Officer 4 Chris Hedgecorth, LtCol Maxwell stood up the barracks to provide recovering Marines a place to heal together. The unqualified success of this program, and the insights learned from its founding, led directly to the creation of the US Marine Corps Wounded Warrior Regiment.

Today, LtCol Maxwell and his wife run the SemperMax Support Fund (www.sempermax.org) to continue that legacy of team healing, and to bring Veterans, wounded, ill, injured, and families together to learn from each other and to move forward.

LtCol Maxwell has a Bachelor of Science degree in Industrial Engineering from Texas A&M University (College Station, Texas), as well as a Master's degree in Operations Analysis from the Naval Postgraduate School (Monterey, California).

LtCol Maxwell's awards include the Legion of Merit, Bronze Star Medal, Purple Heart, Navy/Marine Corps Commendation Medal (3), Navy/Marine Corps Achievement Medal (2), Global War on Terrorism Expeditionary Medal, Global War on Terrorism Service Medal, Iraq Campaign Medal, the Sea Service Deployment Ribbon (6), and others. He has also been recognized with The Marine Corps League's Military Order of the Iron Mike Award, the R. Lee Ermey's Ooh Rah Award, the President of the Veterans Leadership Program of Western Pennsylvania Award, Esquire Magazine's Best and Brightest Recognition, the Mack McKinney Award, and the Bobby Simpson Memorial Award.

His awards and decorations include the Purple Heart, Meritorious Service Medal, three Army Commendation Medals, seven Army Achievement Medals, Army Reserve Component Achievement Medal, two National Defense Service Medals, Korea Defense Service Medal, Iraq Campaign Medal with Campaign Star, Global War on Terrorism Service Medal, Noncommissioned Officer Professional Development Ribbon, Army Service Ribbon, five Army Overseas Service Ribbons, Combat Action Badge, Parachute Rigger Badge, Parachutist Badge, and Air Assault Badge.

While the MHS [Military Health System] is highly valued as a system of care, we also recognize that it remains a microcosm of American medicine. We are buffeted by some of the same challenges as our civilian peers. We must migrate from a system of healthcare to a system of health.

★ ★ ★

LIEUTENANT GENERAL DOUGLAS ROBB
DEFENSE HEALTH AGENCY
CONGRESSIONAL TESTIMONY
APRIL 14, 2014

Chapter Seven

Sexuality and Intimacy

STANLEY H. DUCHARME, PhD*; REBECCA P. CAMERON, PhD†; and
LINDA R. MONA, PhD‡

---

*Clinical Psychologist, Departments of Rehabilitation Medicine and Urology, Boston
University School of Medicine, 725 Albany Street, Suite 3B, Boston, Massachusetts
02118

†Assistant Professor, Department of Psychology, California State University, 6000 J
Street, Sacramento, California 95819-6007

‡Clinical Psychologist, Behavioral Health, VA Long Beach Healthcare System, 5901
East 7th Street, Long Beach, California 90822

INTRODUCTION

Sexuality and intimacy are important aspects of personal and interpersonal well-being and resilience. Yet, these highly valued areas of
functioning may present challenges for Veterans and returning military
personnel who have experienced significant illness or who have acquired a
disability.[1] Healthy sexuality is often portrayed as something very narrowly
defined and inextricably linked to being able-bodied, young, and conven-
tionally attractive (Figure 7-1). In fact, people with disabilities are often
stereotyped as asexual, even childlike. The reality of resilient sexuality is far
different from these requirements and stereotypes, and instead involves partnership, flexibility, and pleasure.[2] The goals of this chapter are to affirm that
sexuality and intimacy can be viewed from a much broader vantage point
than is typically presented and to provide straightforward information about
sexuality and sexual functioning so that Veterans and Military personnel can

Figure 7-1. *Healthy Sexuality Is Inextricably Linked to Being Able-bodied, Young, and Attractive.*

PHOTOGRAPH: DACOWITS. *DEFENSE ADVISORY COMMITTEE ON WOMEN IN THE SERVICES: 1951–2013, 62 YEARS OF DACOWITS– 2013 REPORT.* WASHINGTON, DC: DEPARTMENT OF DEFENSE; 2013.

be empowered in their sexual experiences and knowledgeable when they talk to their healthcare providers about this topic.

SEXUALITY AND INTIMACY

Military service, deployment, and combat create particular challenges for relationships and for the development of a sense of sexual well-being (Figure 7-2). Military service can have profound effects on social, psychological, and physical aspects of sexual functioning because of long separations from loved ones, exposure to sexual harassment and traumatic events, and experiences of physical injury and disability. Given that the majority of people entering the military are young adults, military service may have a significant impact on sexual development and identity formation.[3]

For couples, military service-related separations lead to communication and role changes. For example, the partner who remains at home must fill in the gaps apparent in household management. Also, in the case of parents, the partner who remains home must attend to gaps apparent in childrearing responsibilities. These adjustments often require renegotiation when deployments end and responsibilities shift back to the traditional family format. In the case of significant illness or acquired disability, there are direct effects on the physical aspects of sexual functioning and psychological effects via changes to body image or identity. Intimacy may also suffer because it may be difficult to nurture the erotic aspects of a relationship when an able-bodied partner takes on significant caregiving or assistance tasks for an ill or injured partner or a partner with a disability.

Despite the potential for sexual difficulties among active and returning military personnel, few healthcare providers have the knowledge and comfort level to address issues of sexuality. Although healthcare providers need to incorporate questions regard-

FIGURE 7-2. *Military Service Can Also Affect the Family.* PHOTOGRAPH. COURTESY OF THE NATIONAL MILITARY FAMILY ASSOCIATION, ALEXANDRIA, VIRGINIA.

ing sexual functioning into their intake assessments, this is not always done as standard practice.[4] In particular, healthcare providers may be inadequately trained to assess and respond to sexuality concerns among patients with disabilities. Those healthcare providers who become comfortable and knowledgeable about sexuality may be able to substantially improve psychological and physical functioning through appropriate interventions and/or referrals to specialists.

At the very least, healthcare providers should ask active and returning Veterans about past and recent sexual abuse, molestation, and harassment. They should inquire as to relationship status, as well as past and present sexual difficulties in the areas of erections, orgasms, premature ejaculation, pain during sexual intercourse, lubrication, and sexual desire. Issues regarding fertility may also be a concern and should be addressed whenever relevant. Healthcare providers should always be sensitive to the presence of psychological issues, including body image concerns, depression, anxiety, and relationship stress that might contribute to sexual adjustment difficulties. It is important for providers to find a balance in addressing physical and emotional concerns, as well as issues regarding the relationship. For some individuals, fears regarding failure, performance, body image, or issues of mistrust may result in an avoidance of relationships.

In mainstream culture, people with disabilities are rarely perceived as having sexual needs and enjoying an active sexual life. Instead, there is the false perception that one's sexual interest and abilities are lost with the onset of a chronic illness or disability.[5] These outdated and negative views of disability tend to focus on issues of loss and deficit rather than on a more positive model in which disability is seen as an opportunity for growth and well-being.

In contrast, a modern approach to disability views people with disabilities as adults, with the right to make their own decisions and choose their own path in life; and whose physical, sensory, cognitive, or psychological impairments or differences *become* disabling in a world that fails to prioritize their full participation.[6,7] If our environments were designed for universal access or with functional impairments in mind, there would be less disability.

Similarly, a modern view of sexuality and disability understands sexuality as an opportunity for creativity and self-expression, joy and pleasure, and intimacy and connection. People with disabilities often grow in sexual well-being as they become

- clearer about their sexual needs, values, and priorities;
- more comfortable with vulnerability and human imperfection;
- more open in their communication with partners;
- more direct about sexual expression; and
- more flexible in their strategies for pleasure.

Figure 7-3. *Genital Wounds Primarily From Improvised Explosive Device Blasts.* GRAPHIC: COURTESY OF THE US ARMY, OFFICE OF THE SURGEON GENERAL.

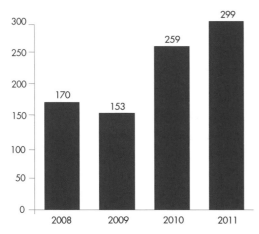

Sexual expression may require preparation, or even assistance, and sex aids like toys, positioning pillows, and lubricants may be helpful.[8–10]

For the returning Veteran, it may be important to take a proactive stance in locating a healthcare provider who has a more modern view of disability and who feels comfortable and knowledgeable in addressing sexuality issues. In general, it is important that issues of sexuality be prioritized as a standard part of medical and behavioral healthcare. If this is not done as a routine part of a comprehensive evaluation, the Veteran may have to take the initiative in raising the topic.

Because, unfortunately, many healthcare professionals continue to be uncomfortable about discussing issues relating to sexuality, it is important that the Veteran be aware of basic genital anatomy and be observant of any potential sexually related issues that may occur (Figure 7-3). These issues include the possibility of infections, masses, or symptoms of sexually transmitted diseases.

MEN'S PHYSICAL SEXUAL HEALTH AND SELF-MONITORING

Good sexual health for men includes conducting regular self-examinations of the penis and scrotum to help ensure that infections or potential cancers are caught and treated early. At least once a month, a man should examine his entire penis and scrotum; compare the testicles; and check for pain, lumps, masses, or any significant changes in skin texture. If there is a foreskin, pull it back and examine the area underneath. Note any signs of redness, rash, or discharge that might be an indication of an infection. The skin of the penis and scrotum can be prone to the growth of bacteria and infection as a result of the warm, moist environment. Anything unusual should be evaluated by a physician. A primary care physician is helpful; but, for deeper concerns, consider seeing a urologist (a specialist who focuses on the urinary tract).[11] For men with various disabilities, self-examinations may be difficult due to pain, limited mobility, or other factors. Often, a personal care attendant can be helpful in these matters.

WOMEN'S PHYSICAL SEXUAL HEALTH AND SELF-MONITORING

Because a woman's genitals are not as visible as a man's, many women are unfamiliar with the structure, shape, and appearance of their genital area. Self-examinations allow each woman to recognize what is normal for her. Thus, she will be able to recognize problems at an early stage and ask relevant questions if a doctor's visit becomes necessary. For women, self-examinations should consist of both a vaginal self-examination and a breast examination.

Undertaking a self-examination of the vulva requires some background reading and some basic instructions from friends or healthcare professionals. Relevant reading materials can usually be obtained from women's health clinics, hospital clinics, physicians' offices, and some pharmacies. In order to perform a thorough self-examination, a woman may need to obtain a speculum, an instrument that will open the walls of the vagina so that she can look inside. Disposable plastic speculums can easily be obtained from a pharmacy or medical supply store. Other materials that a woman may need are a mirror, pillow, flashlight, and a water-soluble gel lubricant. Before beginning, it is important to wash the hands thoroughly and to empty the bladder.

To examine the vulva,

- position the mirror so that the vagina and labia can be viewed;
- note the color, size, and shape of the clitoris, labia, and opening of the vagina; and
- pay attention to any secretions from the vagina.

Vaginal secretions of certain types are normal, and will vary in thickness and consistency according to the phase of the menstrual cycle.

Breast self-examinations are generally painless and simple. However, with a disability they can be difficult. Generally, exams only take a few moments. The best time to do a breast examination is usually a day or two after the menstrual period when any related tenderness and fullness have subsided. It is normally a good idea to perform the exam at the same time each month so that the breast tissue is consistent from one examination to another. In front of a mirror,

- check the size and contour of each breast;
- squeeze (gently) each nipple to check for any unusual discharge; and
- feel the breast for any unusual lumps or thickness, using the three middle fingers of one hand to palpate the breast in a circular motion.

Specific instructions for conducting breast and vaginal examinations should be obtained from a physician or from a women's health clinic. Often, for women with various disabilities, self-examinations may not be possible because of pain, limited mobility, or other factors. In these cases, the assistance of personal care attendants or other trusted individuals may be helpful.

SEXUAL FUNCTIONING AND BIOMEDICAL INTERVENTIONS

Difficulties with how the body functions sexually include decreased desire among men or women; problems with arousal, vaginal lubrication, pain, and orgasm among women; and problems with attaining and maintaining erections and experiencing orgasm among men.[11] Options for treatment of sexual dysfunctions include medications, medical devices, surgery, counseling, and sex therapy. Often, a combination of treatments may provide the best solution. For example, many couples find that medications, such as Viagra

FIGURE 7-4.
Service Member With Counselor. PHOTOGRAPH: PATRICIA DEAL, US ARMY, CARL R. DARNALL ARMY MEDICAL CENTER, OFFICE OF PUBLIC AFFAIRS.

(Pfizer, Inc, New York, NY), are most effective when used in conjunction with couples or relationship counseling.[12]

Problems in reaching orgasm for men and women are another source of distress that is often discussed in sex therapy clinics and urology/gynecology offices.[12] Without sufficient sexual desire and arousal, achieving an orgasm can be difficult. Understanding the range of factors—including cultural factors that may have affected early sexual experiences and current issues (eg, the length of foreplay, encouragement of partner, sexual technique, and the presence of medications)—is important to develop a comprehensive approach to treating women and men with orgasmic difficulties.

Researchers have been focusing on developing biological interventions to increase desire among men and women for whom low desire leads to dissatisfaction. Until the last several years, instruments to measure physiological arousal were inaccurate and of little value. Today, this situation has changed dramatically. New diagnostic tools to measure the degree of arousal and lubrication have now been developed. Armed with these newer strategies, scientists hope that they will gain approval from the US Food and Drug Administration to explore new biological forms of treatment, especially for women.

In addition to the biological issues, sexual well-being and functioning can be affected by problematic relationships, trauma, emotional turmoil, and unresolved issues. Such factors may complicate a healthy and positive sexual life either while in military service or after returning home. Working with a counselor may be beneficial for couples who are seeking to improve their sexual communication or to increase their sense of partnership. In addition, individuals who have undergone experiences and trauma (eg, sexual abuse or harassment) or who are dealing with depression or other emotional concerns may find it helpful to speak with a counselor who can offer suggestions and guidance aimed at improving general and sexual well-being (Figure 7-4).

Seeking a counselor who is disability-affirmative and sex-positive, and who focuses on pleasure and intimacy rather than just dysfunction, can be very helpful.

SEXUAL FUNCTIONING AMONG MEN

Over the last decade, the availability of medical and psychological treatments to improve sexual functioning has grown considerably. Medications, in particular, have become well-known and accepted by the general public, and people have become much more open in discussing difficulties of a sexual nature.[13]

A common sexual experience among men is erectile dysfunction. There are a number of treatments for sexual problems like erection difficulties. Issues such as age, financial resources, relationship status, health issues, and frequency of sexual activity may all play a role in deciding the treatment of choice. For these reasons, seeing a physician (ie, a urologist) may be helpful in deciding which options best fit the life situation of an individual Veteran or Service Member. For example, single men who are dating may prefer treatment methods that can be somewhat more portable and spontaneous. Yet, for other men, certain erection medications may be preferred because of their long-lasting effectiveness or quick-acting characteristics.

As a general rule, it is best to explore the least invasive treatment method before exploring other options that may produce an adverse reaction. Many individuals who choose to pursue interventions to address sexual difficulties such as erectile dysfunction start by talking with a counselor either individually or with their partners. In some cases, reducing anxiety, addressing symptoms of posttraumatic stress disorder (PTSD), improving one's mood, and/or enhancing communication may be enough to provide some relief. This may, in turn, result in a more positive sexual experience either alone or with a partner. It is also important to remember that positive sexual and intimate experiences are not dependent on the presence of an erection. However, there are a number of medical interventions available to men and couples who wish to pursue this approach.

Oral medications to improve erections were first introduced in the United States in 1998. Over time, they have proven to be very effective for many men who do not have significant physical conditions that reduce blood flow to the penis. At the present time, there are four medications that are currently available in the United States:

1. sildenafil (Viagra; Pfizer, New York, NY),
2. vardenafil (Levitra; Bayer AG, Leverkusen, Germany),
3. avanafil (Stendra; Endo International, Inc, Malvern, PA), and
4. tadalafil (Cialis; Eli Lilly and Company, Indianapolis, IN).

These medications have an excellent safety record and have been well toler-ated by most men. Typical adverse reactions sometimes include stuffy nose, blurred vision, and occasional mild muscle ache. However, these medications are not indicated if the man has certain medical conditions (eg, hypotension or low blood pressure) or takes certain medications (eg, nitrates). For this reason, they are given by prescription and should be used under the guidance of a physician.[12] Although similar over-the-counter erection medications are available, there is a danger in taking these medications or herbal supplements because they may contain unknown or potentially harmful substances. In addition, these compounds or herbal treatments often lack a list of ingredients or warning labels.

When oral medications are considered to be ineffective, penile injections are commonly considered the next alternative. The medications are injected into the corporal chambers of the penis and usually include one or several medications that relax the smooth muscles of the penis so that blood flow into the penis can occur more efficiently. After determining the proper dose and receiving training from a urologist, the man and his partner can use this technique at home prior to sexual activity. Some men with intact sensation in the penis report some minor burning in the shaft of the penis. This can be reduced with proper training in the injection technique.[13]

Ideally, a proper dose and mixture of the medication should result in an erection that will last approximately one hour. Should the erection last for several hours, the man is instructed to go to the nearest emergency room where he will be given medications to allow the erection to subside. This con-dition is termed *priapism* and can harm the tissue of the penis if the erection persists for a prolonged period of time. Finally, care should be taken to avoid penile scarring at the injection site. This is usually avoided by applying pres-sure on the injection site for several minutes after injection.

A vacuum constrictive device consists of an elongated tube that is placed over the shaft of the penis. A vacuum is then created in the tube either by a battery-operated device or a manual pumping action. As the vacuum is created in the tube, blood gradually flows into the corporal chambers of the penis. When the penis achieves a satisfactory degree of rigidity, an elastic band or penile ring is slipped off the tube and placed over the base of the penis. The penile ring traps the blood in the shaft of the penis and maintains the erection so that sexual intercourse can occur. The ring should never be left in place for more than 30 minutes; otherwise, blood flow to the penis is inadequate to maintain healthy penile tissue.[13]

In general, vacuum devices tend to be more accepted by men in long-term sexual relationships where spontaneity is not a major concern. Complaints about the vacuum device frequently include comments regarding unnatural erections, coldness of the penis, pain, and difficulty in maintaining an adequate seal at the base of the penis. Although these devices are less popular than they were before the introduction of oral medications, there are still some men for whom this is the preferred treatment strategy.

Because it is so important to remove the ring after sexual intercourse, the vacuum constrictive device is often discouraged if the man has been drinking alcohol or using other medications that may cause fatigue or drowsiness following sexual activity. Alertness and vigilance are necessary to prevent any medical complications from occurring with the use of such devices.[12]

Although penile implants can be highly effective and satisfying, they remain typically the option of last resort for restoring erections because insertion of the penile implant destroys the tissue of the two corporal chambers of the penis. Currently, this method of erection enhancement is generally only used when other options have proven to be ineffective. This is more typical in older men who have medical complications such as diabetes, hypertension, and elevated cholesterol that impact blood flow and tissue integrity. At times, an implant may be a consideration among men who have a long history of polysubstance abuse in which medications or injections are not effective. The decision to have an implant is not one that should be taken lightly and should be decided after other treatments have failed and after a serious discussion with one's partner and a healthcare professional.[12]

There are two types of implants currently on the market:

1. a malleable silicone prosthesis and
2. a more complex inflatable hydraulic prosthesis.

The malleable prosthesis consists of two bendable rods that are surgically implanted in the corporal chambers of the penis. With this device, the penis is always semirigid and ready for sexual intercourse. It only needs to be moved into the correct position for sexual penetration at the appropriate time. The inflatable prosthesis consists of two inflatable chambers that are surgically implanted in the two chambers of the penis. In addition, a fluid reservoir is implanted into the abdominal cavity, and a valve is placed within the scrotal sac. When the man wishes to achieve an erection, either he or his partner squeezes the valve, allowing fluid to enter the inflatable chambers, thereby causing an erection. With a penile implant, orgasm and ejaculation are not affected. Therefore, with adequate stimulation, the man is usually able to reach an orgasm unless there are other issues that may make this difficult.[13]

SEXUAL FUNCTIONING AMONG WOMEN

Epidemiological studies such as the National Health and Social Life Survey suggest that sexual dysfunction affects 30% to 50% of American women.[3] Sexual desire and physiological arousal are areas in which many women experience difficulties; in addition, women may have difficulty experiencing orgasm as readily or as often as they would like. Although women's sexual responses are influenced by multiple factors (including emotions, relationships, trust, comfort, religion, stress, culture, age, and safety), biological factors (eg, hormones [specifically androgens such as testosterone]) may also play a critical role in women's sexual interest. Certain medications (including birth control pills and some antidepressants) may interfere with testosterone levels and result in lower sexual desire. In addition, hysterectomy, breast cancer, childbirth, and menopause all potentially contribute to the depletion of a woman's testosterone level.[12]

There are a range of issues for women who are considering the use of birth control to prevent or delay pregnancy. Choosing a type of birth control method is dependent on personal choice, physical ability to use any given method, and medical issues that might affect the use of any given method. Although contraception is best discussed by both partners in a sexual relationship, most methods are a woman's choice and should be practiced in consultation with a healthcare provider.

The hormonal IUD (intrauterine device) is a small, T-shaped device that is inserted and removed by a trained physician (Figure 7-5). It stays in the uterus for up to 5 years. The IUD releases a small amount of hormone each day that causes the cervical mucus to thicken. This acts as a barrier to prevent sperm from entering the uterus. It may cause some irregular bleeding for a few months and may decrease or eliminate menses over time.

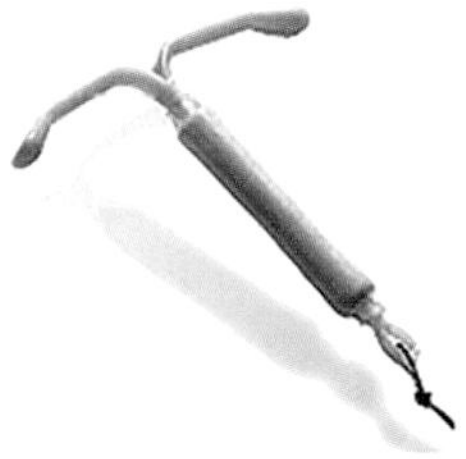

Figure 7-5. *Intrauterine Device (IUD).*

Risks include the possibility of having a reaction to the hormone. Another option is the copper IUD, which is inserted and removed by a physician and can last for up to 10 years. It stops the sperm from reaching and fertilizing the egg. This IUD is sometimes used as an "emergency birth control" because it can be inserted up to 5 days after intercourse to prevent a fertilized egg from implanting in the uterus. With either IUD, there is no need to remember to take a pill and no requirement of fine motor dexterity by the woman or her partner. Both carry the risk of a perforation (small tear) or, rarely, an infection, which may go unnoticed in women with decreased sensation due to a disability.

The diaphragm is a barrier method of birth control that is usually inserted into the vagina by the woman just before having intercourse. Usually, some form of spermicidal gel is placed on the diaphragm before it is inserted. Because both squeezing the tube of gel and inserting the diaphragm require some degree of manual dexterity, this is usually not a choice for women with disabilities that affect hand functioning. Occasionally, in longer term relationships, the device is inserted and removed by the partner.

The subdermal hormonal implant is a small rod, about the size of a matchstick, that is inserted under the skin by a physician. Usually, it is implanted in the upper arm and is effective for up to 3 years. It can cause irregular bleeding for some women. Occasionally, it can affect a woman's mood and sex drive.

The birth control pill is a combination of hormones that are taken orally. Like other hormonal methods, the pill suppresses ovulation, thickens cervical mucus, and thins the lining of the uterus to help block sperm. For maximum effectiveness, it is best if the pill can be taken at the same time each day; the need to remember daily dosages for three weeks each month can be a disadvantage, particularly if a woman has memory or cognitive impairments. The pill can cause nausea, headaches, breast tenderness, and spotting between periods. Some doctors are concerned about giving the pill to women with spinal cord injury (SCI) because of the dangers of developing deep vein thrombosis (blood clots) in the legs, although some physicians feel that newer versions of the pill are safer or that progesterone-only pills have fewer risks for women with disabilities. If considering a hormonal form of birth control, consult with a physician.

The patch is placed on the upper arm, shoulder, abdomen, hip, or upper back. It delivers a combination of hormones that function like the birth control pill, thus suppressing ovulation and blocking sperm. The patch only needs to be changed once per week, offering some advantage over the pill. It has many of the same potential side effects as the pill. If skin under the patch becomes irritated, the location of the patch can be changed. Again, potential risks, such as blood clots, should be reviewed with a physician.

The vaginal ring is inserted into the vagina and slowly releases hormones into the body. Typically, the ring is inserted by the woman or her partner, and some degree of manual dexterity is required for proper positioning. In addition, the use of hormones requires a consideration of individual risks versus benefits.

The condom is a barrier method and is presently the only form of male contraception. Female condoms exist, but can be difficult to insert and possibly difficult to fit for some women who have atrophy in vaginal muscles due to certain disabilities. Both male and female condoms offer protection against sexually transmitted infections. Condoms may limit spontaneity because they are used just prior to intercourse. On the plus side, they have few side effects, except in the case of latex allergies. Male condoms involve men in the birth control process more directly than some of the other forms of birth control discussed, because either partner can roll the condom over the penis at the appropriate time. Using condoms effectively involves good communication between partners and a sense of mutual responsibility for sexual health.

PSYCHOLOGICAL HEALTH AND DISABILITY ISSUES

DEPRESSION
Although circulatory and hormonal issues are important factors in sexual health, emotional issues also play a large role in the quality of sexual functioning. Certain psychological disorders (eg, depression) often contribute to sexual problems and can interfere with pleasure and intimacy. Depression can also complicate physical functioning among people with chronic illnesses or disability.

Individuals with clinical depression vary in the daily pattern of their symptoms; some people feel worse in the morning and better as the day goes on, whereas others experience the opposite pattern. Because increasing pleasurable and rewarding activities may be a part of the treatment or recovery process, engaging in intimate activities might be helpful for some people. Considering time of day and aiming for sensual pleasure rather than orgasm or even intercourse may increase the chances of a positive experience.

Clinical depression has long been shown to negatively affect sexual functioning. Depression can reduce overall energy levels, as well as sexual desire, and can make it more difficult to experience pleasure. Becoming sexually aroused is often difficult for those who are feeling depressed. Although people who are depressed may have feelings of shame or embarrassment about it, depression is commonplace in today's society (Figure 7-6). Untreated depression, however, can be self-defeating and potentially dangerous. Typically, counseling and medications either alone or in combination with one another are the most common and effective treatments of depression. These treatments can significantly improve appetite and sleep, restore energy, and ultimately renew sexual interest.

However, further complicating the direct effects of depression on libido is the fact that many antidepressants also have sexual side effects. Commonly used antidepressants (eg, Prozac, Zoloft, Paxil, and others) can influence sexual functioning by

- reducing sexual interest,
- decreasing the ability to achieve erections,
- reducing vaginal lubrication,
- prohibiting male ejaculation, and
- diminishing the capacity for orgasm in both men and women.

FIGURE 7-6. *Depression Can Complicate Physical Functioning and Negatively Affect Sexual Functioning.* PHOTOGRAPH: PFC PAIGE PENDLETON, 1ST BRIGADE COMBAT TEAM, OFFICE OF PUBLIC AFFAIRS, 1ST CAVALRY DIVISION.

Medications may be indicated if suicidal ideation is present or if the individual with a disability is neglecting self-care routines. It should be noted, however, that the efficacy of antidepressant medication has not been adequately studied in double-blind randomized trials in the population of people with disabilities.[14] As such, psychotropic medications should be used sparingly in favor of a more active, person-centered approach. The process of adjustment may be enhanced by a behavioral appraisal and coping process instead of or in conjunction with medications. Behavioral techniques to reduce depression and anxiety may include guided imagery, relaxation training, or cognitive behavioral therapy.

In addition to depression, other reactions (eg, anger, hostility, and withdrawal) are often seen as well. One study demonstrated that 28% of Veterans who received rehabilitation between 1997 and 2007 were diagnosed with depression. Among people with SCI and depression,

70% were also diagnosed with another psychiatric disorder, with PTSD and anxiety disorders being the most common.[15] These can be short lived or can be present throughout rehabilitation. For some people, there is an absence of depression, which is often confusing to staff members and other members of the rehabilitation team. However, there is no convincing evidence that the absence of strong negative emotions or depression indicates a poor psychological adjustment in the future.

POSTTRAUMATIC STRESS DISORDER
Increasingly, over the past few decades, psychologists have explored and recognized the occurrence of PTSD among people with disabilities and returning Veterans.[16] Traumatic events may include a previous time in which a person was exposed to actual or threatened death, serious injury, or sexual violation. PTSD is an array of psychological and physiological reactions that are expected, normal reactions to a life threat, but that persist beyond a normal period of recovery. It is not uncommon for symptoms of PTSD to persist for many years.

The traumatic nature of deployment and exposure to combat would appear to place individuals at risk for symptoms of this psychiatric disorder. Typical symptoms experienced by people with PTSD often include flashbacks; nightmares; problems sleeping; hypervigilance; and intrusive recollections of the event, along with efforts to avoid thoughts, feelings, or recollections of that event. This effort at avoidance is credited with the chronicity of the disorder because it leads to inaccurate interpretations of the event and increased psychological distress.

Many returning Service Members and Veterans of recent conflicts experience PTSD. This disorder has been associated with high rates of relationship difficulties, as well as sexual dysfunction.[3,17,18] These difficulties are related to biological, cognitive, behavioral, and emotional effects of PTSD. PTSD is often treated with psychotherapy, which may be supplemented with medications (including antidepressants). Cognitive behavioral therapy—and other forms of psychotherapy that focus on changing problematic thought processes and disruptive behavioral patterns—is often utilized to decrease the anxiety, guilt, anger, and disconnection that are part of PTSD. In addition, couples therapy may help. Couples who work together to resolve intimacy issues related to PTSD and to create emotional safety in their relationship may find this to be an important part of the overall healing process for the Service Member or Veteran with PTSD.[1]

Traumatic Brain Injury and Service-Related Physical Disabilities

Traumatic brain injury is the result of concussive injuries that have affected almost 20% of Operation Enduring Freedom and Operation Iraqi Freedom Veterans.[19] Like PTSD, it can affect relationships and sexual functioning through physical, psychological, and relationship changes. These include lower sex drive and problems in sexual functioning, such as disruptions to arousal and problems with orgasm.[1] Counseling can help couples identify the ways in which traumatic brain injury may be affecting their relationship and develop coping strategies that facilitate their sexual connection.

Military service-related disabilities are varied, and include SCI, amputation, and sensory impairments. Due to the prevalence of injuries sustained from improvised explosive devices, injuries may include damage to or loss of genitalia or other injuries to the genitourinary system.[20,21] These kinds of injuries can have profound effects on sexual well-being by changing

- body image,
- physical sexual responsiveness,
- relationship roles, and
- well-being.[1,22]

Ultimately, changes to the former structure and dynamics of life create a shift in the relationship dynamics within the partner dyad, and the caregiver often assumes the dual role of lover and caregiver. This shift in relationship dynamics can create conflict between the couple, which puts the relationship under strain.

Adapting to these changes can involve an initial period of grieving and adjustment. Ultimately, sexual well-being may involve redefining what it means to be a sexy, sensual person; and conventional, outward attractiveness may matter less than one's inner experience. Approaches to sexual expression may need to expand to include a wider range of pleasure- and intimacy-enhancing behaviors.

Sexuality after a disability is a topic that has been widely explored and should be well understood by the mental health professional working with returning Veterans and other military personnel.[23] In addition to education, people with a disability may need specific suggestions regarding exploration and resuming sexual activities. In many cases, sensate focus exercises and improved communication may help a couple to avoid the performance anxiety often associated with intercourse. Early after injury, mutual pleasuring and sexual exploration may be the preferred method to gain sexual confidence and resume sexual activity in a safe, nonthreatening manner.

Couples may benefit from therapy that is disability-affirming to redefine their assumptions about and approach to sexual expression. A variety of counseling strategies (including cognitive, behavioral, and mindfulness) can help individuals and couples with disabilities to challenge negative thinking, develop good self-care and relationship-care strategies, plan for enjoyable sexual expression, and learn to be fully present in their current experiences.

In addition to disability-affirmative counseling, sex therapy can help clients learn techniques to improve sexual functioning. Masters and Johnson[23] developed a treatment plan that removed all pressures from the couple and gradually encouraged people to focus on the feelings and sensations of sexual pleasure. With this technique, termed *sensate focus*, individuals and couples are encouraged to enjoy their physical responses and to disengage from their thoughts, including worries and judgments that could interfere with sexual experience.[22] Additional sex therapy techniques include specific strategies for overcoming difficulties with orgasm and erectile functioning. A disability-affirmative sex therapist can develop a specific, tailored treatment plan to improve sexual functioning and maximize sexual enjoyment and pleasure whether in solo sexual activities (eg, masturbation) or in partnered sexual encounters.[1]

COMMUNICATION

For those in relationships, increasing a sense of partnership and shared responsibility for sexual intimacy is critically important. It can be challenging for many Veterans to talk honestly about sex with their partners. Sometimes, people find it easier to discuss these topics with same-gender friends. Part of that may have to do with embarrassment or self-consciousness, but there can also be differences in what men and women tend to focus on when discussing sex. Although we will suggest some generalizations about gender differences in communication style about sexuality, it is important to recognize that individual men and women vary considerably and may not match these generalities.

To the extent that there are gender differences, however, men may focus on the physical aspects of sex. They may focus on the mechanics of sex and on issues like positions, erections, and orgasm. This can be problematic when it leads to all-or-nothing thinking about the "correct" way to have sex (eg, sex must include erection, penetration, and orgasm; men must be physically and psychologically ready for sex at any time, etc). For men whose physical or psychological functioning during or after military service does not match these preconceived ideas, there may be a risk of feeling like a failure and experiencing distress. Being overly concerned with performance (eg, the ability to delay orgasm) can interfere with sexual pleasure and satisfaction.

In contrast, for many women, sexual priorities emphasize a sense of closeness, emotions, intimacy, and sharing in addition to or as an integral part of the physical pleasures. Feeling connected in a loving way may be more important than the sexual position, the intensity of an orgasm, or the rigidity of an erection.

When there are differences in priorities, focus, or communication style within a couple's relationship, these differences can become either a source of conflict or a means of helping one another to grow in intimacy by exploring each other's perspectives. It is important to note that these individual differences are not completely gender-linked. Thus, in same-gender relationships, as in heterosexual relationships, these differing foci and values may still be present and affect communication and intimacy.

However difficult it may be, sexual intimacy benefits from a certain amount of talk and honest communication. For example, in new relationships, partners may have to ask about sexually transmitted infections and negotiate the use of condoms or other safe sex strategies. This is also true for anyone whose sexual functioning is affected by their disability. People who have changes in functioning with regard to desire, arousal, lubrication, erections, ejaculation, or orgasms may have to explain how things work now and what their partners can expect. They may also want to talk about how partners can be helpful and what kind of assistance they can provide.

When physical or emotional factors lead to fatigue, planning for intimacy may be helpful. Although it may limit spontaneity, partners can plan to enjoy sexual activities when they are well rested and refreshed. Sexual activities in the morning may be more satisfying for some because nighttime blood flow that leads to nocturnal erections for men, combined with the physical and mental relaxation of sleep, may facilitate sexual responsiveness. Later in the day, partners can try a short nap before making love. If making love in the evening, having sex before eating a heavy meal or before drinking alcohol may be more satisfying. For men using Viagra, taking it on an empty stomach when well rested may maximize effects.

Sexual partners should be realistic about their desires and communicate these to each other. Although men in particular may internalize societal messages about being ready for sex at any time, it may be important to challenge these expectations and help men to internalize that it is actually okay for men to not be in the mood for sex or to realize that they are too tired at a given time. Partners who are not in the mood for sex should not try to fake it. By assisting Veterans and their partners with developing comfort and facility in communicating their needs and desires, these newly developed skills can reduce performance anxiety and lessen the chance that sexual encounters will end in disappointment and frustration.

Veterans' sexual expressions or attitudes about sex may be affected by past sexual trauma. Sexual trauma may affect interest in sex or overall comfort regarding sex. Assisting Veterans in performing even short discussions with their partners may be important. Gradually becoming more comfortable in tolerating the emotional vulnerability that accompanies conversations related to sex is critical. This allows the development of emotional closeness, safety, and intimacy within the relationship. Behavioral healthcare providers may be particularly helpful in working with Veterans who have a history of trauma to develop resilience in this area.

Because open communication about sex is so important for a positive sexual encounter, it may be helpful to coach Veterans to keep the following principles in mind:

- Focus on communication goals. They may help in those difficult moments when Veterans are trying to figure out what to say or how to say it. Ultimately, the most important thing to remember is to be honest in talking about sex.
- Do not hesitate to share insecurities or anxieties. Put any ego aside and let true feelings come through. This is not the time to be defensive or to appear to have it all together. It is a time to be clear, open, and honest.
- Express your needs from a personal perspective by sharing private information with your partner. This includes talking from the first person and using words like "I" and "my." Over time, you will find that talking about yourself will put your partner at ease and will be much more constructive.

People with disabilities should avoid waiting until the very last moment to explain how their bodies work and what their partners can do to provide some assistance. It is more comfortable and intimate to be sexual when partners know what to expect about each other's functioning. Conversations about sex are best and more natural when they unfold gradually over time. Sharing a little bit about one's sexual needs and desires is best when both partners feel close and emotionally connected.

Each partner should not only express his or her own feelings, but also listen to their partner's feelings. Each partner should have an open mind, realizing that difficulties in sexual intimacy involve both parties. It can be helpful to think about what can be personally changed rather than trying to lessen discomfort by making excuses, blaming, or distancing oneself from the concerns that are being expressed. Listen with an open mind and with compassion for your partner's vulnerability.

Pay close attention to verbal and nonverbal responses. Take each other's feelings into consideration and be open to any questions that come up. Be sensitive to each other's reactions and be willing to have a conversation according to each partner's willingness and openness to hear the information that is being communicated.

Do not be afraid to say things such as "that feels nice" or "I like it when you touch me here." Partners can suggest different things to try and let each other know when they are enjoying something. Be careful not say to a partner that they are doing things wrong, and partners should avoid sounding like they are shouting out orders or instructions in bed.

Although it is important to explain about things like positions, erections, lubrication, and orgasms, partners should not forget to leave time to talk about their feelings. Share some positive feelings, including feelings about the relationship. Sexual encounters are times to be vulnerable by letting one's guard down. If sex is stressful, partners should communicate that sex is an anxiety-provoking experience. Do not fake a level of comfort or experience; be genuine. Partners should let each other know that this may be a time of discovery for both of them and enjoy the journey together.

If conversations about sex are rare in a relationship, there is a good chance that they will be more awkward and difficult than if the topic is discussed regularly. Frequent conversations about sex become increasingly relaxed. Try to have conversations about sex on a regular basis to become more at ease and natural with the topic. It is important to remember that good sex is a goal and it takes some time, effort, and communication to get there. Sex is not going to be perfect every time, and, in fact, "good-enough sex" is a better goal than aiming for perfection.[2] As a matter of course, some sexual encounters are going to be more enjoyable than others. By communicating consistently about sex, there is a better chance for mutual pleasure during each sexual encounter.

SUMMARY

Achieving sexual intimacy and pleasure proves to be challenging for many people, and those who have served often face additional challenges related to the practical, psychological, relational, and medical consequences of their service. Resilience in the face of those challenges includes arming oneself with knowledge about the workings of the sexual system and about options for medical interventions that may enhance sexual functioning. Resilience also means being willing to challenge ideas that can be limiting. An important first step is recognizing that disability is a function of the interplay between impairments and environments that are not designed to be universally accessible. Sexual expression and fulfillment are important to people with disabilities, and sexual well-being is a function of creative engagement in understanding your body and your relationship. Self-care, medical care, counseling, and sex therapy are all important strategies for achieving sexual well-being. In addition, it is important to be prepared to seek out healthcare providers who support you in your treatment goals and who are disability-affirmative and supportive of sexual expression.

REFERENCES

1. Cameron RP, Mona LR, Syme ML, et al. Sexuality among wounded Veterans of Operation Enduring Freedom (OEF), Operation Iraqi Freedom (OIF), and Operation New Dawn (OND): implications for rehabilitation psychologists. *Rehabil Psychol.* 2011;56:289–301.
2. Metz ME, McCarthy BW. The "good-enough sex" model for couple sexual satisfaction. *Sex Relation Ther.* 2007;22:351–362.
3. Allen ES, Rhoades GK, Stanley SM, Markman HJ. Hitting home: relationships between recent deployment, posttraumatic stress symptoms, and marital functioning for Army couples. *J Fam Psychol.* 2010;24:280–288.
4. Reissing ED, Di Giulio G. Practicing clinical psychologists' provision of sexual health care services. *Prof Psychol Res Pract.* 2010;41:57–63.
5. Olkin R. *What Psychotherapists Should Know About Disability.* New York, NY: Guilford; 1999.
6. Mona LR, Cameron RP, Fuentes AJ. Broadening paradigms of disability research to clinical practice: implications for conceptualization and application. In: Hagglund KJ, Heinemann A, eds. *Handbook of Applied Disability and Rehabilitation Research.* New York, NY: Springer; 2006: 75–102.
7. National Institute on Disability and Rehabilitation Research. *NIDRR Long-Range Plan 1999–2003.* Washington, DC: Office of Special Education and Rehabilitative Services; 2000.
8. Mona LR. Sexual options for people with disabilities: using personal assistance services for sexual expression. *Women Ther.* 2003;26:211–220.
9. Syme ML, Mona LR, Cameron RP. Sexual health and well-being after cancer: applying the sexual health model. *Couns Psychol.* 2013;41:268–285.
10. Mona LR, Syme ML, Cameron RP, et al. Sexuality and disability: a disability-affirmative approach to sex therapy. In: Binik YM, Hall KSK, eds. *Principles and Practices of Sex Therapy* (5th ed). New York, NY: Guilford; 2014.
11. Ducharme S, Gill K. *Sexuality After Spinal Cord Injury: Answers to Your Questions.* Baltimore, MD: Paul Brookes Publishing Co; 1997: 7–8, 69–70, 82–90.

12. Ducharme S, Kewman D, Chase T, et al. *Sexuality and Reproductive Health in Adults with Spinal Cord Injury: A Clinical Practice Guideline for Health-care Professionals.* Washington, DC: Consortium for Spinal Cord Medicine, Paralyzed Veterans of America; 2010: 28–33.

13. Ducharme S. Sexuality and spinal cord injury. In: Nesathurai S, ed. *The Rehabilitation of People with Spinal Cord Injury: A House Officer's Guide* (2nd ed). Boston, MA: Artbuckle Academic Publishers; 2000: 83–89.

14. Elliott TR, Frank RG. Depression following spinal cord injury. *Arch Phys Med Rehabil.* 1996;77:816–823.

15. Ullrich P, Smith B, Blow F, Valenstein M, Weaver F. Depression, healthcare utilization and comorbid psychiatric disorders after spinal cord injury. *J Spinal Cord Med.* 2014;37:40–45.

16. Radnitz C, Schlein I, Walczak S, et al. The prevalence of post-traumatic stress disorder in Veterans with spinal cord injury. *SCI Psychol Proc.* 1995;8:145–149.

17. Cosgrove DJ, Gordon Z, Bernie JE, et al. Sexual dysfunction in combat Veterans with post-traumatic stress disorder. *Urology.* 2002;60:881–884.

18. Letourneau EJ, Schewe PA, Frueh BC. Preliminary evaluation of sexual problems in combat Veterans with PTSD. *J Trauma Stress.* 1997;10:125–132.

19. Tanielian T, Jaycox L, eds. *Invisible Wounds of War: Psychological and Cognitive Injuries, Their Consequences, and Services to Assist Recovery.* Santa Monica, CA: RAND Center for Military Health Policy Research; 2008.

20. Bray JR. Genitourinary trauma: a battle cry for integrated collaborative Veteran-centric care. *J Mens Health.* 2013;10:121–123.

21. Han JS, Edney MT, Gonzalez CM. Genitourinary trauma in the modern era of warfare. *J Mens Health.* 2013;10:124–129.

22. Mona LR, Cameron RP, Goldwaser G, Miller AR, Syme ML, Fraley SS. Prescription for pleasure: exploring sex positive approaches in women with spinal cord injury. *Top Spinal Cord Inj Rehabil.* 2009;15:15–29.

23. Masters WH, Johnson VE. *Human Sexual Response.* New York, NY: Little Brown and Company; 1966.

RETIRED MARINE CORPS SERGEANT BAREN BERG knows that second chances are possible. His high school wrestling career ended in disappointment, when he was ruled ineligible for competition after arriving at school too late in the semester to qualify. The reality of his career on the mat being over was harsh. He had been recruited by top college programs and was looking forward to the opportunity to participate in collegiate wrestling. This was no longer possible, so he left high school and received his GED shortly after.

Responding to the declaration of war in Iraq, Berg joined the US Marine Corps in 2003. After training, he found himself on the front lines of a historical battle with India Company, 3rd Battalion, 5th Marines. During the battle, Berg was rendered unconscious by an explosion. This incident was later declared the cause of his mild traumatic brain injury.

Upon returning home from the war, Berg was accepted as a full-time student at Penn State University and, before long, he walked right on to the wrestling team. Later that year, he won his first college match. Berg even received an award for Scholastic Athletic Achievement for making the dean's list while competing in Division 1 athletics. However, the elation of reaching these milestones was short lived. There was an ongoing war inside his head, and he found himself surrounded by problems with relationships and colleagues on campus. He tried self-medicating with alcohol, but soon found himself in real trouble with the law.

Berg's command leadership recognized his need for treatment. After a stint at the National Naval Medical Center in 2007, he enrolled at Clarion University looking for another chance.

On May 21, 2009, Berg graduated, wearing his Marine dress blue uniform as a symbolic gesture of respect. When the commencement keynote speaker posed the question, "How many of you plan on serving your country after graduation?," Berg slowly raised his white-gloved hand. Looking around, he realized he was the only one raising his hand. Slowly, a thunderous clap erupted throughout the building, and everyone rose to their feet while he remained sitting completely in shock. It was a beautiful close to that chapter in his life.

In 2011, Berg deployed once again to Helmand Providence, Afghanistan, as an E-5 Sergeant. While there, he trained, developed, and mentored Marines. Simultaneously, he earned a Master's degree in science. During his demobilization, an examination determined that he had sustained a mild traumatic brain injury during his first deployment. He was also diagnosed with posttraumatic stress disorder. Healthcare providers informed him that new technologies were available for treatment that had not been in place in 2007.

After leaving the Marine Corps in 2013, Berg was selected as a Presidential Management Fellow. His family then relocated to Washington, DC. Despite facing difficulty within the workplace due to a lack of accommodations, he authored reports and drafted solutions to help shape policies and strategies for other Veterans. Finally, in 2014, Berg started his own business (A Few Good Leaders) to help other Veterans through the recovery process.

Currently, Baren Berg is working as a consultant by helping other Veterans start their own businesses; is pursuing a PhD in Workforce Development at Penn State; and is a member of Penn State's Ability Athletes and Team Semper Fi for running, wrestling, and Brazilian jiu-jitsu.

If wounded, injured, or ill, we will seek out every available resource to restore Marines to health.

★ ★ ★

GENERAL JAMES F. AMOS
COMMANDANT OF THE MARINE CORPS

CHAPTER EIGHT

The Role of Sports and Recreation in Promoting Successful Reintegration

RORY A. COOPER, PhD*; MICHAEL MUSHETT, MS†; and THOMAS WILLIAMS, PhD‡

*Director and Senior Career Scientist, Human Engineering Research Laboratories, Rehabilitation Research and Development Service, US Department of Veterans Affairs, 6425 Penn Avenue, Pittsburgh, Pennsylvania 15206, and Distinguished Professor and FISA Foundation–Paralyzed Veterans of America Chair, Department of Rehabilitation Science and Technology, University of Pittsburgh, 6425 Penn Avenue, Suite 400, Pittsburgh, Pennsylvania 15206

†Executive Director, Turnstone Center for Children, 3320 North Clinton Street, Fort Wayne, Indiana 46805

‡Director, Senior Leader Development and Resiliency, US Army War College, 122 Forbes Avenue, Carlisle, Pennsylvania 17013

INTRODUCTION

We build the comprehensive physical, mental, emotional, and spiritual resiliency of our Soldiers, Civilians, and their Families to enable them to thrive personally and professionally.

GENERAL RAY ODIERNO
US ARMY, CHIEF OF STAFF

Sports and recreation are important components of military life and therefore can serve as an excellent modality in the rehabilitation and reintegration of Service Members and Veterans with disabilities.[1] They help emphasize a commitment to a team effort while effectively providing motivation, purpose, and emotional reward for remaining physically active, which is increasingly recognized as important for all of us. Sports and recreation can help to make Service Members and Veterans become more efficient, effective, and self-aware. This enhances their ability to perform as Service Members or to become successful Veterans in their communities. An holistic approach is required that includes physical, mental, and behavioral components to build resilience, maintain health through the benefits of physical activity, and maximize the likelihood of successful reintegration.[2] Military and Veteran healthcare providers and communities need to both understand and leverage the various military programs focused on enhancing resiliency to develop fitness, confidence, and resilience.[3] These programs include the mental, physical, and emotional readiness to confront the challenges of continuation on duty or to succeed as a Veteran in civilian communities.

This increased understanding of military resiliency programs raises the acceptability and likelihood for the success of an approach that then helps Service Members and Veterans gain greater self-awareness; achieve the ability to sustain themselves long-term; and find the most effective and efficient ways of living, learning, and reintegrating. Successful rehabilitation and reintegration involve learning about personal strengths and weaknesses, and channeling physical and mental strength to achieve goals. Rehabilitation and reintegration require learning to manage stamina and maintain motivation during periods of physical and mental stress. This helps to ensure that our approaches build on the mental and physical resiliency that our military service resiliency programs seek to promote.

Movement is essential to maintaining both physical and mental health. Furthermore, sports and recreation

- help to improve or maintain health,
- build communities, and
- change perceptions of disability and impairment.

Participating in sports and recreation early in the rehabilitation and reintegration process helps to build a healthy perception of self, improve self-confidence, and increase strength and stamina. Although many individuals have good intentions to stay active, participation in sports and recreational activities may positively influence the social cognitions to increase peer-motivated, leisure-time physical activity opportunities that move individuals from "intention" to "activity."[4] Many organizations and military communities provide a wide variety of opportunities for sports and recreation. Fortunately, nearly anyone can participate in some activity, and many activities can be performed with friends and family both with and without disabilities. Integrated activities also help to promote connections to other people with and without disabilities. Importantly, individuals often underestimate the positive impact that increased physical activity will have because they too often focus on the unpleasantness and/or difficulties that are associated with "getting started."[5] All of us need to focus some of our efforts onto three factors that have a significant impact on our physical and mental health:

1. attaining adequate sleep,
2. performing regular exercise, and
3. maintaining a healthy diet.

Given the importance of overall health and well-being, successful reintegration of wounded, injured, and ill Service Members and Veterans and their families is dependent on the Performance Triad of Sleep, Activity, and Nutrition that promotes successful rehabilitation, healthy behaviors, and informed decisions. Teaching Service Members and Veterans to incorporate healthy sleep, activity, and nutrition behaviors can help to optimize the performance of their bodies and brains. An important goal of performance in rehabilitation and reintegration involves focusing on developing more mentally and physically resilient spouses, parents, Service Members, and Veterans to help set the conditions for better decision-making, stronger relationships, and higher overall effectiveness in outcomes.[6]

A BRIEF HISTORY OF ADAPTIVE SPORTS IN REHABILITATION AND REINTEGRATION

The concept of adaptive sports and recreation as a component of rehabilitation dates back nearly 100 years. After the First World War, wounded Service Members began returning to their home countries.[7] At the same time, in many Western countries, a self-sufficiency movement was taking place. In the United States, this movement was in part stimulated by the rising costs of caring for Veterans of the American Civil War, because the US Congress had become concerned that Civil War pensions were consuming a growing portion of the federal budget.[7] Thus, people began to think that wounded, injured, and ill Veterans could return to productive roles in society if they were given the proper training and equipment.[8]

Walter Reed Army Medical Center (Washington, DC) was at the forefront of this movement. At Walter Reed, wounded Veterans were provided with a program of exercise and adaptive sports, which was the precursor to the physical therapy and physical medicine and rehabilitation programs that we use today.[9] To implement the program, the Army hired graduates of physical education programs, many of whom were women, who worked with Army physicians to adapt baseball, volleyball, and other sports for Veterans with disabilities. Often, physical education instructors participated in the sports alongside with or competed against the Veterans. Along with the sports and recreation programs, Wounded Warriors were required to learn to cook and clean for themselves, and repair their prosthetic devices. Self-sufficiency was equated with being manly and whole, and became the goal of rehabilitation.[10]

This model of rehabilitation became formalized during World War II; by this time, physical therapy, occupational therapy, and physical medicine and rehabilitation programs had become established. Sports, exercise, and learning to maintain one's equipment were standard, with two very important changes:[10]

1. there was greater emphasis placed on vocational rehabilitation, and
2. (because of the need for trained Soldiers) there was the opportunity to continue on active duty after being severely wounded and undergoing rehabilitation.

With the advent of new treatments and medications, Veterans with wounds such as spinal cord injuries showed an improved rate of survival and faced the challenge of determining if and how they could return to their homes and families.[11] The demands of new Veterans with disabilities—primarily Veterans with major limb amputations and spinal cord injuries—led to investment in assistive device research in the United States and other countries.[12]

In 1948, Sir Ludwig Guttman searched for a means to improve the fitness of wounded Veterans under his care while at the Stoke Mandeville Hospital in England.[13] He created competitions in various sports and included Veterans who used wheelchairs. His methods caught on in several other countries and led to the first international competition in 1952. As the competitions gained momentum, more countries joined and eventually the Paralympics was established. In 1989, the International Paralympic Committee was founded, which entered into a cooperative agreement with the International Olympic

Committee to share venues.[13] Today, the Paralympics provides a world-class showcase for people with disabilities around the world to exhibit their sporting prowess. Many of these world-class athletes are military Veterans.

In 1981, the US Department of Veterans Affairs (VA) created the National Veterans Wheelchair Games in part to celebrate the International Year of People with Disabilities, but also to use sports as a vehicle for rehabilitation and reintegration of wounded, injured, and ill Veterans.[14] Today, the National Veterans Wheelchair Games (NVWG) include Veterans from the United States, Puerto Rico, and Great Britain. It has become the world's largest annual wheelchair sporting event and is an integral part of the VA's rehabilitation and reintegration programs. Furthermore, the NVWG served as a model for public–private partnerships, and the Paralyzed Veterans of America cohost the games each year. In 1986, the VA partnered with the Disabled American Veterans to create the National Disabled Veterans Winter Sports Clinic that introduces wounded, injured, and ill Veterans to adaptive winter sports.[15] In 2010, the US Paralympics, the Department of Defense, and the VA—along with a number of corporate and not-for-profit partners—created the Warrior Games using the NVWG and Paralympics as models.[16] The Warrior Games use sporting competition teams from the Army, Navy/Coast Guard, Air Force, and Marine Corps to promote healthy activity, rehabilitation, and successful reintegration. All of these events are held annually, but are supported by year-round programs at local Veteran and military medical centers.

IMPORTANCE OF SPORTS AND RECREATION IN REHABILITATION AND REINTEGRATION

The primary goals of rehabilitation and reintegration are to restore as much function as possible and to learn compensatory strategies for lost functions or those yet to be restored. The military and the VA are at the forefront of advancing rehabilitation and reintegration, and they rely heavily on sports and recreation for this purpose. For civilians, insurance reimbursement restrictions for private rehabilitation centers has led to the focus being on learning basic skills that allow people to return home; and, if that fails, they allow people to be transferred to a long-term care facility. However, the military and VA target higher goals for wounded, injured, and ill Service Members and Veterans, with the ultimate goal of returning Service Members to duty or helping Veterans to become successful members of their communities. To attain either of these goals, physical and mental agility are important, and can be promoted through sports and recreation. For example, being able to walk with a prosthetic limb may be sufficient to return home, but more is required to return to duty or to become a fully contributing member of society. One would need to learn how to run and negotiate rough terrain using a prosthetic limb in order to return to duty, and one would need to learn to carry a child or to walk on a hiking trail to more fully participate in society.

Either of the aforementioned goals requires the completion of a series of smaller steps that, when added together, make significant progress. Sports and recreation can help to teach such practical skills as doing a "wheelie" in a wheelchair. The ability to do a "wheelie" is an important skill necessary for negotiating curbs and for progressing over uneven terrain. Sports and recreation also help those with disabilities to relearn teamwork and restore esprit de corps. At the Warrior Games, participants transform into athletes and develop a strengthened affinity for their respective branches of the military service. The sense of making a valuable contribution through participation in sports has a powerful effect on self-esteem and self-confidence.

BENEFITS OF SPORTS AND RECREATION FOR SUCCESSFUL REINTEGRATION

Without regular exercise, the body begins to lose strength and stamina, making it more susceptible to injury and illness.[17] Even within the Military community, there are many people who do not get sufficient exercise, and the problem is much worse among Veterans and the general population.[18] Obesity and overall poor health are a growing epidemic within the United States, and people with physical or cognitive impairments are at even greater risk.[19,20] Partially, this is due to a shortage of accessible facilities and the low availability of adaptive equipment. Fortunately, this is less of a problem for Veterans because the VA recognizes the need to promote health and fitness, and hence provides adaptive equipment.

Adaptive sports and recreation are important modalities in the rehabilitation of wounded, injured, and ill Veterans and Military personnel.[21] During the initial phases of rehabilitation, adaptive sports and recreation are used to rebuild strength and stamina due to deconditioning from inactivity. After prolonged bedrest or minimal activity, the body begins to become weaker, stiffer, and fatigue more easily. These are common barriers to successful rehabilitation and reintegration because most forms of assistive devices require energy for mobility and other activities. Cognitive impairments can lead to changes in balance, coordination, and stamina.[22] Therefore, an exercise routine that involves some aerobic activity, strength training, and flexibility training is important. Sports and recreational activities can serve to augment an exercise routine to build these attributes. Sports also have the added benefit of being fun, competitive, and can make exercise more enjoyable. Further, they can improve endurance, strength, flexibility, mental acuity, and coordination. Scientific studies have shown that sports and recreation are also effective at reducing the symptoms of depression.[23] Nearly all sports have been adapted for people with various disabilities; therefore, most rehabilitation programs for military and Veterans include a variety of sports and recreation opportunities to help people find something that they enjoy and in which they can participate when they return home to their communities. Events like the NVWG and the Warrior Games reflect this philosophy and, combined, offer nearly 15 different adaptive sports that are only a small subset of the possible activities.

Rebuilding a healthy self-image, learning confidence, and developing skill building are important outcomes that can be constructed through adaptive sports and recreation.[24] For example, wheelchair basketball is a great way for wheelchair users to

- build their mobility skills,
- learn balance,
- develop a sense of the position and movement of the chair in space, and
- learn to multitask by moving and dribbling or moving and shooting.

These skills translate directly into better mobility on crowded sidewalks or when crossing busy streets. Sitting volleyball helps to teach balance, coordination, and cooperation. Learned confidence helps us to take on new challenges and get closer to the goal of successful reintegration into the community. Integrated activities are also excellent for rehabilitation. At the National Disabled Veterans Winter Sports Clinic (NDVWSC), Veterans are matched with an instructor who has the training and skills that matches their particular needs. Together, they go out onto the ski slopes with other skiers, and this provides many benefits.

- Learning or relearning to ski builds strength, balance, agility, coordination, and self-confidence.
- It requires rapid integration of multiple skills and processes.
- The activity is fun, and the Veteran is participating in an activity along with other people of varying skill levels, as well as varying physical and mental abilities.
- Often, a day of skiing can achieve practical rehabilitation goals that cannot be achieved through weeks of clinical therapy.

Sports and recreation also help to build on existing relationships or increase the number of supportive relationships.[25] These relationships can be peer-to-peer, within families, or within a mixed group of people with and without impairments. Sports and recreation help to build unit cohesion and are a defining feature of the Military community. These relationships are essential for building social capital and overcoming physical and emotional barriers. They are also excellent learning opportunities. For example, during a wheelchair track meet, the elevators broke down and the athletes were stuck on some of the upper floors of the dormitory where they were staying. Many of the athletes had experienced similar circumstances before and began to descend the stairs in their wheelchairs using a handrail. Other athletes had never done this before and wondered how people were getting down the stairs in their wheelchairs. This situation provided an opportunity for the more experienced athletes to mentor the new wheelchair users and, eventually, everyone was able to get down the stairs.

Similarly, when watching a group learn to play wheelchair basketball, new players quickly learn that if their chairs tip over, they can roll onto their backs and call another player over to roll them back up, instead of crawling out and working to climb back into the chair (thus disrupting the game). Often, relationships established through sports and recreation activities last for years, or even a lifetime. These shared experiences help to form bonds and promote the health of participants. At the NVWG, teams participating in wheelchair rugby are established by having a group of officials assign players to teams: blue team, black team, red team, etc. The goal is to spread the players by skill level equally across all of the teams. Ideally, this results in each team having an equal number of outstanding players, good players, and novices.

Once assignments are made, each team meets and selects a captain, and then the tournament begins. Because the teams are relatively evenly matched, an interesting phenomenon occurs nearly every year: *the group that comes together as a team the fastest nearly always wins the tournament.* The key is to use all of the talents of the team and to support each other to win. If one ego dominates, more often than not the team will lose the tournament. Therefore, the concept of winning is as much about building functional relationships as it is about playing the game.

MAINTAINING HEALTHY EXERCISE HABITS OVER A LIFETIME

Rehabilitation and reintegration are lifetime processes. Although acute rehabilitation after becoming wounded, injured, or ill may take weeks to months, the follow-up often takes a lifetime because physical, sensory, and cognitive impairments are not static. As people age with a disability, there may be the need from time to time to make adjustments or even to undergo another rehabilitation stay. Therefore, it is important to maintain a routine of exercise across the life span. This is best accomplished by learning healthy sports and recreation habits and incorporating them into a daily routine. For most people, simply walking or propelling a wheelchair is insufficient exercise to remain healthy. As people age, they tend to lose

- stamina,
- strength, and
- flexibility.

Therefore, these three factors need to be incorporated into an exercise regimen that may include adaptive sports and recreation.

People with disabilities tend to be more sedentary than the general population and are at greater risk for the health-related risks of deconditioning. This can be excessively troubling for Veterans who use prosthetic limbs or wheelchairs as a source of mobility because these devices often require more energy for ambulation. For health maintenance, about 1 hour of activity per day with a heart rate elevated above 60% of maximum heart rate is a good rule to follow.[26] However, it is best to consult a physician before beginning or making a significant change in an exercise routine. A recreation therapist or physical therapist can be an excellent resource when planning an exercise routine or when learning adaptive sports.

Sports and recreation can reduce the risk of developing secondary conditions related to an impairment.[27] Common secondary conditions include joint injuries, skin breakdown, and neuropathies.[28] Often, a routine that includes building or maintaining strength improves or maintains cardiovascular fitness, and promotes muscle balance will help to mitigate the risk of developing a secondary condition that can exacerbate the impact of the original impairment.[29] When a person has a physical impairment, the person develops strategies using other muscles and joints to compensate for the deficit in another part of the body. This can lead to strain on these joint and limbs, resulting in pain and new injuries over time. To help prevent this from happening, it is important to maintain balance across the joints.

If the muscles on one side of the joint become notably stronger than the other side, the imbalance places strain and can result in injury. For example, wheelchair propulsion primarily uses the anterior muscles of the arms, chest, and shoulders. Subsequently, the posterior muscles in the arms, shoulder, and back may become weaker by comparison. This is often evident by a rounding of the shoulders forward. This muscle imbalance can lead to injury, often manifested when performing some other activity such as a transfer, where a tear may occur in one of the weaker muscles, tendons, or ligaments. Exercise also helps with blood flow to the limbs. As we age, our skin becomes less supple, and blood flow is reduced. Exercise can help to slow or reverse this process. Individuals who have scarring from burns or who use prosthetic limbs are at greater risk of skin breakdown as they age. Therefore, a nonweight-bearing exercise routine, such as swimming, may be helpful in promoting skin health.

Success leads to increased confidence and a greater willingness to set new goals. Moreover, a skewed perception of personal capabilities brought on by low self-esteem may be more limiting than a physical, sensory, or cognitive impairment. This is particularly important in Veterans and Service Members. Many persons who have served in the military put a high value on physical prowess and their ability to handle difficult and stressful situations. For this reason, Veterans with traumatic and acquired disabilities are at increased risk for decreased self-esteem due to alterations in self-perception related to traumatic and acquired disabilities. Adaptive sports, exercise, and recreation provide effective modes through which self-esteem can be enhanced by providing the individual with

- a meaningful mastery experience,
- positive interactions with others, and
- an improved perception of the physical self.[30]

There also seems to be a positive relationship between sports, exercise, and recreation and achieving educational and career goals.[31] This is likely due to regular participation in sports, exercise, and recreation, which promotes improved physical health and mental well-being. More colleges and universities are offering adaptive sports and recreation programs for their students with disabilities, in part because of the requirements of the Americans with Disabilities Act, but also because of the greater demand by students with disabilities for access to this important aspect of campus life. Sports and recreation are an important part of career advancement in some professions, where important social relationships are established on the golf course, tennis court, or even while walking or jogging. Sports and recreation are an integral part of the military culture and lifestyle.

PROVIDING SPORTS AND RECREATION OPPORTUNITIES: CREATING INCUSIVE ACTIVITIES

When a wounded, injured, or ill Service Member or Veteran returns to his or her Military or civilian community, it is important to have inclusive sports and recreation activities available and to ensure the widest possible participation by people of all abilities. When people have fun together participating in healthy activities, it builds supportive relationships that benefit the individual participants, as well as strengthens the community as a whole. Strong communities are communities in which everyone has a sense of belonging. This does not mean that everyone has to be alike or contribute in the same way, but it is important that the needs of all are considered. However, such strong, participatory communities are unfortunately currently not the norm in US society. It will take time and effort on everyone's part to transition communities (both Military and civilian) to offer more inclusive sports and recreation activities in which people of all ages and abilities can participate together in an array of programs.

The Army Ten-Miler and the Marine Corps Marathon are examples of inclusive activities that are important components of the military rehabilitation process. They promote full inclusion of the Military community to include the wounded, injured, and ill, as well as the civilian community. These events are often set as fitness goals for wounded, injured, and ill Service Members. They allow people to participate using necessary assistive devices (eg, wheelchairs, handcycles, prosthetic limbs, etc) and include events for people of wide age ranges and abilities. Military communities place great value on promoting health across the age span, and offer a wide variety of free and low-cost sports and recreation programs.

Integrated and team-building activities are important for forming cohesiveness of units and communities. For several decades, people with disabilities have been expanding the number of adaptations for sports and recreation, and nearly every form of sport or recreational activity can be modified to be accessible to people with a variety of impairments. There are some activities that lend themselves naturally to being inclusive. For example, sitting volleyball is a Paralympic sport for individuals with lower limb amputations or impairments; however, it can be a lot of fun when played as a unit or even when played as a community with games arranged for people with and without impairments. Further, little equipment beyond a gym floor, a net the height of that used in tennis, and a volleyball are needed. If wheelchairs are available, wheelchair basketball can also be a great activity for people of varying physical abilities. In some cases, equipment may already be available.

Many gyms are equipped with spinning cycles and arm ergometers that can be used together to create programs for people of all abilities.

Healthy communities promote the welfare of their members. The design of communities can help to promote activity among members, as well as healthy lifestyle habits. This can be accomplished by offering formal programming and assistance with more everyday conveniences that encourage people to incorporate more movement into their daily lives (eg, walkways to local facilities, bicycle paths, and local shopping opportunities). Low- or no-cost community facilities can also play an important role. Gyms, swimming pools, and ball fields can further encourage activity and health. The key is to create a culture that values participation in sports, exercise, and recreation as a natural part of daily living.[32] The military values these activities, but everyone must assume a role for them to become a core part of the community.

ORGANIZATIONS PROVIDING SPORTS AND RECREATION OPPORTUNITIES

The adaptive sports movement as we know it was founded as a rehabilitation and reintegration tool for wounded World War II Veterans. It provided rehabilitation, postrehabilitation, and reintegration support to Service Members who sustained physical and cognitive injuries.[13] Currently, Veterans with disabilities are introduced to adaptive sports during their rehabilitation and reintegration programs at military treatment facilities and subsequent engagement in sports at VA medical centers. Long-term participation takes place in an individual's home and in civilian or Military communities. Community-based providers of adaptive sports programs are the "hometown anchors" and catalysts for lifetime sporting opportunities. These program providers include the following:

- not-for-profit organizations,
- parks and recreation departments,
- military or Veteran service organizations,
- rehabilitation facilities, and
- colleges and universities.

Table 8-1 is a sampling of "best practice" program resources, but this list is by no means complete or comprehensive.

Table 8-1. *Program Resources*

Program	Web Site	Description
USA Paralympic Resource Network	findaclub. usparalympics.org	The USA Paralympic Resource Network is designed to connect individuals with disabilities, including Service Members and Veterans, to ongoing programs in their communities. The network links individuals with disabilities to community-based adaptive sport program providers. The site includes a national listing of programs that are searchable by state and zip code.
Veterans Administration Adaptive Sports Program—Advance Sports Club Finder	va.gov/ adaptivesports/ va_clubAdvanced Finder.asp	The Advance Sports Club Finder connects disabled Veterans and youth and adults with disabilities with community-based programs—such as the Paralympic Sports Clubs—that have been developed to provide sports programming and physical activity opportunities regardless of skill level. All programs and activities at these organizations are based in the community and are run by local organizations.
SportsAbilities	sportsabilities.com	SportsAbilities touts itself as "the premier resource for people with disabilities to find recreational, advocacy, support, and adaptive sporting activities in the nation." They list activity calendars for every state and 25 different activity categories ranging from team sports to social gatherings.
Paralyzed Veterans of America (PVA)	pva.org	PVA fights for the needs of spinal cord-injured Veterans and ensures that their members receive the quality care and benefits they have earned through their military service. The organization is also engaged in spinal cord research, public education and sports, and recreation. PVA is also co-presenter of the National Veterans Wheelchair Games, the largest annual wheelchair sport event in the world.
Team Semper Fi/ Semper Fi Fund	semperfifund.org	The idea for Team Semper Fi was inspired by the wounded Marines and Sailors who refused to let their challenges prevent them from competing in athletic events. The team is made up of military personnel who have overcome significant challenges in their service to our country and who have embraced the fighting athletic spirit of those on the road to recovery. The Semper Fi Fund provides coaches, specialized sporting equipment, entry fees, and travel expenses to athletic events. Team members are also given the opportunity to receive high-level training from former and current Olympic and Paralympic athletes through a partnership with US Paralympics.

TABLE 8-1. *Program Resources,* continued

Wounded Warrior Project	woundedwarrior project.org	Through partnerships with high-quality, specialized disabled sports providers, the Wounded Warrior Project delivers dynamic and engaging year-round sports and fitness programs to help injured Service Members gain confidence and independence while adapting to life after injury. With adaptive equipment and trained instructors, Warriors can participate in almost any sport or fitness activity, moving them beyond rehabilitation and toward a full and productive life. These programs are designed to encompass all areas of fitness and exercise, including nutrition and physical training, to build a healthy and fit lifestyle.
Disabled Sports USA	disabledsports usa.org	The mission of Disabled Sports USA is to provide national leadership and opportunities for individuals with disabilities to develop independence, confidence, and fitness through participation in community sports, recreation, and educational programs. Each year, Disabled Sports USA serves more than 60,000 youth, Wounded Warriors, and civilian adults through a nationwide network of more than 100 community-based chapters in 37 states in more than 40 different sports. Sports include alpine and nordic skiing, snowboarding, biathlon, kayaking, water skiing, sailing, scuba, surfing, rafting, outrigger canoeing, fishing, hiking, golf, athletics, archery, cycling, running/wheeling, rock climbing, equestrian, and others.
Wheelchair & Ambulatory Sports, USA (WASUSA)	adaptivesportsusa.org	The mission of WASUSA is to provide multisport and recreational opportunities for individuals with a disability by facilitating, advocating, and developing a national community-based outreach program; providing resources and education; conducting regional and national competitions; and providing access to international competitions in conjunction with the International Wheelchair & Amputee Sports Federation. WASUSA offers programs in archery, handcycling, powerlifting, shooting, swimming, table tennis, and track & field.

Table 8-1. *Program Resources*, continued

US Association of Blind Athletes (USABA)	usaba.org	USABA provides life-enriching sports opportunities for individuals with a visual impairment. A member of the US Olympic Committee, USABA provides athletic opportunities in various sports, including—but not limited to—track and field, nordic and alpine skiing, biathlon, judo, wrestling, swimming, tandem cycling, powerlifting, and goalball (a team sport for the blind and visually impaired).
BlazeSports America	blazesports.org	By cultivating local, state, national, and international strategic partnerships with like-minded organizations, BlazeSports America is advancing the equality, visibility, and human rights of people with physical disabilities through sport. The mission of BlazeSports America is to change the lives of children and adults with physical disabilities through sport. Operation Blaze offers a wide range of sports and activities for Veterans and active-duty Service Members with physical disabilities. These programs are offered free of charge and provide excellent year-round health, fitness, and social opportunities.
Challenged Athletes Foundation (CAF)	challengedathletes.org	It is the mission of the CAF to provide opportunities and support to people with physical disabilities so they can pursue active lifestyles through physical fitness and competitive athletics. Operation Rebound funds equipment, training, and travel expenses that can help injured troops and first responders to harness the healing power of sports. Sports clinics are held throughout the year at military medical centers and other locations in the community. Expert coaches and CAF elite athletes provide instruction and mentorship to introduce beginner athletes to a range of sports, including bicycling, handcycling, running, swimming, basketball, etc.

SUMMARY

A responsive and reliable healthcare system and community support system can positively and proactively improve reintegration and resilience. It can also influence the health of Service Members, Veterans, and their families. Approaches that focus on adaptive programs to enhance physical and mental resiliency are very familiar to our Veterans and their families. They can serve as great motivational foundations for their reintegration and overall well-being.

REFERENCES

1. East W. *A Historical Review and Analysis of Army Physical Readiness Training and Assessment.* Fort Leavenworth, KS: Combat Studies Institute Press; 2013: 2.
2. Shih RA, Meadows SO, Martin, MT. *Medical Fitness and Resilience: A Review of Relevant Constructs, Measures, and Links to Well-Being.* Santa Monica, CA: RAND; 2013: 5–8.
3. Jonas WB, O'Connor FG, Deuster P, et al. Why total force fitness? *Mil Med.* 2010;175:6–8.
4. Latimer-Cheung AE, Arbour-Nicitopoulos KP, Brawley LR, et al. Developing physical activity interventions for adults with spinal cord injury. Part 2: motivational counseling and peer-mediated interventions for people intending to be active. *Rehabil Psychol.* 2013;58:307–315.
5. Ruby MB, Dunn EW, Perrino A, Gillis R, Viel S. The invisible benefits of exercise. *Health Psychol.* 2011;30:67–74.
6. Stevenson JE, Kortte KB, Salorio CF, Rohe DE. Assessment in rehabilitation psychology. In: Geisinger KF, Bracken BA, Carlson JF, et al, eds. *APA Handbook of Testing and Assessment in Psychology, Vol 2: Testing and Assessment in Clinical and Counseling Psychology.* Washington, DC: American Psychological Association; 2013: 501–521.
7. Linker B. *War's Waste: Rehabilitation in World War I America.* Chicago, IL: University of Chicago Press; 2011.
8. Sabatier CJ. Education options. In: Ainspan ND, Penk WE, eds. *Returning Wars' Wounded, Injured, and Ill: A Reference Handbook.* Westport, CT: Praeger Security International; 2008: 139–159.
9. Eldar R, Jelic M. The association of rehabilitation and war. *Disabil Rehabil.* 2003;25:1019–1023.
10. Rusk HA. A world to care for. *Am J Phys Med Rehabil.* 1974;53:86.
11. Le CT, Price M. Survival from spinal cord injury. *J Chronic Dis.* 1982;35: 487–492.
12. Geiger RL. *Research and Relevant Knowledge: American Research Universities Since World War II.* New York, NY: Oxford University Press; 1993.
13. Steadward RD, Peterson CJ. *Paralympics: Where Heroes Come.* Edmonton, Ontario, Canada: One Shot Holdings; 1997.

14. Steadward R, Walsh C. Training and fitness programs for disabled athletes: past, present and future. In: Sherrill C, ed. *Sport and Disabled Athletes: The 1984 Olympic Scientific Congress Proceedings*. Champaign, IL: Human Kinetics; 1986: 9.

15. Laskowski ER. Snow skiing for the physically disabled. *Mayo Clin Proc.* 1991;66:160–172.

16. Goff M. Adapted sport programs for veterans with disabilities. *J Phys Educ Recreat Dance.* 2012;83:27–28.

17. Mastro J, Ahrens C, Statton N. Using role models to help celebrate paralympic sport. *J Phys Educ Recreat Dance.* 2012;83:28–30.

18. Nelson KM. The burden of obesity among a national probability sample of veterans. *J Gen Int Med.* 2006;21:915–919.

19. Dixon-Ibarra A, Horner-Johnson W. Disability status as an antecedent to chronic conditions: National Health Interview Survey, 2006–2012. *Prev Chronic Dis.* 2014;11:130251.

20. Hsieh K, Rimmer JH, Heller T. Obesity and associated risk factors in adults with intellectual disability. *J Intellect Disabil Res.* 2014;58:851–863.

21. Messinger SD. Sports, disability, and the reframing of the post-injury soldier. In: Warren N, Manderson L, eds. *Reframing Disability and Quality of Life: A Global Perspective*. New York, NY: Springer Science; 2013: 163–178.

22. Dault MC, Dugas C. Evaluation of a specific balance and coordination programme for individuals with a traumatic brain injury. *Brain Inj.* 2002;16:231–244.

23. Rimer J, Dwan K, Lawlor DA, et al. Exercise for depression. *Cochrane Database Syst Rev 7.* 2012;7:CD004366.

24. Sporner ML, Fitzgerald SG, Dicianno BE, et al. Psychosocial impact of participation in the National Veterans Wheelchair Games and Winter Sports Clinic. *Disabil Rehabil.* 2009;31:410–418.

25. Lundberg N, Bennett J, Smith S. Outcomes of adaptive sports and recreation participation among Veterans returning from combat with acquired disability. *Ther Recreat J.* 2011;45:105–120.

26. Huonker M, Schmid A, Schmidt-Trucksass A, Grathwohl D, Keul J. Size and blood flow of central and peripheral arteries in highly trained able-bodied and disabled athletes. *J Appl Physiol.* 2003;95:685–691.

27. Cooper RA. Wheelchair racing sports science: a review. *J Rehabil Res Dev.* 1990;27:295–312.

28. Webborn N, Willick S, Reeser JC. Injuries among disabled athletes during the 2002 Winter Paralympic Games. *Med Sci Sports Exerc.* 2006;38:811–815.

29. Marge M. Health promotion for persons with disabilities: moving beyond rehabilitation. *Am J Health Promot.* 1988;2:29–44.

30. Pensgaard AM, Sorensen M. Empowerment through the sport context: a model to guide research for individuals with disability. *Adapt Phys Act Q.* 2002;19:48–67.

31. Zabrinskie RB, Lundberg NR, Groff DG. Quality of life and identity: the benefits of community-based therapeutic recreation and adaptive sports program. *Ther Recreat J.* 2005;39:176.

32. Hargreaves J, ed. *Sport, Culture and Ideology*. London, UK: Routledge & Kegan Paul; 1982: 30–32.

Retired Army
National Guard
Sergeant Major
JoAnn Tresco
After combat, no one
is ever the same. When
JoAnn Tresco came home
from Iraq, her boss of
5 years—himself a war
Veteran—asked her, "What
happened to the smart
lady that used to run this
place? Don't you remember
anything?" Although only
1 year had passed since she had left the busy training center that she ran with
an iron hand, it seemed like 10 years had gone by when she returned.

"Trying to remember anything was like trudging through thick sand," said
JoAnn. "I changed." Her combat tour had sapped her of her vitality, trust,
and all of her zest for life she had been known for. Although she hoped that
it did not show, it did.

Back in Iraq, completely by accident, JoAnn had discovered salsa dancing.
She credits learning to salsa dance with having improved her life in the
midst of a war zone. Her unimproved base in Iraq had no MWR (Morale,
Welfare, and Recreation), no gym, and nothing to do. However, deploying
with a large Hispanic community had its benefits, and she soon realized that
dancing took her out of her wartime reality and moved her heart to a better
place.

"When I took someone's hand to dance, the synergy of our movement
connected me to another human being at a time and a place where
connections were nearly impossible," explained JoAnn. "When I salsa
danced in Iraq, I was able to forget the war, forget where I was, immerse
myself into the music, and, for a time, my heart was free." So, she
concluded, if dancing could help her in Iraq, maybe it could help her back

home as well. She soon began taking ballroom dance lessons.

"That began a partnership with dance that has saved my life." Working with her was dance instructor Jonathan Kopatz, an Airborne Ranger with the 82nd Airborne Division. He challenged JoAnn to move with grace and elegance; to trust him while dancing

figures that demanded that she put herself completely in his hands; to learn to instinctively follow his lead without hesitation; and to show emotion on her face and convey emotion with her arms that showed her vulnerability. Each of those things enabled JoAnn to relearn how to feel, to soften, to love, and to move.

"I discovered that the showcases that I danced in with Jon gave me different opportunities to use courage and presence as a beautiful woman," said JoAnn. "In the process, I began to extend my arms and body into delicate lines that soothed my soul."

Today, after retiring from the Pennsylvania Army National Guard after 34 years of service, JoAnn Tresco is the owner and operator of PA DanceSport

Ballroom (Hummelstown, PA), the very ballroom that gave her the gift of dance. After 12 years of operation, the owners of the ballroom offered JoAnn the opportunity to buy the business and continue to use her training and management skills to help others. As the owner, she continues to work with Jonathan Kopatz, Premier Instructor at the ballroom, to improve her dancing and to teach others to dance. She has now joined him as the newest member of the instructional staff and has defined the mission of the business as "enhancing lives through dance."

"Whenever I step onto a ballroom floor, I step into a safe space where I can feel and move without any pain or threat of attack. I leave whatever is troubling me behind. It doesn't follow me onto the floor. . . . When I begin to dance, the cry of my soul is to 'make my heart a better place.' Dance does just that."

Who wouldn't consider themselves fortunate
to stay in [the] . . . ranks and claim the title of a
United States Marine for even just one day.

★ ★ ★

GENERAL JOSEPH F. DUNFORD, JR.
MARINE CORPS BASE
WASHINGTON, DC
SEPTEMBER 24, 2015

CHAPTER NINE

Virtual Reality and Telemedicine to Support Reintegration and Health Maintenance

DEEPAN C. KAMARAJ, MD, MS*, and RORY A. COOPER, PhD†

*Research Associate, Human Engineering Research Laboratories, Rehabilitation Research and Development Service, US Department of Veterans Affairs, 6425 Penn Avenue, Pittsburgh, Pennsylvania 15206, and Graduate Student Researcher, Department of Rehabilitation Science and Technology, School of Health and Rehabilitation Sciences, University of Pittsburgh, 4028 Forbes Tower, Pittsburgh, Pennsylvania 15260

†Director and Senior Career Scientist, Human Engineering Research Laboratories, Rehabilitation Research and Development Service, US Department of Veterans Affairs, 6425 Penn Avenue, Pittsburgh, Pennsylvania 15206, and Distinguished Professor and FISA Foundation–Paralyzed Veterans of America Chair, Department of Rehabilitation Science and Technology, University of Pittsburgh, 6425 Penn Avenue, Suite 400, Pittsburgh, Pennsylvania 15206

INTRODUCTION

A virtual environment (VE) is a simulation of a real world that is generated through computer software and is experienced by the user through a human–machine interface.[1] This phenomenon of human–machine interaction that allows users to engage in different tasks in real time is referred to as virtual reality (VR).[2] A VR-based system is comprised of multiple hardware and software devices that work in unison to provide varying degrees of complexity and a sense of "presence" in the VE. Presence is conceptualized as the subjective perception that the virtual world is somewhat real,[3] meaning that "At some level and to some degree . . . objects, events, entities, and environments are perceived as if the technology was not involved in the experience."[3,4(p1)] In the real world, we gain knowledge about our environment directly through our senses—vision, hearing, touch, proprioception, and smell. By contrast, in the VR-based system, we use these same senses to obtain information about the VE through the human–machine interface.[1] This interface provides information specific to one or more senses, depending on the type of device used by a specific configuration of a VR-based system, which is then used to guide interactions of the participant within the VE.[1]

With the dawn of evidenced-based medicine, there is growing literature supporting the scientific rationale for the use of VR-based systems, specifically in the realm of rehabilitation. The applications of VR-based systems are thought to impact two key areas of rehabilitation—(1) motor learning in the context of musculoskeletal injuries or disorders[1]; and (2) exposure therapy in the context of mental illnesses, such as posttraumatic stress disorder (PTSD), anxiety disorders, and phobias.[3,5,6]

The three key concepts of motor learning include the following:

1.   repetition,
2.   feedback, and
3.   motivation.

They are affected by VR.[1] VR-based systems act as powerful tools to promote repetitive practice, provide feedback about performance, and supply motivation to endure practice.[1] In addition, there is strong evidence suggesting that motor skills learned in the VE transcend and improve real-world performance of similar tasks.[7–9] Similarly, VR exposure therapy (VRET) facilitates emotional engagement of patients with PTSD (or other phobic disorders) during exposures to the multiple sensory stimuli in the VE.[10] The presence provided by a VE facilitates the emotional processing of memories related to a similar life event[10] (eg, a traumatic situation that happens to many Veterans). By allowing gradual exposure to these feared environments or traumatic life events—according to the needs of each patient—VR can be used in situations that are difficult to control or that are unpredictable, which could put the patient at risk if the exposures were performed in a real situation.[3]

The advent of better design and the increasing availability of sustainable and reliable technology have made VR-based therapy regimens much more readily available and advantageous in comparison to standard therapy.[1,2,11–14]

The ability of VR and gaming-based technology to provide different interactive environments that can be progressively challenging, considering the user's capacity to perform a task, has been utilized to address the same underlying deficit over time. This feature—combined with the ability to monitor users' performance—has proven to be a vital adjunct to the evidence-based, real-world rehabilitation regimen.[15,16] Virtual worlds also provide a controlled setting in which users can confidently perform tasks or movements that may compromise safety in the real world,[17] thus enabling activities that may not otherwise be attempted.[15,16] Although resources (time, space, and money) become a challenge to replicate a variety of environmental conditions required to perform tasks in the real world, a VR-based system can be easily modified to accommodate the needs of the individual through adjusting the user interface. In addition, VR-based systems enable the manipulation of multiple forms of sensory feedback (visual, auditory, and force) to enhance the learning experience or to focus attention on particular aspects of task performance to more closely reflect the user's goals in the real world.[15,16]

Although VR-based systems simulating a presence within an environment can be advantageous when inducing learning behavior, they can also potentially induce *cybersickness* (a constellation of motion sickness-like symptoms) among users.[1] Common symptoms of cybersickness include the following:

- nausea,
- vomiting,
- headache,
- somnolence,
- loss of balance, and
- altered eye–hand coordination.[1]

However, it is essential to note that, with newer equipment and better technology, the incidence of cybersickness has greatly decreased. In spite of this decrease in incidence, the effects of different VR systems on various patient populations to potentially induce cybersickness are still widely questioned and studied to understand and design better VR-based systems.[18,19]

These VR systems offer interactive and engaging platforms that increase user motivation for and participation in therapy. VR- and gaming-based technologies (Figure 9-1) have a vast array of applications in rehabilitation and have contributed significantly to the

- treatment of movement disorders,
- musculoskeletal injuries,

FIGURE 9-1. *Virtual reality systems can be used for computer-based gaming.*

- visual impairments,
- cognitive deficits,
- dizziness,
- phobias, and
- pain.[16]

This chapter provides an overview of some of these applications and lists a few resources that provide more information for anyone who might be interested in pursuing VR-based therapy.

VIRTUAL REALITY IN MENTAL HEALTH

VR is an effective tool for delivering exposure therapy to a wide range of mental health conditions, specifically phobias and anxiety disorders (eg, PTSD).[6,20] The *Diagnostic and Statistical Manual of Mental Disorders*, Fourth Edition, characterizes PTSD as causing high-frequency, distressing, intrusive memories, and amnesia about the details of an event.[21] PTSD involves a constant feeling of fear generated by inadequate consolidation of the autobiographical trauma memory.[10,22] To attain adequate processing of the traumatic memory and the consequent extinction of the fear, the memory must be activated, and safe components must be inserted. Prolonged exposure therapy, proven to be highly efficacious in the treatment of PTSD, aims to access the traumatic memory, including information about the traumatic situation and related emotions, thoughts, and behaviors.[10,23,24] This helps the patient to understand the context of the traumatic experience, as well as its impact in the patient's life. The therapy also enables the patient to achieve a realistic perspective about the traumatic event and its aftermath.[10,25] Despite the fact that imaginal exposure therapy stimulates emotional engagement, some patients find it difficult to immerse themselves in the traumatic scene and, therefore, may quit treatment. In some case studies, dropout and nonresponse rates may reach 50%.[10,25] These setbacks lead researchers to explore newer ventures and opportunities to treat PTSD.

In 2001, Rothbaum et al[26] reported that VRET could be used for Vietnam Veterans with PTSD. In a multicase report published in 2007, Beck et al[3] demonstrated that VRET could be used effectively in treating motor vehicle accident-related PTSD. In the same year, a quasiexperimental waitlist-controlled study of survivors of the 9/11 World Trade Center attack showed that VR is an effective treatment tool for enhancing exposure therapy for both civilians and disaster workers with PTSD. VR may be especially useful to those patients who cannot engage in imaginal exposure therapy.[27] Case studies have been reported indicating that clinical outcomes for VR exposure with individual Veterans[28] and active duty Soldiers[29] have been very positive. In 2011, Reger et al[6]—in a study of 24 active duty Soldier participants—found that 62% of patients reported a reliable change of 11 points or more in comparison to their pretreated, self-reported symptoms on the PTSD Checklist–Military Version.

The success of these studies prompted researchers to utilize VR-based therapy in combination with other resources (eg, telehealth). Stetz et al[30] studied the usefulness of VR technology in a sample of medics ($n = 60$). This study examined the emotional levels of participants in one of three groups:

1. saving a virtual patient (*VR group*),
2. practicing relaxation techniques only (*coping or CT [coping training] group*), or
3. participating in a group that practiced relaxation techniques while attempting to save the patient (*CT/VR group*).

The VR group showed higher levels of hostility than the rest of the groups, suggesting an effective immersion and thus greater inoculation potential due to interaction with the VR world. The following year, the same researchers demonstrated that many individuals who practiced relaxation via VR scenarios would continue to practice after the conclusion of the study, which suggests participant buy-in.[30]

There is growing supportive evidence to demonstrate that VR-based therapy is effective in treating mental illness. Functional magnetic resonance imaging helps researchers to better understand the neurological pathways involved in PTSD. With functional magnetic resonance imaging, measured activation of the amygdala, prefrontal cortex, and anterior cingulate gyrus following exposure therapy for PTSD showed significant improvement (or normalization), and such evidence is continuing to grow.[31]

VIRTUAL REALITY IN PHYSICAL HEALTH AND REHABILITATION

NEUROMUSCULAR REHABILITATION

VR for neuromuscular rehabilitation has been studied extensively among able-bodied individuals and among people with specific conditions, such as amputations, traumatic brain injury, and vestibular dysfunction. VR has two broad groups of applications in the realm of neuromuscular rehabilitation:

1. *VR aids in the study of biomechanical parameters that assist with identifying and studying injury prevention strategies.* With increasing availability of complex VR-based simulators, such as the Computer-Assisted Rehabilitation ENvironment (CAREN),[32] studying the biomechanics of human movement and motion has soared to new heights (Figure 9-2). Beltran et al[33] used CAREN to study the margins of stability among individuals with transtibial amputations. They concluded that, based on the mean margin of stability, unilateral transtibial amputation was shown to have affected lateral walking stability during platform perturbations.[33] Similarly, Beurskens et al[34] studied the dynamic stability of individuals with transtibial amputation walking in destabilizing environments. They demonstrated that, in the absence of other comorbidities, patients with unilateral transtibial amputation appear to retain sufficient sensory and motor functions to maintain overall upper body stability during walking, even when substantially challenged.[34]

2. *VR has been useful in providing a training platform to deliver motor rehabilitation that promotes such injury prevention strategies in addition*

FIGURE 9-2. *The Computer-Assisted Rehabilitation ENvironment (CAREN) system in use.*

to strength training regimen. For example, Park et al[35] conducted a study to determine the effect of VR-based exercise using the Nintendo Wii Fit (Kyoto, Japan) on the muscle activities of the trunk and lower extremities of normal adults. Participants of the study were 24 normal adults who were divided into a VR exercise group (VREG; $n = 12$) and a stable surface exercise group (SEG; $n = 12$). The exercises of the VREG using the Nintendo Wii Fit and the SEG using a stable surface were conducted three times a week for 6 weeks. Electromyography was used to measure the activity of the following muscles:

- tibialis anterior (TA),
- medial gastrocnemius (MG),
- erector spinae, and
- rectus abdominis.

VREG showed significant within-group differences in TA and MG muscle activities, whereas the SEG showed a significant difference in the muscle activity of the MG. VR exercise using the Nintendo Wii Fit was an effective intervention for the muscle activities of the TA and MG in normal adults.[35]

DRIVING REHABILITATION

Driving is an activity that most people identify as being an important part of their lives. For many people, driving is essential to maintain functional independence. Cognitive deficits, motor impairments, and visual changes have all been linked to poor driving. Consequently, there are numerous clinical conditions that could negatively affect driving skills. Increasingly, rehabilitation physicians are asked to make difficult decisions about the driving safety of their patients, but there are no well-established guidelines for determining when a patient should relinquish or reinstate his/her driver's license.

The gold standard for assessing driving ability is an on-road assessment. However, there are a number of potential problems with this method of evaluation. In addition to the issue of safety, such evaluations can also be costly, stressful, and time-consuming. Furthermore, for safety and practical reasons, road tests do not always allow assessors to evaluate driving ability in challenging driving conditions (eg, in heavy traffic, at night, or in various types of weather). Road tests infrequently allow for the observation of critical, but low-frequency, events (eg, collision avoidance or a pedestrian in the road). Although neuropsychological test performance can predict driving ability, it has been recommended that neuropsychological assessments not be used in isolation when determining driving safety because they assess only some components of the underpinnings of successful driving. Driving simulators seem to offer a promising alternative (or addition) to the previously described methods of driving assessment.[36]

It is important to note that simulators have certain input/output parameters, and it is essential for users and clinicians to be familiar with these parameters to understand completely the effect that they have on the Veteran using the system. Driver input parameters (eg, how the driver interacts with the vehicle) reflect the decision-making skills of the person operating the simulator. In addition to driver input variables, it is also common to use vehicle output as an outcome parameter of driving simulators.[36]

Even with an established and standardized set of parameters to evaluate this population, additional sources of information may be useful to make a big-picture determination about the ability to drive safely. Brief screening of motor functioning (eg, strength and reaction time) and visual acuity are also recommended to identify sensory impairments that might negatively impact driving safety. Detection of unsafe drivers may be improved when neuropsychological assessment is used in conjunction with the simulated driving evaluation.

Mobility Rehabilitation

Similar to the applications of VR to improve car driving performance, power wheelchair driving simulators have made significant advancements in recent years to help Veterans learn electric-powered wheelchair driving. To assist people with disabilities in increasing their mobility, a great variety of mobility-supporting devices are available (eg, walking sticks and manual wheelchairs). Powered-mobility devices (eg, electric-powered wheelchairs and electric-powered scooters, discussed in Chapter 3, The Promise of the Future: Assistive Technology, Transportation, and Emerging Technologies) are increasingly seen in daily practice. Training is required for (elderly) people to use these (powered) devices safely and to maintain the required physical condition to participate in daily life. Such training, however, is expensive in terms of human resources, and can potentially be unsafe for both the drivers and their instructors.[37] According to Desbonnet et al,[38] a poorly controlled electric-powered wheelchair can cause severe damage to the furniture at home or injure other persons. They also stated that a large practice area is required when training a person—with a minimum risk of collision injury—how to control an electric-powered wheelchair. VR is an emerging technology that can possibly address the problems encountered in training (elderly) people to handle a mobility device.[36,39–42] Recent work has shown promising results in using such technology for clinical applications and in home use.[43,44] Furthermore, VR could be used as a tool to deliver other tested neurocognitive training modalities that have been known to improve mobility and driving as well.

Advanced VR simulators have also been instrumental in the design and development of newer technology, such as robotic wheelchairs and prosthetic devices. Candiotti et al[43] developed an alternative wheel-legged robotic wheelchair—the Mobility Enhancement RoBot (MeBot)—to address limitations commonly noted among current electric-powered wheelchair designs and to provide better maneuverability in outdoor terrains.[43] MeBot is a novel, electric-powered wheelchair that utilizes a dual system of electric and pneumatic actuators to maintain the seat orientation, which is aimed to reduce the risk of tips and falls. They used the CAREN system to simulate real-world outdoor driving terrains and to demonstrate that the seat orientation controller in MeBot maintained its orientation when driving up and down hills (*pitch angle*) or across slopes (*roll angle*).[43] Similarly, CAREN has also been used either in design and testing of newer prosthetic devices or novel prosthetic simulators that aid along with the design process.[44]

Obesity/Diabetes

Today's epidemic of obesity and diabetes poses challenges to healthcare similar to those facing Soldiers who return with postdeployment mental health issues. These include geographic barriers, social stigma, and the need for behavioral change. Researchers at the University of Southern California's Institute for Creative Technologies (Los Angeles, CA) are adapting their extensive experience with technological solutions into training and techniques that can aid Veterans in need. These techniques show promise for concerns in the growing crisis of *diabesity* (diabetes + obesity). VR has already demonstrated itself as an impactful treatment method for several behavioral and mental health domains. Virtual worlds—the successor technology of original VR—not only inherit many of their predecessor's strengths, but also present the new affordances of accessibility, social connectivity, and avatar usage that pave the way toward future treatment options on a broader scale.[38]

Healthcare Information and Support

People with intellectual disabilities have poor access to healthcare, which may be further compromised by a lack of accessible health information. To be effective, health information must be easily understood and remembered. People with intellectual disabilities learn better from multimodal information sources, and VR offers a three-dimensional, computer-generated environment that can be used for providing information and learning. Rizzo et al[46,47] describe the virtual revolution in the use of VR simulation technology for clinical purposes over the last 15 years. A major movement in clinical VR accompanied by the "birth" of intelligent virtual humans is seen as being the natural consequence of shifts in the social and scientific landscapes. The availability of highly interactive, artificially intelligent, and natural language-capable virtual human agents has resulted in the appearance of seminal research and development in this realm.[45] These virtual human beings can be engineered to interact with the real world in a way that is human-like, in that they can exist in a three-dimensional virtual world, speak to real users, and display reactions that are emotional and akin to human.[46]

People with disabilities also have to contend with deterioration in their health and medical status, putting further burdens on the adaptive resources essential for preserving functional independence and quality of life. The gradual curtailment of functional independence and increased reliance on external factors for transportation can also jeopardize one's access to medical and rehabilitation care. A variety of factors—including economic hardships, medication side effects, loss of caregiving family members, psychosocial disorders, etc—can exacerbate existing challenges. With average life spans in industrialized societies on the rise, these challenges have led to a crisis in care for people with disabilities. Rizzo et al[46] point to evidence that functional motor capacity can be preserved, recovered, or maintained through consistent participation in a motor exercise and rehabilitation regimen. However, outside of the clinical context, independent adherence to such programming is extremely low.[47] To enhance, maintain, and rehabilitate sensorimotor processes essential to enhance quality of life and preserve independence, it is vital to address the needs of the population of those aging with disabilities. Development and promotion of home-based access to low-cost, interactive VR systems to engage and motivate recipients to participate in game-driven physical activities and rehabilitation programming are crucial steps undertaken by the scientific research community to promote better quality of life among Veterans with disabilties.[47]

SUMMARY

Over the past 3 decades, VR and gaming-based technology have made tremendous strides due to significant advancements from the entertainment sector. Recent studies have begun to demonstrate the viable clinical applications of such technology, and shed light on the future that awaits the use of devices that utilize such technology in clinics, particularly in rural and remote settings where accessibility to healthcare has been restricted. This chapter provides a brief overview of such technology and discusses few clinical applications that have demonstrated viable applications of such VR technology.

REFERENCES
1. Holden MK. Virtual environments for motor rehabilitation: review. *Cyberpsychol Behav.* 2005;8(3):187–211. Discussion 2-9.
2. Imam B, Jarus T. Virtual reality rehabilitation from social cognitive and motor learning theoretical perspectives in stroke population. *Rehabil Res Pract.* 2014;2014:594540.
3. Beck JG, Palyo SA, Winer EH, Schwagler BE, Ang EJ. Virtual reality exposure therapy for PTSD symptoms after a road accident: an uncontrolled case series. *Behav Ther.* 2007;38(1):39–48.
4. International Society for Presence Research. ISPR website. The concept of presence: explication statement, 2000. https://ispr.info/about-presence-2/about-presence/.
5. Gregg L, Tarrier N. Virtual reality in mental health: a review of the literature. *Social Psychiatry Psychiatr Epidemiol.* 2007;42(5):343–354.

6. Reger GM, Holloway KM, Candy C, et al. Effectiveness of virtual reality exposure therapy for active duty soldiers in a military mental health clinic. *J Trauma Stress.* 2011;24(1):93–96.

7. Cooper RA, Spaeth DM, Jones DK, Boninger ML, Fitzgerald SG, Guo S. Comparison of virtual and real electric powered wheelchair driving using a position sensing joystick and an isometric joystick. *Med Eng Phys.* 2002;24(10):703–708.

8. Rose FD, Attree EA, Brooks BM, Parslow DM, Penn PR, Ambihaipahan N. Training in virtual environments: transfer to real world tasks and equivalence to real task training. *Ergonomics.* 2000;43(4):494–511.

9. Webster JS, McFarland PT, Rapport LJ, Morrill B, Roades LA, Abadee PS. Computer-assisted training for improving wheelchair mobility in unilateral neglect patients. *Arch Phys Med Rehabil.* 2001;82(6):769–775.

10. Goncalves R, Pedrozo AL, Coutinho ES, Figueira I, Ventura P. Efficacy of virtual reality exposure therapy in the treatment of PTSD: a systematic review. *PLoS One.* 2012;7(12):e48469.

11. Barrera TL, Mott JM, Hofstein RF, Teng EJ. A meta-analytic review of exposure in group cognitive behavioral therapy for posttraumatic stress disorder. *Clin Psychol Rev.* 2013;33(1):24–32.

12. Cho GH, Hwangbo G, Shin HS. The effects of virtual reality-based balance training on balance of the elderly. *J Phys Ther Sci.* 2014;26(4):615–617.

13. Jordan K, Sampson M, King M. Gravity-supported exercise with computer gaming improves arm function in chronic stroke. *Arch Phys Med Rehabil.* 2014;95(8):1484–1489.

14. Mirelman A, Patritti BL, Bonato P, Deutsch JE. Effects of virtual reality training on gait biomechanics of individuals post-stroke. *Gait Posture.* 2010;31(4):433–437.

15. Lewis GN, Rosie JA. Virtual reality games for movement rehabilitation in neurological conditions: how do we meet the needs and expectations of the users? *Disabil Rehabil.* 2012;34(22):1880–1886.

16. Lewis GN, Woods C, Rosie JA, McPherson KM. Virtual reality games for rehabilitation of people with stroke: perspectives from the users. *Disabil Rehabil Assist Technol.* 2011;6(5):453–463.

17. Miller S, Reid D. Doing play: competency, control, and expression. *Cyberpsychol Behav.* 2003;6(6):623–632.

18. Kiryu T, So RH. Sensation of presence and cybersickness in applications of virtual reality for advanced rehabilitation. *J Neuroeng Rehabil.* 2007;4:34.

19. Liu CL. A neuro-fuzzy warning system for combating cybersickness in the elderly caused by the virtual environment on a TFT-LCD. *Appl Ergonom.* 2009;40(3):316–324.

20. Parsons TD, Rizzo AA. Affective outcomes of virtual reality exposure therapy for anxiety and specific phobias: a meta-analysis. *J Behav Ther Exp Psychiatry.* 2008;39(3):250–261.

21. American Psychiatric Association. *Diagnostic and Statistical Manual of Mental Disorders (DSM-IV-TR)*. Arlington, VA: American Psychiatric Association; 2013.
22. Brewin CR, Dalgleish T, Joseph S. A dual representation theory of posttraumatic stress disorder. *Psychol Rev*. 1996;103(4):670–686.
23. Brewin CR, Holmes EA. Psychological theories of posttraumatic stress disorder. *Clin Psychol Rev*. 2003;23(3):339–376.
24. Foa EB, Kozak MJ. Emotional processing of fear: exposure to corrective information. *Psychol Bull*. 1986;99(1):20–35.
25. Schottenbauer MA, Glass CR, Arnkoff DB, Tendick V, Gray SH. Nonresponse and dropout rates in outcome studies on PTSD: review and methodological considerations. *Psychiatry*. 2008;71(2):134–168.
26. Rothbaum BO, Hodges LF, Ready D, Graap K, Alarcon RD. Virtual reality exposure therapy for Vietnam veterans with posttraumatic stress disorder. *J Clin Psychiatry*. 2001;62(8):617–622.
27. Difede J, Cukor J, Jayasinghe N, et al. Virtual reality exposure therapy for the treatment of posttraumatic stress disorder following September 11, 2001. *J Clin Psychiatry*. 2007;68(11):1639–1647.
28. Gerardi M, Rothbaum BO, Ressler K, Heekin M, Rizzo A. Virtual reality exposure therapy using a virtual Iraq: case report. *J Trauma Stress*. 2008;21(2):209–213.
29. Reger GM, Gahm GA. Virtual reality exposure therapy for active duty soldiers. *J Clin Psychol*. 2008;64(8):940–946.
30. Stetz MC, Folen RA, Yamanuha BK. Technology complementing military behavioral health efforts at Tripler Army Medical Center. *J Clin Psychol Med Settings*. 2011;18(2):188–195.
31. Roy MJ, Costanzo ME, Blair JR, Rizzo AA. Compelling evidence that exposure therapy for PTSD normalizes brain function. *Stud Health Technol Inform*. 2014;199:61–65.
32. Isaacson BM, Swanson TM, Pasquina PF. The use of a Computer-Assisted Rehabilitation Environment (CAREN) for enhancing wounded warrior rehabilitation regimens. *J Spinal Cord Med*. 2013;36(4):296–299.
33. Beltran EJ, Dingwell JB, Wilken JM. Margins of stability in young adults with traumatic transtibial amputation walking in destabilizing environments. *J Biomech*. 2014;47(5):1138–1143.
34. Beurskens R, Wilken JM, Dingwell JB. Dynamic stability of individuals with transtibial amputation walking in destabilizing environments. *J Biomech*. 2014;47(7):1675–1681.
35. Park J, Lee D, Lee S. Effect of virtual reality exercise using the Nintendo Wii Fit on muscle activities of the trunk and lower extremities of normal adults. *J Phys Ther Sci*. 2014;26(2):271–273.
36. Kraft M, Amick MM, Barth JT, French LM, Lew HL. A review of driving simulator parameters relevant to the Operation Enduring Freedom/Operation Iraqi Freedom veteran population. *Am J Phys Med Rehabil*. 2010;89(4):336–344.

37. Harrison A, Derwent G, Enticknap A, Rose FD, Attree EA. The role of virtual reality technology in the assessment and training of inexperienced powered wheelchair users. *Disabil Rehabil.* 2002;24(11–12):599–606.

38. Desbonnet M, Cox SL, Rahman A. Development and evaluation of a virtual reality based training system for disabled children. *Proceedings of the European Conference on Disability: Virtual Reality and Associated Technologies 1998: ECDVRAT '98, September 10–11, 1998, Skovde, Sweden.*

39. Kamaraj DC, Dicianno BE, Schmid M, Boyanoski T, Cooper RA. Quantitative assessment of power mobility driving skills. *Proceedings of the Rehabilitation Engineering and Technology Society of North America (RESNA) Conference, June 11, 2014, Indianapolis, IN.*

40. Kamaraj DC, Dicianno B, Youk A, Mahajan HP, Cooper R. Perceived workload between experienced and novice power wheelchair users while using a wheelchair driving simulator. *Arch Phys Med Rehabil.* 2015;96(10):e60–e61.

41. Mahajan HP, Dicianno BE, Cooper RA, Ding D. Assessment of wheelchair driving performance in a virtual reality-based simulator. *J Spinal Cord Med.* 2013;36(4):322–332.

42. Spaeth DM, Mahajan H, Karmarkar A, Collins D, Cooper RA, Boninger ML. Development of a wheelchair virtual driving environment: trials with subjects with traumatic brain injury. *Arch Phys Med Rehabil.* 2008;89(5):996–1003.

43. Candiotti J, Wang H, Chung C-S, et al. Design and evaluation of a seat orientation controller during uneven terrain driving. *Med Eng Phys.* 2016;38:241–247.

44. Ramakrishnan T. *Asymmetric Unilateral Transfemoral Prosthetic Simulator* [dissertation]. Tampa, FL: Department of Mechanical Engineering, University of South Florida; 2014. http://scholarcommons.usf.edu/etd/5111/. Accessed July 7, 2016.

45. Hall V, Conboy-Hill S, Taylor D. Using virtual reality to provide health care information to people with intellectual disabilities: acceptability, usability, and potential utility. *J Med Internet Res.* 2011;13(4):E91.

46. Rizzo AA, Lange B, Buckwalter JG, et al. An intelligent virtual human system for providing healthcare information and support. *Stud Health Technol Inform.* 2011;163:503–509.

47. Rizzo A, Requejo P, Winstein CJ, et al. Virtual reality applications for addressing the needs of those aging with disability. *Stud Health Technol Inform.* 2011;163:510–516.

STAFF SERGEANT
AMBER BLANTON,
PENNSYLVANIA ARMY
NATIONAL GUARD
Sunday, December 12,
2004, is a day Staff Sergeant
Blanton will never forget.
At the time, she was
stationed in Afghanistan
at the Kandahar Airfield,
where she worked as a
Paralegal Specialist for the
25th Infantry Division.
She had already experienced rockets and mortars being shot into the base.
Amber had been in the country for 7 months. It was not unusual for officers
or noncommissioned officers to wake her in the middle of the night and ask
questions about the rules of engagement.

But what was different about the night that would forever change her life
is that when she was summoned to the Tactical Operations Center, she was
told to report immediately. She was told to leave her PT (physical training)
uniform on and dispense with putting on her DCUs (desert camouflage
uniform) as she normally did. When she arrived at the Tactical Operations
Center, her battle buddy (another female) was sitting outside the Commander's Office weeping. "When I saw her crying so hard outside that
office, I was afraid that something had happened to her husband because
they had gotten married right before we deployed," Amber remembers
vividly.

"The CO (Commanding Officer) called me in, and he was crying too,"
Amber states with a note of disbelief. "Jeff's been shot," he said. "What?"
I asked. "I just talked to him on Friday. He was finally cleared to RTD
(return to duty) after the last time he was shot."

Amber's husband, a Lance Corporal in the US Marine Corps, had been
deployed to Iraq after his wife shipped out for Afghanistan. He had been
wounded after he had been in the country for a couple of months. The

wound was serious enough that he was hospitalized for a month before he was allowed to RTD.

"You don't understand," said the CO. "Your husband is dead. He was killed in action during a house-clearing raid. He was the first man in a stack, going up a set of stairs when an enemy combatant shot him multiple times before the Marines could return fire. I'm sorry." Later, SSG Blanton, who just turned 21, would learn that her husband had traded places so that another Marine could have a break. "I'm very proud of him," she says with a glowing smile. "He was very brave."

The whirlwind that followed was a blur. SSG Blanton met her husband's parents for the first time at his funeral. They disagreed about some of the choices she was making for her husband's memorial. They fought one another and the Army, but the young widow persevered.

After the funeral, things began to spin out of control. While she was able to keep her military life squared away, things in her personal life began to unravel. She made choices that were not a part of who she is, ultimately resulting in an unplanned pregnancy. Nine months later, she gave birth to a handsome son.

Now, the combat Veteran, widow, and single mother has found peace. Through counseling and strengthening her faith, SSG Blanton has discovered who she is and what she was meant to do. Her circumstances have led her to stay in the military and mentor young Soldiers, as well as try to be an example of what true resilience looks like.

Our collective strength depends on our people —
their mental and physical resilience is at our core. . . .
We must always treat each other with respect and lead with
integrity. Our soldiers are the crown jewels of the Nation;
we must love them, protect them, and
always keep faith with them.

★ ★ ★

GENERAL MARK A. MILEY
39TH CHIEF OF STAFF OF THE ARMY
AUGUST 28, 2015

Chapter Ten

Community/Peer
Support and Services

AL CONDELUCI, PhD*; RORY A. COOPER, PhD†;
MELVA GOODEN-LEDBETTER, MS‡; and D. JOSHUA MARINO, MS§

*Chief Executive Officer, Community Living and Support Services, 1400 South Braddock Avenue, Pittsburgh, Pennsylvania 15218, and Adjunct Professor, Department of Rehabilitation Sciences and Technology, University of Pittsburgh, 4028 Forbes Tower, Pittsburgh, Pennsylvania 15260

†Director and Senior Career Scientist, Human Engineering Research Laboratories, Rehabilitation Research and Development Service, US Department of Veterans Affairs, 6425 Penn Avenue, Pittsburgh, Pennsylvania 15206, and Distinguished Professor and FISA Foundation–Paralyzed Veterans of America Chair, Department of Rehabilitation Science and Technology, University of Pittsburgh, 6425 Penn Avenue, Suite 400, Pittsburgh, Pennsylvania 15206

‡Chief Professional Officer, Community Living and Support Services, 1400 South Braddock Avenue, Pittsburgh, Pennsylvania 15218, and Field Instructor, Department of Social Work, University of Pittsburgh, 2117 Cathedral of Learning, 4200 Fifth Avenue, Pittsburgh, Pennsylvania 15260

§Veteran Mentor, Human Engineering Research Laboratories, Rehabilitation Research and Development Service, US Department of Veterans Affairs, 6425 Penn Avenue, Pittsburgh, Pennsylvania 15206

INTRODUCTION

Most people know that no one person is an island. This is powerfully true when we think about military service; but, in essence, it is true for anyone. Certainly individuals can achieve much, and are often glamorized and idolized when they do. Individual heroes, inventors, leaders, scientists, etc, have brought accomplishments to our society that have been outstanding. Yet, in the end, it is the synergy of people and community that is often at the core of any individual success. People must recognize that myriad other individuals assisted them in getting where they are. Parents, family, teachers, coaches, priests/rabbis, friends, neighbors, coworkers, supervisors, spouses, children, and many others all play roles in the formation of a person. Community is essential, in greater or lesser degrees, to all that is good in society and life.

The core of our perspective is that when a person joins the military, he or she leaves civilian life and joins a new community of allies who work together to forge a powerful alliance. This "band of brothers" aligns and in a holistic way (inclusive of families) creates a full community experience that supports all those who participate. The longer one commits to the community, the more difficult it is to leave.

There are many examples of how challenging a transition back to civilian life can be for many Service Members and families. The lifestyle and relationships—also known as *social capital*—that people forge, nurture, and then bond around are very difficult to break. As hard as these kinds of transitions are for any long-term military individuals or families, when one adds the compromising developments of a disability, the transition can be even more complex. The ravages of change brought on by disability create both internal and external barriers that can not only be perplexing, but also disconnecting.

HISTORICAL DEVALUATION

In today's society, when the Veteran returns to the community, he/she arrives as a hero and commands a powerful culture of respect. However, in time, this "honeymoon" ends, and the Veteran and his/her family moves out of the spotlight and into the mainstream community. As this transition occurs, the Veteran becomes somewhat anonymous; rather than being seen as a war hero, the Veteran is instead seen as the obvious (or not so obvious) effects of his/her disabilities. This can be a setup for devaluation.

All forms of discrimination and devaluation have some common tracks that are easily seen. Subsequently, devalued people are

- labeled and stereotyped,
- congregated in formal ways into their own space,
- thought to be a problem or pose a threat to those in authority,
- seen through their label or difference from those in authority, and
- regarded as a cost to society in either material or economic ways.

Perhaps the most discriminated block of people in the world today are people with disabilities. Every society on Earth has had difficulty including and welcoming people with disabilities. Although progress has been made, the climate for inclusion and full community participation for people with disabilities is still a major challenge. People with disabilities, including our Veterans and Wounded Warriors, are clearly caught in this web of devaluation. In spite of services, treatment, legal rights (eg, Americans With Disabilities Act), and charitable approaches, people with disabilities may be viewed quite harshly:

- *People with disabilities are quickly labeled.* Usually these labels are medical in nature and create huge cultural stereotypes. Once labeled, people with disabilities become that label in the greater community. Terms such as *Jerry's Kids, TBIs, CPs, MRs,* and *VA Retreads* are all labels that seemingly identify a class of people. These labels begin to dwarf any similarity that people might have to others.
- *People with disabilities are still readily institutionalized.* Although these institutions have shifted from large, gothic settings to smaller group facilities, they are still institutions in format. Public funding for community supports for people with disabilities is only offered as a "waiver" to the institutional bias of Medicaid.
- *People with disabilities are thought to be a problem for society.* Our federal and state governments offer funds to address the "disability problem." Beyond this, citizens have grown cautious of having people with disabilities move into their neighborhoods via group homes. Even with the Fair Housing Act, some communities actually have ordinances that specify how much distance must be allowed between homes or places where people with disabilities live. For any given classification of disability, there are efforts to promote funding to address the problems posed by that disability. To this extent, disability has economic costs to society.

INCLUSION

One of the major goals of rehabilitation and reintegration is inclusion. Inclusion is defined as *being incorporated and welcomed back into the community the way one is*. Inclusion is not "integration." On one hand, the concept of integration demands that people fit in, be alike, and reach for similar standards. However, the notion of having to fit in or be like the majority is not realistic in the disability rights movement. To expect people who might not be able to achieve a sense of similarity to be like the majority is insensitive and inappropriate.

On the other hand, inclusion is the concept of bringing people into the community regardless of their differences. Rather than attempting to change or alter their differences, or trying to create a forced similarity, inclusion suggests that people join in *as they are*. Inclusion respects differences and honors diversity, but still allows for full community participation. It is a term that implies a welcoming to all.

In thinking about traditional efforts to achieve inclusion for the Wounded Warrior, the emphasis is typically on functional or technical elements. The system has been lured into thinking if only people would be able to walk, talk, or think better, these gains would lead to greater options for success in the community. Consequently, the majority of programs for Veterans with disabilities focus on these technical or clinical efforts. Still, Wounded Warriors, and to a large extent their families, find themselves excluded from the greater community. The traditional medical/clinical model of Veterans Administration (and civilian) rehabilitation has not achieved the outcomes that everyone wants. In some simple way, this should not seem strange or odd because the nature of the medical/clinical model is to exclude. To address inclusion or to create an inclusive rehabilitation effort is to find ways for people to become included in their communities as they are. To suggest that people must pass some readiness test, be fully fixed, or jump through any other hoop is to focus energy on the wrong aspects. Thus, the microscopic medical model format of most typical Wounded Warrior programs is often a detriment to inclusion rather than a path to the community.

THE MEDICAL MODEL

The lens that society has generally used to address disabilities is found in *medical models*. The framework for treatment and the overarching perceptions that typical members of a community have about disability are that of illness or sickness. As regards the Wounded Warrior, the medical model is prominent and influential.

Many theorists have looked at the medical model as a framework for services. This framework is summarized by the *medical paradigm*[1] as follows:

- *the problem*—the person with the condition,
- *core of the problem*—rests in the person,
- *actions of the paradigm*—to classify/congregate/treat,
- *power person*—the expert (doctor or therapist), and
- *goal of the paradigm*—to fix/heal/change the patient.

Because the medical paradigm is so persuasive in human services, a deeper examination is warranted. Consider the following variables[2]:

- The professional is the expert and is in charge of care/treatment.
- Care/treatment is administered through a chain of authority.
- The person who receives treatment is labeled and expected to cooperate.
- The main purpose of entry to the paradigm is to restore or fix the person to fit in.
- The ailment that brings the person to the paradigm is labeled via a diagnosis.
- Literature examination and research are performed and utilized to understand the specific features of the ailment.
- The patient is usually congregated with others in like situations.
- The expert/professional typically has the control.
- The ailment is normally overshadowed through the therapeutic approach.
- The ailment can only be treated by the expert or his/her agent.
- The expert usually has some credentials or license to treat the ailment.
- The patient is exempt from any real responsibility.
- Most aspects of the ailment are treated in separate and distinct facilities designed for the ailment.

Further exploration of the medical model identifies the following six aspects: (1) deficiency orientation, (2) cause and effect, (3) treatment from a diagnosis, (4) the sick role, (5) microchange, and (6) clinical efficacy. Each of these aspects has both internal and external ramifications. Internally, they begin to shape how the "patient" sees him- or herself and creates a "sickness identity." Externally, these elements begin to shape how the greater community comes to think about, and then treat, people with disabilities.

- *Deficiency orientation*: Without question, medical paradigms focus on what is wrong with the person. They focus on problems, abnormalities, deficits, and struggles. Classic medical interpretations ask:
  —What is wrong with you?
  —Where does it hurt?
  —How long have you had this problem?

- *Cause and effect*: Because medical paradigms are scientific in nature, they usually function from a point of cause and effect. Simply, as the paradigm prompts a study and analysis of the ailment, it is drawn to make predictions about what to expect. This focus on predictability is not necessarily negative; however, when coupled with a deficiency orientation, it has a tendency to lean toward the negative.

- *Treatment from a diagnosis*: Most people with disabilities have some diagnosis that sets them apart from the norm. This diagnosis defines the parameters of the deviance and gives the expert some anchor to understand the ailment. Indeed, the labeling process creates an entire tone about the person and sets everyone up to expect certain events to occur. In this process, the professional begins to look for problems.

- *The sick role*: Perhaps the most powerful manifestation of the medical paradigm is found in review of the concept of the sick role. Here, the person is given the authority to be sick and to surrender autonomy to the agent of the paradigm in order to be made better. In most cases, it is the paradigm that defines what is well and what is sick. Further, only the paradigm can decide if sickness has indeed turned to wellness. It sets the rules, decides who fits, determines what the outcomes should be, establishes its own mechanisms to measure success, and then retains authority to proclaim wellness.[3]

- *Microchange*: A key point in the medical model is that of fixing people. The onus for change rests squarely on the shoulders of the patient. It is he or she who must change, adapt, or adjust to the existing world. Very little attention is paid to macro (environmental) change.

- *Clinical efficacy*: This concept relates to the strong drive that medical model agents have to validate their practice. Most agents of the medical paradigm must have a license or some sort of sanction to practice. To achieve this, the budding professional must put in countless hours of schooling and tutelage under the direction of those thought to be "masters." However, these same masters, in a way, are guardians of the paradigm. They are rewarded and validated by the paradigm so that protection and defensiveness are not difficult to understand.

Although the medical model is not bad in and of itself, the goal of rehabilitation and reintegration is not to eradicate sickness, but to return the Wounded Warrior to his/her community, and to help change the community to accept and respect differences of Veterans with disabilities.

THE BIOPSYCHOSOCIAL MODEL

In May 2001, the World Health Organization (WHO) published the *International Classification of Functioning, Disability, and Health* (ICF), a revision and update of the *International Classification of Impairments, Disabilities, and Handicaps*[4] (ICIDH) first published in 1980. In looking at models of disability and the nature in which it is approached in countries and cultures around the world, the WHO set out to create a standardized method in which levels of functioning could be identified. As they approached health from two domains (health, health-related), the ICF conformed strongly to the *biopsychosocial model of disability*.

Although clinicians have conformed to past treatment paradigms based on the medical model, the ICF sought to address disability in a more inclusive, holistic manner. Instead of viewing the disability purely as a medical or mental state that requires curing in the traditional sense, the WHO identified the three domains that combine to form the disability as a whole:

1. physical and biochemical presentations of a disability are considered to be in the biological domain;
2. a person's mood, behavior, and outlook fall under the psychological aspects of disability; and
3. the nature in which disability impacts an individual's interactions with society, to include barriers they may encounter, is considered as social implications.

By accounting for all aspects of a disability and not only the physical, clinicians can provide a more comprehensive treatment plan and facilitate inclusion and full participation in society. Rehabilitation and reintegration efforts should be provided by a team of health professionals, including physicians, psychiatrists, social workers, and counselors. This approach of viewing and treating disability as a multifaceted, intricate system affords numerous avenues of providing accommodations and support while always putting the individual, not the disability, first. Applying this model of disability to efforts of reintegration and inclusion is not only beneficial to the individual, but also to the community and society in general.

INTERDEPENDENCE

Framing a philosophy for community reintegration requires a paradigm beyond the medical model. To this extent, the *interdependence paradigm* has been suggested.[1] The term interdependence implies an interconnection or interrelationship between two entities and a connection or partnership between these entities that maximizes potential for both groups.

Interdependence is about relationships that lead to mutual acceptance and respect. Although it recognizes that all people have differences, as a paradigm it promotes an acceptance and empowerment for all. It also suggests a fabric effect in which diverse people come together in a synergistic way to create an upward effect for all. As we prepare individuals to return to a civilian community, the services that are designed to be offered in the community must be addressed from an interdependent model.

The framework of the interdependence paradigm consists of the following:

- *the problem*—limited or nonexistent service and lack of community acceptance,
- *core of the problem*—in the system or community,
- *actions of the paradigm*—creates supports and empowers,
- *power person*—person with the disability, and
- *goal of the paradigm*—develop relationships (eg, social capital).

A comparison of paradigms reveals the following:

Treatment Paradigm	Biopsychosocial Paradigm	Interdependence Paradigm
Focuses on deficiencies	Focuses on interaction of factors	Focuses on capacities
Stresses congregation	Stresses relationships	Stresses relationships
Driven by the expert/professional	Driven by the person/disability	Driven by the person/disability
Promotes that the person is "fixed"	Promotes multifaceted approaches	Promotes micro-/macrochange

SELF-DETERMINATION

Self-determination is a key concept in understanding and utilizing an interdependent model. Building on the concept of consumer choice and control, self-determination means that Warriors or Veterans have authority over how, where, and with whom their lives will be lived. They also have control of the resources needed for their support.

Many self-determination researchers agree that the concept revolves around four critical principles:

1. *Freedom*: The ability to plan a life with support rather than be referred to a program.
2. *Authority*: The ability to control a certain sum of dollars to purchase support.
3. *Support*: Through the use of resources, arranging formal and informal support to live within the community.
4. *Responsibility*: Accepting a role within the community through competitive employment, organizational affiliations, and general caring for others within the community; and accountability for spending public dollars in life-enhancing ways.

Recently, a number of states have begun to incorporate the concept of self-determination into the publicly funded human service system. The key actions they recommend to achieve self-determination include the following:

*   transfer financial control to the consumer through individual budgets;
*   use person-centered planning to encourage individual choice;
*   promote cooperation and collaboration;
*   develop awareness of community activities and resources;
*   encourage communication and information sharing;
*   change laws, rules, policies, and procedures to empower people;
*   promote training, education, and leadership development for people with disabilities;
*   use data gathering and analysis; and
*   incorporate quality enhancement and evaluation activities.

Beyond these items, self-determination is a principle that will continue to influence rehabilitation and community resources. To this extent, an understanding of the community is critical to framing a philosophy of treatment. It is imperative to know that rehabilitation is not really the target or endpoint of our efforts; it is the successful return to community.

COMMUNITY AND SOCIAL CAPITAL

A community is a network of different people who come together on a regular basis for some common cause or celebration. Traditional notions of communities bring to mind a shared geography. However, with the advent of the information age, people from around the world can join together in a virtual community (eg, message boards, social media groups, online role-playing games). A community is in actuality based on the relationships that form, not on the space. The term *culture* is analogous to community, but culture relates more to the intricacies in the way of life manifested by the community. People who bind together around a common cause create a community. However, as soon as they begin to establish common symbols, values, language, and norms, they become a culture. Thus, from this perspective, culture is the learned and shared ways that members of the community act among themselves and interact with other communities.

Social capital is a term that describes not only the notion of friendship and connectedness, but also the value that these relationships bring to our lives. Like physical capital (the tools used by communities), or human capital (the people power brought to a situation), social capital is the value brought on by our relationships. Clearly, all people have some form or network of social capital, but sociologists have come to realize its power and potency only fairly recently.

Social capital is critical to individual success and achievement, but its potency is even more advanced. Sociologists have now confirmed that it is related to the following critical issues: health, happiness, achievement, and prosocial behavior.

- *Health*: The evidence is now conclusive that the more social capital a person has, the healthier that person is. Theorists contend that it is due to the scientific principle of *stress buffering*.[5] Thus, the more relationships one has, the lower the stress levels because there are more people to offer emotional support. Although acute stress is associated with short-term, positive immune response, chronic stress adversely affects the immune system.[6] As chronic stressors are negated or minimalized, the individual's stress level declines and his/her overall health improves. Simply put, friends make a person healthier.
- *Happiness*: Over the years, psychologists have initiated the practice of *positive psychology*. In this arena, they are always measuring and gauging factors related to happiness. These factors may vary from culture to

culture, but the one constant is the variable of social capital. It is difficult to be happy when one is isolated.

- *Achievement*: Studies have concluded that people who are connected and liked are promoted more quickly and go further than sullen and disconnected people. Likewise, test scores in high schools and colleges are finding that connected students do better.[7-9]
- *Prosocial Behavior*: Everyone wants a society in which people are honest, fair, tolerant, and kind. These prosocial behaviors create a better, more caring community. Evidence is now clear that these positive behaviors increase in settings where people know each other and have some basic relationship.[10,11] Although people often think that institutions or organizations are keys to their safety, in reality it is social capital that these bodies provide that keeps them secure in their identity and place in the community as a whole. The opportunity for relationships that community offers is at the core; circles of support and the reciprocity they create are the most important aspects in both safety and health.

RETURNING TO COMMUNITY AND BUILDING SOCIAL CAPITAL

The challenge of building social capital in the community is best understood when thinking of the concept of a bridge. Bridges are interesting structures because they blend two important notions: (1) the simplicity of connecting two points and (2) the complexity of the engineering necessary to make the connection. The challenge of reconnecting people to a community is simple as we try to find ways for people who are disconnected to be reunited. The complexity is in making this happen.

With this metaphor of a bridge, the change agent can consider that the individual with a disability is on one side of reality and the community is on the other side. The goal for rehabilitation is to assist the person with the disability to move from being excluded on the one side to joining the community at large on the other side. In this example, the gap between the Veteran and the community can be represented in the problems or deficiencies the person is seen as having.

When considering this metaphor, it seems clear that the problem or the reason that the Veteran with a disability is distant from the community is due to his/her differences, disability, or perceived problem. Given this reality, the medical model suggests that the best way to get people from one side to the other is to focus on the problem or, in this case, the disability. In most human service programs, this is exactly how the issue of inclusion is addressed.

Conventional wisdom (ie, the medical model) tries to mitigate the differences so that the person can be more easily included into the community. This conventional approach is a linear, microscopic approach to the inclusion of people with disabilities. It suggests that if problems can be fixed or masked, the Veteran will be more likely to become included. Although this approach has been practiced for years, it has not led to viable community inclusion. Even though people have been moved *into* the community, they have not really become *of* the community.

A rethinking of the approach is necessary. Consider the example of a disconnection between two points: A and B. If there is a river in the way (point A), one might see the river as a problem. We might seek out help from an engineer as to how we might mitigate or get rid of the river so that we can pass to point B safely. In some ways, this is how the medical model frames the problem of inclusion for Veterans with disabilities. It suggests that the way to get people included in the community is to fix the problems they have (ie, fill in the river).

However, when we use the metaphor of a bridge, the challenge changes from *seeing* the river as a problem to *thinking* about what other ways we might safely pass over it. Obviously, the focus turns to what it might take to build a bridge. With this shift in thinking, the river is not a problem, but a reality to be addressed based on the strength and stability of the shorelines where we plan to anchor the bridge. Consequently, the more important factors are not the problems posed by the river, but the strength that can be garnered to build the bridge.

The creation of a real shift in culture demands that the people supporting Veterans think about four critical steps: (1) find the passion or point of connection, (2) find the venue or connection point, (3) understand the elements of culture, and (4) find or enlist the gatekeeper.[12] These steps are contrary to the medical model and are in many ways contrary to how most human service systems relate to people with disabilities.

Step 1: Find the Passion or Point of Connection

Finding the key points of strength and passion is the first step to cultural shifting. To build a strong bridge, there must be a solid foundation to ensure that the bridge will be safe for passage. The passage of people, products, or ideas into the culture requires the same strength. Consequently, we must identify all that is strong or good about that which we hope to shift the culture toward.

In many cases, people know their passions and interests. For others, this is a discovery process. An interest inventory is powerful because it is not only empowering, but can also set the groundwork for the possibilities of community connections. This process is the same one often used with children in that the process of looking at connectors is one already used by parents. One primary effort as a parent is to discover the interests and capacities of children to connect them to communities that celebrate those same interests.

Step 2: Find the Venue or Connection Point

With cultural shifting, once the change agent has identified the positive capacities for inclusion or incorporation, the next critical step is to find the place that the person, idea, or product will relate to. In other words, find the setting where the Veteran might discover like-minded people who set the stage for building social capital.

The concept of venue and connection point has a clear importance. To find a framework of new friends, one has a better chance of connection by taking up a hobby, passion, or capacity, and joining up with others who share that same passion. There are many interactive Web sites (eg, Meetup.com) or smartphone apps that allow people to identify their interests and locality, and then introduce them to a variety of clubs, groups, or associations that correspond to their wants/needs.

Simply, people tend to gather for all kinds of reasons and interests. For every capacity or passion, there is a place where people gather to celebrate these passions. Such places can offer a starting point for acquiring new social capital.

Step 3: Understand the Elements of Culture

From a sociological perspective, the elements of a culture are defined by the practices and beliefs that a community assimilates as its own. These include symbols recognized by the group as having certain meanings; a shared system of laws, values, and norms; and language/dialect. Within the context of interdependence, the key elements of culture include rituals, patterns, jargon, and memory:

- *Rituals*: These are the deeply embedded behaviors of the culture that the members expect others to uphold. These behaviors can be formal actions or symbolic activities that members just pick up. A vivid example can be found with religious institutions. All cultures are ritualistic; however, churches demand common actions, signs, and movements that create commonality and similarity among and between members.

- *Patterns*: The patterns of a culture refer to the movements and social space occupied by the members. Patterns are captured in how the members relate to each other as they go about the business of their culture. Patterns almost always revolve around the territory occupied by the members. As territorial animals, we are very rigid and defensive of that which we have laid stake to when joining the culture.

- *Jargon*: This relates to the language, words, expressions, and phrasing members of the culture use to describe or discuss that which they hold as important. Oftentimes, these words might be technical or very specific to the cultural theme. Other times, the jargon might manifest in sayings or expressions that are not technical, but are widely understood by other members and become important to the exchange of the culture. Understanding the jargon of the culture helps one make an easy transition into the community.

- *Memory*: This refers to the collective history of the culture. The memory is honored in formal ways by producing yearbooks, annual reports, and other official documents or celebrations that chronicle the actions of the culture. Other types of informal memory also happen within cultures through the weaving and telling of stories or anecdotes. Both of these approaches create a living history of the culture and establish the bond that causes members to want to continue the work and fully participate in the culture. Memory leads to communal wisdom.

Step 4: Find or Enlist the Gatekeeper

The final step in building social capital revolves around the *gatekeeper*. The only way new people successfully enter an existing community is when they are introduced and endorsed by a viable gatekeeper. A gatekeeper is an indigenous member of the community who has either formal or informal influence within the culture. These gatekeepers can be formally elected or selected leaders, or they might be one of the members everyone can count on to get things done. Further, gatekeepers can either be positive or negative or assertive or unassertive about the person, idea, or product being introduced.

The gatekeepers are powerful because they transition their influence to the person, idea, or product they are endorsing or rejecting. This transition of influence is the first step to the inclusion of the new thing into the culture. The mere fact that the gatekeeper likes or dislikes the idea is enough to sway other members to the gatekeeper's side.

To effectively shift a culture to accept something new requires that the change agent identify and then enlist a gatekeeper to facilitate the passage. When the gatekeeper endorses a person, other members observe this and subsequently align their thoughts with the gatekeeper's. The more enthusiastic the gatekeeper is about the new person, the more apt others are to be the same. Although finding and enlisting gatekeepers may be difficult, it is an essential ingredient for building relationships and shifting the culture.

COMMUNITY RESOURCES AND SUPPORT

Community resources are vital to Veterans with a cognitive, emotional, or physical disability in order for them to make a smooth transition to civilian life. Social capital and community inclusion can be complemented by the community support chosen. With these types of support, the transition back to the community is more successful.

Community support services can be framed in a number of ways. One framework is nonprofit agencies that are mission driven to support people with disabilities around community support needs. These nonprofit agencies are guided by volunteer board members and are funded through contracts and donations through governments, local sources, corporate, etc. There are also many for-profit companies that have been developed to meet human services needs. These companies differ from nonprofits in that they are usually privately owned and are profit motivated. Lastly, there are government-supported organizations that are funded by tax dollars, such as the Veterans Administration and its services. Along with these support organizations, there are other governmental bodies that can be helpful to Veterans, but one might have to meet certain criteria to be eligible.

Community support services can include, but are not limited to, attendant care, transportation, accessible housing, and vocational support. The amount of support needed to be successful in the community will vary from person to person; that is why it is critical that Veterans know their passions and interests. Although the abundance of services available from state to state may vary, most states offer the core community resources that will assist the Veteran with living in the community of his/her choice. In more rural areas, Veterans may be more reliant on family and neighbors to assist them in the community. Building a successful community support team that consists of family, friends, and neighbors will be important to ongoing participation in the community.

Attendant Care

Attendant care provides personal care assistance in the Veteran's home. The attendant can assist with helping the Veteran complete all activities of daily living, including light housekeeping and assistance in the community (eg, grocery shopping, banking, attending medical appointments, etc). In some states, home- and community-based services are prevalent. The Veteran can access these services through any home health care agency or human service agency that may also provide the service. State resources like the Center for Independent Living can provide a number of community options to a person seeking these types of services.

Transportation

Transportation is a key component to community success. If one does not have access to transportation, it is difficult to participate in the community. The Veteran will need to access what transportation options are available. The options may include public transportation, paratransit, driving with accessibility, and reliance on community resources to provide the transportation. If a Veteran is interested in transportation support, several options might be explored. Driving oneself is certainly the ultimate option. However, the Veteran will need to evaluate if this is an option for him/her. If accessibility is required, driver's evaluations can be obtained to assist the person with evaluating what assistive technology will be required to drive a car. One might need hand controls or wheelchair accessibility. All of these features can be built in to accommodate the Veteran. Public transportation is available in many communities, including paratransit systems that provide door-to-door transportation to seniors and people with disabilities. If these options are not feasible, and the family lives in a very rural area, then purchasing a vehicle with a conversion package would allow for accessible transportation. The conversion package will provide needed accessibility to the vehicle, thus making it easier for the Veteran to travel.

Accessible Housing

Accessible, affordable, and safe housing is another component to community success. All people want safe and affordable housing. People, regardless of their situation, want to live in the community and stay in their homes. To participate in the community, one must be able to navigate his/her home and the community. Thus, a person who has physical and/or cognitive challenges may now find it difficult to negotiate his/her home without support. In this instance, the Veteran will want to evaluate his/her home for accessibility and/

or the need for home modifications, assistive technology, or durable medical equipment that might allow the Veteran to maintain independence.

Vocational Support

Most adults want to feel productive and know that they are making a difference. Participation in the community for some may include having a job, returning to school, or volunteering in the community. Whatever their choice, there are many resources that are available to assist with making a decision of how they can now contribute to the community. Adults may want to return to their previous employers or seek a new career choice. These individuals may have to make some vocational compromises in the job they did before or they may be able only to do a part of the job or transfer their skills to do work in the same field, but in a different capacity.[13]

When considering the community and how to access available community resources, many resources are available, such as the following:

- *Aging and Disability Resource Centers (ADRCs)*: Many states have an ADRC that serves as a one-stop shop that can assist Veterans in connecting to state resources. The ADRC consists of many collaborative agencies that provide a variety of services and information that can help Veterans obtain the services they need.
- *Association of Assistive Technology*: Assistive technology is a critical growing area to the success of the Veteran being able to live, work, and participate in the community. This resource can help the Veteran gather information on resources for equipment, potential funding for assistive technology, and home modifications.
- *Bureau of Vocational Rehabilitation*: Many states have a vocational rehabilitation service that can assist Veterans with evaluating employment readiness, education, and job placement.
- *Brain Injury Association of America*: The Brain Injury Association of America is an excellent resource to provide information to Veterans regarding living with a brain injury, locating a local brain injury association in their state, and utilizing the services that are available for people with brain injury.
- *National Center for Independent Living (NCIL)*: NCIL can lead Veterans to the Center for Independent Living (CIL) that is available in their state. The services that the CIL offers include attendant care, housing, vocational options, etc. They can also lead Veterans to many other resources that are available within their states.

- *National Association for Mental Illness (NAMI)*: NAMI advocates for access to services, treatment, support, and research. The organization will find information about your local NAMI organization, as well as other services for Veterans with mental health issues.
- *US Department of Veterans Affairs*: Veterans should utilize the resources that are available within the Veterans Administration system. However, if the area where the Veteran resides has limited resources, then contacting the previously described resources will assist the Veteran with developing a comprehensive support system in addition to benefits from the Veterans Administration.

SUMMARY

What we know about social capital is that it works. A person remaining in his/her home and community is by far the better option to facility-based care. The strategies that are previously suggested are designed to assist the person and/or family with making those community connections one step at a time. Successful community reintegration will start with a plan that includes knowing what one wants/needs, exploring all of those agencies that can help assess their desires, and, lastly, implementing the plan. Anyone can complete this process with little to no assistance from others, or the Veteran might want to consider eliciting the assistance of a person who can help facilitate the connections that he/she needs to make.

In whatever manner the Veteran chooses to approach community inclusion and build social capital/relationships, failure should never be an option. This process can be successful when it is recognized that there is more than one way to the mountain's summit. Thus, exploring all options is critical; if one option does not work, then try another way. Community participation does not limit people based on ability because options are many and diverse.

Veterans have served their country well, and now their community is available to serve them. As they approach exploring various options in their communities, Veterans should remember to be patient, positive, and enthusiastic about available opportunities. Further, it is more important to be creative, to reach out, and to be unafraid to take risks.

REFERENCES

1. Condeluci A. *Interdependence: The Route to Community.* 2nd ed. Boca Raton, FL: CRC Press; 1995.
2. Zola IK. Reasons for non-compliance and failure of the elderly to seek care. In: Moskowitz RW, Haug M, eds. *Arthritis and the Elderly.* New York, NY: Springer; 1986.
3. Illich I. *Limits to Medicine; Medical Nemesis: The Expropriation of Health.* London, UK: Marion Boyars Publishers; 1976.
4. World Health Organization. *International Classification of Functioning, Disability, and Health.* Geneva, Switzerland: WHO; 2001.
5. Segerstrom SC, Miller GE. Psychological stress and the human immune system: a meta-analytic study of 30 years of inquiry. *Psychol Bull.* 2004;130(4):601–630.
6. Bowen K, Uchino B, Birmingham W, Carlisle M, Smith T, Light K. The stress-buffering effects of functional social support on ambulatory blood pressure. *Health Psychol* [serial online]. 2014;33(11):1440–1443.
7. Brouwer J, Jansen E, Flache A, Hofman A. The impact of social capital on self-efficacy and study success among first-year university students. *Learn Individ Differ.* 2016;52:109–118.
8. Lai G, Wong O, Feng X. Family, school, and access to social capital among high school students in urban Nanjing. *Am Behav Sci.* 2015;59(8):946–960.
9. Sands MM, Heilbronner NN. The impact of direct involvement I and direct involvement II experiences on secondary school students' social capital, as measured by co-cognitive factors of the Operation Houndstooth Intervention Theory. *Gifted Child Q.* 2014;58(4):297–310.
10. Parsons CA, Jacobson JA, Krupp DB. Self-resemblance and social rejection. *Evol Psychol.* 2016;14(4):1–8.
11. Virdee G, Frederick T, Tarasoff LA, McKenzie K, Davidson L, Kidd SA. Exploring the contours of religion and spirituality in creating community: a focus on persons with psychosis. *J Commun Psychol.* 2016;44(8):1081–1087.
12. Condeluci A, Burke K, Gooden-Ledbetter M, Evans McGuirck M, Ortman D. *Together Is Better: A Guide to Fostering Community Inclusion for Individuals with Disabilities.* Pittsburgh, PA: United Cerebral Palsy; 2004.
13. Condeluci A, Gooden Ledbetter MG, Ortman D, Fromknecht J, DeFries M. Social capital: a view from the field. *J Vocat Rehabil.* 2008;29:133–139.

Private Second Class (PV2) Greg Crouse joined the US Army right out of high school. He served overseas as a Cannon Crewman on a howitzer battery. While on a weekend furlough, Greg was struck (as a pedestrian) by a drunk motorcyclist. He ruptured his stomach, cracked his hips, shattered his left femur in four places, and severed his left leg below the knee. Crouse was heli-lifted to the nearest hospital for treatment, flatlining twice, once on the helicopter en route and once on the operating table.

He underwent recovery and physical therapy stateside for more than 18 months. He suffered

through nerve damage, hip infections, numerous skin grafts, and learning to walk again. After his honorable discharge, Greg drifted aimlessly and fell into a bleak period of drugs and alcohol during the 1990s. He did not find himself again until after regaining his sobriety in 2000. Also, he discovered that he enjoyed participating in adaptive sports alongside other disabled Veterans and adaptive athletes in 2001.

In 2003, at a disabled sports event, Crouse uncovered a passion for canoeing. Soon after, he was introduced to Coach Cheance Adair who trained and tutored him in the ancient South Pacific Islander art of outrigger canoeing. He began traveling with her and other disabled athletes to various venues where they exhibited outrigger canoe racing as a possible Paralympic event, and sought consideration for this sport from the Paralympic Committee. After entering several demonstration-only events in Hawaii, California, and Pennsylvania, an adaptive division was then accepted on a Championship level beginning in 2008. Greg was part of the first races to compete for an Adaptive Class Medal, earning a Silver Medal with a 6-man adaptive crew. Thanks to these efforts, Paracanoe was accepted as a Paralympic sport in 2010.

Greg has been actively working with the adaptive program PossAbilities at Loma Linda University Health, and the program participants have awakened a new passion in him. He seeks to share his failures and triumphs with anyone dealing with an adversity in life. With the support of PossAbilities, he has become a Registered Amputee Peer Counselor, enlightening amputees during their bleak periods of body acceptance and the psychological readjustments that lie ahead. He has spoken with foster children, academically at-risk youth, and posttraumatic stress disorder transitional soldiers about the parallels of losing a limb and overcoming adversity in one's life, yet choosing not to let that adversity define you as a person. He was voted as PossAbilities' Member of the Year, and inducted into the Hall of Heroes for PossAbilities and the Loma Linda Medical Rehabilitation Centers.

Greg Crouse has also been called on to coach at disabled activity camps around the country. He has worked with the Wounded Warrior Project, the Endeavor Games, and various camps introducing water sports to Wounded

Soldiers and their families. He is also a spokesman for hiring Veterans and speaks to prospective employers about the benefits of employing a Veteran.

He has branched out into the community, seeking to share outrigger canoeing with fellow disabled Veterans and other adaptive athletes. He has joined a local Southern California "able-bodied" team, Imua Outrigger Canoe Club (Newport Beach, California), and competes on the local race circuit. Greg also finds time to coach the kids in his canoe club and mentor new paddlers, whether able-bodied or disabled-bodied. He successfully used the employment grants and education processes to become an Orthotic Technician and returned to school later in life to earn a degree in Communications.

Greg is a husband and father, supported and encouraged by his wife, Aimee, and his three children Krystal, Kasey, and Chase.

Crouse has won the US National Rudderless Single Man Canoe title three times (2012, 2013, and 2014), taking a Gold Medal in the 200 meter, 500 meter, and the 5 kilometer. He has also proudly represented Team USA eight times in outrigger canoeing in international competition, appearing at races held in Hawaii (2004), California (2008), Poland (2010 and 2012), New Caledonia (2010), Canada (2012), Germany (2013), and Brazil (2014). Greg has partnered with PossAbilities and strives to achieve his ultimate goal of securing the first ever Open Men's "Para-canoe" selection in the 2016 Paralympic Games in Rio de Janeiro.

Greg Crouse loves his family and his new lease on life, and proudly serves the United States as a Para-athlete and Adaptive Mentor.

The fact is, whether in prosthetics, geriatrics,
PTSD and TBI treatment, or polytrauma care—to say nothing
of disability and education benefits, home loans or homeless
rescues, and final honors in our national cemeteries—
there's no other one institution like the VA positioned to deliver
a broad spectrum of Veteran-specific care and services to the
one percent of our population that currently serves in uniform.

★ ★ ★

ROBERT MACDONALD
SECRETARY OF THE US DEPARTMENT OF VETERANS AFFAIRS
OCTOBER 20, 2014

CHAPTER ELEVEN

Financial Management

DANIEL J. FISHER, MHA*; JOSEPH A. WINEMAN, MHA, DMD, ABGD†; and RANDY LEVANDER‡

---

*Colonel (Retired), US Army; Assistant Chair for Administration and Operations, Department of Rehabilitation Science and Technology, University of Pittsburgh, School of Health and Rehabilitation Sciences, 6425 Penn Avenue, Suite 401, Pittsburgh, Pennsylvania 15206

†Colonel (Retired), US Army; CEO, Wineman Dental, 1701 North Green Valley Parkway, Suite 4D, Henderson, Nevada 89074

‡Technical Sergeant, US Air Force; Veterans Treatment Court Coordinator; also US Air Force Combat Arms Instructor, Financial Coach, and Advocate for Veterans, Pittsburgh, Pennsylvania

---

INTRODUCTION

This chapter is devoted to the financial health and well-being of not only Service Members and Veterans, but also all Americans. Having a good understanding of the key elements associated with a strong financial foundation is critical for resilience and effective reintegration. It is also important for personal and professional well-being. In addition, we will discuss the fundamentals of financial management and planning, give helpful hints about developing a working monthly personal budget, provide an overview of the fundamental financial vehicles used to obtain and maintain financial stability and independence, and explain how to avoid some of the most-often encountered financial pitfalls. We all face financial challenges throughout life. The good news is that understanding the basics can significantly decrease the bumps in the road and help keep you on the path to financial stability.

As you assess your current situation, you must begin to face the reality of your personal finances, whether entering active duty, reenlisting, serving overseas, recovering from injuries, or transitioning out of the military. Each stage brings new concerns, including financial issues. Fortunately, there are a variety of programs and benefits, both in and out of the military, that can help along the way.

MILITARY TRANSITION PLANNING

Departing the military can be planned or unexpected. When the Service Member makes the decision to leave the military, it often takes 12 to 18 months to develop a comprehensive plan that can prevent a lot of potential headaches. However, when someone else makes the decision or when there are circumstances beyond the Service Member's control, the departure can be laden with problems. Having a 3- to 6-month cash reserve for living expenses can make the transition easier.

How can one accumulate such an amount? Pay yourself first. Allocating between 2% to 5% of each and every paycheck into a *contingency fund* or *an emergency fund* can help when the unexpected occurs. All members of the military know that even the best-written operation orders can change at any time, but having a contingency plan can greatly increase your chances of success.

So what constitutes an emergency? The transmission goes out in your car, or the wind blows the roof off of your house and you have to pay the deductible on your homeowners insurance, or you lose your job, etc. The emergency fund should be reserved for true, unplanned events and circumstances. Therefore, consider opening a separate savings or money market account for this fund with a bank that you do not normally go to for most of your primary banking needs. This money should be accessible for emergencies, but not so easily accessible that it ends up being used for other things. Having the contingency money available to cover your transition expenses will help to alleviate the stresses caused by a life-changing event.

The biggest challenge for the departing Service Member is often the lack of predictability in his/her daily life. From knowing where to be, what to wear, where to go to get healthcare, where to buy food, where to exercise or knowing one's salary, many things change when one enters the civilian sector.

In addition, it often takes significant time and effort to obtain a civilian job. Although there has been substantial progress made with helping Veterans find meaningful civilian employment, Veterans can and often do experience lengthy delays in landing well-paying jobs. Whereas some Military Occupation Specialties and Areas of Concentration are transferable, some human resource directors do not necessarily understand how military leadership and real-world experience translate into the civilian workforce.

There are a number of programs available to help Veterans transition to civilian employment. Many of these programs will be explored later in this chapter. Service Members departing active duty and choosing to relocate to a new geographical area may wish to consider working with a respected headhunting company tailored to their specific area of expertise. Some Service Members may want to return to their hometown for additional family support. However, a satisfying job that pays a decent income may be the determining factor in where they choose to move.

FOLLOWING A TRAUMATIC INJURY OR ILLNESS

Following a traumatic injury or illness, Service Members and their families not only find themselves having to deal with immediate physical effects, but also addressing the long-term personal impact and changes. One of the more significant impacts is the possible negative financial effect caused by traumatic injury or illness, including the possibility of losing a job; the need to transition from the military; the dependence on family members to stay at home and care for a loved one; and the burden of having to supply home modifications, medical equipment, assistive technology, etc. Generally, individuals and families do not have the financial means to withstand a financial impact of that magnitude.

Fortunately, the military has programs in place to decrease or defer some of the financial burdens, such as programs that help to pay for

- medical care,
- prosthetics,
- orthotics,
- transportation,
- vehicle modification,
- home modification,
- adaptive sports equipment, etc.

While still on active duty, Service Members continue to receive income and medical care with often little modification. After transitioning from the military, many things change, such as medical care that often transitions to the Department of Veterans Affairs (VA) healthcare system for individuals with service-connected disabilities. Veterans may be eligible for a broad range of benefits and services, including monetary disability compensation, based on their discharge from active military service.

During the transition process, Service Members need to work with their local military treatment facility to conduct a final physical and document any illnesses or injuries that may have occurred or been aggravated while serving in the military. Once an individual transfers out of the military, this information is the basis for determining a service-connected disability rating and for determining eligibility requirements within the VA healthcare system. Eligibility for VA benefits, including medical benefits, varies greatly. Veterans receive VA care and medication at no cost for any condition that may be related to their combat service. Individuals can apply for VA enrollment online at https://www.1010ez.med.va.gov/sec/vha/1010ez/. Veterans are not required to enroll, but are urged to do so to permit better planning of future health resources. Disability compensation benefits are not subject to federal or state income tax.

As previously noted, there are numerous benefit programs available to help address the financial and personal impacts of military service-related illness or injury. There are myriad Veterans benefit-related websites available online. A good starting point is eBenefits at http://www.ebenefits.va.gov/. This site allows Service Members, Veterans, and their families to manage their government benefits online. Additionally, the VA has personnel to assist individuals transitioning from military to civilian life who can be reached at the nearest VA office or by calling 1-800-827-1000.

Another good starting point is the National Resource Directory at http://www.nrd.gov/. This website brings together countless services and resources to support the recovery, rehabilitation, and community reintegration of Wounded Warriors.

Military OneSource provides Wounded Warrior specialty consultation services. Through this service, Wounded Warriors and their families can access immediate assistance with issues related to healthcare, facilities, or benefits. Specialty consultants work collaboratively with the services' Wounded Warrior programs and the VA to ensure that callers are promptly connected to resources that can help address their needs. To reach a consultant, call 1-800-342-9647. Additional information is also available at http://www.militaryonesource.mil.

OTHER TRANSITION ASSISTANCE

There are many programs available to Veterans specifically developed to assist with transition from the military and programs developed to aid injured and ill Veterans. Additional programs come from other federal agencies, such as the VA, the Internal Revenue Service, the US Department of Housing and Urban Development Veterans Resource Center, and the US Department of Health and Human Services. In addition, there are many others programs and benefits that originate from profit and not-for-profit organizations around the country.

SOLDIER FOR LIFE-TRANSITION ASSISTANCE PROGRAM

The Soldier for Life-Transition Assistance Program (SFL-TAP) is designed to assist Service Members as they transition from military to civilian life. The program includes information on job searching, employment, training, and VA benefits. Active duty Service Members and Mobilized Reserve Component Soldiers are eligible to receive transition assistance for up to 180 days following separation or retirement from active duty. After the 180-day window, active duty Army, Reserve, or National Guard SFL-TAP services are available for life to the retiree and eligible family members on a space-available basis. Additional information is also available at SFL-TAP at https://www.sfl-tap.army.mil/.

COMBAT-RELATED SPECIAL COMPENSATION

Individuals with combat-related disabilities may be eligible for a tax-free monthly payment titled Combat-Related Special Compensation (CRSC). This payment helps restore retired pay lost with a VA disability compensation offset. Veterans must apply for CRSC through their branch of service. Additional information can be found in the *VA Health Benefits Handbook*[1] or at http://www.va.gov/opa/publications/benefits_book/benefits_chap02.asp.

HOUSING GRANTS FOR DISABLED VETERANS

Eligible Service Members or Veterans may be entitled to a housing grant from the VA to adapt a home they already own or reside in; to build a new, specially adapted house; or to buy a house and modify it to meet their disability-related requirements (see Chapter 13 for an in-depth discussion of accessible home considerations). Depending on the severity of the illness or injury and for certain permanent disabilities, individuals can receive up to $70,465 through Specially Adapted Housing (SAH) grants that assist in building a new, specially adapted home. If a Veteran chooses to modify an existing home, or purchase a residence already equipped with special features, then the VA may approve up to $14,093 for the cost of necessary adaptations. This program is known as the Special Housing Adaptation (SHA) grant. In addition, if a Service Member or Veteran is living temporarily in a home owned by a family member, he/she may be eligible for a Temporary Residence Adaptation in the form of either a $30,934 SAH grant or a $5,523 SHA grant, depending on the severity of the illness or injuries. The Home Improvement and Structural Alternations (HISA) program provides up to $6,800 to make medically necessary improvements and structural alterations to a Veteran's primary residence. Veterans may also be entitled to a direct loan from the VA to supplement the grant to acquire a specially adapted home.

These grant and loan amounts are adjusted every October 1 based on a cost-of-construction index. For more information on these programs, consult the handbook on *Federal Benefits for Veterans, Dependents and Survivors.*[2] Additional information is also available at http://www.benefits.va.gov/homeloans/adaptedhousing.asp.

Automobile Allowance and Training

If a Veteran or Service Member has a service-connected disability that results in a permanent loss of vision of both eyes or a permanent impairment of use of one or both hands or feet, he/she may be eligible for a one-time payment of approximately $20,000 toward the purchase of an automobile or other form of transportation. In addition, individuals may be eligible for a full range of services, including driver's evaluations and training, repair, replacement, or reinstallation of automobile adaptive equipment (AAE) for the safe operation of a vehicle purchased with VA assistance. To apply, contact a VA regional office at 1-800-827-1000 or the nearest VA healthcare facility.

Allowance for Aid and Attendance and Housebound Pension Benefits

A Veteran may be eligible for additional disability compensation or pension payments if it is determined that he/she requires regular aid and attendance from another person or is permanently housebound.

To access the VA Aid and Attendance and Housebound Pension Benefits, you must write to the VA regional office where you filed a claim for pension benefits or any VA regional office. It is important to include copies of any evidence that validates the need for this type of care. Additional information can be found at http://www.benefits.va.gov/pension/aid_attendance_housebound.asp.

VOCATIONAL REHABILITATION AND EMPLOYMENT

One VA program that has the potential of being a significant benefit during transition is the Vocational Rehabilitation and Employment program (also known as Voc Rehab). The program provides service-connected Veterans with the tools necessary to prepare them to achieve independence or to obtain/maintain appropriate employment. Based on needs of the individual, the program may assist with providing additional education or training for employment, job development and placement services, and on-the-job training. Benefits may also include a subsistence allowance for a determined number of months during the training period.

EDUCATION AND TRAINING

The education and training benefits program is quite extensive and has tremendous potential to aid Service Members and Veterans in acquiring an education and obtaining a head start in the transition process. Eligibility requirements can be complex and may vary based on when individuals served and length of active duty service. However, generally, Veterans may receive extensive education benefits under the Montgomery GI Bill and receive up to 36 months of tuition entitlement and monthly housing allowance under the Post 9/11 GI Bill (2001). Chapter 12 has a detailed discussion of educational benefits. Additional information is available at www.benefits.va.gov/gibill or by calling 1-888-GI-Bill-1 (1-888-442-4551).

RECREATION THERAPY SERVICES

The VA also recognizes that there are a number of positive health outcomes resulting from participation in recreational therapy programs (see Chapter 8). The VA supports this effort by providing or lending equipment through the Adaptive Sports Program. If a Service Member is particularly interested in a specific sport, a detailed assessment is conducted. In various circumstances, the VA can also assist with the purchase of equipment, including sport prostheses, mono-skis, sport model wheelchairs, sledges for sled hockey, and other adaptive sports equipment.

CONDUCTING A CURRENT FINANCIAL ASSESSMENT

Whether you are a current Service Member or a Veteran, if you have questions about your financial state of affairs, one of the most important things you can do for yourself (and for your family) is to conduct a financial assessment. Even if you are financially up to date, it is a good idea to reassess yourself to see where you stand. This will give you a big picture view of your current financial status and help you plan more effectively for the future.

Where to Begin

Start with some questions to honestly assess your finances:

- How much do you make and what are your routine monthly expenses?
- If you are part of a family unit, does anyone else bring in an income?
- Are all bills paid on time and in full each month?
- Is the checkbook balanced? If so, how often?
- Are you a saver or an impulse buyer?
- How much cash do you have immediately available in case of an emergency (not using credit cards)?
- Are you saving money every month?

The importance of maintaining financial stability cannot be overlooked. In a survey of 4,500 couples, researchers at Kansas State University found that no matter how much income a family has, fights about money are the biggest contributors to divorce.[3] The study also revealed that couples take longer to recover from an argument about finances than any other issue because these disagreements tend to last longer (more information available at http://www.k-state.edu/media/newsreleases/jul13/predictingdivorce71113.html).

Military couples are no different; financial trouble can affect your relationship with your spouse and interfere with your military career or your post-military life. If you are worried about a possible repossession of your car or foreclosure of your home, staying focused while on the job can be difficult. When you add in deployment to a hostile wartime environment, your personal stress level can increase exponentially. The best solution is to remain on a solid financial footing at all times.

Many of us think that we know where our money goes each month, but few of us can actually list all of the ways we spend our monthly income. The best way to complete this task is to sit down with a notebook, a calculator, the monthly bills, and credit and debit statements for the month. Next, start listing exactly how your monthly finances are divided. If you are not that organized, start at the beginning of the month and keep a spending journal. Record when, where, and how much is spent for the entire month. Most people can tell you what they pay in monthly rent or mortgage and perhaps what they spend for car payments. However, few of us know the exact amount of our cell phone bill, utility costs, or monthly transportation expenses. Track everything. At the end of the month, simply add up all of your expenses and deduct the amount from your total monthly take-home income. This will provide you with a great starting point and help you to determine if you are living above or within your means.

PREPARING A BUDGET

Spending Plan

The first step in preparing a budget is to develop a personal spending plan. It is designed to help outline where income is earned and how it is spent. The key element in the spending plan is learning to incorporate reasonable financial goals. These goals (eg, saving money for a new home, car, or vacation) help individuals determine how much money should be diverted from living expenses into savings and investments. By combining income and expenses with financial goals, a road map for monitoring spending can be created to help determine the most appropriate methods for saving. By documenting and categorizing all sources of spending, we can better understand whether funds are being spent on items that detract from our ability to save and reach financial stability. Additional information is also available at http://www. investopedia.com/terms/p/personal-spending-plan.asp.

Most American families know that they should create a monthly budget and stick to it in order to achieve their financial goals. Individuals and families need to know where every dollar goes each month. The only way to truly monitor every dollar is to create a monthly budget and follow it. When possible, couples should create budgets together to increase communication and to set up a "hierarchy of expenses." An honest discussion of expenses should result in a prioritized list with either the current dollar amount or proposed dollar amount available to spend attached specifically to that item. Consider listing the expenses in the order of need:

- food,
- utilities,
- transportation,
- shelter,
- insurance, etc.

(*Note*: Most people agree that food is the top priority.) Single individuals will have greater flexibility in spending, but may also face greater temptations to go off-budget.

Avoiding Pitfalls

Tracking and decreasing items that detract from our ability to save require effort and discipline. They are key factors in avoiding the pitfalls that allow debt to accumulate. Try to avoid making unnecessary purchases. Take a step back before you make an impulsive purchase, and then take action to prevent damage to your budget.

For example, rather than purchasing a new car just because your neighbor recently bought one, consider the impact on your spending plan. Be wary of the urge to have the latest and greatest items. If your goal is to get out and stay out of debt, then *discipline* will play a major role in your daily financial life. Financial discipline will help you to assess your goals and consequences when faced with a decision that could potentially run you off course.

Having a credit card is very convenient because you do not have to carry a lot of cash to make purchases. Establishing a good line of credit also helps with securing loans for big purchases. However, along with the advantages also come the disadvantages. Because you do not have to carry around large sums of money and you may have funds available on your card, you may be tempted to buy something impulsively. Before you know it, you hardly recognize your spending plan any more. Maintaining discipline with credit card purchases is key to successfully having credit cards, as well as tracking what purchases you make, knowing what the interest rates are, paying charges on time, and being aware of not spending more than you can afford.

Housing

Housing costs normally take the biggest bite out of a budget. The US Bureau of Labor Statistics reported that about 34% of Americans' spending goes toward housing costs, with 38% of individuals renting.[4] Potential lenders use this budget line item to determine how much mortgage you qualify for. Potential lenders should limit your basic housing expenses (including mortgage payment, real estate taxes, and homeowners insurance) to not more than 30% of your gross annual income. This is a limit, not the goal. There are also numerous hidden costs associated with homeownership. In addition to monthly mortgage payments, there are costs for landscaping, water, gas, garbage, maintenance, etc, that quickly increase monthly expenses. Keeping housing expenses as low as possible, while living comfortably, should be the target.

Transportation

Transportation is normally the second largest expense in a household budget, although this amount can vary depending on your personal situation. The transportation expenses of the average American two-car household account

FIGURE 11-1. *Simple Monthly Budget.*

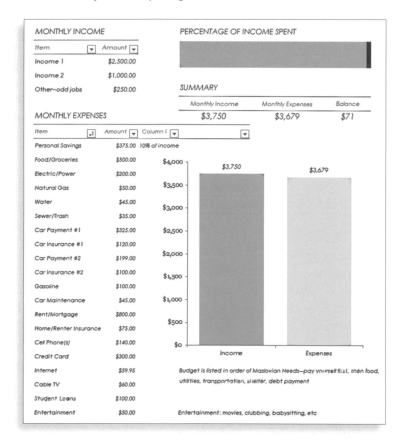

for more than 17% of the overall budget.[4] This expense may run as low as 10% or as high as 20% if you work from a home-based office, use public transportation frequently, own your vehicles outright, are making payments on one or more cars, or have an extended commute.[4]

Food

A large chunk of most household budgets goes toward food. Although budgeting 15% to 20% of your expenditures for food is acceptable, food spending for most Americans is closer to 13% of their overall expenditures.[4] At-home food consumption accounts for almost 60% of all food costs, whereas eating out absorbs the remaining 40%.[4]

Savings, Insurance, and Healthcare

Personal savings, life insurance, healthcare expenses, retirement savings, and cash contributions can take a toll on your budget; but, nonetheless, they are important line items. Life insurance and retirement amount to more than 10% of the average household budget. Healthcare is roughly 6%, and cash contributions are almost 4%.[4] Although Americans sometimes falter when it comes to personal savings, you should budget from 5% to 10% of your budget toward it. Many experts recommend taking a "pay yourself first" attitude when it comes to savings to ensure that you have enough reserves built up in case the unforeseen happens.

Personal Expenses

Roughly 10% of the average American's spending is for

- clothing,
- personal care services,
- gym memberships,
- education,
- reading,
- entertainment,
- tobacco,
- alcoholic beverages, and
- other miscellaneous expenses.[4]

Entertainment costs should not include meals eaten away from home. They should be incorporated into your food budget.

Figure 11-1 is an example of a personal monthly budget report. It is only an illustration of possible monthly expenses. This will vary from month to month and year to year. The working budget report must accurately reflect your *true* monthly income and expenses.

PAYING DOWN DEBTS

After you have mapped out a budget and reviewed your finances, you may feel a little discouraged if you still carry debt. However, like most things in life, motivation is often the key to success. What motivates people to get their financial house in order differs per individual (eg, never-ending bills, countless sleepless nights, trouble with relationships, wanting a long-awaited vacation, etc). Whatever it is that provides inspiration, turn it into a positive motivator.

If your goal is to pay off debt, it goes without saying that you should not accumulate more. Therefore, it is imperative for you to be a disciplined spender and bank a small cash cushion to use for unexpected expenses. Everyone should have an emergency fund of at least $1,000 (or one month's pay would be better) to use for such occurrences.

First, break the habit of paying only the minimum required each month. Paying the minimum—usually 2% to 3% of the outstanding balance—only prolongs payoff. It is precisely what the banks want you to do. The longer you take to repay the charges, the more interest they make, and the less cash you have in your pocket. Instead, pay as much as you can each month. If your minimum payment is $100, double that to $200 or more. Examine your normal expenses, and see if you can find the money to do that. For example, you may want to brown bag your lunch, eliminate buying coffee daily, or perhaps even give up happy hour. By making small, daily sacrifices, you will accumulate the extra dollars to put toward your debt payments.

Second, take a long, hard look at all of your credit card interest rates. Identify the one with the lowest rate and consider transferring the balance from a higher interest card to a lower interest card. If your entire balance is too large to fit on one low-interest card, pay at least the minimum amounts due on all of your cards except one. Pay a majority of your debt repayments against that one credit card, and pay it off as quickly as possible. When the balance on that card reaches zero, move on to the next card with the same aggressive repayment plan. Some financial experts suggest you first attack the account with the highest interest rate, regardless of its balance. Other experts suggest attacking the smallest debt first.

If you are someone who is really motivated by numbers, you will realize the account that is doing you the most damage is the one with the highest interest rate. If the account with the highest interest is utilizing more than 30% of that credit line, focus on repaying that one first to get it under that threshold. Doing so will improve your credit score because *debt utilization*—which is how much you owe compared with how much available credit you have—is an important factor in determining your score. The lower your debt utilization, the better.

You could also cash out your savings (while maintaining your emergency fund) and use the proceeds toward debt repayment. Even when debt interest is at 12%, your savings account would have to pay more than 18% before federal and state taxes to equal that outflow of dollars. Pay off the debt, and it is the same as getting that 18% return without any risk on your part. The higher the interest rate on your debt, the more attractive repayment versus savings becomes.

Whatever method you choose to repay your debts, simply do it over and over again. As the debts disappear, you will be energized by the satisfaction that you get from accomplishing your goal. This method of repayment is called *snowballing*. As your debts decrease, the amount of money you have to pay them with increases. Sooner, rather than later, your debts are eliminated. Plan the work and work the plan.

If you have depleted your savings and cannot keep up with your payments, let your creditors know your situation. Ask for a new and lower repayment schedule, request a lower interest rate, and appeal to their desire to receive payment. Faced with the prospect that you may resort to such a drastic step, many creditors will be willing to work with you in order to protect themselves against a total loss. Bankruptcy should be your last resort.

SAVINGS AND INVESTMENT CONCEPTS AND TOOLS

Some components of saving and investing can be much like planning for a combat operation. Reverse planning that takes place when writing a military operation order is similar to establishing a savings or retirement investment goal and working backward on paper prior to executing your plan. The concept of "defense in depth" can be easily related to diversification of assets with investments. We will examine these and other savings and investment concepts in the next sections.

Emergency Savings
In military training, we strategize and rehearse our operations. In life, we plan by budgeting and by being disciplined with our spending. Having some money tucked away for emergency savings will have a great psychological impact on your life. The stress that is relieved by knowing that you have a safety net is much like the comfort that is felt by knowing that close air support or a quick reaction force is nearby.

Most financial experts recommend that you have 3 to 6 months of expenses saved in an emergency or "rainy day" fund. This probably seems like a significant amount of money to save. Thus, you should start by setting an initial emergency savings goal of at least $1,000. Then, you should consider opening a savings account at a different bank from the one where you do most of your banking. This money should be accessible to you for emergencies, but not too easily accessible or for nonemergencies.

INVESTING FOR RETIREMENT

With the exception of military retirement, those days of working for the same company for more than 40 years, retiring, and then collecting a pension are pretty much in the past. Nowadays, it takes disciplined saving and investing using a combination of *Individual Retirement Accounts* (IRAs), such as a Traditional IRA or a Roth IRA, and *employer-sponsored plans*, such as the 401(k), the Thrift Savings Plan, or the 403(b). These types of accounts or plans are usually defined by the Internal Revenue Service and provide different features based on how they are defined in the Internal Revenue Code (eg, a 401(k) is called a 401(k) because it is in Section 401(k) of the Internal Revenue Code).

All of these types of accounts have to be funded by some kind of underlying investment, such as mutual funds, bonds, annuities, or CDs (Certificates of Deposit). Accounts such as the 401(k), 403(b), and defined benefit pensions are considered as employer-sponsored plans, whereas a Traditional IRA and a Roth IRA are accounts that you own individually through an investment company away from the workplace. IRAs can be opened through banks, insurance companies, or investment firms. The IRA or employer-sponsored plan is just an account. There has to be some type of investment that funds it.

A *stock* is one share of ownership in a company that may sell thousands of shares of their stock (pieces of ownership in the business) in an effort to raise money to be used by the company. A *mutual fund* is a collection of stocks of various companies. Each fund has a fund manager that buys and sells the various stocks within the fund to keep the fund moving toward its objective. Mutual funds are designed to spread the risk of possible investment losses across the various stocks that it owns. You could buy individual stocks in a single company. However, putting all of your eggs in one basket would be a risky scenario. Instead, you could invest in a mutual fund that holds hundreds of shares of a variety of companies' stocks. Most funds will hold stocks from a hundred or more different companies.

A term that should be considered by an investor when analyzing the investment objectives of various funds is *risk tolerance*. When purchasing investments, each investor needs to consider how much risk he/she is willing to take and how much he/she could endure the potential for losses versus the potential for gains. Periodically, an investment company will require an investor to complete a risk tolerance questionnaire that is composed of a series of questions to help an investor determine risk tolerance. Something to consider when determining risk is the investor's "time horizon" or length of time until the investor will have until he/she needs to begin using the money that was invested. For example, a 25-year-old individual could take significantly more risk with investments than a 55-year-old individual because the 25-year-old would have much more time to endure the ups and downs of the stock market, whereas the 55-year-old (who is approaching retirement) should consider safer investments because there is a much shorter time available until he/she will have to begin using the money invested for retirement.

Another common term that is used with mutual funds is *load*. Basically, the load is a sales charge that is imposed by the fund company. It is the cost to buy shares of the fund. There are three types of funds:

1. *Front-end load fund*: a sales charge that is attributed when you initially buy the shares.
2. *Back-end load fund*: a sales charge that is paid when you sell or redeem your shares of the fund; frequently, the sales charge that you would have to pay decreases for every year that you own the shares.
3. *No-load fund*: a fund that does not impose sales charges; an investor is more likely to purchase a no-load fund directly from an investment company that does not have sales agents.

The Traditional IRA and the Roth IRA are often discussed in retirement planning. Comparing these types of IRAs is similar to comparing the use of a B-52 on an airstrike versus a constant barrage of ground artillery. Both IRAs will achieve a similar result, but there are pros and cons to each. The greatest difference between the two is *how taxation works*. With Traditional IRAs, the federal government has not yet taxed the money that has been invested, and the contributions may be tax-deductible for the year that the contribution is made to the IRA. However, when you retire, the distributions will be taxed at your ordinary income tax rate. In contrast, the contributions that you make to a Roth IRA have already been taxed. Therefore, based on current tax law, the distributions will not be taxed when you take them in retirement. *Be sure to consult with an accountant before making decisions on investments that may impact your tax situation.*

Diversification of assets can be thought of as "defense-in-depth" of your investment portfolio. Basically, *diversification* is spreading your monetary assets across high-, medium-, and low-risk investments to achieve the desired outcomes of protecting your investments. You might consider having some high-risk investments in your portfolio that have the potential to make tremendous gains. However, you should be aware that large losses are also a possibility. Your investment portfolio should contain some medium-risk investments that have a moderate potential for gain and less potential for loss. The investment portfolio should also contain some low-risk investments (eg, bonds) to create some stability as a backup force in the event that the other investments sustain major losses. This is the "don't put all of your eggs in one basket" concept.

INSURANCE

Most people spend little time learning about insurance (whether automobile, homeowners, renters, flood, health, life, or disability) or even reviewing their own policies. It is important to keep in mind that one brief moment can be financially devastating if you do not have the proper insurance coverage. Consider taking time to review all of your insurance policies with a qualified insurance professional at least once each year and anytime a major life event occurs (eg, marriage, birth of a child, divorce, purchase of a home, etc).

AUTO INSURANCE

Even though automobile insurance policies will differ slightly from state to state, all of them require that you carry some level of liability coverage. Liability coverage is the most important coverage on your automobile policy because it pays for the damages that you might cause. This coverage is typically broken down into

- *bodily injury liability*—pays for injuries to another person or people due to an automobile accident, and
- *property damage liability*—covers the damage to another vehicle, someone's house, or other property.

Call your automobile insurance company to get prices on increasing your liability coverage. You will probably be surprised at how inexpensive it is to increase your liability coverage. In addition, remember that minimum coverage does not always mean minimum prices.

Other important coverages to consider on your automobile insurance policy include comprehensive, collision, medical payments, towing, and rental reimbursement. Be sure to evaluate each item and understand how it might relate to your circumstances when shopping for or reviewing your automobile insurance policy.

Homeowners Insurance

When most people think of homeowners insurance, the typical fear associated with it is a large house fire. Although "total-loss" house fires do occur, they only represent a small number of actual homeowners insurance claims. The majority of homeowners insurance claims are typically only a few thousand dollars and involve events such as the wind ripping shingles off of the roof, a tree falling on the house, water damage from a broken pipe, etc.

Some of the major elements to consider with homeowners insurance are

- dwelling amount,
- contents coverage,
- liability coverage,
- deductible, and
- replacement cost versus actual cash value (ACV) coverage.

Dwelling Amount

With most homeowners insurance policies, many things are based on the dwelling coverage amount or the amount that the house itself is insured for. The dwelling coverage amount is based on a replacement cost figure. This replacement cost figure is a calculation of what it would cost to rebuild the home completely using like kind and quality materials. Often, people will confuse replacement cost with market value (the amount you could sell your home for) and, quite frequently, the replacement cost figure is significantly higher than the market value.

Contents Coverage

The contents coverage amount is typically determined as a percentage of the dwelling amount. Thus, if the dwelling coverage on your homeowners policy is $200,000 and your policy provides 75% for contents coverage, then you would have $150,000 of contents coverage.

Liability Coverage

The liability coverage on a homeowners policy provides coverage for many different types of incidents that could occur on or off the premises of your home. The policyholder selects the amount of coverage on the policy: the available coverage amounts are typically $100,000, $300,000, or $500,000. Some of the most common claims that occur under homeowners insurance liability coverage are dog bites and slips and falls. Typically, some type of negligence has to occur for claims to be paid under homeowners liability coverage.

Deductible

The deductible is how much the policyholder is responsible for contributing to repair the damage when the policyholder files a claim. For example, if there was a windstorm and your roof sustained $4,000 worth of damage and you had a $1,000 deductible, you would pay $1,000 and your insurance company would pay $3,000 to fix your roof if you had replacement cost coverage. Keep in mind that increasing your deductible will *decrease* your premium, but it also *increases* the amount that you are responsible for paying if you file a claim.

Replacement Cost Versus Actual Cash Value Coverage

When choosing various options on your homeowners insurance policy, you may have the opportunity to select from replacement cost or ACV coverage. You will find that ACV costs significantly less than replacement cost coverage because ACV provides significantly less coverage and, often, mortgage companies may not accept ACV coverage. Basically, ACV coverage is replacement cost coverage minus depreciation. If you had a $4,000 damaged roof claim and a $1,000 deductible, with ACV coverage the insurance company would then subtract money from that $3,000, depending on the age of the roof. For example, if your roof is 15 years old and is expected to last 30 years, the insurance company could reduce your payment by 50%. Now your $4,000 roof claim just turned into you paying $2,500 (your $1,000 deductible plus $1,500 in depreciation) and your insurance company paying $1,500 to have your roof repaired. In most cases, selecting replacement cost coverage will be your best option.

Keep in mind that homeowners insurance policies, like any other insurance policies, will have exclusions, limitations, items that are covered, and items that are not covered. Do not fall into the trap of believing that your homeowners policy will cover anything and everything that could go wrong with your house. Be sure to read the policy booklet that is mailed to you with your homeowners policy declarations page.

RENTERS INSURANCE

A renters insurance policy is very similar to a homeowners insurance policy minus the coverage for the dwelling or house. It is primarily intended to cover contents and liability. Many people believe that the landlord's insurance will cover their contents in the event of a loss, such as a fire; however, this is probably not the case. Renters can purchase renters insurance policies very inexpensively that may also cover "loss of use," which may pay for you to stay somewhere else temporarily while damage is being repaired at the apartment or house that you are renting.

Life Insurance

Life insurance is often a topic that most people do not want to discuss. Fortunately, the military has made life insurance easy to obtain with Service-member's Group Life Insurance (SGLI). *What options exist when leaving the military?* Most importantly, you need to figure out how much life insurance you should have, then determine where you are going to get it.

Liabilities

Liability primarily includes any money that you owe to anyone else that should be paid in the event of your death. Therefore, make a total of all mortgage payments, vehicle loans, credit card balances, loans from family members, and any other money owed to anyone else.

Income

One of the major reasons to have life insurance is to allow your dependents to maintain a similar standard of living after your death. Consider what life would be like for your family if they did not have your income. Something that is often overlooked in life insurance planning is the "income" of a non-working spouse. For example, if you lost your nonworking spouse, would you need money to pay for child care or for someone to prepare meals and do shopping that you do not have time to do?

Final Expenses

Most people think of "final expenses" as funeral expenses. Even though funeral expenses need to be discussed, final expenses go beyond just that. Consider spending about $5,000 per person for cremation expenses and $10,000 to $15,000 for a burial. However, also consider if some money should be included for things such as uncovered medical bills, charitable giving, and other miscellaneous fees (eg, changing vehicle registrations, drafting a new will for surviving dependents, etc). If you are currently setting aside money for your children's education, your life insurance plan should incorporate a strategy that completes that education fund in the event of a premature death. Consider your surviving spouse as well. If you died, would he/she need to go back to school in order to enter the workforce?

Once you have calculated how much life insurance you (and your spouse, if applicable) should have, consider where that life insurance will come from. Keep in mind that some of your life insurance may come from more than one of these sources. Some elements to consider when deciding where your life insurance will come from are cost, medical history, and portability.

Service Members Group Life Insurance to Veterans Group Life Insurance
Upon separation or retirement, Service Members are given the option to
convert their SGLI to Veterans Group Life Insurance (VGLI). If this option
is exercised at the time of separation, there is no medical underwriting or
proof of good health that is necessary. However, if you wait, you will have to
medically qualify. The option to convert SGLI to VGLI might make sense for
Veterans who have health issues that might prevent them from purchasing individually owned life insurance. Keep in mind that the rates increase on VGLI
policies every 5 years, so they can be very expensive later in life.

Group Life Insurance

Most civilian employers will offer group life insurance as part of a benefits
package. Group life insurance is typically inexpensive. However, if it has a
portability option (an option to take it with you when you leave that employer), the cost of the new policy will be significantly more expensive.

Individually Owned Life Insurance

These types of policies are purchased through a private insurance company
(eg, automobile or homeowners insurance). Most individually owned policies
require medical underwriting, and some will require a brief physical. The
costs of these policies depend on the type of policy that is purchased. The
types of individually owned life insurance policies are *term* and *permanent*
(including whole life, universal life, and variable). The simplest way to understand the differences in these types of life insurance is to compare renting an
apartment versus owning a home.

Term life insurance is similar to renting an apartment. With an apartment, you sign a lease that allows you to live there for a certain period of
time, a term. You purchase term life insurance policies in specified terms
such as 10, 20, or 30 years. Also, like an apartment, you are not building
any equity in a term life insurance policy. Term life insurance policies are less
expensive than permanent policies, just as renting an apartment would be less
expensive than owning a home, in most cases. With permanent life insurance
policies, you have life insurance coverage, but you are also accumulating cash
value. This cash value is similar to equity in a home that could be withdrawn
or borrowed against.

Often, the best-case scenario is owning a combination of these types of
life insurance policies. Owning a large amount of term life insurance to cover
temporary needs (eg, a mortgage or having children at home) and owning a
smaller amount of permanent life insurance to cover permanent needs (eg,
final expenses) can be a great life insurance planning solution. Any group life

insurance that you have through an employer could come into play for any gaps in your plan that are not covered by the other policies.

Certainly, insurance is typically not a topic that most people get overly excited about. However, neglecting your insurance plans can have a devastating impact on your overall financial plan, and they can have quite an impact on your family's well-being.

CAREGIVER CHALLENGES, CONSIDERATIONS, AND ASSISTANCE

Caring for a wounded Service Member or Veteran can add a new set of financial issues. Although thousands of Service Members have been wounded in military conflicts, advancements in battlefield medicine have allowed many of our most seriously injured troops to survive catastrophic injuries. These wounds result in traumatic brain injuries, loss of limbs, permanent paralysis, loss of sight, severe burns, and other invisible wounds. Consequently, many of these Service Members will ultimately need long-term, perhaps around-the-clock, care and support.

Most Americans are unaware of the challenges faced by the families of Wounded Warriors. Before the service-related injury, their lives were packed with normalcy—a predictable 5-day work week, the occasional 4-day training holidays, trips to the field, planning for vacations, and dreaming about life after the military. Then, suddenly, families receive word that their loved ones have been gravely injured or wounded, and the normalcy of everyday life ends. The Elizabeth Dole Foundation commissioned the RAND Corporation to assess the needs of the military caregivers and made the following statement:

> Those caregivers often toil in relative obscurity, and they are challenging to count or describe. They are spouses, parents, children, and relatives of the wounded veteran, but many coworkers, neighbors, and friends also take on responsibilities. They provide care and assistance, promoting faster recovery for their loved ones and thus saving our nation millions of dollars in health care costs. However, the personal impact of providing this care is enormous. The time required can result in lost jobs, lost wages, and a possible loss of health insurance; in addition the physical and emotional toll can be substantial.[5]

The report presented information gleaned from military caregivers themselves and from policymakers and program officials who either directly support, or advocate on behalf of, military caregivers. It also provided a snap-shot of the number and characteristics of military caregivers, the roles they serve, the physical and emotional impact caregiving has on their lives, and the resources available to them.

The RAND report estimates between 275,000 and 1 million men and women have cared, or are caring for, wounded, ill, or injured Service Members and Veterans, but the actual number may be even more. Caregivers perform a wide variety of roles and functions in support of their Wounded Warriors, including the following:

- assisting with the normal activities of daily living,
- serving as mental health counselors,
- advocating for new and better treatment, and
- even serving as the family's legal and financial representatives. [5]

All totaled, these functions or services equate to more than a full-time job.

According to the 2010 report[6] released by the National Alliance of Caregiving (Bethesda, MD) and the United Health Foundation (Winnetonka, MN), caring for a Wounded Warrior can have a significant impact on a person's professional life. Approximately 59% of these caregivers have stopped working to provide the around-the-clock care needed by the family member. Additionally, about 28% of caregivers who still work outside the home report they have voluntarily accepted a reduction in pay/benefits to have the flexibility they need to care for an injured Veteran.[6] Even though their take-home income decreases, their medical expenses skyrocket. The RAND Corporation estimates that the family caregiver's out-of-pocket medical expenses are 2.5 times higher than their noncaregiver counterparts. [5] Unfortunately, VA services support a small portion of the 1.1 million caregivers nationwide.

POSSIBLE CAREGIVING EXPENSES

There are many types of additional expenses that can crop up when caring for a loved one. Although this list is not exhaustive, it gives an idea of the kinds of financial challenges that may need to be addressed:

- *Medications, equipment, and co-pays*—Costs of medications, medical adaptive equipment, and co-pays for doctor visits can quickly add up. Although co-pays might not seem like much for each visit, they can put a dent in your wallet if you are visiting many doctors and specialists.

- *Home modification costs*—It may be necessary to make modifications to your home so that it is suitable for your loved one. Ramps to entrances, wider doorframes, and grab bars may be needed to help you and your loved one navigate around home.
- *Caregiving services (respite, day services)*—If you work, you may have to find services for your loved one while you are away, or you may just need a break for your own emotional well-being from time to time.
- *Travel/transportation fees*—If your loved one uses a wheelchair or requires transportation via stretcher, traveling to each doctor's appointment or outing could incur additional costs if you need to hire a service each time to get you there and back home.
- *Reduced work hours, reduced pay, or loss of job for the caregiver*—Your caregiving responsibilities may mean that you have less time for your own work or career. You might need to reduce your hours, take a lower paying position, or even take a leave of absence.

FINANCIAL AND JOB SUPPORT TO CAREGIVERS

The policy landscape is undergoing changes in this domain. However, these changes are still relatively new, and whether they effectively address needs is unclear. In recent years, lawmakers have amended the Family Medical Leave Act (FMLA) to permit family members of "covered" Service Members up to 26 work weeks of leave to care for their Service Member. In 2010, this was extended to include family members of Veterans. These amendments do not provide direct financial remediation for the long-term needs of caregivers. A 2012 report[7] from the Quadrennial Review of Military Compensation (QRMC) addressed this issue specifically.

The QRMC highlighted two programs currently in their infancy that attempt to alleviate potential negative financial consequences associated with caregiving:

1. the Department of Defense's (DoD's) Special Compensation for Assistance with Activities of Daily Living (SCAADL) program and
2. the VA Program of Comprehensive Assistance for Family Caregivers.

These new programs are slated for caregivers who assist their Service Members or Veterans with activities of daily living (eg, feeding, dressing bathing, grooming, toileting, transferring, etc). Although important, these programs are in the early stages of implementation and serve only a small fraction of military caregivers.[8] In addition, as noted in the QRMC report, the programs are already disjointed.[8]

For example, each program imposes different eligibility criteria: the *DoD definition covers injuries and illnesses,* but the *VA definition only covers injuries* (eg, physical injury, traumatic brain injury, psychological trauma, or other mental disorders). The VA also requires that the caregiver be a family member or live with the care recipient and that the caregiver has already provided at least 6 months of continuous assistance. SCAADL imposes neither of these requirements.[8]

SCAADL was authorized by the National Defense Authorization Act in fiscal year 2010. This special monthly compensation is for Service Members who incur a permanent catastrophic injury or illness. SCAADL helps offset the loss of income by a primary caregiver who provides nonmedical care, support, and assistance for the Service Member.

Some nonprofit organizations offer retreats intended to engage both caregivers and their Veterans or Service Members. Military-specific online support communities and forums are also available. Although some caregivers noted that it was difficult to carve out time to attend a retreat or group meeting, many caregivers emphasized that interacting with other caregivers was critically important to them.

RESOURCES FOR CAREGIVERS

Once you have a better sense of the kinds of costs that might arise while caring for your loved one, it is time to develop a sound spending plan that takes both anticipated and unanticipated expenses into account. There are a number of military benefits and resources available to help you take some of the financial stress out of caregiving.

If your loved one is covered under TRICARE, he/she may be eligible to receive home healthcare benefits. The TRICARE website (http://www.tricare. mil) has a wealth of information and can help you determine the benefit eligibility of your loved one. If your loved one meets the eligibility requirements for Medicare or Medicaid caregiving and financial management for the Wounded Warrior, financial coverage may be available for medical costs, transportation, respite care, home modifications, and equipment expenses. Additional information is also available at the Centers for Medicare & Medicaid Services at https://www.cms.gov.

TAKE ADVANTAGE OF THE RESOURCES

Caregiving is a demanding responsibility. Worrying about your finances should not keep you from caring for your loved one and yourself. If you also find that you need some support while undertaking your role as a military caregiver, consider reaching out for help. You can access nonmedical counseling services through Military OneSource (http://www.militaryonesource.mil or by calling 800-342-9647).

FINANCIAL COUNSELING SUPPORT

If you live on or near your military installation, you can reach out to the installation personal financial management program. A financial counselor can help you develop a spending plan that works for you while taking into account those often unanticipated expenses. The program also offers workshops and classes that might be helpful as well. If you are not located near an installation, you can also access financial counseling services through Military OneSource or through the Military and Family Life Counselor (MFLC) program. Contact information for MFLCs can be accessed through your military and family support center. All of these services are provided at no cost to Service Members and their families.

MILITARY RELIEF SOCIETIES

Each service has a private, nonprofit organization that assists families in times of need. Areas of assistance may include the following:

- emergency transportation;
- help with medical bills, child care expenses, food, rent, utilities, and other household bills;
- vehicle repair; and
- family emergency assistance.

For more information on the relief societies, contact the Army Emergency Relief (http://www.aerhq.com), the Navy–Marine Corps Relief Society (http://www.nmcrs.org), or the Air Force Aid Society (http://www.afas.org).

WOUNDED WARRIOR PROGRAMS

The military's Wounded Warrior programs provide assistance and advocacy for severely wounded, ill, and injured Service Members, Veterans, and their families. These programs assist Service Members and their families as they return to duty or transition to civilian life.

Each of the individual branches of service operates a Wounded Warrior program to assist Service Members and their families with nonmedical issues associated with the transition back to duty or to civilian life. The Wounded

Warrior programs work with the Service Member and his/her medical team to develop a comprehensive recovery plan that addresses specific recovery, rehabilitation, and reintegration goals. These programs provide lifetime support for the Service Member. Eligibility for participation in the program does not conclude when the Service Member is discharged from a military treatment facility. Typical nonmedical support provided by the Wounded Warrior programs may include, but is not limited to, assistance with the following:

- pay and personnel issues,
- invitational travel orders,
- lodging and housing adaptations for the Wounded Warrior,
- child and youth care arrangements,
- transportation needs,
- legal and guardianship issues,
- education and training benefits,
- respite care, and
- traumatic brain injury/posttraumatic stress support services.

Eligibility for Wounded Warrior programs is not limited to those with combat injuries. These programs also assist those battling serious illnesses or who are injured in accidents. Generally, the military Wounded Warrior programs support Service Members who incur a serious illness or injury requiring long-term care that may result in a Medical Evaluation Board/Physical Evaluation Board to determine fitness for duty.

SUMMARY

Keeping one's financial house in order is a key factor to reducing stress and living a more joyful life. Dealing with financial issues is never easy, regardless of one's personal situation in life or financial means. However, financial challenges should be addressed as soon as they arise and before they become a crisis. Achieving or even maintaining financial stability frequently requires initiative and often aggressive action; it does not happen on its own. Fortunately, Service Members and Veterans are not on their own. There are many useful tools and invaluable resources available to assist them. Take full advantage of existing programs and benefits. Remember to have a plan, be positive, and stay resilient.

References

1. US Department of Veterans Affairs/Veterans Health Administration. *Veterans Health Benefits Handbook*. Washington, DC: DVA/VHA; 2014. Chapter 2.

2. Department of Veterans Affairs. *Federal Benefits for Veterans, Dependents and Survivors*. Washington, DC: DVA; 2014. Chapter 2.

3. Researcher finds correlation between financial arguments, decreased relationship satisfaction [press release]. Manhattan, KS: Kansas State University, News and Communications Services; July 12, 2013.

4. Reichenberger A. Consumer Expenditure Survey. A comparison of 25 years of consumer expenditures by homeowners and renters. U.S. Bureau of Labor Statistics: Beyond the Numbers, October 2012, vol 1, no 15, p 4. http//www.bls.gov/opub/btn/volume-1/a-comparisonof-25-years-of-consumer-expenditures-by-homeownersand-renters.htm. Accessed December 8, 2015.

5. Tanielian T, Ramchand R, Fisher MP, Sims CS, Harris RS, Harrell MC. *Military Caregivers: Cornerstones of Support for Our Nation's Wounded, Ill, and Injured Veterans*. Santa Monica, CA: RAND Corporation; 2013. http://www.rand.org/pubs/research_reports/RR244.html. Accessed August 15, 2016.

6. National Alliance for Caregiving and the United Health Foundation. http://www.caregiving.org/data/2010_Caregivers_of_Veterans_FULLREPORT_WEB_FINAL.pdf. Accessed December 8, 2015.

7. Office of the Under Secretary of Defense. *The Eleventh Quadrennial Review of Military Compensation—Main Report*. Washington, DC: Author; June 2012: 293 pp. Accession Number ADA563239.

8. Special Compensation for Assistance with Activities of Daily Living (SCAADL) Eligibility. DD Form 2948, September 2011. http://www.wtc.army.mil/documents/factsheets/wtc_SCAADL_fact_sheet.pdf. Accessed December 8, 2015.

CHIEF WARRANT OFFICER 2 SHERMAN GILLUMS, JR When Sherman Gillums, Jr received his orders to transfer to 1st Marine Division in December 2001, months after the 9/11 attacks, he imagined that he could end up catastrophically injured in some way. However, when he awoke after 3 days of unconsciousness following a vehicle multiple rollover at Marine Corps Base Camp Pendleton in February 2002, the journey he had anticipated began in a way he had not expected. Now, the 12-year Veteran of the US Marine Corps—who had trained more than 400 recruits as a drill instructor and earned distinction as the first Warrant Officer to complete the grueling Marine Corps Martial Arts Instructor–Trainer Program—faced his greatest test: overcoming his own mortality.

The sound of the artificial ventilator that kept his now paralyzed body breathing brought him to consciousness on February 23, 2002 at Scripps Memorial Hospital in San Diego. His C5/C6 cervical vertebrae had been fractured from the rollover. The broken pieces had to be surgically removed to relieve pressure on his spinal cord, and a titanium cage was placed around his spine to hold it together. Within days, he had completely lost function in his legs, arms, and bodily systems.

Shortly after transferring to the San Diego VA Medical Center to begin rehabilitation, Gillums began a 4-month journey where major setbacks and incremental progress would typify the course of rehabilitation. It would take numerous bouts of passing out due to hypotension whenever his nurses sat him up before he could even imagine getting into a wheelchair, much less push one. His first bout with autonomic dysreflexia, an extremely painful residual effect of spinal cord injury, brought new meaning to the definition of

pain tolerance. Simple tasks like eating independently called for Herculean endurance and mental energy beyond that he had once marshaled to complete ten 54-hour, 48-mile crucible exercises during his 2-year tour as a drill instructor.

Reintegrating back into his world meant adapting to his new normal, and he did. Soon, the mat-to-wheelchair transfers got easier for him. Using his spasticity to dress while he lay on his back became second nature. Maneuvering his wheelchair eventually required more motivation than pain as he got stronger. These successes would condition him for greater tests of his will where living, not just surviving, was the end game.

For Gillums, living meant finding the will to push beyond the embryonic protection of the VA Medical Center and back out into a world full of challenges. It pushed him to win two Gold Medals at the National Veterans Wheelchair Games and ski the Black Diamond slopes in Aspen, Colorado. It pushed him across the stage at the University of San Diego, where he earned a graduate degree in business. It pushed him down the aisle at the St. Regis Hotel where he married his wife, Tammie.

Sherman's will now pushes him in his tireless advocacy for Veterans with severe disabilities across the country, in national media, and on Capitol Hill. Most importantly, it pushes Chief Warrant Officer Gillums to the bedsides of the many recovering Warriors whose paths to spinal cord injury would go through freeways, battlefields, and training bases. He hopes that all of them will see his life as a case study in resilience worth emulating.

Despite the fact that the current unemployment rate for
Veterans has dropped, those with catastrophic disabilities are still
six to eight times more likely to remain unemployed
despite having a desire to work.
This reality is linked to a number of factors, starting with low
self-expectations on the Veteran's part. But employers
have contributed as well, by submitting to stigmas and misperceptions
about drawbacks of hiring "less than perfect" Veterans.

★ ★ ★

AL KOVACK JR.
PRESIDENT, PARALYZED VETERANS OF AMERICA
CONGRESSIONAL TESTIMONY
MAY 20, 2015

Chapter Twelve

Education and Employment

MARY R. GOLDBERG, PhD*; ANNE E. BARRY, MS, CRC†;
MARIA MILLEVILLE, MEd‡; MICHELLE L. SPORNER, PhD, CRC§;
RON DRACH¥; ALLEN LEWIS, PhD, CRC ¶; and
BRIAN BILSKI, BS#

*Education and Outreach Coordinator, Rehabilitation Research and Development Service, US Department of Veterans Affairs, 6425 Penn Avenue, Pittsburgh, Pennsylvania 15206

†Rehabilitation Counselor, Office of Vocational Rehabilitation, 531 Penn Avenue, Pittsburgh, Pennsylvania 15222

‡Principal, Up Next LLC, 1200 Richmond Street, Pittsburgh, Pennsylvania 15218

§Assistant Professor, Department of Rehabilitation Science and Technology, University of Pittsburgh, 5044 Forbes Tower, Pittsburgh, Pennsylvania 15260

¥Sergeant (Retired), US Army; President, Drach Consulting, 7600 River Falls Drive, Potomac, Maryland 20854; formerly, Director, Government and Legislative Affairs, Department of Labor, Washington, DC

¶Dean and Professor, State University of New York Downstate Medical Center, College of Health Related Professions, 450 Clarkson Avenue, Brooklyn, New York 11203

#President, Veteran Integration Solutions, 17529 Deer Isle Circle, Winter Garden, Florida 34787; formerly, Colonel (Retired), US Marine Corps; Consultant/Economic Liaison, US Department of Veterans Affairs, Jacksonville, Florida

INTRODUCTION

How do today's Service Members and Veterans receive benefits to obtain an appropriate education to pursue their career goals? Do programs exist to support Service Members and Veterans' training and job seeking efforts? How can supporters and facilitators of Service Members and Veterans' transitional success assist in these efforts? To address the current state of Service Members and Veterans' education and employment, it is helpful to understand the history of Veterans' benefits and what programs have been created over time to address education and employment issues. This chapter will provide an overview of the following three issues: (1) employment and career opportunities, (2) benefits of volunteering and being active, and (3) vocational training and education. Special emphasis on programs and initiatives for those with primary disabilities emerging from current conflicts, posttraumatic stress disorder (PTSD), and traumatic brain injury (TBI) will also be examined.

BACKGROUND

THE HISTORY OF VETERANS' EDUCATION

In Abraham Lincoln's second inaugural address, he charged the US government with the responsibility "to care for him who shall have borne the battle and for his widow, and his orphan." The year of Lincoln's address was 1865, but the history of the care for the country's Military Veterans dates many years prior. The laws, initiatives, and programs dedicated to the Military Servicemen and women have a rich and complex evolution—adapting, transforming, and conforming to the current social and military landscape of the nation. Following World War I, the foundational legislation for educational and vocational training for Veterans surfaced. The legislative responses that provided educational benefits to Veterans emerged following military involvement in war and conflict. These legislations were reformed and reflected the Veteran population's needs at that time.

In 1918, the Soldier's Rehabilitation Act was passed, thus broadening the scope of care offered to Veterans by the government. The Vocational Rehabilitation Act established the Federal Board for Vocational Education, an independent agency. In the years to follow, the Disabled Veterans' Rehabilitation Act of 1943 was passed, focusing on job training for Veterans with disabilities. In 1944, the Servicemen's Readjustment Act was signed into effect by President Franklin D Roosevelt in response to the needs created by World War II.

The Servicemen's Readjustment Act, also known as "the GI Bill of Rights," included three key provisions for Service Members and Veterans:

1. up to 4 years of benefits for education or training;
2. home, farm, or small business loans with no down payment; and
3. unemployment compensation of $20/week for up to 1 year.

The educational benefits allocated payment of up to $500 for tuition and funding for books, student fees, and supplies. Additionally, those who were eligible received a monthly allowance. Total participation in the premier GI Bill was approximately half of eligible Veterans.

The Korean War called for adjustment and accommodations for Service Members and Veterans. The 1952 Veterans' Readjustment Assistance Act (or Korean GI Bill) redefined the allocations and benefits. Unemployment compensation, insurance, job training, and home loans still existed, and were similar to the previous GI Bill. However, the educational benefits were more limited, restricting education benefits to a maximum of 36 months as opposed to the previously allotted 48 months. Instead of payment directly for tuition, Veterans received monthly subsistence checks that could be used for tuition. At the termination of these benefits in 1956, 7.8 million Veterans were receiving educational training, and 5.9 million were guaranteed home loans, totaling approximately 50 billion dollars.

In 1966, Congress passed the Veterans' Readjustment Benefits Act (or Vietnam GI Bill). The 1966 GI Bill reinstated educational benefits, providing 10 months of education for every 1 month of military service. The Vietnam GI Bill was received with unprecedented success. Participation during the years following the Vietnam War was 76%, whereas participation for the Korean GI Bill was 43.4%. Once again, the educational assistance offered to Veterans continued to evolve in the post-Vietnam era with the passage of the Veterans Educational Assistance Program (VEAP) Act of 1977. VEAP emerged following the transition in the military from the draft to voluntary service. The provisional option was made by VEAP that Servicemen could pay into their educational fund, with their dollars matched 2:1 with federal dollars up to $2,700.

In the late 1960s, there was a shortage in military recruitment, and the government addressed this problem by increasing educational benefits in the hope of attracting more recruits. The Veterans Education Assistance Act of 1984 (or the Montgomery GI Bill) was passed. The Montgomery GI Bill provided $300/month for 36 months to eligible Veterans. Eligibility included those who served 3 years active duty or 2 years active duty and 4 years in the Reserves. It was later expanded to include those who committed to 6 years in the Reserves.

America's involvement in the Persian Gulf ushered in new amendments to the GI Bill for Veterans. In March 1991, the Supplemental Authorization and Personnel Benefits Act increased the monthly allowance for Veterans receiving educational benefits. About 10 years later, the United States would find itself involved the Global War on Terrorism after the September 11, 2001 terrorist attacks. This war, like others in American history, would challenge the existing legislation and call for the evolution of educational benefits that would come in the form of the Post-9/11 GI Bill: the Veterans Educational
Assistance Act of 2008.[1,2]

Veterans Education Today: Education, Retention, Graduation, and Employment

The Post-9/11 GI Bill was one of the most significant pieces of legislation in terms of educational benefits since the conception of the first GI Bill in 1944. Increased benefits offered to Veterans include full tuition and fee coverage for in-state public undergraduate institutions. Out-of-state choices, private institutions, and graduate schooling are also available for coverage if an agreement is made by the institution and the Department of Veterans Affairs (VA) to match funds to cover costs.[3] Today, estimates of those using the Post-9/11 GI Bill are approximately 760,000 Service Members and Veterans. This number is only expected to increase because there are now approximately 2 million Veterans who will be returning home as a result of the winding down of American involvement in the Middle East. In a recent study conducted by the Iraq and Afghanistan Veterans of America organization and Prudential Financial, Inc, the majority of Veterans reported education as a priority; 44% reported themselves as full- or part-time students.[4,5] The US Bureau of Labor Statistics (BLS) reported in 2010 that 45.9% of Veterans who have served since September 2001 have some college education and that 23.4% have received a Bachelor's degree, leaving only 30.7% of Veterans without any form of postsecondary education.

Currently, the Post-9/11 GI Bill is just 6 years old. Due to its infancy, there is little data available about its current standing and long-term success. Student Veteran retention in postsecondary education is an important area with an unfortunate lack of data. Although reliable and complete data are not available, reports are inconsistent and unreliable.[6] However, this situation is

FIGURE 12-1. *Unemployment Rate (Total Annual Average Percentage).*
DATA SOURCE: BUREAU OF LABOR STATISTICS.

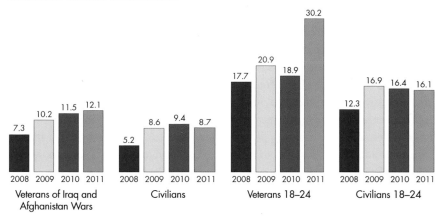

| Veterans of Iraq and Afghanistan Wars | Civilians | Veterans 18–24 | Civilians 18–24 |

being remedied. In 2010, a press release by the Student Veterans of America (SVA) announced a collaborative effort between the VA, SVA, and National Student Clearinghouse to track the success of student Veterans to include retention, graduation, and employment outcomes. Additionally, President Obama signed an executive order in April 2012 that mandated documentation of outcomes and the rate of graduation among student Veterans. In 2013, the BLS reported that unemployment rates for Veterans with postsecondary education credentials are lower than those without these credentials (Figure 12-1).[7] However, in the same report, an ironic trend emerged showing that, although the use of the Post-9/11 GI Bill is increasing, so is the unemployment rate of Post-9/11 Veterans. Currently, the unemployment rate for male Veterans is 4.5%, 5.4% for female Veterans, and 5.8% for their non-Veteran counterparts. Veterans under the age of 24 years have the highest unemployment rate at 13%, which is a highly unfavorable comparison to their non-Veteran peers.[7] Syracuse University's Institute for Veterans and Military Families (IVMF) published a comprehensive Veteran employment situation report in March 2013 that provides a full picture of the Veteran employment landscape.

LEGISLATIVE BACKING
In addition to the various GI Bills and described provisions, there are additional federal laws, policies, and programs that affect enrollment, retention, and employment of Veterans. The Transition Assistance Program (TAP) was created and established as a pilot program in 1990 to offer in-person assistance in the form of a 3-day workshop for Service Members coming off

deployment orders and retiring from the military. Within TAP, the Department of Defense (DoD) offers preseparation counseling; the Department of Labor (DOL) offers briefings regarding employment and reemployment rights as well as job placement trainings, and the VA offers services and education to Veterans with disabilities. In 2011, Congress passed the VOW Act (Veterans Opportunity to Work and Hire Heroes Act of 2011), which mandates that all separating Service Members attend TAP, and that the Department of Labor redesign its portion, the employment workshop.[8]

In 1994, the Uniformed Services Employment and Reemployment Rights Act took effect, and it outlines protections to Veterans and members of the National Guard and Reserves in the way of civilian job rights and employee benefits. The Service Members Civil Relief Act (SCRA) modernized the Soldiers' and Sailors' Civil Relief Act of 1940.[8] In 2003, the Service Members Civil Relief Act offered protection in matters involving rental agreements, security deposits, prepaid rent and insurance, and tax payments for Reservists who were called to active duty.

The Higher Education Relief Opportunities for Students Act of 2003 provides protection against adverse implications of Federal student aid to Service Members and Veterans. It includes special provisions for these students during times of war or national emergency.[8] There is also the Veterans Opportunity to Work Act established in 2007 that expanded training and educational opportunities to Veterans, as well as included incentives for employers to hire Veterans. Similar programs to this include the Yellow Ribbon Reintegration Program, VA for Vets, and Hire Heroes USA. Degree-granting institutions of higher learning participating in the Yellow Ribbon Program agree to make additional funds available for Veterans' education programs without an additional charge to their GI Bill entitlement. VA for Vets helps Veterans and transitioning Military Service Members find federal or nonprofit careers, whereas Hire Heroes USA is dedicated to creating job opportunities for Veterans and their spouses through military transition training and corporate partnerships.

EMPLOYMENT AND CAREER OPPORTUNITIES

The GI Bill has trained and provided employment opportunities to 450,000 engineers, 238,000 teachers, 91,000 scientists, 67,000 doctors, 22,000 dentists, and millions of other Veterans in the workforce. Despite the fact that 69.3% of today's Veterans have a Bachelor's degree or some college education, the unemployment rate for Veterans is on the rise and shows a disparity between Veterans and non-Veterans.[9] The troops serving in America's Global War on Terrorism are coming home, and the longest wartime chapter in America's history is drawing to an end. As a result, there will be potentially hundreds of thousands of Veterans seeking employment and hoping to carve out a new life and vocational identity. Thus, there are many federal initiatives and resources for Veterans pursuing employment.

A supplemental note required when discussing Veterans' employment is that of the disabled Veterans seeking entrance into or already in the workforce. Reports provide numbers ranging from 47,000 to 75,000 Servicemen returning home with service-connected disabilities.[10,11] Moreover, at any given time, there are approximately 200,000 Veterans with disabilities who are trying to find a job.[12] Twenty-five percent of Veterans making up this population are diagnosed with "invisible wounds." These disabilities can include impaired hearing, degenerative vision, traumatic brain injuries, and PTSD.[10] All war-related disabilities require cognizant consideration, respect, and sensitivity from potential employers. In more complicated cases, education and patience may be required as well.

In addition to the Veterans Opportunity to Work program and Hire Heroes USA, there are other noteworthy federal initiatives. In 2011, President Barack Obama signed the American Jobs Act that granted tax credit to businesses that hired unemployed Veterans. An extension of this Act is the Wounded Warrior tax credit provided to those who employ Veterans with service-connected disabilities. Additionally, several organizations and Internet resources exist to aid the job search process for Veterans, as well as for potential employers of Veterans:

- Feds Hire Vets,
- Job Accommodation Network,
- Employer Assistance and Resource Network,
- National Resource Directory, and
- AbleForces.org.

A more comprehensive review of helpful resources can be found in Table 12-1[11] and in Chapter 14 (Overview of Military and Veteran Resources). In 2012, IVMF published "The Business Case for Hiring a Veteran: Beyond the Clichés."[13] This paper identified the strengths, skills, and assets that today's Veterans possess that make them optimal candidates for employers. Common themes that showed up in the IVMF brief were the strong work ethic, sense of mission, leadership, and high levels of trust that are commonly found among Veteran populations. Veterans typically have a strong sense of

Table 12-1. *Summary of Low-Intensity Programs**

Program Name	Services	Types of Assistance
AbilityOne	Provides employment opportunitites for people who are blind or who have other severe disabilities http://www.abilityone.org	Link to opportunities, job placement, and matching
Able Forces	Provides employment opportunities and community-based job preparation training to returning Service Members suffering from severe physical disabilities and psychological disorders http://www.ableforces.org	Link to opportunities, job placement, and matching
Air Force Wounded Warrior HART Program	Assists wounded Airmen with employment placement or employment counseling http://www.af.mil/News/ArticleDisplay/ tabid/223/Article/131091/palace-hart- helps-injured-airmen.aspx	Link to opportunities and job preparation
America's Heroes at Work	Provides information and toolkits to employers hiring Veterans with TBI and PTSD http://www.dol.gov/vets/ahaw	Link to resources for employers
DoDVets	Provides general career information for Veterans with disabilities who are looking for opportunities at the Department of Defense; includes federal employment information, Q&As for Veterans and managers, internships, and education and training programs http://www.godefense.com/veterans	Link to opportunities
EARN	Provides information for employers seeking to recruit and hire employees with disabilities http://www.askearn.org	Link to resources for employers
Entrepreneurship Bootcamp	Offers experiential training in entrepreneurship and small business management to Soldiers, Sailors, Airmen, and Marines with disabilities http://bv.vets.syr.edu	Job preparation
Feds Hire Vets	Provides training information and resources for federal agencies looking to hire Service Members and Veterans http://www.fedshirevets.gov	Link to resources for employers
Hire Heroes USA	Provides links to career opportunities nationwide for returning Service Members, specifically those who have been wounded or with any level of disability http://www.hireheroesusa.org	Link to opportunities, job placement, and matching

JAN	Provides employers with informational assistance on workplace accommodations and the Americans with Disabilities Act http://www.askjan.org	Link to resources for employers
National Resource Directory	Provides access to services and resources that support employment http://www.nationalresourcedirectory.gov	Link to opportunities
VETS	Provides information and resources about employment opportunities and employment rights for individuals with disabilities http://www.dol.gov/vets	Link to opportunities
VetSuccess	Offers services such as helping build job-seeking skills, resume development, and assistance finding and keeping a job http://benefits.va.gov/benefits	Link to opportunities, job preparation, job placement, and matching
Work Support	Provides links to reports, manuals, and resources to accommodate employees with disabilities http://www.worksupport.com	Link to resources for employers
Warrior Care and Transition	Matches injured Warriors with case managers to build personalized work plans and provide job skills training http://www.wtc.army.mil	Job preparation
Wounded Warrior Project	Offers higher education programs, information technology training, and employment assistance services (an extensive employment database is currently under development) http://www.woundedwarriorproject.org	Link to opportunities, job placement, and matching

DoD: Department of Defense; EARN: Employer Assistance and Resource Network; HART: Helping Airmen Recover Together; JAN: Job Accommodation Network; PTSD: posttraumatic stress disorder; Q&As: questions and answers; TBI: traumatic brain injury; Vets: Veterans; VETS: Veterans' Employment and Training Service

*This table provides resources found on the Internet. Due to the nature of online resources, these Web addresses are subject to change without notice. We suggest using a search engine to find any missing resources.

Data source: Reproduced with permission and minor changes from Osilla K, Van Busum K. *Labor Force Reentry: Issues for Injured Service Members and Veterans.* Santa Monica, CA: RAND National Defense Research Institute; 2012.

self-efficacy, a high need for achievement, and the ability to make effective decisions in dynamic situations. They are generally comfortable with autonomy and uncertainty, but remain resilient, mission focused, and driven toward successful outcomes. Their experience provides team-building skills, as well as a commitment to organizational structure and leadership. The majority of Veterans will have had cross-cultural experiences with a rich diversity of work settings and a developed sense of cultural sensitivity.

Furthermore, Veterans have and can leverage their advanced technical training. Their experiences will have often exposed them to accelerated training in highly progressive technology. Several of these skills will adeptly transfer advantageously to the fields of science, technology, engineering, and math.[9]

VETERANS ADMINISTRATION VOCATIONAL REHABILITATION AND EMPLOYMENT

The history of employment services dates back to 1918 with the Vocational Rehabilitation Act. Throughout the century, the basic services outlined in the 1918 Act were renamed and structurally reorganized until they finally landed under Chapter 31 in Title 38 of the Code of Federal Regulations. Chapter 31 is the Vocational Rehabilitation and Employment (VR&E) Program, the mission of which is to prepare, train, attain, and maintain suitable employment for Veterans with a service-connected disability of at least 20%. If the goal of employment is not attainable for a Veteran with a severe disability, then VR&E benefits include identifying realistic living situations, distinguishing rehabilitation and resources to reach that end, and meeting the goal of independent living.

Once a Veteran has received his/her disability rating status and is deemed eligible for Chapter 31 benefits, the Veteran will be able to initiate these services at any point within 12 years of his/her initial eligibility. A Veteran is then entitled to a maximum of 48 months of services, and services include the assignment of a vocational rehabilitation counselor. The counselor and Veteran will work together to establish a *rehabilitation plan*. In this plan, skills, strengths, aptitudes, and interests will be identified. The counselor and Veteran will explore the job market and investigate wage information, demands of the job, and relevant training requirements.[14] Chapter 31 is part of the VA branch known as the Veterans Benefits Administration. The Veterans Health Administration is a sister branch of the Veterans Benefits Administration and houses a separate vocational rehabilitation service for Veterans regardless of disability rating. The program includes the same collaboration and goal setting with a counselor. It offers three primary vocational assistance programs: (1) compensated work therapy, (2) incentive work therapy, and

(3) supported employment. Studies have shown and supported the efficacy of these programs. Veterans who engage in vocational services are more likely to find and maintain competitive employment, earn higher wages, work more days, and have more vocational opportunities than those who do not receive these services.[10,15,16]

EXPLORING NEW OPPORTUNITIES

As previously described, transitioning Service Members tend to possess overall skill sets that show tremendous benefits in the civilian workforce. Some attributes that they bring to an employer are often referred to as *soft skills*, and they include the following:

- commitment and loyalty,
- dedication and focus,
- "get-the-job-done" attitude,
- unsurpassed experience working under pressure,
- experience in conflict resolution,
- multicultural experience,
- security issues on an international scale, and
- ability to work individually or as part of a team.

Often, however, transitioning Service Members have difficulty translating their military experience into civilian language and terminology. Therefore, they also have trouble getting their resumes to the "top of the pile." Because of certain stigma attached to military service, they are sometimes reluctant or unsure about exposing their military history.

Likewise, many Veterans experience difficulty assimilating back into society. The stigma especially impacts those who are living with PTSD and/or TBI. These injuries may generally be invisible and are frequently referred to as the *signature injuries* of Iraq and Afghanistan. As many as one in five Veterans of the Iraq and Afghanistan wars has dealt with depression or stress disorder. Estimates range up to 300,000 with PTSD. Additionally, 19% report they might have experienced a TBI, usually as the result of a roadside bomb. In June 2010, when the Society for Human Resource Management surveyed its members, 46% said they believed PTSD and other mental health issues posed a hiring challenge. Only 22% said the same about combat-related physical disabilities. Although media attention has helped make the diagnoses and treatment of PTSD and TBI government priorities, Veterans believe that it has also contributed to the stigma associated with these wounds.

In an attempt to address the stigma and other issues faced by Veterans with PTSD and TBI, DOL—through a collaborative effort between their Office of Disability Employment Policy and the Veterans' Employment and Training Service—established America's Heroes at Work (http://www.dol. gov/vets/ahaw/). This initiative was designed to educate employers and others about issues related to employment that might impact Veterans with PTSD and TBI. DOL recognized they could not do it alone, and reached out to and received support from the DoD and the VA, as well as from the private sector. DOL established an employment pilot for Veterans with PTSD and TBI, and several employers came forward. From that pilot program, DOL learned that

- the most responsive employers show strong, visible commitment from top-level decision makers;
- individualized workplace flexibility is the key to success and has applicability to the entire workforce;
- work experience, internship, and mentorship opportunities are extremely beneficial to both employers and Veterans;
- TBI/PTSD-related stigma exists among many employers, including those employers used to hiring Veterans; and
- employers are typically unaware of the resources that exist to help them provide appropriate workplace accommodations.

Private Sector Initiatives
President Obama had asked the private sector to hire 100,000 Veterans/ returning Service Members by 2015. The 100,000 Jobs Mission was launched with the goal of hiring 100,000 transitioning Service Members and Military Veterans by 2020. Eleven corporations have joined this mission. Even prior to the President's request, many employers initiated specific outreach efforts to hire not only returning Service Members, but also specifically Wounded Warriors, including those living with PTSD and/or TBI.

Northrop Grumman Corporation (Falls Church, VA) established Operation IMPACT (Injured Military Pursuing Assisted Career Transition), which is focused on Wounded Warriors living with PTSD and/or TBI. British Aerospace (Farnborough, UK) and Marconi Electronic Systems (Chelsmford, UK) have programs for hiring Veterans with PTSD and/or TBI. In addition, Computer Sciences Corporation (Falls Church, VA) developed a program for hiring Veterans, military spouses, spouses of severely wounded and injured Veterans, and caregivers.

JPMorgan Chase & Co (New York, NY) has developed and is executing a holistic Veteran's strategy. Two key elements include a commitment of $7.5 million to (1) provide seed funding for the creation and (2) launch a "first-of-its-kind" Institute for Veterans and Military Families at Syracuse University, as well as the 100,000 Jobs Mission.

The US Chamber of Commerce created a private sector National Veterans Employment Advisory Council, which will be comprised of 25 of America's largest employers, representing every major industry and sector. They also initiated a series of nationwide job fairs to assist job-seeking Veterans.

Federal Sector Initiatives

On November 9, 2009, President Obama issued Executive Order 13518 (Veterans Employment Initiative) calling on federal government agencies to increase their efforts to employ Veterans in the federal workforce. To assist this effort, the Office of Personnel Management established Feds Hire Vets (http://www.usajobs.gov/). This site contains valuable information for job seekers (Veterans) and hiring officials.

Veterans can access federal jobs in several ways, but typically they apply through USAJOBS (https://www.usajobs.gov/). By applying through this portal, eligible Veterans may receive 5 or 10 points added to their passing score of any test or numerical rating. This does not guarantee a job, but does benefit the applicant.

The Veterans Recruitment Appointment allows federal agencies to appoint an otherwise qualified and eligible Veteran to any position up to GS-11 or the equivalent without competing with other applicants (see 38 USC § 4214; 5 CFR Part 307). The VA or any military service branch may also appoint qualified and eligible Veterans who have a disability rating of 30% or more (see 5 USC § 3112; 5 CFR 316.302; 5 CFR 316.402; and 5 CFR 315.707).

The Veterans Employment Opportunity Act (VEOA) of 1998 as amended allows Veterans to apply to announcements that are only open to so-called "status" candidates, which means "current competitive service employees" (Veterans' preference does not apply). VEOA was enacted in recognition that Veterans should have all the rights and benefits in employment accorded to other federal employees. To be eligible for a VEOA appointment, a Veteran must have been granted an honorable or general discharge and must be either preference eligible as defined in Title 5 USC § 2108(3) or be a Veteran who substantially completed three or more years of active service. [For additional information, see the Office of Personnel Management's section on qualifying service (http://www.opm.gov/policy-data-oversight/veterans-services/vetguide/) (PL 105-339, October 31, 1998; 5 USC § 3304f; 5 CFR 315.611;

and 5 CFR 335.106).]

Veterans with disabilities who participate in the VA's VR&E program may be eligible for an appointment with a federal agency in a position for which they have been trained through VR&E (see 5 USC, § 3112; 5 CFR 316.302; 5 CFR 316.402; 5 CFR 315.707; and 5 CFR 315.604). Veterans in the VR&E program may also gain valuable experience through the Non-Paid Work Experience where they may be placed in an internship-type program in a job that is compatible with their training objective (eg, an accounting major can be placed in an accounting-related job, etc). These jobs can be in any federal, state, or local government agency. They will continue receiving their VR&E stipend, but will not be paid by the agency. VR&E also administers the Coming Home to Work program that assists eligible Service Members who are pending medical separation. These Service Members may be placed in the Non-Paid Work Experience and still retain their active duty pay.

DoD operates a similar internship program for wounded, ill, and injured transitioning Service Members called Operation Warfighter (OWF). OWF is a nonpaid internship program within the federal government for returning Service Members while still on active duty in accordance with DoD Instruction 1000.17.[17] The objective of OWF is to place recovering Service Members in a supportive work environment to assist their rehabilitation and to potentially increase career readiness. Originally, OWF opportunities were available only in the Washington, DC, area, but have since been expanded to other geographic areas that have a significant federal employment presence and are near a military treatment facility. Currently, DoD is planning on opening these opportunities to the private sector. Although DoD has refrained from calling OWF an internship program, it allows transitioning wounded, ill, and injured Service Members an opportunity to work at these federal agencies performing meaningful work that garners them valuable civilian work experience. It was never intended to be a placement program, but many of the agencies have employed these Service Members upon discharge. Most, if not all, Veterans in this program are eligible for the Veterans' Recruitment Appointment.

One of the most common and frequent problems reported by transitioning Service Members and employers is that their resumes are often replete with military language that civilian employers (public and private) cannot understand. There are several sites for translation of military skills into the private sector (see section on Private Sector), and one has been developed for the federal sector. The Crosswalk from Military to Federal Civilian Jobs program of the state of Maryland (http://www.dllr.state.md.us/mil2fedjobs/) assists the transitioning Service Member with the ability to write a resume that uses language accessible to federal managers and hiring officials.

EDUCATION AND VOCATIONAL TRAINING

One consequence, albeit generally a positive consequence, of exploring new opportunities is the realization that additional skills are required. The American economy has increasingly required a more highly skilled workforce in recent years, making education instrumental to the Veteran's successful transition to civilian life. For individuals transitioning out of the military, vocational counseling is a critical component in the adjustment to the nonmilitary, civilian workforce. By participating in the broader vocational counseling process, Veterans may discover alternative interests, as well as transferable skills and abilities. Through this process, Veterans may identify alternative education opportunities they previously would not have considered.

On average, individuals with college degrees earn $15,000 to $20,000 more than high school graduates and are more likely to pass on this higher socioeconomic status to their children. Higher earning individuals rate their quality of life as higher than those making lower wages. These individual benefits translate into social benefits. Higher enrollment and graduation of Veterans from colleges and universities and participation in vocational training programs ensure that more qualified professionals will be prepared to enter the modern workforce and contribute to our Nation's economy.

Although research on Veterans' education is just beginning to emerge, it is already known that Veterans have difficulty transitioning to a college environment for various reasons, including the following: having the inability to relate to traditional students, having service-connected disabilities, being a target of antiwar sentiments, and encountering the insensitivity of faculty. In addition,

- Only 22% of colleges with services for Veterans and active duty Service Members provide comprehensive transition programs that link those services together.
- Only 33% of higher education institutions offer special programs for Veterans with disabilities.[18]
- Only 23% offer special services and programs for Veterans with invisible disabilities (eg, TBI and PTSD).[18] Invisible disabilities can translate into poor academic performance and lead to student Veterans dropping out of school. Only 2 of 5 colleges provide training for faculty and staff working with this population.[19]

With support from the President, DoD, the VA, DOL, and the Department of Education, stakeholders in Veterans' education have worked together to identify strategies and to establish clear guidelines that colleges and universities should follow to best serve Veterans. These support structures should also help them reach their academic and career goals while attending to their rehabilitation needs and recognizing their status as nontraditional students. The outcome of their efforts is depicted in the *8 Keys to Success*:

1. create a culture of trust and connectedness across the campus community to promote well-being and success for Veterans;
2. ensure consistent and sustained support from campus leadership;
3. implement an early alert system to ensure that all Veterans receive academic, career, and financial advice before challenges become overwhelming;
4. coordinate and centralize campus efforts for all Veterans, together with the creation of a designated space (even if limited in size);
5. collaborate with local communities and organizations, including government agencies, to align and coordinate various services for Veterans;
6. use a uniform set of data tools to collect and track information on Veterans, including demographics, retention, and degree completion;
7. provide comprehensive professional development for faculty and staff on issues and challenges unique to Veterans; and
8. develop systems that ensure sustainability of effective practices for Veterans.[20]

Currently, more than 250 higher educational institutions have adopted the 8 Keys to Success,[20] and the number of colleges expected to adopt the keys continues to grow. When choosing a college, a Service Member is encouraged to check whether that institution of choice has adopted the 8 Keys to Success.

Although more institutions are making their campuses Veteran-friendly by raising awareness of Veterans' issues on campus and centralizing services for Veterans, a few offer comprehensive transition programs that do not only direct Veterans to resources available outside of the institution, but also provide those services in-house, thus expediting the transition process. Such intensive training programs are available at the academic and vocational levels, and can accommodate Veterans and Service Members with various interests and career aspirations.

Experiential Learning for Veterans in Assistive Technology and Engineering

The ELeVATE (Experiential Learning for Veterans in Assistive Technology and Engineering) program at the University of Pittsburgh is an evidence-based comprehensive transition program for Veterans interested in pursuing a career in the fields of engineering and technology. ELeVATE is based on a three-phased approach, with each phase consisting of various interventions:

- *phase 1*: corresponds to the first 10 weeks of the program, and focuses on the acquisition of skills necessary to succeed in a demanding and unfamiliar academic environment;
- *phase 2*: ELeVATE students apply to and transition to college as they continue to work on their research projects; and
- *phase 3*: students remain connected to the program by mentoring new ELeVATE students while working on their college degree.

Community reintegration, academic preparation, professional development, and vocational rehabilitation are essential components of ELeVATE. Prior to joining ELeVATE, each Veteran is assigned to a mentoring team comprised of a faculty member, a graduate student, and a Veteran community mentor who has successfully reintegrated into civilian society. To ensure that the ELeVATE staff and mentors can provide the necessary support to program participants, regular training sessions are conducted by a rehabilitation counseling professional in which they learn about common injuries, prevailing conditions (eg, TBI and PTSD), and how those conditions affect the Veteran's experience in college. As a result, the ELeVATE program's staff members are knowledgeable about how to coach a student Veteran to best negotiate the rehabilitation process while pursuing higher education or vocational training.

Making the experience meaningful is part of the success of academic transition programs. Participation in rehabilitation science and technology research allows ELeVATE students to engage in technical disciplines while working on projects that can change the lives of people with disabilities (including Veterans and Service Members).

In addition to the research project, ELeVATE students participate in additional lectures and workshops, such as Technologies for Competitive Adaptive Sports, Introduction to Machining Skills, Research Methods, and Oral Presentation Skills. Additional activities include networking events with local employers and field trips to organizations of interest. Each activity presents ELeVATE students with the opportunities to network with professionals in science, technology, engineering, and math, and to explore different career options.

Vocational counseling is an essential component of ELeVATE. Students have comprehensive rehabilitation plans based on their functional and neuropsychological needs, as well as interests, aptitude, and career goals. The plan sets out objectives that must be met at specific time points to achieve more distant goals. As the participants develop a better understanding of their strengths and limitations through the course of the program, they work with the rehabilitation counselor to incorporate their new awareness into their revised rehabilitation plans. Each ELeVATE student meets individually with the rehabilitation counselor at least three times during the 10-week period. Group sessions attended by the students and all ELeVATE staff members are held weekly. The purpose of those sessions is to address any transition-related questions the students might have. The sessions also give the students an opportunity to share their thoughts about their academic experience in a supportive environment.

During educational or vocational counseling, focus should be placed on the strengths of the individual as well as on the challenges they may face or could potentially face. For Veterans with disabilities, an important component of the vocational counseling is to help identify potential strategies an individual could use to promote success in the classroom and on the job. They could include personalized compensatory strategies or workplace accommodations, such as taking frequent breaks, working in a quiet space, or using assistive technology. The Job Accommodation Network is a resource that individuals can use to get tips and tricks to promote employment while working around some of the challenges associated with TBI and PTSD.

Entrepreneurship Bootcamp for Veterans

IVMF at Syracuse University has been a leader in providing education opportunities for transitioning Service Members and Veterans, supporting their families, and working with individuals and institutions to facilitate the successful transition of Veterans into civilian society. The IVMF offers numerous transition tracks for Service Members, Veterans, and their families, thus responding to the unique needs of their program participants.

The IVMF's Entrepreneurship Bootcamp for Veterans (EBV) is a unique program for Veterans with service-connected disabilities who wish to start their own businesses. The program utilizes a three-phase approach, where each phase corresponds to development of specific knowledge and skills necessary for a Veteran's success as a new entrepreneur:

- *phase 1*: participants develop their business concepts while engaging in online training provided by entrepreneurship faculty and graduate students at one of the EBV universities;
- *phase 2*: a 9-day residency at an EBV university, where Veterans participate in entrepreneurship workshops; and

- *phase 3*: participants continue to receive support from the EBV faculty and partnering institutions.

In addition to providing Veterans with disabilities with knowledge and practical skills for starting a successful business, the program helps them establish support networks, further helping them prosper in their new role as entrepreneurs.

The EBV program was recognized by the Secretary of the Army as a "National Best Practice" in 2009 and was featured in *Inc.* magazine as being among the top 10 entrepreneurship programs in the nation. The success of EBV led to the development of more entrepreneurship programs targeting women Veterans, families of Veterans, Reservists and members of the Guard, and active duty Service Members at the earliest stages of the transition process.

VOCATIONAL TRAINING PROGRAMS

According to DOL's *Occupational Outlook Handbook*,[21] many professions that require vocational training, especially those in the technology domain, will be in high demand and will be compensated for at a high rate in just a decade. Several colleges have established programs to accommodate Veterans and Service Members who are interested in manufacturing careers. Typically, such programs include training in an academic environment followed by an on-the-job component that can serve as a springboard to employment or further education.

For example, with support from DOL, 12 state and community colleges in Florida have been part of the Florida TRADE (Transforming Resources for Accelerated Degrees and Employment) program, designed to assist Veterans (among other groups) by providing them with accelerated training (3–6 months) that can lead to internships and employment in manufacturing. The network of employers working with the TRADE colleges is broad, and various certifications are available based on the participants' interests. Vocational training received through the TRADE network can be converted into credits and counted toward an Associate's degree. However, programs like TRADE are not designed specifically for Veterans and might not be right for those Veterans who need more coaching in compensatory strategies as they transition to college and employment. Therefore, it is important for transitioning Service Members and their support networks to be familiar with comprehensive transition programs designed specifically for Veterans with and without disabilities.

Although the need for comprehensive vocational training transition programs for Veterans remains high, only a few institutions currently offer such programs. The Advancing Inclusive Manufacturing (AIM) program at the University of Pittsburgh is designed specifically to aid in the transition of rehabilitating Wounded Warriors and rehabilitating Veterans to machining careers. Over a 12-week period, AIM students learn basic machining principles and practices as they cycle through fundamental areas of fabrication, including carpentry, welding, prototyping, and electronics. Upon completion of the program, AIM students can independently design, develop, and evaluate their own product using established design principles. AIM program training activities include computer-aided design concepts, rapid prototyping, tubing, bending, and machining and milling.

In addition to technical training, the AIM curriculum includes vocational training sessions in which Veterans work on goal setting and career planning. The curriculum is enhanced with workshops on disability support and various areas of assistive technology, including mobility, communication, computer access, and prosthetics and orthotics. AIM training takes place at the Human Engineering Research Laboratories, the VA Center for Wheelchairs and Associated Rehabilitation Technology. The laboratories' training facilities were designed specifically to accommodate a range of physical and cognitive disabilities. After successful completion of the program, AIM trainees are prepared to sit for the National Institute for Metalworking Skills Level 1 Exam and are matched with an employer in the area for on-the job-training experience at local companies, where potential full-time employment can be secured.

TRANSITION PROGRAMS

The SVA (which provides undergraduate Veterans with resources, support, and advocacy) and Kognito Interactive (New York, NY), a developer of role-playing health training simulations) together created evidence-based training modules[22] that allow faculty, staff, and peers to practice how to best provide support to student Veterans when they encounter challenges associated with transitioning to campus and civilian life in general. Training covers a range of topics, including academic challenges, time management, cultural differences, and managing classroom discussions on topics that Veterans might find difficult. This training also presents the viewer with real-life scenarios and provides immediate feedback via an emotionally responsive avatar to help the trainee learn effective communication skills specific to the student Veterans' needs. As more institutions adopt this or other training tools, more will be known about the effectiveness of virtual versus live, in-person training modules. Thus, virtual reality training modules can be a valuable resource at institutions with limited access to rehabilitation counseling professionals.

The number of colleges partnering with the DoD's Defense Activity for Non-Traditional Education Support initiatives, the VA's VetSuccess On Campus, and the VA's Veterans Integration to Academic Leadership programs—designed to aid in the transition process—continues to grow, thus ensuring that more Veterans have knowledge of and access to the resources available to them through the VA.

VOLUNTEERING

Education and employment are key strategies in helping Veterans to achieve an optimal quality of life and return to being productive civilian citizens. However, these strategies do not function in a vacuum, and their value can be magnified when combined with volunteering. There is a relationship between military service and volunteering. Military service renders one more likely to volunteer because it socializes individuals with a concept of civic responsibility from which volunteering is a natural outgrowth.[23] Formal volunteer programs that target Veterans have been shown to be successful. For example, Veterans with disabilities who have volunteered for The Mission Continues program have reported enhanced educational and career development.[24] Seven of 10 Veterans participating in this program continued their education, 8 of 10 were successful in transferring military competencies into civilian employment, and 9 of 10 were able to develop professional networks to benefit future career development.[24]

Volunteering can augment the education strategy by offering an immediate complement to didactic learning by bridging theory learned in the classroom with actual practice in an authentic context. Furthermore, volunteering provides "in vivo" exposure to real-world work even before the Veteran is able to gain such exposure on a paid and gainful basis (ie, in a real job). Ultimately, volunteering represents experiential learning and jump-starts the process of building social capital (ie, developing an effective social network). The combination of meaningful employment and a well-developed personal and/or professional network can pave the way for the Veteran to achieve an enviable quality of life.

Volunteering is experiential learning because it occurs within the milieu of a real-work setting. Experiential learning aligns well with adult learning theory (ie, *andragogy*). The concept of andragogy was developed by Malcolm Knowles.[25] In contrast to pedagogy that addresses teaching of children, andragogy assumes that adult learners

FIGURE 12-2. *The Veteran Opportunity Cycle.*

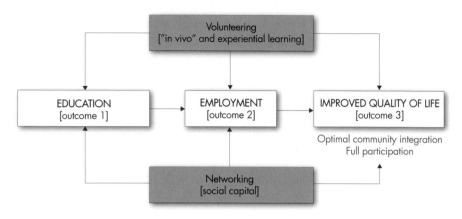

- have life experience that stimulates learning,
- are self-directed in learning,
- are ready to learn based on advanced social roles and development, and
- can apply learning immediately.

The life experience of adults is a key ingredient that, when combined with the learning task, can result in a *teachable moment*. Robert Havighurst popularized the teachable moment concept in the 1950s.[26] The experiential learning that occurs through volunteering inherently links to the adult learning theory and the concept of the teachable moment. This attribute, combined with the volitional aspect of volunteering (ie, the fact that volunteering is freely chosen by the Veteran), means that it has the potential to be an efficacious approach for enhancing the community reintegration of Veterans.

Beyond the experiential learning involved in volunteering is the need for the Veteran to build an effective network of individuals who provide social and professional support (ie, social capital). Such a network can provide strategic guidance, connection, and entry into situations that can boost the Veteran's development. Often, Veterans do not take full advantage of networking opportunities because of either faulty understanding of its power or lack of practice, thus leaving networking skills underdeveloped.[27] The positive impact of both volunteering and networking on the key outcomes of education, employment, and quality of life can render the Veteran optimally prepared for a successful postmilitary lifestyle (Figure 12-2). Such a lifestyle is characterized by the Veteran who is

- empowered and self-determining;
- prepared professionally through specific education, and volunteer and employment experiences;
- self-sufficient;
- able to participate in all desirable life pursuits; and
- in possession of a well-developed amount of social capital for personal, social, and professional purposes.

Therefore, from a holistic perspective, volunteering helps the Veteran to fully seize a commensurate share of the American dream as a civilian.

SUMMARY

This chapter provides an assortment of opportunities for Veterans to consider as they are transitioning to the civilian world. This transition often requires the acquisition of new skills that may be obtained through a community college or university, by volunteering, or through a private or federal sector work training program, and financed through a variety of disability and/or military benefits. Collaborations between educators, counselors, administrators, employers, and human resources personnel may provide the optimal level of support required for educational and employment retention. A multitude of research opportunities, many aimed at best practice development, exist to continue to better understand and meet the needs of this population. As more transparent data emerge, additional federal and private programs may be created to address the Veterans' most pertinent needs. This not only benefits Veterans and their future education and employment pathways, but also high-need employment areas, including (but not limited to) the science, technology, engineering, and math sectors.

References

1. Stanley M. College education and the midcentury GI bills. *Q J Econ.* 2003;118(2):671–708.

2. Department of Veterans Affairs. VA history in brief. http://www.va.gov/opa/ publications/archives/docs/history_in_brief.pdf. Accessed June 23, 2015.

3. O'Herrin E. Enhancing Veteran success in higher education. *Peer Rev.* 2011;13(1):15–18.

4. Institute for Veterans and Military Families. The business case for hiring a Veteran: beyond the cliches. http://nvti.ucdenver.edu/resources/resourceLibrary/pdfs/ Syracuse%20Business%20Case%20to%20Hire%20a%20Vet.pdf. Accessed February 2, 2015.

5. Prudential Financial, Inc., Afghanistan and Iraq Veterans' of America. Veterans employment challenges: perceptions and experiences of transitioning from military to civilian life. http://www.prudential.com/documents/public/Veterans EmploymentChallenges.pdf. Accessed February 2, 2015.

6. Sander L. As GI bill expands, so do calls for tracking Veterans' academic success. *Chron High Educ.* 2012;59(17):3.

7. Bureau of Labor Statistics. *Employment Situation of Veterans—2015.* Washington, DC: US Department of Labor; March 22, 2016. News Release USDL-16-0611.

8. Veterans Opportunity to Work Act to Hire Heroes Act of 2011. *The VOW Act.* Washington, DC: House Committee on Veterans' Affairs; November 21, 2011.

9. Mitcham M. *Academic Recognition of Military Experience in STEM Education.* Washington, DC: American Council on Education; 2013.

10. Twamley EW, Baker DG, Norman SB, Pittman JE, Lohr JB, Resnick SG. Veterans Health Administration vocational services for Operation Iraqi Freedom/Operation Enduring Freedom Veterans with mental health conditions. *J Rehabil Res Dev.* 2013;50(5):663–670.

11. Osilla K, Van Busum K. *Labor Force Reentry: Issues for Injured Service Members and Veterans.* Santa Monica, CA: RAND National Defense Research Institute; 2012.

12. Ruh D, Spicer P, Vaughan K. Helping Veterans with disabilities transition to employment. *J Postsecond Educ Disabil.* 2009;22(1):67–75.

13. Institute for Veterans and Military Families. *The Business Case for Hiring a Veteran: Beyond the Clichés.* Syracuse, NY: 2012.

14. Crane B, Scott C, Davis C. *Veterans' Benefits: The Vocational Rehabilitation and Employment Program* (RL34627). Washington, DC: Congressional Research Service; 2008.

15. Frain MP, Malachy B, Bethel M. A roadmap for rehabilitation counseling to serve military Veterans with disabilities. *J Rehabil.* 2010;76(1):13–21.

16. Burnett-Zeigler I, Valenstein M, Ilgen M, Blow AJ, Gorman LA, Zivin K. Civilian

employment among recently returning Afghanistan and Iraq National Guard Veterans. *Mil Med.* 2011;176(6):639–646.

17. Cooper RA, Pasquina P, Drach R, eds. *Warrior Transition Leader: Medical Rehabilitation Handbook.* Washington, DC: Borden Institute; 2011.

18. Cook BJ, Kim Y. *From Soldier to Student: Easing the Transition of Service Members on Campus.* Washington, DC: American Council on Education; 2009.

19. Redden E. Campus as vet-friendly zones. http://www.insidehighered.com/news/2009/06/05/veterans. Accessed February 2, 2015.

20. Baker S. 8 Keys to Success: Supporting Veterans, military and military families on campus. http://www.whitehouse.gov/blog/2013/08/13/8-keys-success-supporting-veterans-military-and-military-families-campus. Accessed February 2, 2015.

21. Department of Labor. Occupational Outlook Handbook. http://www.bls.gov/ooh/. Accessed February 2, 2015.

22. Kognito Web Site. Creating a supportive campus for student veterans. http://www.kognito.com/products/voc/. Accessed February 2, 2015.

23. Nesbit R, Reingold DA. Soldiers to citizens: the link between military service and volunteering. *Public Admin Rev.* 2011;Jan/Feb:67–76.

24. Matthieu MM, Smith ID, McBride AM, Morrow-Howell N. *The Mission Continues: Engaging Post-9/11. Disabled Military Veterans in Civic Service (Research Brief).* St. Louis, MO: Center for Social Development, the George Warren Brown School of Social Work, Washington University; 2011: 1–3. CSD Publication no. 11–25.

25. Knowles MS. *The Modern Practice of Adult Education, Revised and Updated.* Chicago, IL: Follett; 1980.

26. Lewis PH, Lewis AN, Williams FD. Cultural competency in public administration programs. In: Norman-Major KA, Gooden ST, eds. *Cultural Competency for Public Administrators.* New York, NY: M. E. Sharpe; 2012: 244–264.

27. Faulkner ML, Nierenberg A, Abrams M. *Networking for Veterans: A Guidebook for a Successful Military Transition into the Civilian Workforce.* Boston, MA: Pearson Learning Solutions; 2013.

BIBLIOGRAPHY

Lincoln A. *Second Inaugural Address, March 4, 1865.* Washington, DC: The Abraham Lincoln Papers at the Library of Congress, 1837–1897.

SERGEANT D. JOSHUA MARINO enlisted in the US Army in May 2001 and attended Advanced Individual Training at Fort Gordon, Georgia, for the Military Occupational Specialty of 25S (31S), Satellite Communications Systems Operator/Maintainer. Marino quickly advanced to the position of Team Chief at his first duty station in the Republic of Korea. After 3 years, he successfully transferred his skill set to Fort Riley, Kansas, where he was instrumental in standing up the 4th Brigade Combat Team of the 1st Infantry Division. During his deployment to Iraq in 2007–2008, Sergeant Marino was wounded by several mortar blasts in an indirect fire attack, sustaining a traumatic brain injury and multiple concussions. Upon return to garrison, Sergeant Marino continued to train soldiers despite his condition. However, as he worsened, it was determined by a medical evaluation board that he was no longer fit for duty. Thus, he was separated from the Army in 2009.

Josh moved back to his hometown of Pittsburgh, Pennsylvania, and started classes at the University of Pittsburgh using the Chapter 33 Post-9/11 GI Bill. Throughout the following semesters, Josh utilized the many community supports and accommodations made available to him to effectively transition into a career that suited his talents. A dedicated team of professionals within the VA Pittsburgh Healthcare System offered treatment for physical maladies, as well as counseling to advance his social and professional reintegration. In working with the Vocational Rehabilitation

Department, Josh was guided through the process of furthering his education and career. Working to better the quality of life of other Veterans was always his primary goal, with the belief that healing the wounded required not only intellectual know-how, but also a strong sense of empathy that only another Veteran could provide.

After 3 years, he graduated with a BS degree in Social Sciences. He was selected to participate in the Experiential Learning for Veterans in Assistive Technology and Engineering (ELeVATE) program at the Human Engineering Research Laboratories (HERL). Alongside other Veterans in an environment that championed the camaraderie present between former and current

 members of the Armed Forces, Josh was able to experience the inner workings of research studies in assistive technology and rehabilitation, coordinate on a professional article and symposium presentation, and participate in professional development sessions designed to advance his career and reintegration. He excelled in the program—which solidified his intent to pursue graduate school for certification as a Rehabilitation Counselor—with the goal of providing care and understanding to other Veterans when they need it most.

Josh regularly volunteers with Three Rivers Adaptive Sports (TRAS) and numerous annual marathons within the Pittsburgh area. He is currently acting as a peer mentor for program participants at HERL. His most ardent supporters throughout have been his mother, father, and extended family, but especially his wife of 5 years, Dr Rebecca Marino.

It is a moral obligation to our Soldiers and their families that they have a place to heal and transition back to the force and/or transition out.

★ ★ ★

Brigadier General Darryl Williams
Commander, US Army Warrior Transition Command
July 11, 2012

CHAPTER THIRTEEN

Accessible Homes, Communities, and Transportation

CAROL PEREDO LOPEZ, AIA*; LAVINIA FICI PASQUINA, MS†;
AMANDA McALPINE, NCIDQ, LEED AP‡; PATRICK RAKSZAWASKI,
RA§; STEVE BUCHA, AET¥; and PAUL F. PASQUINA, MD¶

Accessibility Design Review Manager, Washington Metropolitan Area Transit Authority, 600 5th Street, NW, Washington, DC 20001

†*Associate Professor of Architecture and Director of Digital Media, The Catholic University of America, 620 Michigan Ave, NE, Washington, DC 20064*

‡*Interior Designer, AE Works Ltd., 6587 Hamilton Avenue, Pittsburgh, Pennsylvania 15206*

§*Project Architect, AE Works Ltd., 6587 Hamilton Avenue, Pittsburgh, Pennsylvania 15206*

¥*Architectural Designer, AE Works Ltd., 6587 Hamilton Avenue, Pittsburgh, Pennsylvania 15206*

¶*Colonel (Retired), Medical Corps, US Army; Chief, Department of Orthopaedics and Rehabilitation, Walter Reed National Military Medical Center, 4494 North Palmer Road, Bethesda, Maryland 20889*

INTRODUCTION

One of the most important goals in achieving successful reintegration after combat-related wounds, injuries, or illnesses may be returning home. Unfortunately, for many injured Service Members and families, their homes were defined by their duty station. For those who medically separate (ETS or Expiration of Term of Service) or retire from the military, one of the first steps to successful return to the community is to decide where to reside. Selecting the right location and community may be challenging and is often influenced by multiple factors, such as

- Where have you previously lived that you enjoyed the most?
- Where do you have the most access to healthy relationships (including family and friends)?
- What vocational opportunities exist in that community?
- What are the options for current or future children in terms of public and private schools?
- What are the local laws regarding state and local income and property taxes for military and disabled Veterans?

The answers to these questions require significant thought; research online or with counselors; and conversations with friends, family, and trusted colleagues who have already successfully made this transition. Although there are significant stresses associated with these decisions, one must recognize that moving is always an option. Because military Service Members are often accustomed to moving, they should not be fearful of this in the future. They should recognize that many families even in the civilian sector frequently relocate based on many of the same factors. To keep relocation as an option in the future, however, sound financial decisions are critical. Committing to a high mortgage rate before first testing a community may put individuals and families at significant financial risk; therefore, one may consider renting prior to committing to purchasing a house.

In addition to previous considerations, those individuals with physical, emotional, and psychological injuries after military service must also carefully assess issues surrounding accessibility, transportation, and independence. This is especially true for individuals with physical or cognitive impairments related to injuries such as amputation, traumatic brain injury, vision or hearing impairment, and paralysis. In addition, those Service Members with significant extremity trauma are at a higher risk of developing issues such as posttraumatic arthritis, overuse injuries, or increased cardiovascular disease with aging. Despite these challenges, it is important to remember that even with their physical, cognitive, or psychological impairments, their ultimate disability is often more reflective of the context of their living environment rather than their ability to walk, see, or hear. Today's advances in adaptive techniques and assistive technology can frequently support substantial independent living even when severe impairments exist, and can substantially decrease disability when these technologies are properly incorporated into the individual's living environment. Furthermore, *smart home technologies* have universal appeal to individuals with and without disabilities, thus making these homes more accessible and affordable as technology advances.[1-3] This chapter provides an in-depth discussion of home, community, and transportation considerations for those with physical, cognitive, and psychological impairments.

ACCESSIBLE HOMES

At the top of the list when selecting a home are usually issues such as

- location,
- number of bedrooms,
- closet and living spaces,
- bathrooms and kitchens, and
- outdoor settings.

However, when accessibility becomes a priority, there are many additional elements that need to be considered. Residential architects report in the 2014 AIA (American Institute of Architects) Home Design Trends Survey that one of the most significant trends in home layouts is improving accessibility. Street-level entries, ramps, broader halls, and open floor plans are all increasing in demand.[4] Wider hallways and fewer steps have been reported as increasing in popularity by almost two-thirds of respondents, whereas 55% of respondents report that increased accessibility into and out of the home by using ramps and on-grade entrances is also becoming more popular. With open layouts and improved accessibility trending, accessible housing options are becoming increasingly available.

SELECTING A HOME
When looking for a home, there are many points to consider and many questions to ask. Although new home design is now trending toward more open,

flexible spaces, there are also many older homes on the market with great features that can provide the required accessibility. To help you find your new home, the following sections detail important features to look for in a community, outside the home, with the interior home design and floor layouts, various building systems, and more.

Community

Community is a very important consideration when selecting a home. Nearby services and amenities, as well as landscaping and lighting, all contribute to creating a feeling of home and belonging while increasing convenience. When considering the neighborhood where a home is located, take time to explore and understand how the location fits into your lifestyle.

The following questions help to identify important key features when examining prospective neighborhoods:

- *What services, activities, and amenities are nearby?*
  Close proximity to a grocery store, pharmacy, post office, hardware store, bank, healthcare, and other services can minimize traveling distance, thus quickly increasing convenience. In urban areas, these services may be able to be accessed without use of a vehicle.
- *Is it easy to travel on the surrounding streets and sidewalks?*
  Although most communities have gone through substantial transformation since the Americans with Disabilities Act (ADA)[5] was enacted, the level of accessibility required will vary depending on individual needs. When looking to relocate, it is important to consider specific items. For example, paths should be examined for level sidewalks, manageable curbs, and functional ramps, as well as lighting on streets.
- *What is the feel of the neighborhood?*
  In addition to seeing what services and amenities are nearby, it is also a good idea to research and ask around about noise and traffic, as well as local/community activities. Is the area noisy at night? Are there regular neighborhood gatherings? Is the community active in supporting social and environmental interests and groups?

Outside the Home

Beyond the community, there are important features *outside* the home to take a closer look at, such as parking and how many steps it takes to get to the front door. These elements might not seem as important as what is *inside* the home, but these features can greatly impact day-to-day activities. Availability of a yard, deck, patio, or front porch can also provide more livable space to host barbecues and other gatherings. Not only is accessibility becoming more attractive to homebuyers, so is their access to outdoor space.[6]

The following questions can help to identify important key outdoor features:

- *What type of parking is available?*
  If you have a vehicle, it is important to examine any driveways, carports, or garages for level surfaces and availability/maneuverability of space. If there is no on-site parking option, look for nearby street parking while considering the volume of traffic and other events that take place in the area that could impact availability.
- *How do I get into the house?*
  Sidewalks, steps, paths, and lighting are main outdoor landscape elements that should be carefully considered. The number of steps, levelness of paths, and amount of lighting can assist in supporting safe and secure home access.
- *Does the outdoor space require a lot of maintenance?*
  Decks, green space, flowers, and trees can help create a personal outdoor oasis, and are also an extension of your home and livable space. Maintenance of these outdoor spaces is important, including the need for lawn services, snow removal, or leaf removal.

These issues are explored in greater depth in the section on Outdoor Spaces.

Interior Home Design and Floor Layout

Inside the home, carefully consider how individual rooms are accessed. Doors and stairs are interior elements to inspect carefully. Specifically, the number of stairs, positioning of handrails, stair treads, adequate lighting, and door handles and locks that impact home mobility and privacy.

Visibility and Comfort

Visibility and comfort are important considerations in creating both a welcoming and accessible home environment. Home systems include windows, air conditioning, heating, plumbing, and electrical work. If building a new home, custom systems can be easily included during construction. If buying an existing home, some compromises may be needed. However, it is fairly simple to incorporate certain elements to help with visibility and enhance comfort.

The following questions can help to identify important key features in home systems:

- *Visibility and Power*: Are outlets, switches, and lights easily accessible?
  The positioning of outlets and light switches is important because the height and location can greatly impact use. Motion sensors and lamps can also enhance the ease of operating and providing ambiance while adding character to living spaces. To support numerous electrical devices—including security and automation systems, multiple computers, and peripheral electronics (as well as charging stations for motorized wheelchairs or electric prostheses)—proper grounding and outlet locations are necessary.

- *Windows and Blinds*: How do they open?
  The type of window, casement or double hung, impacts reach and level of effort to open and close it. Although casement windows can often be opened while seated, double hung windows require a higher reach. Similarly, longer cords and rods make blinds and window coverings easier to use, especially from a wheelchair or short prostheses.

- *Air Conditioning/Heating*: How is the temperature of the home controlled?
  There are a variety of air conditioning/heating systems used in homes. Forced air, radiators, and electric are the most common types. These different systems not only vary in how they adjust temperatures, but also range in utility costs. If you are thinking of buying an existing home, consider asking for information on past utility usage and costs. Temperature regulation can be particularly challenging for individuals with conditions such as brain injury, spinal cord injury, and multiple sclerosis; therefore, independent room cooling or heating systems may be necessary, depending on how many individuals will be occupying the home. Newer technologies, available now through companies like Nest Labs (Palo Alto, CA), provide "learning thermostats" that can be programmed to meet an individual user's needs.[7]

- *Plumbing*: How is water temperature adjusted?
  Typical homes use a storage tank hot water heater. If large amounts of hot water are used at once, it will take time to replenish the hot water supply just as it may take time for warm water to reach the faucet when it is initially turned on. In contrast, *instantaneous water heaters* (or tankless water heaters) heat the water directly at the fixture, but are typically less energy efficient. It is especially important to check that plumbing has insulation, particularly at sinks where the hot water supply is exposed.[8]

Home Layout: Kitchen, Bathroom, and Bedroom

Normally, the kitchen, bathroom, and bedroom are the most used rooms. Looking for key features and asking a few important questions can help you better understand what is best for your personal needs, as well as enhance your living environment substantially.

The following questions can help to examine important key features in these rooms:

- *Navigating the Kitchen: Are key appliances and cabinets positioned for easy access?*
  There are many different types of kitchen layouts that offer a range of features to support easy access. It is important to consider how the kitchen is used currently, compared with the layout wanted. For instance, people who cook a lot should examine whether the kitchen has enough counter space. Are key appliances (eg, microwaves, sinks, ovens, etc) easily reached? Do cabinets offer enough reachable storage?
- *Bathroom: What fixtures and layout options enhance accessibility?*
  The location of toilets, showers, and tubs can impact accessibility, especially for those individuals with limited mobility. Mirrors and grab bars are key features to look for, but also items that can be added or adjusted to meet individual needs. Availability of open, clear floor space is also something important to take into account. When using the bathroom, is there enough space to move about?
- *Bedrooms: What design features can make your bedroom not only more accessible, but also more comfortable?*
  To provide a relaxing, enjoyable space, some key features to consider in a bedroom include the following items that help make the use of lighting, power, and home systems more convenient: positioning of light switches near beds and nightstands, easily reachable storage/closet space, remote control operation of ceiling fans and other home systems, etc.

Miscellaneous Items for Consideration

Small details can help everyone get around the house more easily and make day-to-day activities simpler. The following questions address a few additional items to consider when buying a home:

- *Does the flooring support safe travel throughout the house?*
  Do the floors, carpets, or tiles impair wheelchair or prosthetic mobility? For individuals with frequent headaches, which light and noise may aggravate, are there accessible locations within the home that can be darkened and sound minimized? For individuals with cognitive problems, does an open floor layout support orientation and wayfinding, and also incorporate appropriate privacy?

- *Where is the laundry room located?*
  If possible, laundry machines should be located on a main living level.
  Side-loading machines are more easily accessible for those individuals
  in wheelchairs.
- *Is there adequate security?*
  Doorbells, door latches, peepholes, and security systems that monitor
  intrusion, fire, and carbon monoxide are important features that can be
  adjusted to support a safe, secure, and more accessible home. Many of
  the security devices that are now available can stream images directly to
  a tablet or smartphone. In addition, devices such as the Kwikset Kevo
  Smart Lock (Lakeforest, CA) allow individuals to control door locks with
  Bluetooth technology.[9]

Identifying Elements of the Home That Need Improvement Based on Specific Needs

A common misperception is that "accessible design" only applies to individuals who are wheelchair users. In fact, many individuals benefit from modifications to their home environments to not only improve their independence,
but also to improve overall quality of life, whether from a physical, sensory,
cognitive, or psychological impairment.[10,11]

Hearing Impairment

Simple design considerations can help those with hearing impairments. In a
compartmentalized home with many different rooms, people tend to rely on
speech to get the attention of others. This can be challenging in a situation
where there are one or more people living in the home who are deaf.[12] In
comparison, in an open floor plan, people can more easily see one another,
making communication easier. Also, incorporating lighting and bright colors
can make signing appear more clear. When it comes to finishes, matte paint
helps to reduce glare while supporting visual clarity.

Visual Impairment

For those with visual impairments, contrasting floor textures and colors can
help with wayfinding or room-to-room travel, alerting one to room transitions. In addition to texture and color, lighting can play a big role in helping
to distinguish important areas and features in a home. For example, entrances
and halls with bright, overhead lighting make it easier to find keys and open
doors.[12] Glow-in-the-dark tape is another option that can be placed along
baseboards or stairwells to provide guidance in low levels of light. Along long
corridors, a chair rail can be added for tactile guidance. This is a more subtle
addition than a handrail.

For those with limited mobility and/or eyesight impairments, existing outlets or light switches in hallways can be replaced with a combination night light/control that turns the light portion on when it is dark. Light switches for ceiling-mounted lighting fixtures and fans can be replaced with motion sensor switches that also have remote control or manual override controls. Doorbells, fire alarm systems, and carbon monoxide detectors with light-based alerts can also help enhance safety and awareness of surroundings.

For easy use, lamps should be plugged into outlets with switch control. Different light bulb and lamp color temperatures (warm vs cool light) are also available. Lamp color is measured by the Kelvin scale. Lamps within the 3,000 to 3,500 K range (warm) produce a calm, welcoming, and relaxing atmosphere. Lamps with shades should also be used to prevent direct glare. Advanced technologies now allow options for controlling lighting with a smartphone. They also have options for programming different rooms with different lighting features to change automatically throughout the day, such as the Philips Hue Connected Bulbs (Philips Lighting, B.V., Amsterdam, The Netherlands).[13]

Allergies, Breathing Difficulties, or Temperature Sensitivities

If allergies or temperature sensitivities exist, it is important to consider how the temperature of the home is controlled. As described previously, there are a variety of air conditioning/heating systems used in homes. Forced air, radiators, and electric are the most common. Forced air systems allow for faster adjustments in temperature. However, forced air may cause unwanted breezes or drafts and circulate dust in the home. In contrast, radiators provide slow and steady heat without moving air, but temperature adjustments usually take longer. Most homes have one thermostat for the entire structure. If more acute control is required, through-the-wall or window cooling units can be added, as well as space heaters. Ceiling fans can improve comfort by blowing downward during the summer to provide a cooling effect or blowing upward during the winter to draw room air up and force warm air down. This is especially effective for rooms with high ceilings.

Spinal Cord Injury Care

Individuals with a spinal cord injury or disorder will most likely require an assistive device for mobility, such as a manual or powered wheelchair. During the transition between inpatient rehabilitation and home discharge, most rehabilitation centers have a simulated home environment that allows the individual to engage in therapy directed at ensuring independence and safety at home. Therefore, the more the simulated environment can replicate the patient's home, the better the rehabilitation team can prepare the individual.

Figure 13-1. *Simulated Living Transition Environment.*

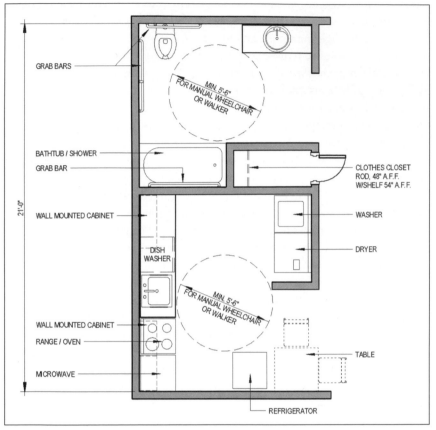

MIN: minimum; A.F.F.: above finish floor

An example of a simulated environment is depicted in Figure 13-1. Important features of the space include

- a minimum diameter of approximately 5½ feet in each space to provide enough clear space to move around,
- grab bars where appropriate in the bathroom for ease of movement,
- placement of the washer and dryer on the main living level, and
- positioning of appliances close to one another to facilitate ease of use.[14]

The following sections discuss improving wheelchair accessibility in the home. Further details are available in the *VA Handbook for Design.*[15]

MAKING A BATHROOM ACCESSIBLE

A bathroom tends to be the most important room in a house, yet it also tends to be the smallest. Because of this issue, many people overlook just how much they use this room and focus on making do with something underwhelming. With the right attention to layout, positioning of doors, and the style of key features (eg, toilets, showers/tubs, sinks, etc), a bathroom can become accessible, and be transformed into a personal spa. Ultimately, this room can not only enhance

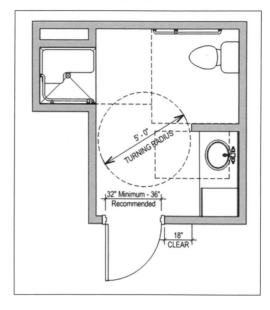

FIGURE 13-2. *Example of Bathroom Layout.*

personal hygiene, but also provide comfort and relaxation. Touchless faucets, heated tile floors, and sliding pocket doors are just a few features that do not require a full bathroom renovation.

Small upgrades (eg, doors and layout, clear floor space, etc) can help make a bathroom not only accessible, but also more comfortable. All included heights and reach ranges listed below are based on ADA standards, but should be tailored to individual needs.

Doors

Access is the first important feature to consider. Doorways at least 32 to 36 inches wide are recommended to make it easy to get in and out of the bathroom. At least 18 inches of clear space should be provided parallel to the doorway on the latch side of the door to help make it easier to access the bathroom. As shown in Figure 13-2,[5] the door should swing out of the bathroom space to make sure it is easy to exit the room.

Layout, Clear Floor Space

To accommodate easy movement within the bathroom and access to key bathroom spaces, a 5-foot-diameter turning radius is recommended, as well as a clear floor space (see Figure 13-2). Enhancing easy turning also improves visibility within the space, which also can be enhanced by placement of ad-

Figure 13-3. *Positioning of Toilets and Grab Bar.*

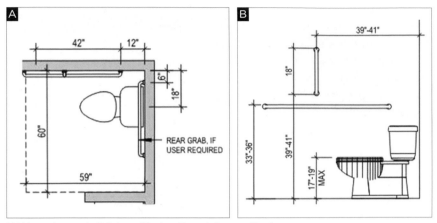

MAX: maximum; A: Toilet positioning; B: grab bar positioning

ditional mirrors. When adding or repositioning mirrors, pay attention to the height and position to best meet individual needs. Tilting mirrors can also provide better visibility.

Toilets

The height and position of a toilet and nearby grab bars are very important in bathroom design and upgrades. ADA toilet seats are recommended to be between 17 and 19 inches above the floor. However, for people who have trouble sitting down, or getting up once seated, a thicker toilet seat can increase the height of the toilet. Horizontal and vertical grab bars can also be added near the toilet. Typical dimensions and positioning of these items are noted in Figure 13-3. However, depending on individual needs and preferences, these heights may require adjusting.

Clear space around the toilet ensures that appropriate space is available to move around in. A clear floor space of at least 60 inches perpendicular to the side wall and 59 inches perpendicular from the rear wall should be provided. The toilet should be located approximately 18 inches off of the adjacent wall. If a wall is not available, the toilet should be located 16 inches off the centerline of the floor with a centered mounted grab bar.[5]

Bathroom Sinks

Careful sink positioning is critical to allow ease of use. Wall-mounted shallow sinks allow more space under the basin, thus improving wheelchair access. If the sink is not in a vanity cabinet, all exposed piping must be insulated to

FIGURE 13-4. *Suggested Sink and Vanity Dimensions.*

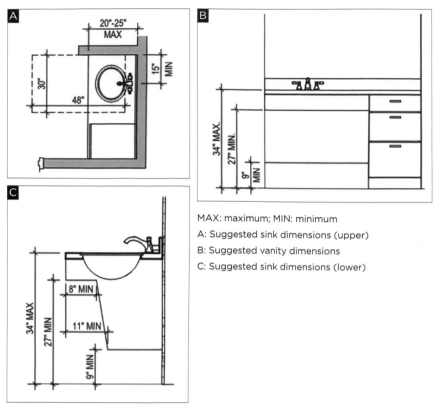

MAX: maximum; MIN: minimum
A: Suggested sink dimensions (upper)
B: Suggested vanity dimensions
C: Suggested sink dimensions (lower)

prevent injury and scalding, if the user comes into contact with the piping. Counters can also be wall-mounted or have minimal structural supports under the counter to further allow wheelchair access. Lever faucets are also easier to operate than knobs. Suggested clearances and positioning are noted in Figure 13-4.[5]

Showers

There are many types of showers and different configurations to meet individual needs. *Transfer-type* and *roll-in showers* are usually the best options for accessible bathrooms. All shower floors should be of a nonslip material to help prevent slips and falls. Flexible hose and handheld showers are also easy upgrades to help with limited mobility.

Transfer-type showers are generally smaller, but at a minimum should be at least 36 inches wide × 36 inches deep (Figure 13-5).[5] Adequate clear floor

Figure 13-5. *Transfer-type Showers.*

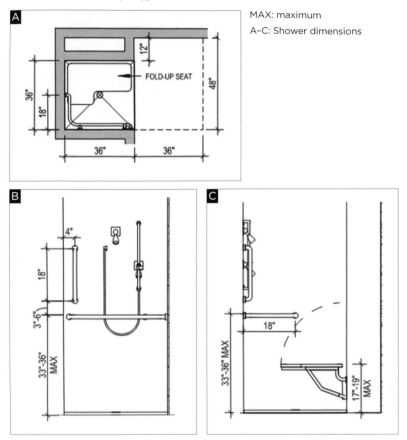

MAX: maximum
A–C: Shower dimensions

space should be provided outside of the shower to help with getting in and out and moving around the bathroom. In transfer-type showers, a fold-up shower seat is recommended for ease of use and comfort. The seat should be mounted 17 to 19 inches above the floor, but should be adjusted based on individual needs. The height and positioning of grab bars in showers are also especially important and should be adjusted to meet personal preference. A horizontal grab bar is best positioned across the control wall and side wall to a point of 18 inches from the control wall. An 18-inch vertical grab bar should also be provided 4 inches from the edge of the shower entrance and above the horizontal grab bar.

Roll-in type showers are best characterized by the lack of any threshold between the shower and the bathroom floor (Figure 13-6). Usually, these

FIGURE 13-6. *Roll-in Showers.*

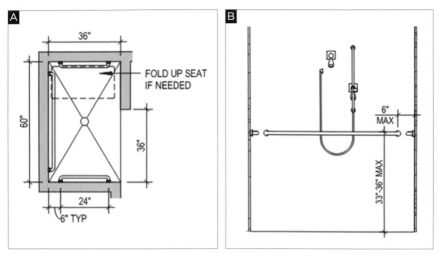

MAX: maximum; TYP: typical

A: Roll-in shower floor plan; B: roll-in shower dimensions

showers are at least 60 inches wide x 36 inches deep. A 36-inch-wide minimum opening can be provided at one end of the compartment if an enclosed shower is desired. For added comfort and to support limited mobility, a fold-up shower seat is an option. If a seat is provided, horizontal grab bars are only needed on the control and opposite side walls.

Bathtubs

With the right positioning and features, bathtubs are also an option in an accessible bathroom. Maximally, tubs should be 17 to 19 inches above the floor. Grab bars are especially important when using tubs. Key heights and positions of grab bars are described later, but should be adjusted based on personal needs and preference.

Horizontal grab bars should be installed along the side wall at 33 to 36 inches above the finish floor. The end of the grab bar should be 12 inches maximum from the control wall and 15 inches from rear wall. Grab bars should be installed on the side wall 8 to 10 inches maximum above the rim of the bathtub. A 24-inch horizontal grab bar should be installed on the control wall at the front edge of the bathtub.

Vertical grab bars of 18 inches should be installed 4 inches from the front edge of the bathtub and 4 inches above the horizontal grab bar (Figure 13-7).

Figure 13-7. *Bathtubs and Grab Bars.*

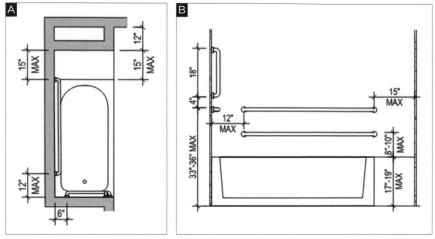

MAX: maximum; A: Bathtub dimensions (top); B: bathtub dimensions (side)

Accessible Kitchens

The kitchen's central role in the home as a place to prepare meals, eat, gather, and entertain should be seriously considered in terms of increasing accessibility. When designing a new or renovating an existing kitchen, the first consideration should be the *layout of space*.[12,15] Several different types of kitchen layouts can include the following:

- *U-shaped kitchen*: With more counter space than a traditional kitchen layout, this kitchen is more convenient for several people (Figure 13-8A).[8,12]
- *L-shaped kitchen*: This type of kitchen provides several work surfaces for people to work with enough space around them. This is the most ideal layout, but, often, the amount of square footage required for this layout is less readily available (see Figure 13-8B).[8,12]
- *Galley-style kitchen*: This layout can fit into a smaller space. Although it provides more entry and exit points to the space, its use is often limiting for individuals using wheelchairs who will have less turning space and typically only a side approach to counters and appliances (see Figure 13-8C).[8,12]

Once the optimal layout has been determined, consideration should be then given to countertop, cabinet, and appliance choices; layout; and configuration. Leaving empty space under countertops around the sink or cooking area is valuable for wheelchair accessibility.

FIGURE 13-8. *Accessible Kitchens.*

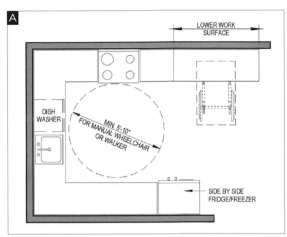

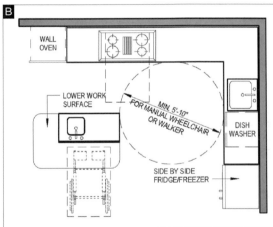

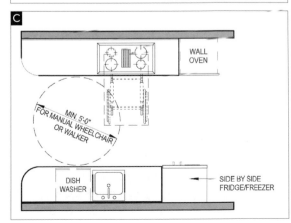

Appliances: Safety and ease of use should be the priority when thinking about kitchen layout and the appliances that are placed in it. Appliances that offer both visual and sound alerts, as well as glare-free and nonreflective controls, are recommended. In addition, appliances with automatic shut-off and other programmable features are generally more accessible to all household members.

In terms of a kitchen layout, the availability of natural light and views to the outdoors are primary considerations that can significantly improve the environment of the space. Window height should *always* be considered. Outdoor views can dramatically enhance the ambiance in the kitchen and provide access to natural light, which can help boost someone's mood, be a

MIN: minimum

A: U-shaped kitchen

B: L-shaped kitchen

C: Galley-style kitchen

part of controlling depression, and just make a person feel better. In addition, lower countertops and sinks are easier for someone in a wheelchair or those with limited mobility to use. When choosing sinks, the depth needs to be considered for ease of reaching. A depth of no more than 5 inches should be considered, and there should be at least 2 to 3 inches of countertop in front of the sink to provide arm support.[15] For easy use, controls for the sink should have paddle or lever faucets rather than knobs. Hands-free or touch-activated faucets are other options for many users.[5] Finally, it would be ideal for the sink and dishwasher to be side by side for ease of use. Although this is a good starting point and rule of thumb, no two people are alike, so these reach ranges and heights may need to be adjusted for each individual.

Refrigerators: Cabinetry is now able to accommodate larger appliances, such as dishwashers and refrigerators. Many times, this design not only creates a seamless concept, but also creates more accessible appliances, specifically for wheelchair users. For example, side-by-side refrigerators with pull-out shelves create flexibility, and pull-out freezers provide more shelving that requires less reach. Microwaves may also be built into the casework at a lower height for ease of accessibility and reach range.

Ovens and Stoves: As previously described, safety and ease of use should be the priority, especially when selecting ovens and stoves. Choosing a cooktop without open flame, such as an induction cooktop, would add the benefit of safety, as well as energy efficiency. Additional features to be aware of when choosing a safe oven or stove are automatic shut-off and cool touch features.[15] Similar to reach ranges of sinks, placement of controls need the same consideration. The controls should be located along the front or side of the unit for both ease and safety. One does not need to reach across the hot surface to properly use the appliance.[8] Finally, cooktops and ovens do not need to be a one-unit appliance. Purchasing and designing cooktops and ovens separately may work best for the space so the cooking surface has a clear area below it (similar to accessible sinks). Models also exist that are height adjustable and have buttons for up/down movement.[16]

Storage: Aside from how the storage is designed, ample storage is able to minimize the need for multiple shopping trips, making it easier on a person with limited mobility. Storage is able to be easily retrofitted into existing kitchens or into standard cabinets. Adjustable shelving, revolving trays, and pull-out/pull-down shelves are able to improve access to stored items. Deep shelves and high, wall-mounted cabinets should be avoided. The standard maximum depth of cabinets is considered to be 25 inches, but, based on personal preference, this may need to be adjusted. Toe spaces under the cabinets should be 9 inches high and 6 inches deep to support closer access points to cabinets and storage.[5]

Assistive Technology: As introduced in Chapter 3 (The Promise of the Future: Assistive Technology, Transportation, and Emerging Technologies), the Cueing Kitchen[2] and KitchenBot are the emerging assistive technologies that will bring additional assistance in the coming years. The Cueing Kitchen is an intelligent coaching system that can guide people with cognitive impairments through steps to prepare a meal independently. The KitchenBot is an integrated robotic kitchen manipulator designed to aid people with upper extremity impairments with common kitchen tasks, such as meal preparation and cleanup.

HALLWAYS, STAIRS, AND DOORS

Inside the home, it is important to assess access to all rooms. An open floor plan minimizes hallways and narrow routes; however, this is not always possible in existing homes. An ideal hallway width is 4 feet, but many homes have much more narrow hallways.[12] With access being a high priority, the minimum width should be 3 feet 8 inches. For dead-end passageways (without space to turn around at the end), an open space of approximately 5 feet in diameter should be created to allow enough turning radius to accommodate wheelchair use. In addition, flooring surfaces should be low-pile dense carpeting or nonslip wood or tile, with consistency between hallways and rooms.

If there are stairs inside the home, it is best to install handrails on both side walls (if possible). Handrails should be sturdy and have no disruptions in continuity (ie, brackets should not interfere with the continuous grasping of the handrail). Stairs are typically 11 inches deep and have a vertical height of 7 inches. Most codes dictate that risers, the vertical height between the steps, must be solid to prevent slips through the back of the steps. Proper lighting is also important in stairwells. A lower amount of light may be adequate if there is a high enough contrast between the edges of the tread and the risers. The goal is to make the edges of the steps visible, which enhances accurate placement of feet on the steps and hands on the railings.

Proper selection of doors also enhances access to the home, as well as to each room. Residential doors are usually 32 inches wide, but older homes may have more narrow openings. Optimally, doors should be at least 36 inches wide to improve access. They should be mounted to open out when exiting small spaces, such as bathrooms. Although residential doors do not typically have automatic closers on them, many storm doors do. These should be adjusted to close slowly. Doors that swing in should have between 18 to 24 inches of clear space on the side of the door with the handle to make it easier to exit the room.[5,8] Switching hardware from knobs to levers can greatly enhance ease of grasp and use.

Floors

Color and texture are important considerations for flooring. Flooring should be slip-resistant, but smooth to make it easier to walk on or maneuver a wheelchair across. Some examples of slip-resistant materials include low-pile carpet, hardwood, laminate, linoleum, rubber, matte and textured ceramics, and cork.[12] By incorporating contrasting colors, walls, floors, and door thresholds are able to help with wayfinding, especially for individuals with vision impairment. They can be even more enhanced with textural contrast. Glare can be disturbing and intolerable for some individuals; therefore, low-matte and low-gloss paint finishes are also recommended. For individuals with vision impairments, materials that enhance echoed sound (eg, hardwood, marble, ceramic, and laminate) can help augment awareness of the space and surroundings. In contrast, for those with hearing impairments, it is important to silence noise. Thus, using flooring such as carpet, cork, or rubber can best support their needs.[12]

Walls

Smooth finishes are recommended to avoid abrasions if they are bumped into. As with flooring, the use of contrasting colors can help identify architectural components, such as the wall and floor, wall and ceiling, wall and door, door handles, wall switches, and wall outlets. Textural contrast is also helpful in identifying primary routes and functional areas.

Bedrooms

In a home with multiple bedrooms, when choosing which bedroom would be best (in addition to size), consider the proximity to the bathroom or egress from the home in an event of an emergency. Also, consider window height and the views to the outdoors for enhanced ambiance.

A space of at least 13 feet x 14 feet is recommended for a bedroom.[17] This amount of space allows for enough clear space even with standard furniture. Open space of about 5 feet on each side of the bed is recommended if possible.[1] To increase convenience, important items such as clothing and storage for medical equipment should be positioned nearby for easy access. Bedroom furniture should be placed to allow easy, unobstructed pathways and reaches for drawers and handles. Legs on furniture have both an aesthetic and functional purpose; they make the room look bigger while also allowing a wheelchair user to approach more closely. Open shelving may also make storing and access to clothes easier.[17]

In addition to furniture placement, the placement of electrical outlets and controls is just as important. The use of three-way switches, for example, gives the individual the freedom to operate lights and other features from both the entry area and by the bed area without excessive moving around.[17] By considering placement of the outlets and controls, advanced technology can be incorporated with ease. For example, if a lift is needed, a ceiling-mounted outlet will provide power without long extension cords or the need to hardwire the electrical system. Because safety is always the top priority, a switch next to the bed can be connected to a communication system that alerts of falls or other care needs.[17]

OUTDOOR SPACES

As described previously, there are important features outside of the home to consider, such as available parking and how many steps are needed to enter the home. These elements might not seem as important as the general interior of the home, but they may have a significant impact on day-to-day activities and quality of life. Ideally, yard and outdoor spaces should be extensions of the home, thus providing—if desired—more enjoyable living spaces with plants, comfortable seating, and recreation or cooking amenities. Accessibility to both interior and exterior spaces is fundamental to an accessible home.

Parking

If there is a driveway, check for a level surface and make sure that there is plenty of width to get in and out of a vehicle. A carport or garage offers protection from the elements. If there is no on-site parking option, look for nearby street parking and consider the volume of traffic and other events that take place in the area that could impact availability.

Access to the Main Entry

Sidewalks, steps, paths, and lighting are main outdoor landscape elements that should be reviewed carefully. Ideally, the number of steps to the front door should be minimized, and either handrails or a ramp may need to be installed to improve home accessibility. Exterior wood stairs should have treads for additional slip resistance. Ample light at entrances, along with markings at any changes in level, helps support safe and secure home access. Any concrete pads or pathways leading to the home should be level. Typically, a ½-inch difference in height is the maximum a wheelchair can get over without assistance.[5,8] Concrete should also be slightly sloped to allow rain to run off without puddling, which in wintertime would form ice.

ACCESSIBLE COMMUNITIES AND TRANSPORTATION

When choosing a community to live in, proximity to work, family, healthcare, and friends is a major factor to consider. Careful analysis of specific elements can help determine whether the community meets a person's accessibility needs. Ideally, a community should be universally accessible; many communities have gone through substantial transformation since the ADA was enacted in 1990. The level of accessibility within a community, however, may vary depending on the individual's needs. Therefore, when looking to relocate or assess the accessibility of a community, it is helpful to consider the following questions:

- *Is the community pedestrian-friendly?* A "walkable" community is generally more accessible for those who use mobility aids (eg, wheelchairs or prosthetics), as well as for those who are blind or who have limited vision. A pedestrian-friendly community has sidewalks, curb cuts, clearly marked crosswalks, and pedestrian signals at busy intersections. Safe pedestrian connections to grocery stores, banks, post offices, parks, and playgrounds make a community more attractive to walking options, so that individuals rely less on vehicular transportation. Communities with transportation nodes (eg, bus stops or train stations) are inherently pedestrian-friendly and are also generally more accessible.
- *Are recreation facilities accessible?* Accessible fields can be used and enjoyed by all individuals with disabilities. Paths without steps or steep slopes provide access to those who rely on wheeled devices and those who use prosthetic limbs. Clearly accessible signs in large fonts, raised lettering, and Braille—along with barrier-free paths—make facilities more accessible for individuals who are blind. Many community pools have lifts to improve access. Some pools have transfer areas where the ledge of the pool is raised 18 inches on the deck side of the pool to ease individual access from a wheelchair. In many community fitness centers, exercise equipment is relatively versatile and has features to allow use by individuals with a variety of disabilities.
- *Are community gardens accessible?* Gardens are popular and can be established in community parks and sometimes on rooftops. Making an existing community garden accessible to a person who cannot bend down to reach the ground surface can be as simple as installing raised planters (ie, where the planter surface is 18 inches above the surrounding ground area). This can be accomplished by using prefabricated raised

containers or by building them on site. Accessible gardens can provide fresh produce, are therapeutic and calming, and can foster community involvement.

• *Are grocery stores accessible?* Shopping for food is a routine. Locating an accessible grocery store or a store that delivers food should be considered. Since the ADA was passed 20 years ago, most grocery stores are accessible. Stores generally have wide aisles to support two-way traffic, which greatly enhances wheelchair mobility. However, shelving height may still be a problem for people of short stature or those individuals using a wheelchair. Store employees are generally available to help shoppers with disabilities and should be called on as needed. Online shopping is also widely available for most goods and services, and home delivery services greatly enhance access. Software programs, such as the JAWS (Job Access With Speech) screen reader, are very helpful for individuals who are blind.

ACCESSIBLE PUBLIC TRANSPORTATION

A community with nodes of public transportation can greatly enhance independence. Since the ADA became law, all public transportation systems are required to be accessible. Detailed information regarding the accessibility of the public transportation system is generally available within the local transportation authority's website. For example, the Washington Metropolitan Area Transit Authority (www.wmata.com) has an accessibility tab on its website that leads to information about all services—including fixed rail, bus services, and the Paratransit Service (called "MetroAccess")—that provide door-to-door aid for qualified individuals. Individuals must reserve rides at least 24 hours before their desired pick-up time. To qualify for this service, customers must present an application signed by a physician certifying that they are not able to use bus and rail services independently. Individuals who qualify are eligible for a MetroAccess Identification Card. Some customers can use fixed-route buses and trains; however, for some trips, they need to supplement their transportation needs with door-to-door service. Reduced fare rates are also generally available for daily users.

City subway/public transportation systems should be fully accessible. Stations should have elevator entrances, accessible fare vending machines, and fare gates. Train platforms should be equipped with safety features—including detectable warning tiles, lighting and audio, and visual information—for those with hearing or vision impairments. Public buses should be able to lower the floor or deploy a ramp to ease access. Many public transportation systems offer free travel training for customers who need orientation on the system. Travel trainers provide customers with disabilities-specific information on how they can best use the bus and rail systems. Real-time subway, train, or bus information should also be available online and accessible from a smartphone or tablet. These should also be compatible with a screen reader. Applications such as NextBus may also be helpful to customers using public transportation. This GPS (Global Positioning System)-enabled application for mobile devices recognizes the location of the nearest stop and informs the user when the bus will arrive.

Taxi Services

Generally, a standard taxi is accessible to people who are blind, deaf, or have cognitive disabilities. Taxi services must provide rides to customers with service animals without adding an additional fee. Unfortunately, there may not be a wide choice of taxi services for people who use wheelchairs or scooters, because the ADA does not require taxi services to purchase or lease wheelchair-accessible automobiles. However, because of public pressure, there has been an increase of wheelchair-accessible taxis in large metropolitan areas. For taxis that are accessible, no additional fare should be added for the services.

Driving, Buying, or Adapting a Car

Technological advances have given people with disabilities greater opportunities for driving independently using adaptive equipment. Depending on the use of adaptive devices, however, certain restrictions may be placed on the license. Although an individual cannot be denied the opportunity to apply for a license due to a disability, there are safety reasons why some drivers have been denied the opportunity to drive a car or have restrictions placed on their license. For example, a person could be denied a license to drive a car with a manual transmission if that person needs to use manual controls for depressing a clutch, braking, and acceleration because it may not be possible to have one hand on the wheel at all times. Before investing in a modification for a vehicle, careful research about the possibility to sustain a driver's license should be considered.

Information pertaining to adaptation of motor vehicles for individuals with disabilities can be found at the National Resource Directory.[18] In addition, the Department of Veterans Affairs (VA) offers a one-time grant of a maximum of $20,114.34 toward the purchase of an accessible automobile. The VA will also pay for adaptive equipment for a vehicle, as well as its maintenance and replacement multiple times during the Veteran's or Service Member's life. To be eligible for these grants, the Service Member or Veteran must have one of the following disabilities:

- loss or permanent loss of use of one or both feet,
- loss or permanent loss of use of one or both hands, or
- severe burn injury.

More information regarding eligibility for a VA vehicle grant or for application forms[19] may be found at http://benefits.va.gov/BENEFITS/factsheets/serviceconnected/Auto.pdf. Additional information on applying for a VA grant can be obtained at http://www.vba.va.gov/pubs/forms/VBA-21-4502-ARE.pdf.

SUMMARY

Injuries or illnesses, particularly those affecting Wounded Warriors and Veterans, may cause significant physical, cognitive, and emotional impairments. The resulting disability from these impairments, however, is largely influenced by one's environment. Modern technologies now support numerous adaptive solutions to enhance functional independence for individuals who have a variety of severe impairments. Numerous resources are currently available at the local, state, and federal levels to help support individuals with disabilities. Tailoring one's home and community to be more accessible helps socialization and promotes successful family and community participation, which is fundamental to long-term health and quality of life. Success begins with being aware of one's deficits and working with dedicated professionals to implement solutions, whether that be building a new home, modifying an existing home, relocating to another community, or just being familiar with and accessing resources that already exist within the community.

NOTE

The information presented in this chapter is based on the current knowledge of the authors and is provided for general information purposes only. Because individual needs vary, we advise readers to consult appropriate professional resources to decide what is safe and appropriate for their specific needs. Any action taken based on the information presented in this chapter is the responsibility of the user.

References

1. Gentry T. Smart homes for people with neurological disability: state of the art. *NeuroRehabilitation.* 2009;25:209–217.

2. Pasquina PF, Pasquina LF, Anderson-Barnes VC, Giuggio JS, Cooper RA. Using architecture and technology to promote improved quality of life for military Service Members with traumatic brain injury. *Phys Med Rehabil Clin North Am.* 2010;21:207–220.

3. Home Smart Home. *Time.* July 7–14, 2014:46–87.

4. American Institute of Architects. 2014 AIA Home Design Trends Survey. AIA website. http://www.aia.org/practicing/AIAB103887. Accessed November 1, 2015.

5. Americans with Disabilities Act. Information and Technical Assistance on the Americans with Disabilities Act. ADA website. http://www.ada.gov/. Accessed November 20, 2015.

6. Baker K. Accessibility and Outdoor Property Improvements Top List of Popular Home Characteristics. American Institute of Architects website. http://www.aia.org/practicing/AIAB103887. Accessed September 20, 2014.

7. Nest Labs. Nest Learning Thermostat. Nest Labs website. https://nest.com/. Accessed November 6, 2015.

8. International Code Council. *Standard for Accessible and Usable Buildings and Facilities.* Washington, DC: ICC; 2007. ICC A117.1-2009 (ANSI).

9. Kwikset Kevo Smart Lock. Kwikset website. http://www.kwikset.com/kevo/default.aspx#.Vj_uTjFOktw. Accessed November 6, 2015.

10. Haux R, Hein A, Kolb G, et al. Information and communication technologies for promoting and sustaining quality of life, health and self-sufficiency in ageing societies—outcomes of the Lower Saxony Research Network Design of Environments for Ageing (GAL). *Inform Health Soc Care.* 2014;39:166–187.

11. Jasiewicz J, Kearns W, Craighead J, Fozard JL, Scott S, McCarthy J Jr. Smart rehabilitation for the 21st century: the Tampa Smart Home for Veterans with traumatic brain injury. *J Rehabil Res Dev.* 2011;48:vii–xviii.

12. Canada Mortgage and Housing Corporation. Accessible and adaptable housing. 2015 Kitchen, Living Spaces Section. CMHC website. http://www.cmhc-schl.gc.ca/en/co/acho/index.cfm. Accessed November 6, 2015.

13. Philips Hue Personal Wireless Lighting. Philips website. http://www.usa.philips.com/c-p/046677426354/hue-personal-wireless-lighting. Accessed November 6, 2015.

14. Department of Veterans Affairs, Office of Construction & Facilities Management. *Design Guide—June 2008: Spinal Cord Injury/ Disorders Center.* US Department of Veterans Affairs website. http://www.cfm.va.gov/til/dGuide/dgSCIDC01.pdf. Accessed December 24, 2015.

15. Veterans Benefits Administration. *VA Handbook for Design: Specially Adapted Housing for Wheelchair Users.* Washington, DC: VBA; August 2009. Pamphlet 26-13.

16. Freedom Lift Systems. Cabinet and Shelving Lifts. Freedom Lift Systems website. https://freedomliftsystems.com/Adjustable-Height-Counter-Lifts. Accessed November 7, 2015.
17. Schwab C. Around the House: Bedroom Addition Provides In-Home Healing. October 2011. http://www.aia.org/aiaucmp/groups/aia/documents/pdf/aiab103880.pdf. Accessed November 20, 2015.
18. National Resource Directory. NRD website. https://m.nrd.gov/transportation_and_travel/vehicle_modifications_and_adaptive_equipment. Accessed December 14, 2015.
19. US Department of Veterans Affairs. VA Benefits Fact Sheets. VA website. htttp://benefits.va.gov/BENEFITS/factsheets/serviceconnected/Auto.pdf. Accessed November 14, 2015.

Gunnery Sergeant James M. Joseph was born in Pittsburgh, Pennsylvania on May 7, 1961. He enlisted in the Marine Corps on May 8, 1979 and attended boot camp at the Marine Corps Recruit Depot in San Diego, California. From 1979 to 1983, he served in the Marine Corps Infantry as a Mortarman. Subsequently, Joseph completed schooling for a lateral move, thus becoming a Small Missile Systems Electro-Optical Repairman. In December 1990, he was ordered to Direct Support Group 2, 1st FSSG (Force Service Support Group) Saudi Arabia, where he was assigned as the Electro-Optical Repair Chief and served as a Breach Guide during Operation Desert Storm.

During the fall of 1994, Joseph was diagnosed with diabetes mellitus. This information was kept confidential and only the Commanding Officers/ First Sergeants of his subsequent units were advised of his health problem. In February 1996, he returned to Okinawa, Japan, for the third time and served as the Fire Control Repair Chief of Ordnance Maintenance Company, Maintenance Battalion, 3rd FSSG. In August 1999, Joseph was assigned to the Marine Corps Detachment at Aberdeen Proving Ground. He served as an Electro-Optical Instructor and as the Senior Marine Instructor.

After becoming insulin-dependent, Gunnery Sergeant Joseph retired from the Active Marine Corps Forces in 2001. Following retirement, he worked as a Machine Technician for the Dialysis Clinic, Inc (Pittsburgh, Pennsylvania). The challenges of working constant shift schedules led Joseph to the Vocational, Rehabilitation, and Education counselors at the Department of Veterans Affairs (VA). Upon qualifying for the Chapter 31 Vocational and Rehabilitation Program, he attended Point Park University and earned a BS degree in Information Technology.

While attending school full time, Joseph was also employed as an Administrative Clerk/Information Technology Specialist at the Human Engineering Research Laboratories, Department of Veterans Affairs. After completing the internal VA job application process, he changed career paths and became an Information Security Officer for the Veterans Benefits Administration in Pittsburgh. Eventually, he became the Facility Chief Information Officer at the Office of Information and Technology for the same organization. As increasing job responsibilities and 24/7/365 on-call status proved to be incompatible with the time requirements needed to deal with taxing, daily diabetic routines, Joseph retired in December 2012.

Finding retirement unfulfilling, Joseph returned to the Human Engineering Research Laboratories and was enrolled in the Advancing Inclusive Manufacturing (AIM) Program. After graduating from AIM, he was encouraged by the program's director to consider changing careers and return to school.

James Joseph is currently a second-year graduate student at the School of Health and Rehabilitation Sciences at the University of Pittsburgh. He is pursuing an MS degree in Clinical Rehabilitation and Mental Health Counseling. He is also a member of the American Legion and the Disabled American Veterans.

The delivery of high-quality, accessible healthcare services
as the foundation of a ready force—
and the life-saving care in the deployed environment is
a force multiplier.

★ ★ ★

HONORABLE JONATHAN WOODSON, MD
ASSISTANT SECRETARY OF DEFENSE HEALTH AFFAIRS
DIRECTOR, TRICARE MANAGEMENT ACTIVITY
OCTOBER 9, 2015

Chapter Fourteen

Overview of Military and Veteran Resources

RORY A. COOPER, PhD*

*Director and Senior Career Scientist, Human Engineering Research Laboratories, Rehabilitation Research and Development Service, US Department of Veterans Affairs, 6425 Penn Avenue, Pittsburgh, Pennsylvania 15206, and Distinguished Professor and FISA Foundation–Paralyzed Veterans of America Chair, Department of Rehabilitation Science and Technology, University of Pittsburgh, 6425 Penn Avenue, Suite 400, Pittsburgh, Pennsylvania 15206

INTRODUCTION

After over a decade of being at war, there has been growth in the number and size of government programs to assist wounded, injured, and ill Service Members, Veterans, and their families. In addition, there have been various government agencies and offices (Exhibit 14-1) that have attempted to meet their needs with varying degrees of success. Some programs have also been created that promise to have a profound effect on the Veteran population (eg, the Post-9/11 GI Bill). A significant challenge that remains is the difficulty in identifying the various programs, sorting through the eligibility requirements, and surmounting the application processes.

Physical and mental health are personal to each of us and require a proactive approach to maintain or improve well-being. This requires people to participate in regular physical activity, good nutrition, and quality sleep. Service Members are accustomed to having a mission and a unit that has an assigned purpose, goal, and specific objectives. Postmilitary life will be most successful if Veterans also set goals and develop long-range objectives,

Exhibit 14-1. *Web Sites to Assist With Health, Reintegration, and Resilience*

National Resource Directory	nrd.gov
Army Medicine	armymedicine.mil
TRICARE	tricare.mil
MyHealtheVet	www.myhealth.va.gov
National Veterans Wheelchair Games	wheelchairgames.org
National Disabled Veterans Winter Sports Clinic	wintersportsclinic.org
National Disabled Veterans Summer Sports Clinic	va.gov/opa/speceven/ssc/
Dietary Guidelines for Americans	www.cnpp.usda.gov/dietary-guidelines
US Department of Agriculture Dietary Guidelines for Americans SuperTracker	choosemyplate.gov/tools-supertracker
American College of Sports Medicine Position Stands	acsm.org/public-information/position-stands
Comprehensive Soldier and Family Fitness program	csf2.army.mil/
Navy and Marine Corps Public Health Center	www.med.navy.mil/sites/nmcphc
Vet Centers	www.vetcenter.va.gov
Association of the United States Army	ausa.org/family
Soldier For Life program	soldierforlife.army.mil
Marine For Life program	www.usmc-mccs.org/services/career/ marine-for-life-network
VA eBenefits	www.ebenefits.va.gov
Veterans' Employment and Training Service	dol.gov/vets/programs
Hero2Hired	h2h.jobs
Hiring Our Heroes	uschamberfoundation.org/hiring-our-heroes
Small Business Administration— Resources for Veterans	sba.gov/offices/headquarters/vbd/resources/4930
Office of Personnel Management— Veterans Services	opm.gov/policy-data-oversight/veterans-services/ vet-guide

Web sites are listed in the order that they appear in the chapter. This exhibit and chapter provide resources found on the Internet. Due to the nature of online resources, these Web addresses are subject to change without notice. We suggest using a search engine to find any missing resources.

Military service ingrains in Veterans the need to pay attention to detail, to look for anything and everything that is wrong or out of place, and to correct it immediately. In the civilian world, this may not always be appreciated and may be viewed by colleagues as criticism.

The first stop for Service Members, Veterans, and their families who are seeking resources should be the National Resource Directory (nrd.gov). The National Resource Directory was established to be an authoritative source of information for wounded, injured, and ill Military and Veteran Service Members, their families, and the people who care for them. These individuals use a wide range of benefits and resources available to them from

- federal, state, and local governments;
- not-for-profit organizations; and
- corporate America.

A collaboration of the Department of Defense, the Department of Labor, and the Department of Veterans Affairs (VA), the National Resource Directory is found as a free online tool that provides access to more than 10,000 resources at the national, state, and local levels.

With the market penetration of smartphones, access to information is literally at the fingertips of users. Smartphone applications include an increasing number of health-related information programs. These applications can be helpful and have been used successfully to assist people in making positive changes in their lives. There are a growing number of devices that assist with maintaining health and fitness that communicate with or complement smartphones.

HEALTH-RELATED RESOURCES

There are a number of sponsored resources from the Department of Defense and the VA to help promote a healthy lifestyle. The US Army offers several programs. Information can be found at the Army Medicine Web site (army medicine.mil). This site includes some participatory challenges for individuals, families, and friends. Army Medicine encourages soldiers and their families to

- take 10,000 steps per day for at least 30 days,
- eat 8 servings of fruits and vegetables over 8 days, and
- sleep 8 hours per day for at least 8 days in sequence.

TRICARE (tricare.mil) offers information on health and wellness. This site provides information about the location of military treatment facilities and wellness centers. TRICARE provides information on what benefits are covered, contact information for doctors, cost estimates, steps to take when there are changes in life events, and health and wellness information. TRICARE also offers information on health and wellness, as well as on the following:

- alcohol awareness,
- tobacco cessation,
- preventative services,
- getting fit, and
- healthy partners.

The VA offers information and programs to help promote the health and well-being of Veterans. The primary online pathway for helping Veterans to manage their health is via MyHealtheVet (www.myhealth.va.gov). This online resource enables Veterans to manage their medical priorities through an online prescription refill service, personal health journal, and links to federal and VA benefits. In addition, the VA also provides various health support services to help Veterans maintain physical and mental wellness (Exhibit 14-2).

For Veterans with disabilities, the VA offers a number of national events to promote participation in healthy sports and recreation activities. Among these are the National Veterans Wheelchair Games (wheelchairgames.org), the National Disabled Veterans Winter Sports Clinic (wintersportsclinic.org), and the National Disabled Veterans Summer Sports Clinic (va.gov/opa/speceven/ssc).

The US Department of Agriculture and the US Department of Health and Human Services prepare and distribute Dietary Guidelines for Americans (www.cnpp.usda.gov/dietary-guidelines) every 5 years. These guidelines provide advice about consuming fewer calories, making informed food choices, and being physically active to attain and maintain a healthy weight, reduce the risk of chronic disease, and promote overall health. The US Department of Agriculture offers the "supertracker" (choosemyplate.gov/tools-super tracker) to help people follow a healthy diet plan. The supertracker provides examples of daily food plans, suggestions on tracking calories, information on how to best allocate calories, and tips on how to interpret food labels. A very useful aspect of this tool is an explanation of empty calories and solid fats.

EXHIBIT 14-2. *MyHealtheVet*

MyHealtheVet helps to maintain physical and mental wellness through the following:

- support for blind and low-vision Veterans and their families;
- support and services for those who care for Veterans;
- attention to the spiritual health needs of Veterans;
- short-stay and long-stay nursing home care for Veterans who are medically and mentally stable;
- a vocational rehabilitation program that endeavors to match and support work to ready Veterans for competitive jobs;
- advocating for health promotion, disease prevention, and health education for our Nation's Veterans;
- geriatric and extended care services for Veterans, including noninstitutional and institutional options;
- a variety of resources, programs, and benefits offered by the VA to assist Veterans who are homeless;
- maintenance and improvement of the health and well-being of Veterans through excellence in healthcare, social services, education, and research;
- remaining a Center of Excellence for research and education on the prevention, understanding, and treatment of posttraumatic stress disorder;
- a source of prosthetic and orthotic services, sensory aids, medical equipment, and support services for Veterans;
- improvement of access to and quality of care for Veterans living in rural areas;
- resources and tools to help smokers quit;
- treatments addressing all types of problems related to substance use, from unhealthy use of alcohol to life-threatening addictions;
- the Veterans Crisis Line (dial 1-800-273-8255 and press 1), a toll-free, confidential resource that connects Veterans in crisis and their families and friends with qualified, caring VA responders;
- the MOVE! Weight Management Program, which helps Veterans to lose weight, keep it off, and improve their health; and
- implementation of positive changes in the provision of care for all female Veterans.

The American College of Sports Medicine (acsm.org/public-information/position-stands) provides time and intensity recommendations for cardiorespiratory, resistance, neuromotor, and flexibility exercises.[1] Their guidelines offer guidance on improving and maintaining health, strength, endurance, flexibility, coordination, and agility. The American College of Sports Medicine recommends a minimum of 150 minutes of weekly exercise, which may be obtained by exercising longer on days when time is available or breaking workouts into several increments of 10 minutes or more throughout a day.

RESILIENCE-RELATED RESOURCES

Serving in the military may present challenges to the people serving and their families, especially during deployment or mobilization. Service in the Armed Forces requires working long hours in the face of difficult and sometimes life-threatening issues that may place severe pressures on the people serving, as well as their families. Operational and wartime missions can have physiological and psychological effects on how Service Members, Military Civilians, and their families think, feel, and act. Therefore, the military provides tools and resources to help people become more resilient.

The US Army offers the Comprehensive Soldier and Family Fitness program (csf2.army.mil) that is designed to build resilience and enhance the performance of Soldiers, their families, and Army civilians. This program also provides hands-on training and self-development tools to members of the Army to help them cope with adversity, perform better in stressful situations, and thrive in all aspects of life. It also offers an online self-assessment and self-development tool (known as ArmyFit) for Soldiers, family members, and Army civilians that includes videos, information, and links to people or organizations. Similarly, the Navy and Marine Corps provide both in-person and online services to members of the Armed Forces and their families through the Navy and Marine Corps Public Health Center (www.med.navy.mil/sites/nmcphc).

Service Members can become more resilient by working on several key factors:

- incorporating role flexibility into their toolkit to encourage being able to function in multiple roles;
- practicing active coping strategies;
- maintaining communication/contact with friends and family during deployment;
- setting realistic expectations; and
- building strong, supportive, and healthy relationships.

REUNION AND REINTEGRATION RESOURCES

Reunion and reintegration after deployment are not always easy. A broad range of counseling, outreach, and referral services for Veterans and their families may be needed. Services may include individual and group counseling (eg,

Exhibit 14-3. *Association of the United States Army*

To promote successful reintegration, the Association of the United States Army provides the following list of expectations:

- expect to have mixed emotions about being home,
- expect to see changes in your partner,
- expect you and your family members to need reassurance as you readjust,
- expect the spouse/parent who remained home to want to help with family maintenance,
- expect your partner to remember the promises made while you were separated,
- expect your partner to need some romance and pampering,
- expect your partner to feel a mix of anger and resentment if she/he had a difficult time while you were gone,
- expect you and your partner to experience some physical and emotional fatigue after the initial reunion,
- expect adjustments to take from several weeks to several months, and
- expect to feel some sadness or depression.

in areas such as posttraumatic stress disorder), alcohol and drug assessment, and suicide prevention referrals. Readjusting to a "new normal" is a transition involving some level of stress. After a deployment, and especially if there is also a prolonged hospitalization or recovery, everything at home will not be the same. People change with time, and members of the Armed Forces are affected by each deployment. Reintegration is a process of adjustment to a new normal that can last from days to years, depending on the circumstances. If a Service Member returns with a major disability, such as a limb amputation, adjustment and reintegration can be extensive. Deployment—especially when severe wounds, injury, or illness result—can strengthen or strain relationships. Patience and flexibility can improve chances for successful reintegration.

The VA provides Vet Centers (www.vetcenter.va.gov) to welcome home war Veterans by providing readjustment counseling in a caring manner. Vet Centers assist Veterans and their families with a successful postwar adjustment in or near the communities where they live. The Association of the United States Army (ausa.org/family) has produced a set of materials to help Service Members and families with successful reintegration and with building strong families. The Association provides a list of *expectations* to help promote successful reintegration (Exhibit 14-3).

Some people find it hard to talk about deployment activities. Everyone develops their own coping strategies. However, it may be helpful to talk with a trusted friend, family member, or healthcare professional. It is acceptable and may be desirable to talk about deployment and disability experiences. Appropriate sharing with family and friends can be a powerful source of support and help with reintegration and readjustment. Sharing with other people may be a helpful coping strategy that is often recommended by physicians and psychologists.

Service Members, when undergoing reintegration, may demonstrate one or more of the following: low frustration tolerance, anger management issues, difficulties in coping and self-regulation, hypervigilance, social withdrawal, and higher risk for alcohol and other substance abuse. Service Members had a concrete purpose in their units, but they may lose this sense of purpose upon reentry into a civilian community.

The Army and Marine Corps have programs to help Soldiers and Marines with successful reintegration into civilian life, including the Soldier For Life (soldierforlife.army.mil) and the Marine For Life (www.usmc-mccs.org/services/career/marine-for-life-network) programs. These programs provide links wherein Veterans can turn for information on

- benefits, education, and career opportunities;
- fitness and health;
- family services;
- mental health services;
- suicide prevention;
- posttraumatic stress disorder; and
- traumatic brain injury.

These resources and connections can help Soldiers and Marines obtain the necessary training and qualifications and make the needed connections to be successful in their efforts to reintegrate into civilian life. Veterans embody the traits that employers seek—they have years of outstanding training and are disciplined leaders, loyal team members, and hard workers. The Soldiers For Life and Marines For Life programs provide Veterans with the tools to be successful members of their communities by using the resources and training from the Army or Marine Corps, while readily having access to the wide network of civilian entities that will support them.

BENEFIT RESOURCES

A challenge that many Veterans face, and that may ultimately cause them hardship, is not immediately accepting that they have earned the benefits offered to them by the military and the VA. It is often in the nature of Military Service Members and Veterans to be modest and self-sufficient. Veterans must accept that they have earned the benefits that they receive, and come to accept that there is nothing wrong with applying for and receiving them. Many of the procedures for securing Veterans benefits are complex and can be confusing, even for those who know them well. Many Veterans benefits have deadlines for applying. In some cases—including some kinds of insurance, education, and other important benefits—once the deadlines expire, there is no recourse. Do not try to apply for benefits on your own, especially those from the VA. There are Veterans service organizations that provide excellent assistance at no cost.

Military service is a hazardous profession, not only when serving in hostile regions that can impact your body and mind, but also during training and when exposed to the materials and substances with which Service Members come into contact with that can impact health, often long into the future. Therefore, it is important to enroll in the VA as soon as you are eligible. VA service connection is often the gateway to VA healthcare, even if only needed in the future. If the VA grants service connection, even at a 0% rating, the Veteran will have the condition recorded and may be eligible for increased compensation if the service-connected condition worsens over time.

The VA provides an online gateway to benefits information known as eBenefits (www.ebenefits.va.gov) that every Veteran should review, in addition to contacting a credentialed service officer at one of the national Veteran service organizations. The eBenefits Web site provides links and information to apply for benefits, to learn about and apply for the post-9/11 GI Bill, to extend TRICARE benefits, and to sign up for MyHealtheVet. VA benefits cover a broad range of domains that include

- healthcare,
- life insurance,
- education,
- employment,
- self-employment,
- compensation,
- burial, and
- assistance for qualified dependents.

The VA offers a home loan guaranty program to help individuals obtain a home loan at favorable interest rates and terms, often with no or very little down payment. Some states also have a state-level Veteran-specific home loan program, including Alaska, California, Oregon, Texas, and Wisconsin. Many state housing agencies also offer home loan assistance and other housing programs that Veterans may qualify for, even though they are not Veteran-specific. Many of the VA benefit programs have deadlines or time limits; therefore, it is best to start early and exercise due diligence.

Most states and US territories provide benefits, programs, and services to Active Duty, Reserve, and National Guard Military Service Members; Veterans; and dependents. All 50 states—as well as Washington, DC, Puerto Rico, American Samoa, Guam, the Northern Mariana Islands, and the US Virgin Islands—have services for Veterans operating at the local level that offer a complex array of benefits, programs, and resources that may supplement or complement those provided by the federal government or that are specific to a certain state or territory. Reserve and National Guard members or Veterans who may not qualify for federal Veterans benefits may still qualify for state or territory programs.

EMPLOYMENT RESOURCES

Military experiences help to shape Veterans for a lifetime. Much of military life is about teamwork and unified efforts to achieve a common mission or objective. A high level of cooperation and selfless service often becomes ingrained in Veterans. It is important to understand that much of society is based on competition and not on cooperation. The level of competitiveness experienced in postmilitary life may feel unfamiliar or even oppressive.

The Department of Defense, the VA, and the Department of Labor offer employment assistance programs for Veterans and employers who would like to hire them. The Department of Labor's Veterans' Employment and Training Service (dol.gov/vets/programs) offers employment and training services to eligible Veterans through a noncompetitive Jobs for Veterans State Grants program. In this program, funds are allocated to State Workforce Agencies in direct proportion to the number of Veterans seeking employment within their state. The Uniformed Services Employment and Reemployment Rights Act protects civilian job rights and benefits for Veterans and members of Reserve components. The Uniformed Services Employment and Reemployment Rights Act also provides enforcement mechanisms, and includes federal government employees and those employees eligible to receive Department of Labor assistance in processing claims. Under the Vietnam Era Veterans' Readjustment Assistance Act of 1974, federal contractors and subcontractors must track and report annually to the Department of Labor the number of employees in their workforces who belong to the categories of Veterans covered under the affirmative action provisions of the Vietnam Era Veterans' Readjustment Assistance Act.

Hero2Hired (H2H; h2h.jobs) is a Department of Defense program that provides Reserve Component Service Members with a tool to connect to and find jobs with military-friendly companies. H2H offers career exploration tools, military-to-civilian skills translations, education and training resources, and a mobile app. If Reserve Component Service Members are unsure about what they want to do, H2H offers a short skills and interests survey to help determine career types that may fit the Service Member's background.

The US Chamber of Commerce offers a Hiring Our Heroes (HOH; uschamberfoundation.org/hiring-our-heroes) program. HOH is a nationwide initiative to help Veterans, transitioning Service Members, and military spouses find employment opportunities. HOH works through the network of state and local chambers and strategic partners from the public, private, and nonprofit sectors. HOH deploys two overriding strategies: (1) grassroots engagement and (2) public–private partnerships.

The Small Business Administration–Resources for Veterans (sba.gov/offices/headquarters/vbd/resources/4930) offers a number of opportunities for Veterans. The Small Business Administration has 16 resource centers around the country that provide services (exclusively for Veterans), such as mentoring, training, business preparation, and more. Veterans may qualify for government contracting to grow a small business. Service-Disabled Veteran-Owned Small Businesses may be able to become a part of the Service-Disabled Veteran-Owned Small Business Concern program. This procurement program provides that federal contracting officers may restrict competition to the Service-Disabled Veteran-Owned Small Business Concern and award a sole-source or set aside a contract wherein specific criteria are met.

The Office of Personnel Management–Veterans Services (opm.gov/policy-data-oversight/veterans-services/vet-guide) handles programs that provide some degree of preference for qualified Veterans in appointments to federal jobs. The US Congress has enacted laws to prevent Veterans seeking federal employment from being penalized for their time in military service. Veterans' preference recognizes the economic loss suffered by citizens who have served their country in the Armed Forces, restores Veterans to a favorable competitive position for government employment, and acknowledges the larger obligation owed to disabled Veterans.

Veterans' preference is codified in various provisions of Title 5, United States Code. Veterans who are disabled or who served on active duty in the

Armed Forces during certain specified time periods or in military campaigns are entitled to preference in hiring and also in retention during reductions in force. In addition to receiving preference in competitive appointments, Veterans may be considered for special noncompetitive appointments for which only they are eligible.

SUMMARY

There are thousands of organizations, programs, resources, and Web sites to assist with health, reintegration, and resilience. Only a small fraction of them are covered within this chapter. However, those selected are among the most used and have been based on the latest clinical and scientific evidence. More information and continuous updates are also available through the Defense Health Agency's programs, presentations, seminars, and Web-based resources.[2]

References
1.   Garber CE, Blissmer B, Deschenes MR, et al. Quantity and quality of exercise for developing and maintaining cardiorespiratory, musculoskeletal, and neuromotor fitness in apparently healthy adults: guidance for prescribing exercise. *Med Sci Sports Exerc.* 2011;4:1334–1359.
2.   Joint Chiefs of Staff Web site. Sea of Goodwill: Matching the Donor to Need—White Paper. http://www.jcs.mil/Portals/36/Documents/WarriorFamilySupport/SOGW_donor_to_need.pdf. Accessed July 7, 2015.

MIKE SAVICKI grew up in Franklin, Massachusetts, as the eldest of three children. He attended Franklin High School and was a member of the varsity soccer, basketball, and track teams. In school, he also discovered creative writing and science. Mike attended Tufts University in Medford, Massachusetts, and earned a BA in political science and international relations. During his 4 years there, he was a member of the Zeta Psi fraternity, and played varsity soccer, club rugby, and volleyball. At the same time, Mike also completed a 4-year Navy ROTC (Reserve Officers' Training Corps) scholarship program at Massachusetts Institute of Technology in nearby Cambridge. He also ran two Boston Athletic Association Boston Marathons because, well, there are just some things in college one has to do.

In November 1990, while training to become a US Navy F-14 fighter pilot, Mike Savicki sustained a severe spinal cord injury after diving into the waters off Pensacola Beach, Florida. In an instant, the then 22-year-old went from being a fit, active, promising Naval officer—commissioned as the top flight candidate in the nation's number one ROTC college graduating class—to an individual with a severe spinal cord injury who was challenged with learning to live life again using a wheelchair. As the United States sent its soldiers and sailors to the Persian Gulf, Mike was transferred from a Florida hospital's intensive care unit to the Veterans Affairs Hospital in West Roxbury, Massachusetts.

After completing 7 months of rehabilitation in a Veterans Affairs spinal cord injury unit, Savicki relocated from his family home in Massachusetts to attend graduate school at Duke University in North Carolina. Along the way, as he regained his independence, earned an MBA, and delivered

the commencement address, Savicki became involved in wheelchair sports. Competitions took him across the United States and around the globe to various countries, including Australia, New Zealand, and Vietnam.

Now, over half his life later, Savicki continues to pursue his passion. Not only is he an 18-time finisher (and 5-time division winner) of the prestigious Boston Athletic Association Boston Marathon (making him the only person to have completed the marathon on foot and subsequently in a wheelchair), he has also earned more than 85 Gold Medals in the National Wheelchair Veterans Games (the nation's largest annual sporting event for athletes with disabilities). A triathlete since 1999, Savicki became the first quadriplegic to finish the 70.3-mile Beach to Battleship Half Ironman Triathlon in his home state of North Carolina in 2009. He also played quad rugby—a Paralympic sport more popularly known as Murderball—for 13 years and spent 3 years as a high-performance program member competing for a spot on the Athens 2004 Paralympic team.

Mike's success extends well beyond athletics. After receiving his MBA, he accepted a full-time job as a Management Consultant at Public Consulting Group, Inc, in Charlotte, North Carolina. From there, he landed a job as Deputy Director of World T.E.A.M. Sports, a nonprofit for people with and without disabilities. In his free time, he began freelance writing and has since profiled a broad spectrum of professional athletes, political figures, and comedians.

Savicki is currently the Founder and Chief of Scratching Post Commu-nications, which offers creative communications services, consulting, and public relations for businesses and individuals. He is the recipient of the Tufts University Distinguished Alumni Award and the National Veterans

Wheelchair Games' Spirit of the Games Award. For 4 years, he has served as spokesperson for National Mobility Awareness Month.

Mike Savicki was married in 2010. He and his wife, Sarah, welcomed a baby girl into their lives shortly thereafter.

Overcoming adversity, marathons, triathlons, degrees, companies, teams, books, magazines, speeches, advocacy efforts in DC, and fighter jets? "That's nothing," he says. The real challenge? Keeping up with a toddler whose life is unfolding each and every day.

We don't differentiate between the combat wounded or just plain sick — people who may have fallen off a ladder or who have cancer. We're going to take care of you until you transition back to duty or return to civilian life.

★ ★ ★

COLONEL WILLARD BUHL
COMMANDER, US MARINE CORPS
WOUNDED WARRIOR REGIMENT
FEBRUARY 26, 2014

CHAPTER FIFTEEN

The Role of Service Organizations and Volunteers

S. ELAINE EITLER, MEd, IAST,* and WILLIAM M. LAKE, BS†

*Assistive/Special Education Technologist/Education Specialist, Curriculum and Instruction Information Technology, George Mason University, 4400 University Drive, Fairfax, Virginia 22030

†Colonel (Retired), US Marine Corps; Rehabilitation Counseling Graduate Student, School of Allied Health Professions, Rehabilitation Counseling, Virginia Commonwealth University, 821 West Franklin Street, Richmond, Virginia 23284; formerly, Director, Marine For Life Injured Support Program, Headquarters, US Marine Corps

INTRODUCTION

The World Health Organization defines quality of life as "the perception by individuals of their position in life, in the context of the culture and value systems in which they live and in relation to their goals, expectations, standards and concerns."[1(p1)] Inevitably, perceptions may change as individuals transition from military service and reintegrate into civilian communities. Admiral Michael Mullen, former Chairman of the Joint Chiefs of Staff, has said that improving reintegration for Veterans and Service Members is the goal toward which we all strive.[2] Embarking on a "new normal" is a challenge some individuals find exhilarating. Others find the process daunting and feel that it creates an overwhelming sense of vulnerability.

Berglass and Harrell[3] note that, "As a veteran grows increasingly comfortable with life after military service and achieves better social and personal relationships, health and satisfaction of material needs, and purpose in life, he or she may become increasingly well."[3(p1)] Facilitating a successful reintegration requires resilience. Traits of resilience—such as courage, patience, self-efficacy, and self-control—allow persons to achieve success in the face of adversity. With each success, quality of life is enhanced.

The impact of reintegration expands beyond individual needs. When dealing with the many physical and cognitive challenges associated with new disabilities, individuals need assistance from support networks that share their core beliefs. These networks must confirm to the individual that no matter how much has changed, their needs and potential remain important, and the possibility for a bright future lies ahead.

A *holistic reintegration plan* can heighten the likelihood of positive outcomes. Inclusive plans place emphasis on the individual's physical and cognitive health, material needs (eg, housing, financial, legal, spiritual, etc), and sense of purpose. The plan also focuses on the stakeholders in the individual's rehabilitation (ie, family, friends, and social networks). Having a dialogue about expectations during the reintegration plan is vital to fulfilling the individual's needs in the key areas of social and human capital (Figure 15-1).

VOLUNTEERISM

Statistics released by the Bureau of Labor Statistics in February 2013 reported that 64.5 million Americans were involved in a volunteer activity. Motivation to participate in volunteerism is as varied as the millions of individuals who engage in connecting with a cause. Clary et al[4] described the Volunteer Functions Inventory (VFI) motives, which are widely regarded as the most credible measures of volunteer motivation. The VFI explores six decision-making, functional factors related to volunteerism by measuring 30 motivations to engage in unpaid helping activities.[4] As designated by Clary et al, the VFI motives are as follows:

1. *protective*—a way of protecting the ego from the difficulties of life;
2. *values*—a way to express one's altruistic and humanitarian values;
3. *career*—a way to improve career prospects;
4. *social*—a way to develop and strengthen social ties;
5. *understanding*—a way to gain knowledge, skills, and abilities; and
6. *enhancement*—a way to help the ego grow and develop.

Figure 15-1. *Holistic Reintegration.*

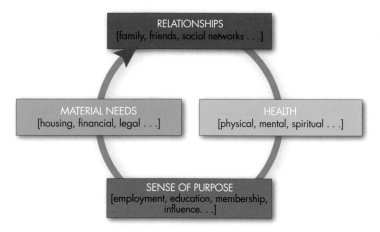

Whether engaged in volunteer activities or receiving assistance, persons must determine how to pair personal motivation with expectations and goals. Utilizing motivation inventory tools, such as the VFI, allows organizations and volunteers to match motivational needs to an array of volunteer tasks, thus increasing the likelihood of a more positive volunteer experience. Expanding horizons can be a means of positively impacting quality of life for oneself and others. However, in the quest for success, mistakes will be made. Dale Carnegie said that, "The successful man will profit from his mistakes and try again in a different way."[5(p1)] In essence, mistakes or missteps should not be roadblocks to achieving desired outcomes. Sharing successes and failures will help others to develop their own unique coping strategies and lead to improved personal volunteer outcomes.

SOCIAL AND HUMAN CAPITAL

Though modernized, the terms *social capital* and *human capital* are not new concepts. In 1865, Alexis de Tocqueville coined the phrase "habits of the heart," which described caring for one another's well-being as a means to feel socially connected and useful.[6] Studies conducted on the impact of social capital on quality of life were summarized by academic Robert Putnam who defined social capital as "the collective value of all social networks and the inclinations that arise from these networks to do things for each other."[7] Putnam concluded that such connectedness is necessary for the safety and security of individuals and communities. In addition to Putnam's formal definition, social capital has been described as professional contacts, networks, employment leads, and social relationships. The works of Tocqueville, Putnam, and others support the age-old notion that people not only want to be needed, but also *need* to be needed.

Theodore Schultz coined the phrase "human capital" in the 1960s. Human capital encompasses intangible concepts, such as ability, skill level, knowledge, leadership, and work experience. Many individuals believe that investing in these concepts by training and educating individuals improves human capacity and the quality of production output.

In a 2010 report by Copeland and Sutherland, "No single agency or organization has the manpower, resources, or intellectual capital to provide a lifetime of care and support to our military families."[8(p7)] The adage "there is strength in numbers" can be appropriately applied to the reintegration process. Currently, Veterans and Service Members benefit from popular support of American citizens to ease the strain that their service has on their well-being. The *Sea of Goodwill* report places emphasis on the "capacity of greatness" that lies within our military personnel, their families, and the societies they reintegrate into and how this symbiotic relationship between each of these groups can benefit each of them. The report also focuses on ways to empower Veterans and Service Members by providing opportunities through education, employment, and healthcare and by connecting them with the services that will support their specific needs. Stakeholders involved in reintegrating Veterans and Service Members into society are often driven by a wide variety of motivations, including patriotism, social awareness, and sometimes personal financial benefit. The stakeholders involved in an individual's rehabilitation need to constantly measure the effectiveness of resources and make adjustments in the best interest of each individual Veteran.

CONSIDERATIONS FOR SELECTING A TRANSITION SERVICE PROVIDER

When selecting from the multitude of service providers, consideration should be given to the following questions:

- Does the provider identify with the breadth of needs?
- Does the provider understand that needs are unique to a particular individual (ie, one size does not fit all)?

TABLE 15-1. *Typical Scenarios of Service Delivery*

RURAL	URBAN
Roving providers	Facility-based providers
Referral-based services	Self-sustained/in-house services
Nonprofit transport	Public transportation
Services provided via phone and social networking	Services provided person-to-person
Services available through local for-profit and not-for-profit chapters	Services provided in local, state, and federal government centers
Telemedicine and telerehabilitation delivery utilized	Medicine and rehabilitation delivery person-to-person

- Is the provider aware that needs may be defined by generational perceptions/attitudes?
- Does the provider have the ability to change with the times, evaluate outcomes, and learn from mistakes?
- Is the provider well informed and have an evidence-based action plan?
- Does the provider have connectivity and collaborate with other organizations?
- Does the provider have a concise understanding of military culture?
- Is the provider a catalyst for advocacy?
- Does the provider help individuals understand how their proficiencies align with their needs?
- Does the provider offer incentives for reintegration?

Reintegration is a long-term prospect, not a one-time event. A commitment to prioritizing short- and long-term goals will require compromise and tolerance. Advocating for the rehabilitating individual will require stakeholders to be assertive and persistent. A determined course of action needs to be logical and organized. Developing coordinated, seamless, evidence-based approaches and setting common goals for a reintegration strategy will benefit all decision-makers. The benefits of developing a coordinated approach may include, but not be limited to:

- reducing duplicative efforts,
- promoting connectedness,
- alleviating feelings of being overwhelmed and confused,
- empowering stakeholders with ownership of ideas,

- decreasing stressors,
- increasing communication and cooperation,
- allowing more efficient allocation of resources,
- avoiding influences from unnecessary bureaucracy, and
- helping to identify barriers.

The acronym FOB may be helpful in assembling a plan. As described in the *Warrior Transition Leader* handbook,[9] F = Forward thinking, O = looking for Opportunities, and B = Building a new life.

Each transition is unique to individual circumstances. Not all programs will be beneficial or comprehensive in meeting an individual's needs. For example, leveraging sustained service of care will require familiarity with the location in which the individual resides, since the availability of resources, areas of expertise travel time, and delivery of services and/or resources in urban areas may differ from that of rural settings (Table 15-1). Diversity will be necessary to enhance the likelihood of desired outcomes. The ideal program will help individuals think about the future, find opportunities, and begin the journey of building their new reality.

VOLUNTEER PROGRAMS

No one is useless in this world who lightens the burdens of another.

Charles Dickens

Having a sense of purpose often results in improved self-respect and elevated levels of pride. Sense of purpose may be associated with work or activities, such as gainful employment, unpaid labor, or volunteerism. A Veteran's sense of purpose may be different than an active Service Member's. The change of roles inherent in transitioning from active duty to Veteran status may challenge Veterans' perceptions of themselves or create confusion as to their value to society. Participation in volunteer activities can enrich social and human capital, thus elevating the sense of purpose.

The advantages and benefits of engaging in volunteerism as a provider of services or assistance will vary for all participants. Volunteer assistance can provide encouragement to individuals who may have experienced helplessness. Productivity within a community is empowering and can be therapeutic. Service can positively impact learned behaviors and skill sets. Volunteering may spark rediscovery of a passion or discovery of new competencies and interests.

FIGURE 15-2. *A Symbiotic Relationship: Volunteerism–Human Capital–Social Capital.*

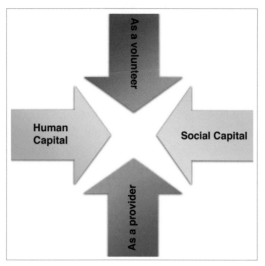

In 2012, Secretary of Labor Hilda L. Solis[10] remarked that volunteerism cannot replace formal job training and is not a replacement for compensated employment. Yet, in a competitive job market, volunteerism might give individuals a leg up on the competition by improving one's social and human capital.[10]

WHAT HUMAN OR SOCIAL CAPTIAL DO YOU BRING TO THE TABLE?

Anecdotal evidence asserts a symbiotic relationship in which volunteerism can lead to employment and employment can lead to volunteerism (Figure 15-2). Findings from the 2013 study by Spera et al[11] conclude that individuals who have volunteer experience have 27% better odds of securing employment. This study also found that persons without a high school diploma, but who have volunteer experience, have a 51% greater chance of obtaining employment. Data from this study suggest that education and volunteerism impact social and human capital. This research provides reasonable justification that involvement in social/volunteer activities and education can improve quality of life.[9]

In contrast, passivity can be an agent for feelings of loneliness, anxiety, disassociation, and powerlessness. Passivity can lead individuals to engage in behaviors detrimental to their well-being and quality of life, such as eating and sleeping disorders, substance abuse, emotional distress, and deliberate self-harm. Sustained apathy frequently leads to a person's mental and physical health spiraling out of control, and has the potential of creating instability and roadblocks to successful reintegration.

Volunteerism allows for an active social life and opportunities to learn new concepts and skills. When a decision has been made to opt in to the arena of volunteerism, it is important for participants to prepare themselves for their mission. Outreach efforts are not a one-size-fits-all proposition. Reintegrating Veterans and Service Members will bring different life experiences to the table. Stakeholders need to develop a genuine understanding of the challenges that Service Members faced while on active duty. Care providers also need to have working knowledge, beyond generalities, of the population they wish to serve. Understanding the lingo or common language prior to volunteering is a valuable asset in building rapport. Likewise, knowing that others understand the journey from military to civilian life is comforting to those embarking on the process. Although age-appropriate connections may stimulate mutual trust between providers and receivers, others will find fulfillment in working across generations. Interacting with those who have had similar life experiences will help individuals create social bonds and build meaningful friendships. Providers and volunteers should respect comfort levels. They should play to strengths and leverage risk taking.

Terra Zvara, a former Red Cross Volunteer, noted that contributions should provide guidance, not handholding (T. Zvara, personal communication, June 2013). Zvara cautioned caregivers not to underestimate individuals needing assistance. She warned that one's limitations or shortcomings should not be a barrier to volunteerism because everyone has skill sets and natural abilities that can make a difference. Barbara van Dahlen[12] confirmed this notion, and stated that Service Members diagnosed and undiagnosed with medical needs (eg, posttraumatic stress disorder, traumatic brain injury, and spinal cord injury) can be affected by their experiences while serving; however, their service-related diagnoses should not preclude success at their endeavors.[10]

Recipients of help may need nurturing to overcome the stigma associated with asking for aid. Reluctance to seek assistance is a common behavior among those who have served. Reticence may indicate that the individual has not acquired strategies that support behaviors necessary to manage significant life changes. Persons navigating reintegration will profit from associating with role models who demonstrate these skills and have the ability to instill them in others. This is especially true for Veterans who have transitioned from highly structured military environments to civilian routines.

Experienced volunteer and former Wounded Warrior assistive technology advisor Emily Davis reported that recipients of assistance frequently shared expressions of appreciation for being supported by volunteers who had life experiences and opinions independent of military service (E. Davis, personal communication, June 2013). She noted that Veterans and Service Members often expressed that their relationships with civilians provided an autonomous safe haven where they could speak openly and take risks that they may not have felt comfortable doing in front of their military comrades.

COMPASSION FATIGUE

The role of a volunteer is not always auspicious. In this realm of support, the occurrence of burnout is common. It is not unusual for volunteers to feel isolated from their regular social networks. Relationships with certain individuals may be physically and/or emotionally challenging. Often persons needing assistance with the reintegration process have visible and invisible wounds that impact volunteer collaboration. The relationship between provider and recipient can stimulate stressors detrimental to the caregiver's well-being, and these empathetic responses may result in symptoms of physical or mental distress in a volunteer. Many times, these signs go unnoticed, even by those closest to the person.

Time committed to volunteer work should not be regarded as burdensome. When providing aid is perceived as onerous, the caregiver usually becomes ineffective. When stakeholders recognize and validate compassion fatigue, volunteers may be better equipped to mitigate effects to their interpersonal relationships and well-being. Knowing the warning signals may help to prevent this type of exhaustion.

According to Susanne Babbel,[13] caregivers suffering from compassion fatigue may find themselves:

- feeling disassociated,
- feeling angry,
- having anxiety,
- experiencing sleep disturbances and having nightmares, and
- feeling powerless.

To combat compassion fatigue or burnout, caregivers should share successes and acknowledge failures. Instead of complaining, caregivers should have meaningful communications daily with good listeners. Caregivers need

T a b l e 1 5 - 2 . *Web Site Resources*

WEB SITE	WEB ADDRESS
Blue Star Families	bluestarfam.org
Corporation for National and Community Service	volunteeringinamerica.gov/national
Give an Hour	giveanhour.org
Independent Sector	independentsector.org
The National Resource Directory	nrd.gov
Wounded Warrior Project	woundedwarriorproject.org

to come to terms with fears and anger. They should balance time volunteering with time spent on personal interests/hobbies. Scheduling quiet alone time may help volunteers recalibrate the effectiveness of their efforts. Maintaining a healthy diet and a regular exercise regime may also help minimize the phenomenon of compassion fatigue.

DIVERSITY OF VOLUNTEER PROGRAMS

Camaraderie is revered in the service. This mutual respect for colleagues has led many to become involved in assisting with reintegration. An abundance of volunteer programs are available for the Veteran or Service Member during and after reintegration. Selecting a program will depend on physical location, physical abilities, and personal preferences. Networking with others is a viable means of connecting with an organization.

In this chapter, we have divided organizations into three entities: (1) Military and Veteran organizations, (2) umbrella organizations, and (3) wraparound programs. The goals of organizations are typically outlined in their history or mission statement. The goals of some organizations are wide-ranging, whereas others are genre-specific.

M i l i t a r y a n d V e t e r a n O r g a n i z a t i o n s

Preparing for and actively navigating the reintegration process takes perseverance. This is particularly true when the Service Members begin to establish a record of benefits they are afforded as compensation for their time in service. Throughout the transition period, both the reintegrating individuals and their stakeholders will rely heavily on government and volunteer organizations.

Service Members moving from active duty to Veteran status will participate in the Transition Assistance Program (TAP). TAP attendance is required for all separating Service Members. Its main focus is on the individual leaving service. The TAP experience provides professional and moral support to colleagues as they move from the military community to the Veteran or civilian community. TAP educates participants on a wide variety of topics and assists in the compilation of a paperwork trail associated with separation. TAP also provides guidance in helping individuals identify a civilian career path and teaches skills associated with building a professional resume. TAP also assists in the application for Veteran benefits. In the past, TAP has been criticized as not being effective; however, TAP has undergone a major overhaul and is a valuable part of departing military service.

Many organizations are connected with every branch of the military, and many others are connected to one specific military branch. Some organizations are more visible than others, but all seek a better quality of life for those who are serving or have served our nation, including those with both seen and unseen injuries. These organizations have an intimate understanding of Veteran concerns. Personal mentors, peer support groups, and programs focused on athletics and hobbies are also available to facilitate connectedness with other Veterans. Participation in any of these programs as either a volunteer or a recipient of services may help to restore and boost one's confidence and resilience.

As noted in the previous chapter, an important resource for both active duty and Veteran Service Members is the National Resource Directory (see http://www.nrd.gov/). This directory provides a cornucopia of resources dedicated to successful reintegration of troops and their families (Table 15-2).

One hurdle that transitioning individuals face is how to translate their highly specialized military skill sets to the civilian sector. Often, this translation is complicated by physical and/or cognitive injuries acquired while serving. There are numerous organizations focused on matching skill sets to needs. Usually, these organizations are well versed in service-related injuries and the needs of individuals living with these disabilities. The process can be intimidating, but Veterans have found relief when accessing available programs. As part of the transition, individuals may benefit from educating themselves about the spectrum of not-for-profit organizations whose missions share passions similar to their own, and other groups that provide service to ease the anxiety generated by change. Stakeholders must diligently examine each organization to determine if the match will fit the criteria they have set for improving their quality of life (Exhibit 15-1).

Exhibit 15-1. *Examples of Organizations Involved in Bettering Quality of Life for Service Members and Their Caregivers*

The American Legion
>The focus of the American Legion is active duty Service Members, Veterans, and communities. The American Legion is dedicated to promoting patriotism and strengthening communities through mentor programs and sponsorships.
>For more information, visit legion.org/heroes

Disabled American Veterans
>As a Veterans Rights advocate, the Disabled American Veterans provides assistance and outreach to Veterans with disabilities and their families.
>For more information, visit dav.org

The Mission Continues
>Bringing Veterans and civilians together, the guiding principles of The Mission Continues are "work hard, trust, learn and grow, respect, and have fun."
>For more information, visit missioncontinues.org

Paralyzed Veterans of America
>The Paralyzed Veterans of America has spent decades advocating for Veterans and empowering Veterans with injuries to realize a life of independence.
>For more information, visit pva.org

Team Rubicon
>The members of Team Rubicon are focused on utilizing the skills of Veterans to respond to the needs of communities devastated by disasters.
>For more information, visit teamrubiconusa.org

United Service Organizations
>The United Service Organizations is dedicated to lifting the spirits of Service Members worldwide. This organization provides a tangible way for Americans to thank those who protect their freedoms.
>For more information, visit uso.org

Umbrella Organizations

For the purpose of this chapter, umbrella organizations are defined as entities that pool resources to provide expertise and coordinate activities or actions. These differ from the aforementioned groups in that they have no specific military ties. Yet, many of these groups have a storied history in delivering services to Service Members and Veterans.

Veterans may have sustained injuries that make it difficult to achieve their goals or partake in desired activities. Such constraints may be related to a Vet-

EXHIBIT 15-2. *Examples of Organizations With a Rich History of Volunteer Activity*

Easter Seals
> For more than 100 years, Easter Seals has assisted individuals and individuals with disabilities and special needs and their families. Easter Seals' emphasis is on medical rehabilitation, employment and training, child services, adult and senior services, and recreation.
> For more information, visit easterseals.com

Paralympics, US Olympic Committee
> Based in Colorado Springs, the mission of the US Olympic and Paralympic Committees is to support athletic endeavors by providing assistance with funding, insurance, tuition grants, and career services.
> For more information, visit teamusa.org

The Peace Corps
> The Peace Corps' goals focus mainly on training and promoting an international understanding of Americans.
> For more information, visit peacecorps.gov

Red Cross
> The main focus areas of the American Red Cross are to administer disaster relief; support American military families; provide lifesaving blood, health, and safety services; and supply international services. Their network's mission is to prevent and alleviate suffering and hardship.
> For more information, visit redcross.org

Teach for America
> Teach for America provides training and career development to potential leaders who will invest in providing education for underserved communities.
> For more information, visit teachforamerica.org

eran's environment, status/position, or health. Some umbrella organizations provide a wide range of services specific to rejuvenating personal interests. Others are designed to teach new skills (Exhibit 15-2).

WRAPAROUND PROGRAMS

Wraparound programs are typically community-based collaborations that provide services to individuals and their families in a specific geographical area. Traditionally, these programs embrace persons in need and provide nonjudgmental and unconditional care. Services provided are as varied as the multiple agencies involved in developing customized plans and creative solutions to support those in need. In general, these agencies tend to have a more intimate relationship with clients. Frequently, these programs are discovered through personal interactions that stakeholders have within their communities (ie, school systems, places of worship, civic associations, etc). This type of networking may create opportunities that may not be realized in working with larger service organizations.

Some examples of wraparound programs include the following:

- community outreach,
- civic organizations,
- philanthropic organizations,
- business organizations,
- faith-based organizations,
- family assistance providers,
- internships,
- mentorships,
- social media forums,
- peer-to-peer outreach, and
- advocacy groups.

SUMMARY

Al Condeluci—author, consultant, and CEO of Community Living and Support Services of Pittsburgh—described the structure of a bridge merging "two important notions, the simplicity of connecting two points and the complexity of the engineering necessary to make the connection."[14] In Condeluci's bridge metaphor, he implores persons on one side of a river (ie, point A) trying to reach the other side (ie, point B) to "seek out help from an engineer as to how we might mitigate or get rid of the river so we can pass to point B safely."[14(p2)] It is not a provider or volunteer's responsibility to change the world; commitment should be based on realizing a desired quality of life. As Condeluci so eloquently states, "The river is not a problem, but a reality to be addressed based on the strength and stability of the shorelines where we plan to anchor the bridge."[14(p2)] Whether acting as the recipient of assistance or as the volunteer who delivers support, one should be the agent of change, the engineer of strength, and the creator of stability.

REFERENCES
1. World Health Organization. WHOQOL: measuring quality of life. WHO Web site. http://www.who.int/healthinfo/survey/whoqol-qualityoflife/en/. Accessed July 24, 2015.
2. Belanger M, Magoon M, Weepie N, et al. The path to healthy homecomings. http://www.boozallen.com/content/dam/boozallen/media/file/Path_To_Healthy_Homecomings.pdf. Accessed February 2, 2015.
3. Berglass N, Harrell MC. Well after service: Veteran reintegration and American communities. http://www.cnas.org/sites/default/files/publications-pdf/CNAS_WellAfterService_BerglassHarrell.pdf. Accessed February 2, 2015.
4. Clary E, Snyder M, Ridge RD, et al. Understanding and assessing the motivations of volunteers: a functional approach. *J Pers Social Psychol*. 1998;74:1516–1530.
5. Carnegie D. The motivational speakers hall of fame. GetMotivation Web site. http://getmotivation.com/dale-carnegie-hof.html. Accessed July 2013.
6. Tocqueville A, Bender T, eds. *Democracy in America*. New York, NY: McGraw-Hill Companies; 1981.
7. Putnam RD. *Bowling Alone: The Collapse and Revival of American Community*. New York, NY: Simon & Schuster; 2000: 19.
8. Copeland JW, Sutherland DW. Sea of goodwill: matching the donor to the need. http://usarmy.vo.llnwd.net/e2/rv5_downloads/features/soldierforlife/White_Paper-Sea_of_Goodwill_17MAY2010.pdf. Accessed September 2013.
9. Cooper RA, Pasquina PF, Drach R, eds. *Warrior Transition Leader: Medical Rehabilitation Handbook*. Washington, DC: Department of the Army, Office of The Surgeon General, Borden Institute; 2011.
10. Solis HL. Remarks for the Honorable Hilda L. Solis: White House Conference on Expanding Opportunity Through Volunteering. http://www.dol.gov/_sec/media/speeches/20120419_WH.htm. Accessed July 14, 2013.
11. Spera C, Ghertner R, Nerino A, DiTommaso A. Volunteering as a pathway to employment: does volunteering increase odds of finding a job for the out of work? http://www.nationalservice.gov/ impact-our-nation/research-and-reports/volunteering-pathway-employment-report. Accessed August 2013.
12. Van Dahlen B. The value of Veterans' service back home. *Time*. June 2013.
13. Babbel S. Bodily symptoms of empathy. *Psychology Today*. July 2012.
14. Condeluci A. *Cultural Shifting: Community Leadership and Change*. St Augustine, FL: Training Resources Network; 2002.

GUNNERY SERGEANT MATTHEW HANNAN served for 15 years active duty in the US Marine Corps from September 18, 1995 to October 30, 2010. He was medically separated after an injury he sustained in Fallujah, Iraq, on January 21, 2007. He served his entire career as an Intelligence Analyst/Intelligence Chief. Matthew was directly involved in Combat Operations in Tirana, Albania, and the Al Anbar Province of Iraq. He also participated with humanitarian operations in the Mediterranean Sea, with tsunami relief efforts in 2005, and with operations in the Caribbean Sea in 1996.

While in the Marine Corps, Gunnery Sergeant Hannan was stationed with various operational forces that include (but are not limited to) Joint Special Operations Command, US Forces in Korea, 2nd Marine Aircraft Wing, 2nd Marine Division, Marine Forces South, Joint Interagency Task Force South, and III Marine Expeditionary Force.

After his medical separation, he participated in an internship that was offered through the Veterans Affairs Vocational Rehabilitation Clinic with the Human Engineering Research Laboratories (HERL) in the ELeVATE Program (Experiential Learning for Veterans in Assistive Technology and Engineering). Matthew is currently working on his undergraduate degree in Public Service (Nonprofit Management). He has plans to apply to the Master's degree program in Rehabilitative Counseling at the University of Pittsburgh, while working as a research assistant at HERL.

Hannan is an active member in the Veterans of Foreign Wars (VFW) Post 92, Disabled American Veterans, American Legion Post 868, and the Marine Corps League Post 827. He also volunteers as an Assistant Team Leader for Semper Fi Odyssey, acts as a peer mentor for the Wounded Warrior Project, is a Student Ambassador and Veteran Advisor to the College of General Studies, and is a youth mentor and wrestling coach with the Shadyside Boys & Girls Club of Western Pennsylvania. Matthew is currently the President of Pitt Vets, which is the Student Veterans of America Chapter at the University of Pittsburgh.

The quality of our men and women in uniform
directly contributes to our roles as the world's
pre-eminent fighting force.

★ ★ ★

HONORABLE JESSICA WRIGHT
UNDER SECRETARY OF DEFENSE FOR PERSONNEL AND READINESS
MARCH 25, 2014

Chapter Sixteen

Culture and Reintegration of Veterans

ALLEN LEWIS, PhD, CRC*; SETH MESSINGER, PhD†;
TWYLLA KIRCHEN, PhD, OTR/L‡; JEANNE WENOS, Ped§; and
SHELLY BROWN, MEd¥

*Dean and Professor, State University of New York Downstate Medical Center,
College of Health Related Professions, 450 Clarkson Avenue, Brooklyn,
New York 11203

†Research Director, Center for Rehabilitation Sciences Research, Department of
Rehabilitation, Uniformed Services University of the Health Sciences, 4301 Jones
Bridge Road, Bethesda, Maryland 20814

‡Director, Occupational Therapy Program, College of Health and Behavioral Studies,
Department of Health Sciences, James Madison University, 800 South Main Street,
Harrisonburg, Virginia 22807

§Assistant Professor, Occupational Therapy Program, College of Health and
Behavioral Studies, Department of Health Sciences, James Madison University,
800 South Main Street, Harrisonburg, Virginia 22807

¥Doctoral Candidate, Graduate School of Education, Duquesne University,
600 Forbes Avenue, Pittsburgh, Pennsylvania 15282

INTRODUCTION

This chapter addresses the role that culture plays in the reintegration of Veterans to civilian life in the United States. It addresses the concept of culture, pluralism in the United States, and the many cultural dimensions in today's military. The role of culture for individuals entering and exiting the military, unique considerations regarding women in the military, barriers to Military Family reintegration, along with strategies to address the barriers are also examined. The chapter concludes with a discussion of the role of culture in promoting Service Member reidentification as a healthy civilian.

THE CONCEPT OF CULTURE

A useful way to approach the concept of culture, particularly in this chapter, is to think of it as a set of enduring constructions that provide a framework for perception and meaning among people who share a world, however loosely or narrowly defined. Culture can be described as a series of "scapes" that link people across space and time, even if they are quite distant from one another.[1] An example is the broadly shared dispositions, habits, and values of investment bankers or electronic music devotees across the globe. Military Service Members are another example. There is a wide range in technology and skill among uniformed Service Members from different nations, but there is a sense that individuals who are Service Members share certain beliefs and skills that have drawn them into their career.[2] Simply watching documentaries, such as *Restrepo* (a 2010 film about an American Army unit) and *Armadillo* (a 2010 film about a Danish Army unit), bears this out.

This concept of culture is also a process. Culture as a set of ideas and dispositions is unevenly distributed across a society or group.[3,4] For instance, people draw on sets of shared meanings, but do not always invest them with the same significance. Furthermore, they may share sets of shared meanings and also have several that overlap with entirely separate communities.[5] The concept of culture has typically been used to explain commonalities in societies. However, in the last couple of decades, researchers have become intrigued about the way that culture can highlight differences within communities.[3,6,7]

PLURALISM IN THE UNITED STATES

The United States, which has always been pluralistic or culturally diverse, is becoming demonstratively more so. Some estimates place the white population slipping into the minority position within the next several decades.[8,9] However, it is easy to overstate this process in part because the notions of race, ethnicity, and color in the United States have historically been very fluid. In the 19th century, many categories of people who are now included within the white category were seen in starkly different terms.[10,11] US immigration continues to be a major source of diversity, with rapid increases among individuals from Asia and Latin America accounting for the majority of new citizens. Along with ethnic, racial, and religious diversity, there is increasing acknowledgment of sexual and gender diversity in the United States. In terms of the military, the most significant change reflecting this diversity has been the end of the "don't ask, don't tell" (DADT) era in 2013 that officially opened the military to recruits regardless of sexual orientation.

THE MANY FACES OF CULTURE IN TODAY'S MILITARY

When demographic information about active duty US military personnel is available, it is usually broken down into two categories: (1) enlisted personnel and (2) officers. Although divisions among the service branches and other qualifiers are often noted, it is the division between the officers and the enlisted personnel that permeates almost every demographic data point. A distinction is made, however, when measuring educational achievement within the military. For reference, there are approximately 1,196,897 enlisted Service Members and 232,139 officers within the entirety of US Department of Defense (DoD) personnel.[12]

RACE AND ETHNICITY
Although the military exhibits some diversity, whites make up approximately 74.6% of the entire active duty force and minorities make up 25.4%, of which 17.8% are black.[12] These proportions, though not equivalent, do trend with race and ethnicity rates among the civilian population and have a similar distribution within both the enlisted and officer realms.[12] Combat fatalities are also proportional to these rates.[13] It appears that whereas minorities do tend to be underrepresented, the distribution mirrors that of the civilian population in both raw numbers and placement of different races among duty stations, rank, and responsibility.

GENDER
Female Service Members are significantly underrepresented in the US military. The service-wide enlisted female percentage is 14%, with the Air Force having the highest percentage of women at 19.9% and the Marine Corps having

the lowest percentage at 6.2%.[12] Among officers, the service-wide percentage is 15.3%, slightly better than the percentage among the enlisted population.[12] Again, the Air Force has the highest representation of female officers at 18.3% and the Marine Corps has the lowest representation of female officers at 5.8%.[12] Since 1980, approximately 5% of active duty military fatalities have been women.[13] Until recently, women were not allowed to deploy to frontline combat roles. Thus, this may explain their underrepresentation in the military. This thinking may account for the difference in recruitment numbers of women among branches, as well as the disproportionate representation of women in officer roles. The lack of combat roles for women is almost certainly responsible for the disproportionately low incidence of active duty fatalities.

SEXUAL ORIENTATION

Under DADT, gay and lesbian Service Members could be separated from service if they revealed their sexual orientation while in the military. Because of this practice, there was a disincentive for homosexual Service Members to reveal themselves. Therefore, this population remained unrecorded in any demographic data that the DoD released, which obscures their representation in the military.[14] However, with the recent repeal of DADT, we can reasonably expect the issue to be studied more thoroughly in the future.

RELIGIOUS/SPIRITUAL AFFILIATION

Information regarding religious and spiritual affiliation within the military was reported by the Military Leadership Diversity Commission.[15] In that report, data from the Religious Identification and Practices Survey (RIPS) revealed greater religious diversity within the ranks of military personnel younger than age 40 years, compared with Military Personnel older than age 40 years. The current military also reports greater religious diversity than previous generations, including those from the "Greatest Generation" who served during World War II.[16] Religiosity in the military was studied in the context of diversity by the Defense Equal Opportunity Management Institute (DEOMI). Faith groups were identified by DEOMI, the Defense Manpower Data Center, the American Religious Identification Survey, and the Pew Research Center's Religious Landscape Survey as Protestant (variety of denominations), Catholic, Orthodox, other Christian, and Jewish (roughly 75%).[17] Also included was a smaller percentage of Muslim, Pagan, Eastern, Humanist, and other less common affiliations. Depending on the source used, 12% (as reported by the Pew Research Center) to 25% (as reported by RIPS) were identified as having no religious affiliation.

Religious beliefs are thought to be central to a person's worldview and are influential to choices that individuals make in life, including the shaping of values that influence one's judgment.[18] Because of the diverse expression of religiosity in the military, clinicians working with individuals in the military must be mindful of the contributions of individual belief systems to patterns of thinking.[19] Resilience or the lack of it may manifest from healthy and unhealthy beliefs regarding religiosity and spirituality.[19] One study measured intrinsic religiosity of Military Veterans using a three-item questionnaire of perceptions of a strong sense of God's presence, the importance of one's religion linked to its provision for meaning to life, and the vital importance of having a relationship with God. Veterans, likewise, reported having an internal sense of allegiance to their personal religious beliefs.[20]

The military reports its struggle to holistically embrace human diversity while maintaining standards of excellence surrounding

- character,
- obedience,
- unit cohesion,
- *esprit de corps*, and
- mission readiness

for which matters of religion and spirituality pose a particular challenge.[15] Issues of harassment within the military surrounding the expression of one's religious beliefs have been reported.[19] However, the spiritual element is designated as one of four dimensions of a Service Member's well-being that comprise mission readiness[21]:

1. assessment of emotional, social, family, and spiritual fitness;
2. universal resiliency training;
3. individualized training; and
4. training of master resilience trainers.

Part of the Army's Comprehensive Soldier and Family Fitness program includes a relatively new component—*spiritual fitness*—added to the approach for maintaining holistic health and wellness.[21] The pendulum appears to be swinging back to the rediscovery of spiritual practices of healing, substantiated by reports of patients desiring prayer time with their physician; experiencing deep satisfaction with spiritual means of reframing injury or illness; and seeking alternative therapies that address the mind and spirit, in addition to treating physical ailments of the body.[22]

Social Economic Status

Socioeconomic status (SES) among Service Members is difficult to determine because many of its usual factors are not recorded by the DoD, and the SES indicators that are recorded tend to hold less meaning than similar measures used to compare groups in the civilian population. This occurs because the use of these tools between Service Members in the same branch does not yield much variation in quality of life. Factors such as homogenized healthcare and the enforcement of uniform lifestyle standards that are regulated by individual commands in keeping with the standards of that branch are contributory components. Comparisons among branches encounter similar problems because each military branch has to adhere to basic military-wide standards. Factors that are recorded can be useful when comparing the SES of Service Members to that of their civilian counterparts. For example, 92.5% of Service Members among all military branches have a high school diploma or above, and 89.3% of Service Members have a BA/BS or above.[12] The only outlier in this sample is the Coast Guard, which decreases the service-wide BA/BS attainment average to 53.4%.[12] With the exception of the Coast Guard at the college level, military educational achievements at these levels are significantly higher than those of the civilian population.[23]

Culture and the Military Family

The Military Family may consist of the Service Member, his or her spouse, children, and, at times, extended family members (eg, parents, other relatives, etc). Kirchen and Hersch[24] conducted a qualitative study that examined the lived experiences of World War II, Korean War, and Vietnam Veterans who had recently transitioned to a long-term care facility. One of the most salient themes that emerged from analysis of the phenomenological data was the importance of the Military Family. Participants in the study identified strong, supportive families as being the most important factor in their ability to cope with frequent deployments and other stressors associated with military life.[24] *Fitness for duty* is a term used to describe a Service Member's physical and mental health in relation to his or her ability to deploy or perform duties stateside. There is a direct correlation between the strength of the family support system and a Service Member's ability to perform his or her duties as assigned.[25] Wang et al[26] examined the association between military divorce with mental, behavioral, and physical health outcomes. They found that compared to those who remained married, recently divorced individuals were significantly more likely to screen positive for new-onset posttraumatic stress disorder, depression, smoking initiation, binge drinking, alcohol-related problems, and moderate weight gain.[26]

There are numerous factors that affect the sustainability of the Military Family unit. However, the stress of being able to kill, avoiding being killed, caring for the wounded, and witnessing death and injury are all part of military service. Additional military occupational stressors include frequent relocation, separation from family, and being constantly available. Although other occupations may have similar stressors, the stressors identified here are salient features of military service.[27] It is not surprising that divorce rates for military couples from October 1, 2006 to October 1, 2007 were approximately 25,000 failed marriages of 755,000 married active duty troops.[17] As such, military leaders recognize the importance of keeping Service Members healthy and deployable through fostering strong and committed Military Families.

CULTURE AND THE MILITARY: THE PARADOX

One of the main cultural processes associated with the military (aside from its power as a tool for social mobility both geographically and through SES) is that it is a machine for producing specific kinds of uniformity. The raw material of this uniformity is the diverse social landscape of the United States.

ENTERING THE MILITARY AND THE ROLE OF CULTURE

One way to understand the process of entering the military is to see it as a ritual of initiation. Victor Turner[28] introduced a model of the ritual process that was drawn from his work with an African people known as the Ndembu. Basically, Turner argued that rituals occur in three stages: (1) separation, (2) transition, and (3) reincorporation. A problem with this work is that it can be infinitely recursive (thus every transfer of duty station can serve as an initiation ritual). Nonetheless, when considering the significant moments of military life, this three-part approach is quite useful.[28]

The first stage of the ritual process, *separation*, can be seen vividly in the entry into military service at the basic training level. Participants in an ongoing study at Walter Reed Army Medical Center described how going to their basic training locations had some features of a pilgrimage. These individuals went to a common airport or other facility on their own. Often, they would meet up with guides at USO (United Service Organization) offices in airports (that provide a public welcome and hospitality space for Service Members) and then be sent on their way. When they finally arrived at their in-processing location, they experienced a sharp breach with the lives they were leaving. For example,

- they had to get rid of their clothes,
- they had to have their hair shorn, and
- they had to be moved through a whole series of events designed to strip them of their individuality (eg, receiving uniform clothing, being yelled at as a group, moving rapidly through medical examinations, etc).[29]

Turner referred to the second stage of the ritual process (*transition*) as liminality, or a time out of time. For example, features that would have differentiated military recruits prior to entry are erased. This is seen in the physical experiences previously described, but also in other ways. For instance, race, ethnicity, and, to some extent, gender are erased as instructors herd, exhort, and berate recruits through a wildly varied series of physical and mental exercises. Individuals described experiencing routine lack of sleep, eating unpalatable food, and being constantly reminded that they were separated from their familiar lives. (This is reinforced by quite literally cutting off recruits from friends and family for the duration of their basic training.) Furthermore, instructors deliberately seek to sow doubt about families of the recruits, especially friends, in an effort to coerce recruits into seeing their comrades and other Military Service Members as their "true" families.[30]

Although all of this may bear strong similarities to examples of negative conditioning, there is also a positive conditioning aspect of this training. Throughout basic training, differences that might have stratified recruits in their home environments are dissolved in favor of membership in the wider service branch. Recruits experience changes in their bodies, cognitions, and capacities. They become stronger and more fit, able to excel at a wide variety of mechanical and physical skills, and perceive risks and dangers in their environment that they might have been unaware of in their former lives. The recruits have the experience of camaraderie, as well as an enhanced sense of personal prestige and status at having succeeded in being welcomed (at the end of training) into a very highly regarded institution.

Reincorporation, or the third stage of the ritual process, has recruits becoming fully accredited members of their service branch in a public ceremony that welcomes parents and friends to the military installation where they trained. Here, newly minted Soldiers, Sailors, Airmen, and Marines are able to give their loved ones a tour, show off their new bodies in their crisp uniforms, and, perhaps more importantly, give a demonstration of their new bearing as Service Members. These experiences are reproduced, though with likely diminished intensity, as Service Members move on to advanced training and are then assigned from one unit to another.

Service Members have often pointed out that individuals who have not experienced deployment or combat are relatively ill-treated compared to other members of the unit. This has the effect, perhaps intended, of encouraging these inexperienced Service Members to eagerly await their upcoming deployment.

Exiting the Military and the Role of Culture

Military service offers a very durable platform for identity among Service Members. The durability of this identity is visible in material culture. Clothing, hats, bumper stickers, and license plates can all be tools with which to share the military component of one's biography. More subtly, though more importantly, military training becomes integrated into an individual's embodied sense of being in the world after Service Members leave the military and reintegrate into civilian society.[29,31] Military training and combat exposure may both act as barriers to social reintegration.[32,33] This problem has emerged, to some extent, as a stigma (given the number of suicides among Veterans and active duty personnel, and the sensationalizing of crimes committed by Veterans) that may follow Veterans as they negotiate their pathway to civilian life.

Veterans of Vietnam, Iraq, and Afghanistan have all shared the burden of being viewed with some suspicion by the public. This is in part motivated by accounts of poor social reintegration through criminal or suicidal behavior by some Veterans.[34] Currently, the question of social reintegration is nationally prominent and is accompanied by accounts of antisocial behavior by individual Veterans. For example, a Navy Veteran allegedly perpetrated a mass shooting at the Navy Yard in Washington, DC. This alleged shooter had never deployed to a combat theater, but this fact may be obscured simply because he was a Veteran.

Paradoxically, Veterans may also struggle with the ways that they are positively valued in public life. Veterans are often held up as models of civic participation. In addition, they are also often referred to as heroes. This intense measure of public approval can be constraining for Veterans who may be struggling with reintegration challenges or who simply want to return anonymously to civilian life. It can be a challenge to live normally in a community or even attend sporting or other public events. Frequently, it can be difficult being called on when a master of ceremonies asks all Veterans to raise their hands or stand up to receive public ovations. One Veteran discussed the uncomfortable situation of being offered money as a token of gratitude for his military service.[2] After attempting to gently refuse a proffered $20 bill, the well-wisher lightly tossed the bill into the open window of the Veteran's car, necessitating him to crawl around on the floor to find it later. Although this may seem like a rare circumstance, it is nonetheless indicative of some of the potential challenges faced by Service Members who become a kind of condensed symbol for civilians rather than fully accepted as realized human beings.

UNIQUE CONSIDERATIONS OF WOMEN AND REINTEGRATION

HISTORICAL PERSPECTIVE

Women have served in every war and conflict in United States history, from undercover spies in the Revolutionary War to combat pilots in Afghanistan.[35] The first formal recognition of women in the military occurred in 1901 with the establishment of the US Army Nurse Corps.[35] The inception of an all-volunteer force in 1973 initiated a dramatic increase of women entering the armed forces. Several historic junctures in US military policy changed the face of women Service Members and expanded opportunities for advancement and combat roles, including:

- 1901   Congress creates the Army Nurse Corps. Participants had no official military rank, received unequal pay, and were not eligible for retirement.
- 1941   The Women's Army Auxiliary Corps was conceived by the US Congress and received full military status in 1943.
- 1951   The Defense Advisory Committee on Women in the services was established.
- 1967   Public Law 90-130 eased restrictions contained in the Women's Armed Services Integration Act, which was passed 19 years earlier, in 1948.
- 1973   The US military becomes all-volunteer.
- 1990s   Access increases for opportunities in combat zones.
- 2011   The Department of Veterans Affairs (VA) and the DoD collaborate on the VA Task Force for Women.

THE FACE OF TODAY'S WOMEN VETERANS

Women represent 8% of Veterans, with the largest percentage (more than 50%) having served in conflicts since 1990.[35] Black women comprised the largest minority of women Veterans at 19%, compared to the overall US population of 12% black women. Conversely, women Veterans from Puerto Rico represented 8% of the women's Veteran population.[35] Further, the average age of women Veterans in 2009 was 48 years, 2 years older than the average age of the general population of US women. The percentage of women Veterans with children under the age of 17 was 39%, slightly higher than the population of US women with children in the same age range.[35]

POSTDEPLOYMENT ISSUES IMPACTING WOMEN
The postdeployment experience of women Veterans is similar to the psychological trauma of men Veterans, with an additional layer of trauma for women who identify as an underrepresented minority. Postdeployment issues can include homelessness, military sexual assault, and posttraumatic stress disorder (PTSD).

Homelessness
According to the *2013 Annual Homeless Assessment Report*[36] to Congress, 8% of the Veteran homeless population are women. The overall rate of chronically homeless Veterans has declined, yet 8% represents approximately 4,400 women Veterans without a consistent home.[36]

Military Sexual Assault
Men and women Service Members can be impacted by sexual trauma, yet women face additional barriers and challenges when reporting incidents and receiving support.[37] Approximately 20% to 40% of women Veterans report incidents of military sexual assault.[38]

Posttraumatic Stress Disorder
Research has shown a high percentage of Veterans with PTSD, including women. In women, a significant amount of comorbidity exists between PTSD and depression, often compounded by military sexual assault.[39] The purpose of the study was to identify barriers to care for women Veterans with PTSD. An interesting finding was determined: 27% of women Veterans did not seek treatment because of a lack of awareness of eligibility or available services.[39]

The study by Lehavot et al[39] concluded that future outreach and education efforts should target women Veterans. Additionally, the study identified that women Veterans had greater access to the Internet and computer usage, thus suggesting that telehealth and computer-based resources may represent an alternative option for care and support.[39]

RECOMMENDATIONS
Several factors contribute to effective return to civilian life following deployment, particularly as it applies to children and youth in Military Families.[40]

The concept of *seamless communities* refers to the need for caregivers, service providers, and community entities to recognize the unique structure of military life, including language, norms, and customs.[40] Additionally, an understanding of the policies that govern access to and usage of resources further supports the concept of seamless communities.[40] As the leading provider of medical and behavioral health services for Veterans, the VA is cognizant of the need for unique services to address the needs of women Veterans. Thus, the VA has developed comprehensive, gender-specific programs and facilities for women Veterans.

The following initiatives for women Veterans support services for physical and mental health; educational opportunities; and procurement of adequate, safe housing.

Homelessness
• Supportive Services for Veteran Families
  https://www.va.gov/homeless/for_women_veterans.asp
• Housing Choice Vouchers
  https://www.va.gov/homeless/hud-vash.asp

General Health
• Center for Women Veterans
  https://www.va.gov/womenvet
• Women Veterans Health Care
  www.womenshealth.va.gov

Military Sexual Trauma and PTSD
• Military Sexual Trauma
  www.mentalhealth.va.gov/msthome.asp
• PTSD: National Center for Posttraumatic Stress Disorder (NCPTSD)
  www.ptsd.va.gov

REINTEGRATION BARRIERS AND STRATEGIES

There are several notable barriers and strategies to overcome the problems associated with reintegration of military families (Table 16-1). A strong case has been made for embedding family-based care for military and Veteran families in the community.[41] This is especially true for family separation from the military, but it will require many civilian resources (including those of the VA) to answer the call. In addition, the family unit is more likely to experi-

TABLE 16-1. *Barriers/Strategies for Military Family Reintegration*

BARRIERS	STRATEGIES/RECOMMENDATIONS
Limited access to medical care	• Consider residing in a location that is within driving distance to a major military hospital or VA medical center
Financial constraints	• Identify states that do not tax military retirement—Service Members who retire from the military • Consider transferring GI Bill benefits to college-age children • Use VA housing benefits to finance a home
Locating employment	• Know that the Service Member and his or her spouse may be eligible to use the GI Bill to obtain a degree or an additional degree • Be aware that hiring preferences exist for Service Members and some spouses within the federal government service employment system
Existing medical conditions (psychological/physical)	• Ensure that all medical conditions are revealed prior to separation from the military • Receive ongoing care and support of all conditions and advocate for additional support from the VA for any service-related conditions that surface postseparation
Social isolation	• Remain in contact with military-related friends through social media, phone, e-mail, and/or visits • Connect with other military-affiliated families in the community • Participate in community-based activities through church, school, or work

VA: US Department of Veterans Affairs

ence high reintegration stress in the presence of PTSD-related symptoms and when the Service Member's mental health is low.[42] Stress factors associated with reintegration most often reported by the Service Member or his or her spouse include the following:

- limited access to medical care,
- financial constraints,
- ability to locate employment for the Service Member and/or the spouse,
- management of chronic medical conditions sustained by the Service Member while on active duty, and
- social isolation within a community that may not understand military culture.

THE ROLE OF CULTURE IN PROMOTING
SOLDIER REIDENTIFICATION AS A HEALTHY CIVILIAN

Resilience (the ability to bounce back from or be insulated from adversity), *social capital* (viable social networks), and *reintegration* (resuming civilian life in a complete and healthy manner) are important and interwoven concepts in the lives of Service Members attempting to successfully reenter civilian society. Reentry requires successful reidentification from a Service Member to a healthy Veteran/civilian member of American society and consists of three dimensions:

1. the role of culture in becoming a Service Member,
2. the natural and multiple stressors that occur as one moves from the role of Service Member to Veteran, and
3. the role of culture in facilitating a smooth transition back to civilian life.

This three-dimension experience is one wherein culture plays a pivotal role in assisting the former Service Member to become successfully reidentified as a healthy civilian.

The process of becoming a Service Member, especially in the early stages of basic training, arguably is intended to mute the cultural identities of individuals who have entered the military and amplify the culture of becoming and being a Service Member. Thus, the prime objective of a Service Member is to become a well-trained fighting machine in which personal autonomy and unique manifestations of personality and self-concept are not allowed to interfere with receiving orders and executing the primary mission of successful combat. Therefore, when an individual enters the military and begins to assume the identity of a Service Member—thus replacing his or her former cultural orientation as a unique individual (a civilian) with that of a Service Member—this is an *intentional process.*

When a Service Member has completed the active duty mission and resumes life as a Veteran/civilian, there are several stressors that typically present themselves as barriers to the process of successfully transitioning back to non-military life, such as medical issues, financial challenges, psychological/emotional adjustments, and social concerns. There is typically a multiplier effect among these countervailing demands/stressors as depicted in Figure 16-1. The problem is that the magnitude of these combined demands and stressors can have a synergistic negative effect on the Service Member attempting reentry into society. To successfully navigate these multiple demands, the Service Member must embrace a cultural identity that can match the demands. Sometimes,

FIGURE 16-1. *Multiple Demands on Soldiers Attempting to Reenter American Society.*

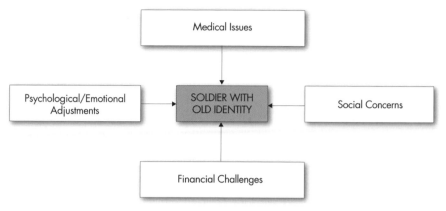

the former identity as a Service Member can manage the demands effectively, and sometimes the Veteran needs to embrace a new cultural identity to match the multiple demands of this new environment. Keep in mind that formerly the military provided a homogenous milieu that addressed medical care, financial remuneration, psychological and emotional self-concept, as well as social capital needs, and all within the self-contained military installation community.

In Figure 16-1, the soldier is being encroached on by four competing stressors: (1) medical issues, (2) social concerns, (3) psychological/emotional adjustments, and (4) financial challenges. Essentially, the identity of being a combat Service Member (ie, old identity) does not help when successfully navigating the demands of the new civilian context. The solution is for the Service Member to engage in a systematic and intentional process of reidentification to regain a multifaceted cultural identity that will successfully match the dimensions of American society. As this happens, the individual's resilience improves, as does the social capital, and, ultimately, the reintegration process will be well underway.

At the core of the reidentification process is the *whole-person model* by Wegscheider-Cruse.[43] She proposes a six-dimensional whole-person concept in the context of helping individuals in their recovery from alcoholism to successfully reenter a life of sustained sobriety. We are not comparing recovery from alcoholism to the reintegration process for a Veteran. However, the Wegscheider-Cruse model has been applied to the population of persons with alcoholism. Thinking more generally about this whole-person model and the process of adjusting to civilian life, the model offers concrete dimensions for consideration. The six dimensions of this model are

1. physical,
2. mental,
3. emotional,
4. social,
5. spiritual, and
6. volitional.

Much like what Wegscheider-Cruse proposed for persons recovering from alcoholism (in the context of reintegrating Veterans), still the goal would be to have each returning Service Member commit to an explicit process of identifying at least one asset in each of the six dimensions and then devote constant attention to a regime of personal development in those areas. The asset in each dimension would serve as a positive foundation on which to build out and continue to develop. As development transpires, the Service Member evolves toward a new cultural orientation in all six dimensions.[43]

Over time, this process of building assets, growing cultural identity, and accomplishing personal development in each of the six dimensions will lead the Service Member to a new identity as a civilian. Thus, the civilian endeavors to function to *full personal potential* physically, mentally, emotionally, socially, spiritually, and volitionally. As this occurs, the individual will automatically become more resilient from having assets and a new identity in each of the six dimensions that serve as natural insulation to adversity. With the person developing a social dimension, the construction of social capital will also be underway. Work on the whole person in each of the six dimensions will lead to a new identity as a *former Service Member*. Thus, this Veteran/civilian is now on his or her way to developing a new and full cultural existence. The Service Member's work in each of the six dimensions of the whole person *becomes a new identity*. Therefore, a beginning cultural orientation (eg, values, beliefs, preferences, and worldview) assists the individual in becoming fully functional in American society, with a stronger sense of reintegration, resiliency, and growing social capital.

SUMMARY

In this chapter, we discussed the role of culture in the reintegration of Veterans. Adequately addressing the full scope of a broad concept such as culture in one chapter is a tall order. Nevertheless, we have attempted to do so, and in so doing have touched on many important aspects of culture in the United States and how those aspects intersect with the experience of being a Veteran while attempting to successfully reenter civilian society. We have defined the concept of culture, discussed the overarching role that culture plays in the pluralistic US landscape, and introduced the salient dimensions of culture that must be considered when working with Veterans. The chapter concludes with a recommended process that can assist the Veteran in effectively reentering civilian society through identification of a holistic set of personal assets that form the basis for developing a new civilian cultural identity.

REFERENCES

1. Appadurai A. *Modernity at Large: Cultural Dimensions of Globalization.* Minneapolis, MN: University of Minnesota Press; 1996.
2. Messinger S. Getting past the accident: explosive devices, limb loss, and refashioning a life in a military medical center. *Med Anthropol Q.* 2010;24(3):281–303.
3. Bourdieu P. *Distinctions: A Social Critique of the Judgment of Taste.* Cambridge, MA: Harvard University Press; 1984.
4. Lave J. *Apprenticeship in Critical Ethnographic Practice (Lewis Henry Morgan Lecture Series).* Chicago, IL: University of Chicago Press; 2011.
5. Kleinman A, Fitz-Henry E. The experiential basis of subjectivity: how individuals change in the face of societal transformation. In: Biehl J, Good B, Kleinman A, eds. *Subjectivity: Ethnographic Investigations.* Berkeley, CA: University of California Press; 2007.
6. Abu-Lughod L. *Recapturing Anthropology: Working in the Present.* Albuquerque, NM: SAR Press; 1991.
7. Kleinman A. Experience and its moral modes: culture, human conditions, and disorder. In: Peterson GB, ed. *The Tanner Lectures on Human Values.* Vol 20. Salt Lake City, UT: University of Utah Press; 1999: 52–65.
8. US Department of Commerce. Population projections of the United States by age, sex, race, and Hispanic origin: 1995 to 2050. http://www.census.gov/prod/1/pop/p25-1130.pdf. Accessed December 23, 2015.
9. US Census Bureau. *Twenty-third Census of the Inhabitants of the United States 2010.* Washington, DC: United States Congress and Secretary of State; 2010.
10. Jacobson MF. *Whiteness of a Different Color: European Immigration and the Alchemy of Race.* Cambridge, MA: Harvard Press; 1999.
11. Roediger D. *Working Toward Whiteness: How America's Immigrants Became White—The Strange Journey from Ellis Island to the Suburbs.* New York, NY: Basic Books; 2006.
12. US Department of Defense. *Defense of Manpower Data Center: Demographics of Active Duty US Military.* Washington, DC: U.S. Department of Defense; 2011.
13. US Department of Defense. *Active Duty Military Deaths—Race/Ethnicity Summary (as of July 25, 2009).* Washington, DC: US Department of Defense; 2009.

14. US Office of the Secretary of Defense. *Sexual Orientation and U.S. Military Personnel Policy: An Update of RAND's 1993 Study.* Santa Monica, CA: RAND Corporation; 2010.

15. US Army Public Health Command. Boosting resilience through spirituality. *Military Leadership Diversity Commission Issue Paper No. 22.* http://mldc.whs. mil. Accessed December 23, 2015.

16. Wansink B, Wansink CS. Are there atheists in foxholes? Combat intensity and religious behavior. *J Relig Health.* 2013;52(3):768–779.

17. Defense Manpower Data Center. U.S. military active duty demographic profile. http://www.slideshare.net/pastinson/us-Military-activeduty-demographic-profile-presentation. Accessed April 9, 2009.

18. Ferman D. Religiosity, selective exposure, and the U.S. military's "don't ask/don't tell" policy. *Southwest Mass Commun J.* 2012;27(2):37–52.

19. Hathaway WL. Religious diversity in the military clinic: four cases. *Mil Psychol.* 2006;18(3):247–257.

20. Schumm WR, Rotz PL. A brief measure of intrinsic religiosity used with a sample of military Veterans. *Psychol Rep.* 2001;88(2):351–352.

21. Pargament KI, Sweeney PJ. Building spiritual fitness in the Army. *Am Psychol.* 2011;66(1):58–64.

22. Karren KJ, Smith NL, Hafen BQ, Jenkins KJ. *Mind, Body, Health: The Effects of Attitudes, Emotions and Relationships.* San Francisco, CA: Benjamin Cummings; 2010: 355–392.

23. Ryan CL, Siebens J. *Educational Attainment in the United States: 2009.* Washington, DC: US Department of Commerce; 2012.

24. Kirchen TM, Hersch G. Understanding person and environment factors that facilitate Veteran adaptation to long-term care. *Phys Occup Ther Geriatr.* 2015;33(3):204–219.

25. Crum-Cianflone N, Fairbank JA, Marmar CR, Schlenger W. The Millennium Cohort Family Study: a prospective evaluation of the health and well-being of military service members and their families. *Int J Meth Psychiatr Res.* 2014;23(3):320–330.

26. Wang L, Seelig A, Wadsworth SM, McMaster H, Alcaraz JE, Crum-Cianflone N. Associations of military divorce with mental, behavioral, and physical health outcomes. *BMC Psychiatry.* 2015;15:128.

27. Adler AB, Castro CA. An occupational mental health model for the military. *Mil Behav Health.* 2013;1(1):41–45.

28. Turner V. *Forest of Symbols: Aspects of Ndembu Ritual.* Ithaca, NY: Cornell University Press; 1970.

29. Messinger S. Vigilance and attention among US service members and Veterans after combat. *Anthropol Conscious.* 2013;24(2):191–207.

30. Burke C. *Camp All-American, Hanoi Jane, and the High-and-Tight: Gender, Folklore, and Changing Military Culture.* Boston, MA: Beacon Press; 2005.

31. Finley E. *Fields of Combat: Understanding PTSD Among Veterans of Iraq and Afghanistan.* Ithaca, NY: Cornell University Press; 2012.

32. Shay J. *Achilles in Vietnam: Combat Trauma and the Undoing of Character.* New York, NY: Simon & Schuster; 1995.

33. Shay J. *Odysseus in America: Combat Trauma and the Trials of Homecoming.* New York, NY: Simon & Schuster; 2003.

34. Sontag D, Alvarez L. Across America, deadly echoes of foreign battles. *New York Times.* January 8, 2008: A1.

35. National Center for Veterans Analysis and Statistics. *America's Women Veterans: Military Service History and VA Benefit Utilization Statistics.* Washington, DC: NCVAS, Department of Veterans Affairs; November 2011.

36. U.S. Department of Housing and Urban Development, Office of Community Planning and Development. *The 2013 Annual Homeless Assessment Report (AHAR) to Congress.* Washington, DC: USDHUD; 2013.

37. Osborne A, Gage L, Roblieski A. Psychological effects of trauma on military women service in the National Guard and Reserves. *Adv Social Work.* 2012;13(1):166–184.

38. Kelly UA, Skelton K, Patel M, Bradley B. More than military sexual trauma: interpersonal violence, PTSD, and mental health in women veterans. *Res Nurs Health.* 2011;34(6):457–467.

39. Lehavot K, Der-Martirosian C, Simpson TL, Sadler AG, Washington DL. Barriers to care for women veterans with posttraumatic stress disorder and depressive symptoms. *Psychol Serv.* 2013;10(2):203–212.

40. Davis B, Blaschke S, Stafford E. Military children, families, and communities: supporting those who serve. *Pediatrics.* 2012;129(S1):S3.

41. Glynn SM. Family-centered care to promote successful community reintegration after war: it takes a nation. *Clin Child Fam Psychol Rev.* 2013;16(4):410–414.

42. Marek L, D'Aniello C. Reintegration stress and family mental health: implications for therapists working with reintegrating military families. *Contemp Fam Ther.* 2014;36(4):443–451.

43. Wegscheider-Cruse S. *Another Chance: Hope and Help for the Alcoholic Family.* Palto Alto, CA: Science and Behavior Books, Inc.; 1981.

PETTY OFFICER 3RD CLASS AL KOVACH, in 1983, was a heavily recruited high school All-American swimmer who chose Indiana University for its decades-long reputation as a swimming powerhouse. Legendary swim coach Dr James E. Counsilman instilled character traits associated with Olympic-class athletes, such as resilience, teamwork, selflessness, and patriotism. Possessing such characteristics might explain why Kovach joined the Navy in 1988 and volunteered for what is recognized by experts as the toughest military training in the world: Basic Underwater Demolition/SEAL training (also known as BUD/S).

Kovach pushed through the physical, mental, and emotional challenges of BUD/S and, following graduation, was assigned to SEAL Team 5 located in Coronado, California. However, his career was cut short in 1991 while on a combat training exercise. Kovach broke his neck in a parachuting accident that resulted in permanent paralysis from his chest down.

While hospitalized, Kovach received a visit from the Paralyzed Veterans of America (PVA), an organization that helped him secure the VA benefits he earned as a result of his military service. Benefits also included a housing grant to make his home wheelchair accessible, a vehicle that was adapted with hand controls, and access to a lifetime of quality healthcare.

Kovach's first employment position following his paralysis was as PVA's Government Relations Director in San Diego, California. The Americans with Disabilities Act was passed in 1990 and gave a voice to 45 million people. It was an exciting time to be in Kovach's position. However, after much contemplation, he chose to go back to his athletic roots and began competing in races.

His first competition was in 1994, and he won four Gold Medals at the National Veterans Wheelchair Games. Kovach went on to become a member of the 1996 US Paralympic Team and subsequently won multiple national titles and set many records on the track.

Kovach quickly transitioned from the track to the road. Not only did he win prestigious races—including the Los Angeles Marathon in 1996 and 1997—but he also expanded his repertoire to include hand-cycling and triathlons. He claimed victories in places as far from home as Australia. With a "been there, done that" attitude, Kovach looked for a greater challenge. Thus, in 1998, he completed a 3,700-mile triathlon that began in Los Angeles and ended 65 days later in New York City. In recognition for his athletic accomplishments, Kovach was honored by the San Diego Hall of Champions as the Disabled Athlete of the Year in 1999.

Multiple injuries have sidelined Kovach's ability to continue competing in triathlons and marathons, but his need for speed endures in many incarnations. He now competes in motorsports and continues to be instrumental in creating adaptive sports programs for children with disabilities.

Kovach recently played a role in putting together a team of paralyzed Veterans, SCUBA professionals, and medical researchers to conduct a pilot study to explore the neurological, psychological, and pulmonary effects of SCUBA on people with spinal cord injury and disease (SCI/D). The remarkable results were documented in a film titled *Sea of Change*.

In recent years, Kovach has chosen to repurpose his skills and abilities, thus turning his attention to supporting his fellow paralyzed Veterans. In 2014, Kovach was elected National President of PVA. As the face and voice of 20,000 Veterans with SCI/D, Kovach has an enormous responsibility that he does not take lightly. After all, it took PVA 70 years to create its stellar reputation as the premier Veterans service organization that is the sole advocate in the realm of healthcare, benefits, research, and civil rights for Veterans with SCI/D. Using the traits and skills learned from his days as a Navy SEAL, Kovach is now leading PVA on a trajectory for success.

There is nothing more gratifying than to care for
these wounded, ill, and injured heroes.

★ ★ ★

LIEUTENANT GENERAL ERIC SCHOOMAKER
COMMANDER, US ARMY MEDICAL COMMAND
US ARMY SURGEON GENERAL
CONGRESSIONAL TESTIMONY
APRIL 21, 2010

Chapter Seventeen

Summary

RORY A. COOPER, PhD*

---

*Director and Senior Career Scientist, Human Engineering Research Laboratories, Rehabilitation Research and Development Service, US Department of Veterans Affairs, 6425 Penn Avenue, Pittsburgh, Pennsylvania 15206, and Distinguished Professor and FISA Foundation–Paralyzed Veterans of America Chair, Department of Rehabilitation Science and Technology, University of Pittsburgh, 6425 Penn Avenue, Suite 400, Pittsburgh, Pennsylvania 15206

INTRODUCTION

We must also remember that conflict is a human endeavor,
ultimately won or lost in the human domain.
The Army operates in the human domain which is the
most important factor in a complex environment.

GENERAL RAYMOND T. ODIERNO
US ARMY, CHIEF OF STAFF
(2011–2015)

There is an understanding gap between American society and the population serving within the military and Veterans. Less than 1% of Americans are serving in uniform, and about 6% of the American population are Military Veterans. This creates challenges for Service Members and Veterans when reintegrating. Although most people are supportive of Service Members and Veterans, they often do not know how best to assist or translate military experience into successful civilian careers. This makes it important for Service Members and Veterans to be resilient and to assist each other with successful reintegration.

RESILIENCE

Planning and effort are required to instill the resilience needed for successful reintegration. Building resilience for successful reintegration, either back into the military service or the civilian community as a successful Veteran, is a multidimensional process. Personal resilience is essential for successful reintegration. Resilience is multidimensional and consists of physical, cognitive, social, and spiritual factors.

Too much stress of any kind can negatively impact a person's resiliency, health, memory, attention, and creativity. Some of the best ways to beat stress include exercising, eating right, getting adequate sleep, having social support through family and friends, and maintaining an optimistic outlook. Resilient people take care of themselves so that they can attack the challenges that face them. Building physical resilience through exercise and a healthy diet can have a positive impact on other components of resilience, especially the physical and mental elements. For example, exercise can improve brain function. Exercise has been shown to improve attention, processing speed, executive functions (eg, planning and organizing), memory, creativity, and flexibility in thinking. Only 20 to 35 minutes of aerobic exercise per day can have a positive effect. Maintaining a balanced diet and promoting a healthy body weight not only benefits resilience, but also slows cognitive declines associated with aging.

REINTEGRATION

Self-awareness is key to building resilience and to successful reintegration. Self-awareness links the complex interplay between leadership, readiness, fitness, and human performance. There are multiple aspects of successful reintegration, including:

- physical and mental health;
- connectedness through positive and supportive relationships with family and/or friends;
- financial stability; and
- a sense of making meaningful contributions to home, work, or society.

The support of organizations, family/friends, and members of the broader community—whether military or civilian—can play a large role in successful reintegration. Service Members and Veterans must recognize that they do not need to face the challenges of reintegration on their own, and should rely on their training and experiences to reach out to and connect with trusted individuals and organizations that will help them to succeed.

Many military and Veterans service organizations (VSOs) provide valuable assistance, with a wide array of programs to assist Service Members and Veterans with reintegration. Most organizations do not charge for their services. There are a number of VSOs that offer a variety of services and programming. Some Veterans are active in multiple organizations, and some Veterans are not interested in any. In any case, it is worthwhile to contact different VSOs and learn about them. These organizations can help Veterans connect to other Veterans, provide recreation and service activities, and assist with employment. This can help with reintegration and also provide a social network to strengthen resistance.

Many employers and colleges provide Veterans with assistance in successful reintegration. Veteran-friendly employers and colleges have offices that provide assistance with applying for positions or enrolling in college. Often, civilian employers have little experience with the military or Veterans and are unsure of how to translate military experiences into civilian job requirements. There are services to help Veterans create civilian-style resumes. However, greater success in securing employment is likely when the company has a Veterans employment specialist within the human resources department or has Veterans on the team with hiring authority.

There are likewise many colleges and universities with small student populations who are Veterans, and these organizations may not be aware of the knowledge gained through military schools and hands-on experiences. This may place Veterans at a disadvantage for admissions and for receiving course credit for prior experience and training. Veteran-friendly colleges and universities typically have an office of Veterans services and may have a chapter of the Student Veterans of America. Some of the services that are particularly beneficial include the following:

- transition assistance programs (eg, access to Veterans benefits, math, and writing skills building, study habits, campus resources),
- counseling and tutoring services,
- Veterans scholarships,
- summer internships with research laboratories and/or industry, and
- placement assistance.

Community colleges are often a good starting point, especially because they may be close to home, offer lower costs, and provide greater flexibility. If the goal is to pursue a 4-year degree or advanced degree, it is important to select a community college with matriculation agreements to 4-year colleges. Employment with or without a college degree can lead to a fulfilling career and greater financial security. However, financial security also requires planning and commitment. Creating and following a budget requires discipline. As a tool, a budget can help to prepare for

- unforeseen circumstances,
- long-term goals (eg, purchasing a home, paying for children's college),
- short-term goals (eg, planning for a vacation, purchasing/replacing an appliance), and
- balancing necessary expenditures (eg, food, housing, utilities, transportation) and discretionary spending (eg, entertainment, dining out).

Managing life balance is important to achieving success and happiness at work, at home, and in the community.

It is important to find healthy and healing pursuits (eg, art, travel, sports, etc). Life is more pleasant when it includes activities that an individual enjoys, and it is even more so when these lead to improved physical and mental health. People have many preferences about the types of activities that they enjoy. Those activities that include families and friends are often more enjoyable and encourage people to participate for many years. It is important to incorporate healthy pursuits, especially physical activity, into our daily routines. Regular aerobic exercise, especially when involved in an activity that one enjoys, can have significant influence on a person's physical and mental health.

SOCIAL NETWORKS

It is difficult to live in isolation, and the lack of a strong social support system can lead to depression and poor health. People who have strong social networks tend to be happier, healthier, and have greater satisfaction with work, home life, and their role with family, friends, and the community. A strong social network does not necessarily equate to a large social network. A strong and supportive relationship with a few close friends and/or family members can be very effective.

A strong social network is an important component of resiliency. Having people who can be relied on to assist in times of challenges or even during a crisis can provide individuals with the confidence to take healthy risks (eg, form new relationships, seek a promotion or a better job, buy a house, or attend college). Close friends and family, especially those with shared experiences and values, who live positive lifestyles, are important to help address problems, answer questions, and make improvements in one's self, relationships, and community. Social networks are also key to finding a satisfying career after serving in the military. Most people learn of and attain career positions and skills through their networks of friends who make connections that lead to appropriate positions that provide opportunities for professional growth. Personal connections can help to overcome the hurdles often faced by Veterans. People who have not served in the military or who may not be familiar with military service may have difficulty interpreting the Veteran's skills and how these skills match to key elements of a position. A Veteran in the organization may be able to help with this issue.

CONNECTION AND SUPPORT

For Service Members or Veterans with disabilities, it is important to remain connected with a specialized team of medical professionals and to participate in regular check-ups. The standard recommendation is annually once a person is living within his/her home community. The Department of Veterans Affairs (VA) maintains a number of specialty clinics and clinical care teams to serve Veterans with limb amputations, spinal cord injuries, polytrauma, posttraumatic stress disorder, vision loss, hearing impairments, etc. The VA is a proponent for the concept that "rehabilitation is a life-long process." Some military treatment facilities also support this premise. It is important to enroll for VA care if and when eligible. Physical, cognitive, and sensory impairments are seldom static, and changes over time may be compensated for through advances in technology, new medications, and periodic reinforcement of therapeutic interventions (eg, counseling, physical therapy, and occupational therapy). At the very least, Service Members and Veterans with disabilities who use assistive devices should remain in contact with their clinical team to remain aware of advances in technology that may help to improve function, comfort, and performance.

Veterans have a long tradition of being engaged in their communities and providing support for worthy causes. In many cases, Veterans are pillars of their communities and apply the skills and experiences that they gained while serving in the military to improve their communities as Veterans. Being engaged in their communities is an obligation that Veterans should accept to contribute toward supporting the needs of Veterans who are less capable of advocating for themselves, to contribute to the understanding of the general public of military service, and to help build inclusive communities where everyone is valued and respected. Veterans of each generation have worked to improve the lives of their successors. The concept of "paying it forward" is important within the Veteran community and helps to ensure that challenges faced by one generation are reduced for subsequent generations.

SUCCESSFUL REINTEGRATION AND RESILIENCY

Successful reintegration and resilience are multifactorial. Ultimately, each Service Member and Veteran must set and assess their personal goals. However, some metrics are generally accepted as measures of progress:

- employment (either paid or volunteer);
- stable, healthy relationships with others;
- frank assessment of oneself and accurate interpretation of perceptions of others;
- physical and mental health;
- spiritual centering;
- ability to withstand change and adversity; and
- making positive contributions.

Building resilience and successfully reintegrating into society may be challenging, especially when not connected to other mutually supportive people with common interests and values. In a notable number of cases, Service Members and Veterans view their lives as being better posttrauma. The concept of posttraumatic growth relates to having an adversity-building character and forging a physically and mentally stronger Service Member or Veteran. A significant number of Service Members and Veterans with severe injuries, such as limb amputations or paralysis due to spinal cord injuries, often find new and rewarding outlets for their talents and discover strengths that they were previously unaware that they had. There are numerous examples, some illustrated in this book, wherein Service Members and Veterans translated adversity into advantage, and transformed their lives and those of their communities through sports, education, entertainment, and employment.

Staff Assistant to the Secretary of the Army, US Army Captain (Retired) Matthew A. Staton was born in Madison Heights, Virginia, and enlisted in the Virginia National Guard as a Simultaneous Membership Program (SMP) cadet with the 29th Infantry Regiment in 1998 while attending Virginia Military Institute for one year. Following graduation, he enlisted as an infantryman (11B) in the US Army. Matthew was stationed in Vicenza, Italy, with the 1st Battalion, 508th Infantry Airborne Combat Team before deciding it was time to pursue a different path in the military. After serving 3 years of active duty, Matt attended Officer Candidate School and was commissioned in September 2002.

Staton traveled to Fort Carson, Colorado, for his first duty assignment after becoming a Second Lieutenant. He deployed to Iraq in July 2003 as the Rifle Platoon Leader of Charlie Company, 1st Battalion, 8th Infantry Regiment. During his deployment, Matt was exposed to multiple IEDs (improvised

explosive devices), resulting in a mild traumatic brain injury, as well as sustaining a gunshot wound to the leg. He continued to serve and recover in multiple roles with the 1-8th Infantry, culminating in commanding the battalion's rear detachment while the unit deployed back to Iraq (2005–2006).

In August 2007, Staton returned to Virginia after completing the Army's Physical Disability Evaluation System and being medically retired from the Army. In September 2007, Matthew began his current service as a Department of the Army civilian and as a direct Advisor/Staff Member to the Secretary of the Army for Ill, Injured, and Combat Wounded Soldiers.

In the years following Matthew's deployment, he and his family learned to cope with the impact of mild traumatic brain injury and posttraumatic

stress disorder, two invisible injuries of war along with the physical injuries he sustained from combat. He has since become a Professional Alpine Disabled Ski Instructor, a Professional Association of Diving Instructor (PADI), and a Handicapped SCUBA Association buddy for individuals with disabilities. He also holds a PADI Master Scuba Diver rating. Matthew currently volunteers with multiple organizations that support people with disabilities. He is married to Jennifer Staton, has a 10-year-old daughter Samantha, and lives in Fredericksburg, Virginia.

Matthew Staton's decorations include the Superior Civilian Service Award, Army Staff Badge, Combat Infantryman Badge, Expert Infantryman Badge, US Airborne Wings, Tunisia Airborne Wings, Hungarian Airborne Wings, Bronze Star Medal with Valor, Bronze Star Medal, Purple Heart, four Army Commendation Medals, five Army Achievement Medals, Army Good Conduct Medal, Army Reserve Components Achievement Medal, Iraq Campaign Medal, Global War on Terrorism Expeditionary Medal, Global War on Terrorism Service Medal, NCO (noncommissioned officer) Professional Development Ribbon, Army Service Ribbon, two Overseas Service Ribbons, and the NATO (North Atlantic Treaty Organization) Medal (Kosovo).

Acknowledgments

MANY PEOPLE PROVIDED GUIDANCE, ADVICE, AND ASSISTANCE in the conceptualization and preparation of this book. The tremendous dedication, selfless service, and commitment to excellence exhibited by the men and women in the Armed Services, Military Veterans, and their families have provided inspiration.

The following people deserve to be recognized for their contributions, motivation, inspiration, guidance, or leadership: Honorable Jessica Wright, Honorable Lynda Davis, Honorable John McHugh, GEN Joseph Dunford, GEN(Ret) James Amos, GEN(Ret) Michael Haige, LTG(Ret) Eric Schoomaker, LTG Patricia Horoho, LTG Gary Cheek, VADM Matthew Nathan, MG Darryl Williams, Mr. Thomas Webb, COL Chris Toner, COL Danny Dudek, Col. Willy Buhl, COL (Ret) John Mayer, COL (Ret) Gregory Boyle, SgtMaj(Ret) Joseph VanFonda, CSM Ly Lac, BG Novell V. Coots, MG John Gronski, SMA(Ret) Ken Preston, SMA(Ret) Jack Tilley, SMA(Ret) Raymond Chandler, SgtMaj Ronald Green, CAPT William B. Adams, Dr. Alice Aiken, GySgt(Ret) James Joseph, GySgt(Ret) Matt Hannan, CSM(Ret) Althea Dixon, MG(Ret) Anthony Cucolo III, COL(Ret) Barbara Springer, CSM(Ret) Benjamin Scott, BG Patrick Sargent, Maj.(Ret) Brian Bilski, COL Christopher Boyle, Mark Campbell, Casey Fisher, COL David Bair, COL Frank Frazier, COL Matthew St. Laurent, COL Colin Greene, Dan Pulz, LTC David Rozelle, CSM David Davenport Sr., Debbie M. Paxton, LtGen(Ret) Doug Robb, Ellyn Dunford, CSM Eugene B. Chance, GEN Frank Grass, GEN(Ret) Frederick Franks, MAJ George Smolinski, COL(Ret) Greg Gadson, COL Craig Trebilcock, Honorable Jack Farley, Honorable James D. Rodriguez, COL(Ret) Jim Ficke, Jim Marszalek, BG John Cho, Col.(Ret) John Hugya, Karen Guenther, Dr. Ken Lee, Lonnie Moore, CAPT Louis Tripoli, LtCol Joseph Allena, LtCol Leland Suttee, LTG Michael Tucker, MajGen Michael Lehnert, CSM(Ret) Malcolm D. Parrish, CSM(Ret) Mark Dennis, Matthew Staton, CSM Matthew Brady, Megan Andros, SgtMaj Michael T. Mack, LTC(Ret) Mike Richardson, MSgt Benjamin Fender, Lt. Nathan Bastien, RADM(Ret) Clarke Orzalli, LTC Paula Smith, SgtMaj(Ret) John Ploskonka,

RADM Joan Hunter, MG(Ret) Richard Stone, BG(Ret) Rick Gibbs, Rocky Bleier, Ron Drach, Seamus Ahern, SgtMaj(Ret) Karlton Kent, Dr. Stephanie Belanger, Stephen Tomlin, MajGen T. S. Jones, Tammy Peppe, Tracey Koehlmoos, COL(Ret) John Shero, COL(Ret) Chuck Scoville, CSM(Ret) Jesu Febo-Colon, Cpl(Ret) Artem Lazukin, CSM(Ret) Bob Gallagher, COL(Ret) Timothy Karcher, Ken Ductor, William R. Cole, and SgtMaj Michael P. Barrett.

All of the authors, editors, and the team at the Borden Institute have earned the most heartfelt "thank you" from the editors, Dr. Cooper, Dr. Pasquina, and D. A. Etter.

Furthermore, all the Service Members and Veterans who contributed their stories to this book deserve special recognition because they serve as examples to all of us that adversity can be transformed into positive growth and lead to a "new normal" that can be rewarding and fulfilling.

Acronyms and Abbreviations

ABS	acrylonitrile butadiene styrene
ACE	Ask, Care, Escort
ACV	actual cash value
ADA	Americans with Disabilities Act
ADAPT	After Deployment: Adaptive Parenting Tools
ADL	activities of daily living
ADRC	Aging and Disability Resource Centers
AIA	American Institute of Architects
AIM	Advancing Inclusive Manufacturing
APA	American Psychiatric Association
AT	assistive technology
ATM	automated teller machine
BG	Brigadier General
BLS	US Bureau of Labor Statistics
BUD/S	Basic Underwater Demolition/SEAL training
CAF	Challenged Athletes Foundation
CAPT	Captain
CAREN	Computer-Assisted Rehabilitation Environment
CART	Communication Access Realtime Translation
CBT	cognitive behavioral therapy
CD	Certificate of Deposit
CHAMP	Consortium for Health and Military Performance
CIL	Center for Independent Living
CO	Commanding Officer
COL/Col.	Colonel
Cpl	Corporal
CRSC	Combat-Related Special Compensation
CSM	Company Sergeant Major
CT	coping training
d	depth
DADT	don't ask, don't tell
DCUs	desert camouflage uniform
DEOMI	Defense Equal Opportunity Management Institute

DoD	Department of Defense/US Department of Defense
DOL	US Department of Labor
EBV	Entrepreneurship Bootcamp for Veterans
ELeVATE	Experiential Learning for Veterans in Assistive Technology and Engineering
EPW	electrical powered wheelchair
ETS	Expiration of Term of Service
FMLA	Family Medical Leave Act
FSB	Forward Support Battalion
FSSG	Force Service Support Group
GEN	General
GPS	Global Positioning System
GySgt	Gunnery Sergeant
H2H	Hero2Hired
HERL	Human Engineering Research Laboratories
HOH	Hiring Our Heroes
IAHP	International Association of Hygienic Physicians
iARM	intelligent Assistive Robotic Manipulator
ICF	International Classification of Functioning, Disability, and Health
IED	improvised explosive device
IMES	implantable myoelectric sensor
IMPACT	Injured Military Pursuing Assisted Career Transition
IRA	Individual Retirement Account
ISO	International Organization for Standardization
IUD	intrauterine device
IVMF	Institute for Veterans and Military Families
JAWS	Jobs Access With Speech
Lt.	Lieutenant
LTC/LtCol	Lieutenant Colonel
LTG/LtGen	Lieutenant General
MAJ/Maj.	Major
MajGen	Major General
MA2R*INES3	Mission, Accountability and Attitude, Responsibility, Integrity, Nourish, Energy, and Synergy/Strive/SMEAC
MBA	master's degree in business administration
MeBot	Mobility Enhancement Robotic wheelchair
MEDCOM	medical communications
MEPS	Military Entrance Processing Station
mFLC	Military and Family Life Counselor

MG	Major General; medial gastrocnemius
MHS	Military Health System
MSgt	Master Sergeant
NAMI	National Association for Mental Illness
NATO	North Atlantic Treaty Organization
NCIL	National Center for Independent Living
NCO	noncommissioned officer
NDVWSC	National Disabled Veterans Winter Sports Clinic
NVWG	National Veterans Wheelchair Games
OEF	Operation Enduring Freedom
OIF	Operation Iraqi Freedom
OT	occupational therapist
OWF	Operation Warfighter
PADI	Professional Association of Diving Instructors
PerMMA	Personal Mobility and Manipulation Appliance
PFC	Private First Class
POW	prisoner of war
PSF	power seating function
PT	physical therapy; physical training
PTSD	posttraumatic stress disorder
PV2	Private Second Class
PVA	Paralyzed Veterans of America
PVC	polyvinyl chloride
QRMC	Quadrennial Review of Military Compensation
RADM	Rear Admiral
RAND	RAND Corporation
RESNA	Rehabilitation Engineering and Assistive Technology Society of North America
RIPS	Religious Identification and Practices Survey
ROTC	Reserve Officers' Training Corp
RTD	return to duty
SAH	Specially Adapted Housing
SCAADL	Special Compensation for Assistance with Activities of Daily Living
SCI	spinal cord injury
SCI/D	spinal cord injury and disease
SCUBA	Self-Contained Underwater Breathing Apparatus
SEG	stable exercise group
SES	socioeconomic status
SFL-TAP	Soldier for Life-Transition Assistance Program
SGLI	Servicemembers Group Life Insurance

SGT	Sergeant
SgtMaj	Sergeant Major
SMA	Sergeant Major of the Army
SMART	specific, measurable, attainable, realistic, and time-bound (goals)
SMEAC	Situation, Mission, Execution, Administration, and Communication
SS	Schutzstaffel
SUV	sports utility vehicle
SVA	Student Veterans of America
TA	tibialis anterior
TAP	Transition Assistance Program
TBI	traumatic brain injury
3D	three-dimensional
TRADE	Transforming Resources for Accelerated Degrees and Employment
TRAS	Three Rivers Adaptive Sports
USA	United States of America
USABA	US Association of Blind Athletes
USMC	US Marine Corps
USO	United Service Organization
VA	Department of Veterans Affairs/US Department of Veterans Affairs
VADM	Vice Admiral
VAULT	Value, Accept, Understand, Love, and Trust
VE	virtual environment
VEAP	Veterans Educational Assistance Program
VEOA	Veterans Employment Opportunity Act
VFI	Volunteer Functions Inventory
VFW	Veterans of Foreign Wars
VGLI	Veterans Group Life Insurance
Voc Rehab	Vocational Rehabilitation and Employment
VR	virtual reality
VR&E	Vocational Rehabilitation and Employment
VREG	virtual reality exercise group
VRET	virtual reality exposure therapy
VSC	Virtual Seating Coach
VSO	Veterans Service Organization
w	width
WASUSA	Wheelchair Ambulatory Sports, USA
WHO	World Health Organization
WTC	Warrior Transition Command
WTL	Warrior Transition Leader
WTU	Warrior Transition Unit
WWP	Wounded Warrior Project

Suggested Reading List

Aiken AB, Belanger AH, eds. *Beyond the Line: Military and Veteran Health Research.* Kingston, Ontario, Canada: McGill-Queen's University Press; 2013.

Aiken AB, Belanger AH, eds. *Shaping the Future: Military and Veteran Health Research.* Kingston, Ontario, Canada: Canadian Institute for Military and Veteran Health Research, Canadian Defense Academy Press; 2011.

Ainspan ND, Penk WE, eds. *When the Warrior Returns: Making the Transition at Home.* Annapolis, MD: Naval Institute Press; 2012.

Anderson B, Mack D. *No Turning Back.* New York, NY: Berkeley Publishing Group; 2011.

Armstrong K, Best S, Domenici P. *Courage After Fire: Coping Strategies for Troops Returning from Iraq and Afghanistan and Their Families.* Berkeley, CA: Ulysses Press; 2006.

Cifu DX, Lew HL. *Handbook of Polytrauma Care and Rehabilitation.* New York, NY: Demos Medical; 2014.

Cleland M, Raines B. *Heart of the Patriot: How I Found the Courage to Survive Vietnam, Walter Reed, and Karl Rove.* New York, NY: Simon & Schuster Paperbacks; 2009.

Cody V. *Your Soldier, Your Army.* Arlington, VA: The Institute of Land Warfare, Association of the US Army; 2005.

Condeluci A. *The Essence of Independence.* Rock Hill, NY: Irwin Siegel Agency, Inc.; 2000.

Cucolo G. *Dog Tags: The History, Personal Stories, Cultural Impact, and Future of Military Identification.* Cleveland, GA: Allen House Publishing; 2011.

Daugherty SJ, ed. *Profile of the U.S. Army: A Reference Handbook.* Arlington, VA: The Association of the United States Army; 2014.

Downs DA, Ilia Murtazashvili I. *Arms and the University: Military Presence and the Civic Education of Non-Military Students.* Cambridge, MA: Cambridge University Press; 2012.

Finkel D. *Thank You for Your Service*. New York, NY: Random House Publishing; 2013.

Future Warfare Division, Army Capabilities Integration Center. *Army Innovation: First Principles and Supporting Essays, Unified Quest—Win in a Complex World*. Fort Eustis, VA: US Army Training and Doctrine Command; 2015.

Headquarters, Department of the Army. *Leadership Development*. Washington, DC: DOA; 2015. Field Manual FM 6-22.

Institute for Veterans and Military Families, Syracuse University. *Guide to Leading Policies, Practices & Resources*. New York, NY: Syracuse University; 2012.

Klein SD, Kemp JD, eds. *What Adults with Disabilities Wish All Parents Knew: Reflections from a Different Journey*. New York, NY: McGraw-Hill Books; 2004.

Lincoln A. *Second Inaugural Address, March 4, 1865*. Washington, DC: The Abraham Lincoln Papers at the Library of Congress, 1837–1897.

Linker B. *War's Waste: Rehabilitation in World War I America*. Chicago, IL: The University of Chicago Press; 2011.

Lynch R, Dagostino M. *Adapt or Die: Leadership Principles from an American General*. Grand Rapids, MI: Baker Books; 2013.

Magnuson PB. *Ring the Night Bell: The Autobiography of a Surgeon*. Boston, MA: Little, Brown and Company; 1960.

Nathan D, Ainspan ND, Penk WE, eds. *Returning Wars' Wounded, Injured, and Ill: A Reference Handbook*. Westport, CT: Praeger Security International; 2008.

Office of Warrior Care Policy. *Caregiver Resource Directory*. Alexandria, VA: The Office of Warrior Care Policy; 2015.

Phillips JW, Falcone P. *Boots and Loafers: Finding Your True North*. Seattle, WA: CreateSpace Independent Publishing Platform; 2014.

Poorman C, ed. *The Next Step: The Rehabilitation Journey After Lower Limb Amputation*. Washington, DC: US Department of Veterans Affairs; 2012.

Rigsby S, Glatzer J. *UnThinkable*. Carol Stream, IL: Tyndale House Publishers, Inc.; 2009.

Rozelle D. *Back in Action: An American Soldier's Story of Courage, Faith and Fortitude*. Washington, DC: Regnery Publishing; 2005.

US Armed Forces. *The Noncommissioned Officer and Petty Officer: Backbone of the Armed Forces*. Washington, DC: National Defense University Press; 2014.

US Army Medical Command. *The Performance Triad Guide*. Washington, DC: Army Medicine; 2015.

Index